The Matter of Virtue

The Matter of Virtue

Women's Ethical Action
from Chaucer to Shakespeare

Holly A. Crocker

PENN

UNIVERSITY OF PENNSYLVANIA PRESS

PHILADELPHIA

Published by
University of Pennsylvania Press
Philadelphia, Pennsylvania 19104-4112
www.upenn.edu/pennpress

Printed in the United States of America on acid-free paper
1 3 5 7 9 10 8 6 4 2

Library of Congress Cataloging-in-Publication Data

Names: Crocker, Holly A. (Holly Adryan), 1971– author.
Title: The matter of virtue : women's ethical action from Chaucer to
    Shakespeare / Holly A. Crocker.
Description: 1st edition. | Philadelphia : University of Pennsylvania Press,
    [2019] | Includes bibliographical references and index.
Identifiers: LCCN 2018056720 | ISBN 9780812251418 (hardcover)
Subjects: LCSH: English poetry—Middle English, 1100–1500—History and
    criticism. | English poetry—Early modern, 1500–1700—History and
    criticism. | Virtue in literature. | Women in literature. | Ethics in
    literature.
Classification: LCC PR311 .C76 2019 | DDC 821/.2099287—dc23
LC record available at https://lccn.loc.gov/2018056720

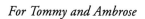

For Tommy and Ambrose

CONTENTS

Virtues That Matter

For use almost can change the stamp of nature.
—Shakespeare, *Hamlet*, III.iv.151.8

Whan that Aprill with his shoures soote
The droghte of March hath perced to the roote,
And bathed every veyne in swich licour
Of which vertu engendred is the flour
—Chaucer, *General Prologue*, I.1–4

This book investigates premodern "vertue," or the embodied excellence that enables women's ethical action in vernacular English poetry between 1343 and 1623.[1] To study this kind of virtue, the following chapters address skepticism regarding women's capacities for ethical action, by which I mean the concrete ability to enact principles that organize an everyday way of life in premodern England. When Hamlet advises his mother to abstain from sex with Claudius, "Assume a virtue if you have it not," he treats virtue as a power that Gertrude might exercise (III.iv.151).[2] Yet, when he concludes his counsel with the remark, "For use *almost* can change the stamp of nature" (my emphasis), he suggests that Gertrude cannot fully enact this or any other virtue (III.iv.151.8). Instead, he imagines Gertrude's virtue as a decorative covering, as "a frock or livery / That aptly is put on" (III.iv.151.4–5). Hamlet renders Gertrude's virtue as superficial, and, by so doing, he forecloses her potential for ethical action. This devaluation of "virtues that matter"—as well as the association of these embodied powers with women—focuses the ensuing argument.

Material Virtue

Like Hamlet, we often refer to virtues as qualities that humans might perform, and for good reason. As this study shall acknowledge, virtues are fundamentally engaged with what it means to be human. Yet, during the period
studied in this book, virtues are also the defining properties of material
things. In medieval and early modern England, a rich vernacular vocabulary
reveals that premodern virtues are physical qualities. Like better-known areas
of virtue ethics, this tradition can also be traced to Aristotle, who claims in
The Physics, "the virtues are perfections of nature."[3] Prominent contemporary
philosophers, including Philippa Foot, Julia Annas, and Rosalind Hursthouse, have argued for virtue's "naturalism," and the argument that follows
in this book arises from their contention that our very species is morally
situated—that the flourishing of the human *qua human* relies on its virtues.[4]
Unlike modern moral philosophers, who by and large focus their discussions
on human excellences, I emphasize one aspect of premodern virtues that
makes this naturalism possible: in premodern English, "virtues" were not
exclusively human. Rather, the *Middle English Dictionary* defines "vertu" as
"an inherent quality of a substance which gives it power."[5] Similarly, early
modern English continued to refer to "vertues" as forces that imbued physical
bodies with vitality and power.[6] From heads to hands, and from rocks to
plants, virtues suffused all material bodies in premodern England.[7]

"Vertues" were not simple or inert characteristics of a physical body.
Jeffrey Jerome Cohen theorizes "vertu" as "life force: reproduction and vitality, affect and intellect and health, that which moves the flesh."[8] *The Peterbor-
ough Lapidary* characterizes "vertu" as proof of divine power: "no man schall
be in / dowte Þat god haþe set & put gret vertu in worde, stone, & erbe, by
the wyche, if it so be þat men be not of mysbeleue & Also owte of dedly
synne, & many [wonder]full mervailes my3t be wrow3t þorow her vertues."[9]
As Mary Carruthers explains, virtue was a "principle of biological energy."[10]
Elsewhere, she notes, "vertu" signified "that innate 'power,' 'energy,' or
'desire' of the soul animating the body, which (as with babies, puppies and
plants) requires channeling, habituation and training."[11] The fourteenth-
century *Dives and Pauper* credits such energies to divine power: "God 3af
gres, trees and herbis diuerse vertuys."[12] We might best understand each of
these virtues as an affordance, or the capacity for a specific body to flourish
in a particular environment. In the most fundamental sense, "vertues" im-
proved the bodies they inhabited.

To distinguish these embodied affordances from other, more traditional characterizations of premodern virtues, throughout this study I shall refer to "material virtues" as the inherent powers of physical bodies commonly referenced in English writings between 1343 and 1623. From the start, I should acknowledge that this practice is somewhat misleading, since, as I have briefly noted above, many contemporary moral theorists think of all virtues as similarly embodied. So what I am describing as "material virtue" would just be "true virtue" as it has more recently come to be understood by key thinkers.[13] I maintain this distinction in order to investigate a discursive habit, which, on account of its everyday, pragmatic emergence in the particular historical milieu of premodern England, might remain unimportant to modern moral philosophers. Material virtue was not the domain of scholastic debate or pastoral teaching (though they did intersect, as I shall subsequently demonstrate). Instead, these inherent bodily powers were central to everyday practices that focused on the natural potencies of physical bodies. Premodern medicine relied on material virtues, for, as John Trevisa's fourteenth-century English translation of Bartholomaeus Anglicus's *De proprietatibus rerum* explains, "A good physician . . . nediþ to knowe complexions, vertues, and worchinges of medicynable þinges."[14] A command of material virtue also requires intimate local knowledge, including the season for the optimal cultivation of healing plants: "Þese herbys . . . mustyn ben gaderyd abowtyn mydsomyr, for þanne þei ben of moste vertu."[15]

This sense of virtue's materiality continued in the early modern period. Herbals as well as medicinal tracts attend to the "vertues" of different plants and potions. The brief broadsheet, *The admirable vertue, property and operation of the quintessence of rosemary flowers and the meanes to vse it for the sickesses and diseases herein mentioned* (1615), equates "vertue" to a physical potency: "Moreouer, the force and vertue thereof extendeth it selfe euen to the sinewes shrunke and weakned."[16] In the more comprehensive *A boke of the propreties of herbes called an herball* (1552), the "vertues" of different plants are associated with distillation, which means that this type of power is thought of as the defining essence of each example included therein.[17] Similarly, *A right profitable booke for all diseases. Called The path-way to health* (1587) describes its contents by referencing virtue as a type of potency, "wherein are to be found most excellent and approoued medicines, of great vertue."[18] The oft-printed *An hospitall for the diseased* (1610), by Thomas Cartwright, also proclaims the powers of its practical wisdom by advertising the "most excellent approoued medicines, as well emplaisters of speciall

vertue . . . for the restitution and preseruation of bodily health."[19] Thinking
of "vertue" as potency is central to medicine's public standing, or so the
English translation of the Latin *Prepositas* (1588) claims: "When men or
women shall, hauing read this booke, see and vnderstand how that there are
in hearbes, plants, gummes &c. such seuerall vertues . . . they will be the
better perswaded to like and esteeme of phisicke then heretofore they haue
done."[20] Virtues are not intangible, theoretical principles; rather, bodies have
the potentialities their virtues enable.

Treating virtue as the animating power of a physical body was not confined to the specialized vocabularies of science, husbandry, or medicine.
Rather, as I shall argue in greater detail, it is also important to literary representations, which seek to bring bodies to life—on the page, on the stage, or
both. The well-known opening of Chaucer's *Canterbury Tales*, from which I
take my second epigraph, affirms the animating power of material virtues:
"Of which vertu engendred is the flour" (I.4).[21] As it does in other instances,
virtue enlivens a physical body. Those animate bodies, in turn, have the
power to affect those around them. Elsewhere in *Hamlet*, when Laertes
observes Ophelia's madness, he curses his eye's natural powers:

Tears seven times salt
Burn out the sense and virtue of mine eye! (IV.v.154)

Ophelia's madness affects Laertes in an intimate, immediate fashion. The
suffering chronicled on the stage, in turn, is designed to move audiences in a
tangible, demonstrable fashion. This influence is moral, insofar as it prompts
Laertes—and insofar as it might provoke the play's spectators—to live in a
different way. The ability for bodies to make a moral difference to one
another is both ethical and physical, for this kind of virtue materializes a
world organized by specific values.

Material virtue's power is centrally connected to representational art, and
its ethical standing. Indeed, although a physical body's power to affect those
around it is well known, this capacity has long founded critiques of the
theater, as well as the literary arts more generally. Augustine, notably, dismisses the theater's ability to evoke pity as a sham form of ethics, since, as he
queries, "But how can the unreal sufferings of the stage possibly move pity."[22]
He claims such spectacles do not evoke true emotions; rather, they are
"merely fictitious," providing a superficial enjoyment that makes no moral
difference to the spectators who watch stage plays.[23] While he allows that

poetry provides greater "food for thought," and recalls how Medea's plight caused him to reflect on moral situations that he might not have otherwise contemplated, earlier in the *Confessions*, when Augustine recounts how he wept for Dido as a youthful reader of Virgil, he condemns his investment in her suicide as a distraction that prevented him from realizing the corrupt condition of his fallen soul.[24]

Despite his disapproval, Augustine confirms that poetic stories bring bodies to life, and shows how those bodies exert moral power over their immediate audiences. Yet, since the ethical demands such bodies issue are not concerned with Christian salvation, Augustine insists this power is wholly negative. The poets and playwrights I study in this book would also meet with Augustine's censure, for they are primarily concerned with imagining how people might lead better lives in the everyday circumstances of premodern England. Even narratives that prioritize Christian salvation are firmly grounded in a material world that is riven with contingency and violence, but has the potential for improvement and reform. This quotidian materialism is due, I suggest, to the sense that human excellence must be set in relation to physical powers that worked, for good or ill, as part of a broader ethical ecology in the premodern world. In a darker affirmation of these physical powers, when Laertes conspires to poison Hamlet he tells Claudius the potion is beyond the powers of any medicine:

> And for that purpose I'll anoint my sword.
> I bought an unction of a mountebank
> So mortal that, but dip a knife in it,
> Where it draws blood no cataplasm so rare,
> Collected from all simples that have virtue
> Under the moon, can save the thing from death
> That is but scratched withal . . . (IV.vii.112–18)

Such references are not just figurative, but mine a vocabulary of practical, material virtue that was believed to suffuse all physical bodies. As the herbals' and medicinals' practical appeals to readers indicate, thinking of virtue as the animate force of a material body was commonplace in early modern England.

One of the central contentions of this book is that material virtue makes an ethical difference in premodern England. If material bodies have inherent, animating powers, then those bodies typically and insistently associated with matter—namely, women—are not passive, inert, and therefore incapable of

ethical action. Rather, bodies exert moral influence by means of their proximity and connection to us. Virtue might very well be transformed on
account of its association with feminine matter. For that reason, I will
ultimately argue that a rival idea of what it means to be human emerges
when we consider virtue in relation to modes of ethical action available to
premodern women. This conception of humanity includes vulnerability,
endurance, and openness to others. Before detailing the difference matter
makes to virtue, in the following section I shall give an overview of virtue's
ethical history, or at least the Western tradition of virtue ethics that extends
from antiquity to the early modern period. I do so principally to highlight
the fact that women's exclusion from virtue ethics is widely acknowledged
by modern philosophers. I do so also to demonstrate how a shift in the
foundation of virtue changes what it means to be human. This shift does
not simply produce a new set of virtues; rather, many of the qualities that
I highlight across this study intersect, and frequently overlap, with familiar
schema. The difference, I contend, derives from thinking of the material
body not as a tool of an empowered agent, whose cultural supremacy is
guaranteed by prevailing social structures. Rather, if we consider physical
bodies as women more frequently experienced them, as fragile and open,
as well as connected and subjected to others, then our virtues will be, like
the worlds we share, transformed.

Heroic Virtue Ethics and the Virtues in Medieval England

As Alasdair MacIntyre acknowledges, the heroic society in which Aristotle
devised his ethical framework was masculinist in its assumptions about who
qualified for *areté*, or virtue.[25] Because "Aristotle believed that women could
not exercise the requisite control over their emotions," they could not be citi-
zens, and therefore they could not cultivate the virtues that accompanied public
life in the polis.[26] Stephen G. Salkever details how virtue in ancient Greek
thought was inseparable from the ideal of virility, and the inveterate misogyny
that structured republican politics.[27] Even if, as Salkever contends, Plato and
Aristotle contest the exclusively male orientation of ancient virtue, he explains
that ancient writers who come after them do not vest "women and womanly
activities [with] a greater dignity."[28] The classical formulation of *virtus*, with its
emphasis on empowered, public action, rendered women's excellences largely
invisible.

This heroic tradition dovetailed with medieval misogyny in a powerful fashion. Indeed, in the long history of virtue ethics, women's association with matter denied them an equal ability to develop virtues derived from ancient thinkers.[29] With his influential *Etymologiae*, Isidore of Seville establishes women's explicit association with matter from the seventh century: "A mother is so named because something is made from her, for the term 'mother' (*mater*) is as if the word were 'matter' (*materia*)."[30] Women's materiality, which for medieval thinkers was associated with the flesh's fallen-ness, meant they could never take up the active, autonomous practices of self-cultivation required for virtues derived from the heroic tradition.[31] For centuries, misogynist writers insisted that women acted according to bodily desires. Physical appetites, not rational dictates, drive women's actions. The thirteenth-century writer Guido Delle Colonne references women's materiality when he insists upon their insatiable desire: "But just as it is known that matter proceeds from form to form, so the dissolute desire of women proceeds from man to man."[32] This does not mean that medieval Christian thinkers adopted earlier understandings of heroic virtue wholesale. Augustine is famously uncomfortable with ancient virtues, because, "the pagan virtues are vices, if glittering ones," as Jennifer A. Herdt explains.[33]

Even so, from the twelfth century onward, Christian thinkers including Peter Abelard and Peter Lombard adopted what came to be known, following Ambrose, as the "cardinal virtues"—Prudence, Justice, Temperance, and Fortitude—which were derived from Plato and Aristotle, then Cicero and Seneca.[34] These were joined with the "theological virtues"—Faith, Hope, and Charity—which were derived from 1 Corinthians 13:13: "And now there remain faith, hope, and charity, these three: but the greatest of these is charity."[35] Thomas Aquinas's *Summa Theologiae* (I–II, q. 49–67) made the elaboration of such qualities central to medieval ethics. In his most fundamental statement, Aquinas says, "Virtue is not in a power of the soul, but in its essence."[36] Yet Aquinas's insistence on the infused nature of virtue affirms that embodiment remained a crux of medieval virtue ethics. He articulated the widely accepted idea that theological virtues were infused into the human soul by divine power, but, in a move that was generally not followed by other philosophers, he also developed a parallel set of cardinal virtues, which he argued were equally infused (this means there were two sets of cardinal virtues in Aquinas's formulation).[37] In the same way that herbs, metals, and other physical bodies were imbued with powers attributed to the divine, the human soul was invested with qualities—the infused virtues—that humans did not cultivate.

Visual art made the cardinal and theological virtues familiar, but medieval depictions also vested them with a gendered embodiment that this book investigates. Indeed, the theological and cardinal virtues were so frequently depicted as women that Barbara Newman argues they formed part of what she characterizes as a "goddess culture" in the High Middle Ages.[38] Nevertheless, because grammatical gender renders ideals including *justitia* and *prudentia* feminine in Latin, and because allegory is often taken to use abstraction to personify such qualities, women's connection to these virtues has frequently been dismissed.[39] My project challenges the dominance of this account by working to uncover the ethical influence of the material body on representations of the theological and cardinal virtues. Yet I should also like to acknowledge that the cardinal and theological virtues were not the only virtues medievals recognized. Despite the prominence of the "seven virtues" tradition, Siegfried Wentzel rightly observes: "Were one to ask Bishop Bradwardine or Geoffrey Chaucer or a real-life Haukyn the Active Man . . . to name the chief virtues[, it] would probably have occasioned a puzzled 'Which ones?' For throughout the Middle Ages, systematic theology as well as popular catechetical instruction recognized two different series of chief virtues, depending on whether 'virtue' was considered as a principle of morally right action, or as a counterpart to or replacement for a specific vice."[40] In the latter formulation, derived from practices of pastoral care, virtues were remedial and arose in direct response to enumerated sins.

The remedial virtues were responsive to actions that occurred in the world, so they were almost invariably imagined as powers that enabled and protected a Christian subject, body *and* soul. The remedial virtues, it is worth emphasizing, were multifaceted. Perhaps because the seven deadly sins could manifest themselves in myriad ways, Wentzel explains, "[the remedial virtues] never became as definitely fixed as did the corresponding list of deadly sins."[41] Two other sets of qualities derived from the Bible were also integrated into considerations of the remedial virtues: the beatitudes of Matthew 5:3–9 (or 11), along with the gifts of the Holy Spirit, from Isaiah 11:2–3. As the invaluable work of Morton Bloomfield, Richard Newhauser, and their respective collaborators demonstrates, there were over 6,500 virtues and vices treatises circulating in Europe between 1100 and 1500.[42] In establishing the genre of the *tractatus de vitiis et virtutibus*, Newhauser underscores its hierarchical organization, but also emphasizes its existence "as an intrinsically open system. . . . it was either subsumed into larger, more expansive forms . . . or was extracted from more inclusive works." For instance, although the Dominican

William Peraldus elaborated two analytically organized *summae*, a tradition of vices and virtues proliferated outside the boundaries of this popular genre.[43] Medieval virtue was multiple, and it was informed by scholastic and pastoral discourses at once.

Important for my purposes, virtues were not rendered as abstract, idealized principles, but, as the thirteenth-century *Summa Virtutum de remediis anime* makes clear, they were described as *remediis* for *morbis ipsius anime*, or "remedies" for "the soul's diseases."[44] Again, since medieval medical discourse classifies virtues as physical powers, we should not regard the use of medicinal vocabulary in a moral treatise as purely figurative. Virtues did things in the world, uniting body and soul through a system of everyday ethics in premodern England. This is because, as medievalists are keenly aware, 1215 saw the greatest pedagogical program ever instituted with the Church's Fourth Lateran Council. Lateran IV's canon, *Omnis utriusque sexus*, which required yearly confession for all Christians, meant that a basic set of spiritual information had to be taught. Answering this need, in 1281 Pecham's syllabus mandated certain rudiments of religious literacy, including instruction in the virtues, for every layperson.[45] Men as well as women were taught the virtues as part of a quotidian ecology of ethical information. These virtues overlapped and intersected: often the remedial, cardinal, and theological virtues are included in a single treatise, and the physical power that "vertu" carried in Middle English is fully utilized by writers seeking to explain the transformational capacities of these qualities.

On account of virtue's multiplicity, if one wanted to trace the ways in which the virtues informed characterizations of literary women in Middle English literature, then one would still have to decide which qualities to include in such a project. I have not followed this path, but instead, I investigate how literary authors, in seeking to represent women's ethical action, end up inventing new virtues through their female characters. This is in part because the ethical standing of these so-called canonical virtues changes over the period featured in this study. Indeed, the transition between the medieval and early modern periods in literary history is an era in the history of philosophy when virtue ethics is said to have declined.[46] Virtue becomes troubled, and is eventually eclipsed by other theorizations, following attacks upon and challenges to virtue by later writers including Luther, Machiavelli, and eventually Hume.[47] Writers from Chaucer to Shakespeare were certainly aware of the traditions of virtue ethics that derived from heroic and stoic writings, as well as scholastic philosophy and pastoral care. They did not bind themselves to these traditions, I maintain, because the creative processes of character formation demand more ethical complexity than *any* schematized set of qualities can provide. For most if not all the literary authors featured here, the motivating concern is formal, not ethical. Writing more complex characters, to be clear, produces more complicated virtues.

Nevertheless, I shall briefly elaborate the reasons why traditional virtue ethics cannot fully account for the material virtues this study uncovers. I do so to emphasize the feminist stakes of the ethical changes I trace across this book. In telling the story of the demise of virtue ethics, scholars usually point to a series of factors, which were established during the period studied here. These include the break between habit and virtue; the rise of rule-based ethics; virtue's superficial, even deceptive status; and an emphasis on the individual as the principal moral agent.[48] These factors, I suggest, arise from treating all virtues like women's virtues. Indeed, "the misfortunes of virtue," to adopt J. B. Schneewind's important formulation, always restricted women's ethical action.[49] This is because these features—which are said to cause virtue's demise in the history of philosophy—structured women's moral lives throughout the history of Western virtue ethics.

Habit, Virtue, and Women's Ethical Action

Intellectual historians confirm that the period treated in this study witnessed one of the most significant revisions to ethics in the history of Western thought, what Katharine Breen terms a "crisis of habit."[50] As Aristotle's *Nicomachean Ethics* maintained, "Moral or ethical virtue is the product of habit. . . . We become just by doing just acts, temperate by doing temperate acts, brave by doing brave acts."[51] Until the High Middle Ages, virtues were the products of habits. Yet, in the late thirteenth and early fourteenth centuries, philosophers as different as Duns Scotus, William of Ockham, and John Buridan destabilized the connection between habit and virtue.[52] Although good acts remained laudable, they said nothing about a person's virtue. A person could perform good or bad acts, in other words, but doing so would not make that person good or bad. Instead, a person's will determined a person's virtue, but volition was completely, and troublingly, severed from action. As a consequence of this ethical revision, even when a person performed good deeds, those deeds might be dismissed as indices of moral character. Or such deeds might be counted as instances of duplicity in a larger performance of deception.

Niccolò Machiavelli rather infamously embraced the impressive, theatrical, and spectacular manifestations of virtue that worried thinkers from Augustine to Luther. For Machiavelli, virtues are simply qualities that are praised by others. They do nothing to reveal the ruler's inner moral state. And, though his *virtù* created new forms of political life for ambitious men, only an elite few were empowered by these theatrical capacities.[53] For the most part, early moderns remained wary of virtue's freighted history. In the fifteenth and sixteenth centuries, thinkers including Gabriel Biel and Martin Luther attempted to reconcile the rift between volition and action that the break between habit and virtue introduced.[54] The focus shifted not to human action, but to God's grace, a *pactum* made with humans that stressed God's preeminence, as well as his mercy.[55] Human action only counts as moral virtue because God agrees to see it as such; and as we see in the writings of anti-Pelagian writers from Augustine onward, there was a persistent insistence that no human deed could ever earn divine favor—human virtue is not based on merit, but on God's free gift of grace. The crisis in habit, because it divides a person's moral character from ethical action, puts virtue under suspicion.

This crisis in habit is significant because, I want to emphasize, it merely extends to everyone a long-standing assumption about women's moral lives. Aristotelian virtue ethics always reserved *consuetudo* (custom) for lesser persons, including women.[56] Used to enforce social and gender divisions, this form of repeated action occupied "lower mental faculties and the habitus . . . higher ones."[57] Because women had no access to the rational capacities that made ethical habits transformative, their good deeds said nothing about their virtue. With his *Enchiridion militis Christiani* (1501; trans. William Tyndale, 1533) Desiderius Erasmus attempts to allay broader worries about virtue by codifying a form of *imitatio Christi*.[58] While Erasmus does not claim that following Christ's perfect model will habituate the soul, such imitation does formulate a code of conduct that affirms humans' struggle to maintain faith in the face of their own frailties. The rise of rule-based ethics, therefore, was a direct response to the late medieval crisis in habit. Here too, though, ethics only expanded to men an assumption that had always been applied to women. Indeed, early thinkers had always insisted that women should practice codified moralized actions. From Christian antiquity and throughout the Middle Ages, male advisers trained their female charges in virtuous rules of conduct. From Tertullian to Jerome, from Jacques de Vitry to Jean Gerson, and from Richard Rolle to Walter Hilton, medieval male writers affirm their relation to an ethical habitus by dispensing moral training to women.[59] The rule-based morality that is often cited as a factor in the broader demise of virtue, then, was always applied to women in the early history of virtue ethics.

Rule-Based Ethics and Conduct Books for Women

While women's virtues had long been directed and supervised by men, the vernacular hybrid situated somewhere between spiritual guide, courtesy manual, and exemplary catalog, which modern scholars now roughly refer to as the "conduct book," arose during the period studied in this project.[60] Emerging in the fourteenth and fifteenth centuries, and gaining cultural importance in the era following, the genre provides guidelines for those wishing to pattern their lives after elite modes of outward presentation.[61] These books aim not just to provide ethical rules, but more importantly, I suggest, to dematerialize virtue, to make it into a set of principles that can never be fully embodied. Indeed, despite their announced practicality, conduct treatises for women present intangible virtues (not particular acts) of worthy figures for ethical imitation. As William Caxton explains in the preface to his 1484 translation of *Le Livre du chevalier de la Tour Landry*, "Emong al other this book is a special doctrine & techyng by which al yong gentyl wymen specially may lerne to bihaue them self vertuously."[62] His *Book of the Knight of the Tower* abstracts the narratives it contains, distilling particular virtues by separating them from the specific conditions of their emergence. Women are told to act like the Virgin Mary in their humility, even if they are not chosen to be "the moder of the sone of God / of whome the regne shold haue none ende." The abstract ideal is then converted into the good behavior recommended for late medieval women: "Euery good woman oughte to humble her self toward god / toward her lord and toward the world."[63] Other narratives extol the virtues of strong, active women, yet the complex particulars that invest model heroines with moral power are downplayed as a means to shape everyday feminine conduct.

And, while the totalized exemplarity of famous women allowed Christine de Pizan to recuperate a number of sullied heroines in her *Cité des dames* (ca. 1405; trans. Henry Pepwell, 1521), the exceptionalism of female worthies remained a distinctive feature of conduct books incorporating such idealized narratives. Christine features the deeds of strong pagan and Christian women, but as Justice explains in her introduction of holy saints' lives, these narratives offer good women lessons for contemplation, not emulation. Though she is installed as the "heede of the kynde of women" to confirm a continuing

history of feminine excellence, Mary, as Queen of Heaven, equally demonstrates "her hyghnesse towarde [regular women's] lytelnesse."[64] Similarly, in
what became the most popular conduct book in Tudor England, *De institu-
tione feminae Christianae* (1523; trans. Richard Hyrde, ca. 1529, as *A very frutefull and pleasant boke called the Instruction of a Christen woman*), the Spanish
humanist Juan Luis Vives instructs unmarried women to model their lives
after the Virgin Mary: "Therfore by my counsaile the mayde shall folowe her
[the Virgin Mary's] example / nat with a faynyng & a dissembling mynde /
but true and stedfaste / leste there be a worse vice lying vnder a colour of
virtue / as hit were a poison vnder an holsome thynge / or a sore vnder a
holle skynne."[65] In recommending the Virgin Mary as a model, Vives's guide
confirms that the virtues prescribed to women have little to do with their
everyday lives.

To this point, after Gaspar objects that the women described in book 3
of Baldassare Castiglione's *Courtyer* are "so farr from vs, that many lyes may
be toulde," Julian turns to contemporary examples. In a great irony, however,
these women are treated with far more abstraction and generalization than
narratives featuring famous women from the legendary or biblical past.[66] Giovanni Boccaccio captures the anxiety that accompanies presentist exemplarity
in his *De claris mulieribus*, for as he tells his eventual addressee, the Countess
of Altavilla, he settled on her after he realized the renown of his initial choice,
Joanna, queen of Sicily and Jerusalem, would outshine "the flickering flame
of my little book so small and weak."[67] To say more, Boccaccio tacitly admits,
would risk comparing this dazzling queen to other women, thereby reducing
her unmatched virtues to everyday conduct. By and large, writers including
Boccaccio and Castiglione do not treat contemporary notables as living,
breathing actors. They are icons, whose agency is suspended by their prized
exemplarity. Through Castiglione's praise of Queen Isabella, the airy virtue
of the court lady gains a living model: "There hath not bine in our time in
the world a more cleere example of true goodnesse, stoutnes of courage,
wisdome, religion, honestie, courteisie, liberalitie, to be bref, of all vertue,
then Queene Isabel."[68]

The disembodied, rule-based ethics formulated by premodern conduct
books rendered virtue as a performance in ways that were problematic for
women in particular. What had been a spontaneous, improvised reaction
became a rote rehearsal of moralized norms that exercised no ethical hold
over individual subjectivity. Worse, if a woman had no ethical investment in
the goods she performed, her virtues might be feigned, or even used to

deceive her immediate audiences. In a rather infamous example, Phillip Stubbes links his critique of the theater to virtue's superficial status in *The anatomie of abuses* (1583). His condemnation does not just affirm that stage plays teach their audiences "to playe the vice"; rather, he argues that women's cosmetics, like their ornate clothing, encourage women to feign virtue, to hide their corruption under the guise of excellence.[69] If virtue becomes scripted, played according to moral rules that say nothing about ethical subjectivity, then the power of this form of ethics, this logic reveals, is wholly negative. Stubbes equally condemns men for ethical emptiness, but he does so by decrying their "effeminat condition, as we may seeme rather nice dames and yonge gyrles, than puissante ag[e]nts, or manlie men, as our Forefathers haue bene."[70] Once again, an ethical practice associated with women degrades virtue more generally. Even if we dismiss Stubbes's attack as inflammatory, his treatise nevertheless shows how the rise of rule-based ethics leads directly to an association between virtue's duplicity and women's corruption.

Women's Corruption and Virtue's Duplicity

In establishing the suspicion of virtue in early modern thought, Michael Moriarty traces a much longer tradition from classical antiquity through the Christian Middle Ages. He does so because early modern writers use a longer tradition to "put forward . . . redescriptions of apparently virtuous behavior as fundamentally vicious."[71] My project begins with the late Middle Ages because by the second half of the fourteenth century, it was clear that virtue's duplicity was connected to women's corruption. This link was present even when it was not immediately apparent. For instance, the fifteenth-century *N-Town Passion Play I* blames virtue's flimsiness on Satan's abuse of language, since he renames the seven deadly sins so that each takes on the guise of virtue:

> Ye shal kalle Pride '[H]oneste,' and 'Naterall Kend' Lechory,
> And Covetise 'Wisdam there tresure is present';
> Wreth 'Manhod,' & Envye callyd 'Chastement'
> (Seyse nere session, lete perjery be chef);
> Glotynye, 'Rest' (let abstinawnce beyn absent);
> And he that wole exorte the[e] to vertu, put hem to repreff.[72]

The practice of *paradiastole*, that is, redescribing the virtues of one's opponent as vices, was a mainstay of classical rhetoric, but the medieval conven-
tion of masking vices as virtues derives from the sermon tradition.[73] And, as
John F. Plummer points out, Satan's deliberate confusion of vice with virtue
has an explicitly gendered history in medieval sermons: "The image of Satan
renaming sins to make them more palatable for mankind is a commonplace
in the fifteenth-century English sermon, and seems to have had its origin in
the popular stories of the devil's marrying of his seven daughters, the deadly
sins, to humanity; in order to make these ugly daughters marriageable, Satan
gave them new names."[74]

The fifteenth-century sermon from the Gloucester Cathedral Library
describes the reoutfitting process for the devil's eldest daughter, Pride: "And
for by cawse that the fende wolde marry hyr to the pepull of the worlde, he
hathe sett on hyr a gay name and now sche is callyd Honestye."[75] Satan's
redescription of vices as virtues in the *N-Town Passion Play I*, just mentioned,
comes after a passage that details women's capacities for deception:

> A beggerys dowtere to make gret purviauns
> To cownterfete a jentylwoman, disgeysyd as she can.[76]

Here as elsewhere, virtue's corruption follows from a woman's duplicity—her
ability to feign worthiness. And, while political theorists have attended to the
ways that Machiavelli adopted *paradiastole* from the ancients, an association
between women's corruption and virtue's duplicity persisted in early modern
England.[77] Barnabe Rich is most engaging in decrying those: "Idle fol|lies of
this madding age, that Time hath now hatched vp, and are long sithens
become so flush and fligge, that they are flowne into the world, and they
haue there nestled them|selues amongst the Chickins of vertue, so disguising
them|selues vnder the habit of vertue, that they are reputed to be of vertues
Broode, and are not easily to be discerned by their plumes, or outward
shew."[78] Vice can look like virtue, Rich warns in *My Ladies Looking Glasse*
(1616), which purports to distinguish "A Good Woman from a Bad, and the
true resemblance of vice, masked vnder the vizard of vertue" (t.p.).

Similarly, Nicholas Breton's *Will of Wit* (1597) accepts virtue's potential
for duplicity:

> For vertue many waies,
> Is made a vice, yet Vertue hath her praise.[79]

This is despite Breton's insistence in *The Soules Immortall Crowne* (1605) that "Vertue is Wisedome's light," a font of glorious truth:

> No, where she loues, it tends but with her life,
> And whe~ she speakes, her Iudgements shewes her wit:
> And, when she writes, her Concords know no strife,
> What choise conceite shall chiefe in honour sit:
> But speake, and write, and looke, and like, and loue,
> All haue their blessings in the heauens aboue.[80]

Virtue's potential for perversion, despite her truth, can be traced to skepticism regarding appearances in early modern culture. Things that are false can appear to be true; that which is corrupt can take on the guise of the unsullied. Even writers who personify virtue, who depict virtue as a woman whose truth is disregarded, even denigrated, by a superficial culture infatuated with debased vices, articulate the fears that many men had about women's capacity for virtue during this period.

In *A dyall for dainty darlings* (1584), William Averell insists that virtue remains true by retaining its inward character. For Averell, "vertue [is] a habite of the hidden minde, [which] appeared not in her externall déedes."[81] Phillip Stubbes seeks to memorialize his young wife's death after childbirth in *A Christal Glas for christian women* (1592), but the virtue he ascribes to Katherine Stubbes in his popular pamphlet hides her from the world: "& so solitary was she giuen, that she would verie seldome or neuer, & that not with|out great constraint (& than not neither, except her husband were in companie) goe abroad with any, either to banquet or feast, to gossip or make merry (as they tearme it) in so much that she hath beene noted to do it in contempt and disdaine of others."[82] Thomas Salter's *Mirrhor of Modestie* (1579) goes further, suggesting that the mirror his treatise presents is "of an other maner of matter, and is of muche more worthe then any Christall Mirrhor; for as the one tea|cheth how to attire the outward bodie, so the other guideth to garnishe the inward mynde, and maketh it meete for vertue."[83] To conclude his treatise, Salter appends "A pretie pithie Dialogue betwene Mercurie, & Ver|tue," which presents virtue as neglected and disrespected by a corrupt, superficial society.[84] For women in the world, then, virtue is hidden by a protective interiority, and makes no outward appearance in deed, or even gesture. When virtue does appear in public, society treats virtue as degraded, unwanted, and suspicious. As these texts collectively demonstrate, early modern English culture confined women's virtue to an inward domain where it had no shaping impact on the world. Outward acts, furthermore, were treated as disguised and misleading vices. Vives points to his own mother-in-law as a perfect model of forbearance, but the patience Clara Cervent displays while nursing her grotesquely ill husband makes her deeds suspect. Readers are clearly meant to marvel at her willing abasement, "And euery day [she] dyd salue and bynde his sore and stynkyng legges and rounnyng of matter." But what of the claim, offered without irony, that she preserved him "with that dolefull body, more like unto a graue, than a body . . . in the whiche space she had two chyldren by hym"?[85] Cervent's miraculous conception reveals a rift between feminine excellence and female embodiment in premodern virtue ethics.

Virtue's Misfortunes and Hamlet's Advice to Gertrude

The familiar story of virtue and its misfortunes confines women's ethical action in premodern England. This does not mean, of course, that the literary authors featured in this study were immune to this powerful tradition. On the contrary, when he advises his mother, Hamlet assumes three of the four factors that led to virtue's demise in conventional accounts of virtue ethics:

> Assume a virtue if you have it not
> That monster custom, who all sense doth eat,
> Of habits devilish, is angel yet in this:
> That to the use of actions fair and good
> He likewise gives a frock or livery
> That aptly is put on. Refrain tonight,
> And that shall lend a kind of easiness
> To the next abstinence, the next more easy—
> For use almost can change the stamp of nature. (III.iv.151.1–9)

For Gertrude, there is a break between habit and virtue, her behavior must be rule-governed, and her good deeds remain suspect due to her inveterate bodily corruption, or what Hamlet refers to as "the stamp of nature."[86]

To resist the benighted materiality of the female body, Hamlet urges Gertrude to follow custom. This is despite the fact that Hamlet earlier imagines this mindless form of behavioral repetition in wholly negative terms, wondering if the rote enactment of cultural expectations has deadened his mother's ability to distinguish right from wrong:

> And let me wring your heart; for so I shall
> If it be made of penetrable stuff,
> If damnèd custom have not brassed it so
> That it is proof and bulwark against sense. (III.iv.34–37)

When he implores Gertrude to avoid Claudius's bed, however, Hamlet emphasizes unthinking custom's positive potential. In the same way that it can corrupt those disposed to good, mindless actions can improve those who might pursue vice. Gertrude's vicious deed is sex with Claudius. If she abstains for one night, Hamlet insists, resistance will become increasingly easy for her. This is notwithstanding Gertrude's desire for Claudius. Importantly, Hamlet does not address Gertrude's desire except as it might be reupholstered by alternative practice. Deep down she might continue to love or want Claudius; but through virtuous action, Gertrude's unvirtuous desire will be masked, even if it is never completely remade. When he sidesteps Gertrude's volitional investment, Hamlet resists any suggestion that Gertrude might cultivate virtue as a "habite of the hidden minde," in Averill's words, above.

Unlike earlier advisers, moreover, Hamlet is not concerned with Gertrude's soul. Her outward practice, not her inward disposition, interests the young prince. Indeed, since he treats virtue as an external covering—as a pleasing outfit that might be donned—he puts faith only in its extrinsic, imposed dimension. Like Claudius, Hamlet sees a distinct break between "th'exterior [and] the inward man" (II.ii.6). Modern scholars have found ample room in this formulation for the emergence of modern interiority, or "that within which passeth show" (I.ii.85).[87] We might therefore assume an expansive terrain of complex interiority would also be extended to women, since, as Kathryn Schwarz sagely observes, "Good women have to know what they are doing."[88] To be sure, Gertrude must will her own alteration to enact Hamlet's recommendations. Yet, according to the familiar story of virtue ethics, women's investment in their own ethical action is rendered moot. Once Gertrude accedes to her son's directives, her volition can be voided by the repetition custom dictates. In fact, the lingering specter of Gertrude's bodily corruption necessitates continued masculine supervision, for Gertrude cannot be trusted to direct her own moral behaviors to ends that count as ethical excellences by premodern society. She will enact only vice, even if she means to perform virtue.

In seeking to forestall what he characterizes as Gertrude's lust, Hamlet justifies his continued control over his mother's behavior by suggesting that she is a creature of appetite. He reasons with her, in other words, even though he believes bodily desires govern her moral choices. The Ghost tells Hamlet that Gertrude's virtue is just a cover for deeper duplicity, since "virtue . . . never will be moved, / Though lewdness court it in a shape of heaven" (I.v.53–54). She is for him "my most seeming-virtuous queen" (I.v.46), or an actor who dons virtue to pursue vice. Like his father, Hamlet treats Gertrude's desire as corporeal, seated in the physical appetites of the lustful (female) body. He refuses to believe her virtue is anything but a superficial ruse, a shallow performance that says nothing about Gertrude's inner character. When women are tutored in virtue, guided by men through the motions that culturally count as goodness, they lose ethical autonomy. If women enact virtues by themselves, however, they gain startling—sometimes threatening—new powers. In thirteenth- and four-teenth-century visual art from German nunneries, Christ is frequently depicted as crucified by feminized virtues.[89] Although this image is meant to enact the allegory of the *Song of Songs*, the nightmare of women's ethical action is realized through the virtues' feminization.

A Different Perspective: Virtue's Organicism

This project investigates alternatives to this nightmarish vision of women's virtues. In part, this is because, as Kathryn Schwarz observes, "a curious pattern" emerges in early modern literatures: "Women pose a threat when they willingly conform to social conventions."[90] Likewise, Glenn Burger ana-lyzes the "performative reading" medieval conduct literature elicits as "a set of practices developed individually by means of an internalized, textually driven process of understanding."[91] As these scholars detail, women often find room to develop ethical subjectivity through even the most prescriptive, rule-based guides, in situations where women's virtue is subject to skepticism, if not outright dismissal. I maintain that this happens when the grounds of virtue become material. Women overturn the prescriptive ideals that demate-rialize their virtues when the physical body is reimagined as a positive resource for ethical action. In recognizing the material body's positive ethical potential, medieval and early modern writers resist virtue's reduction to a superficial guise that might be deployed to mask vice. This struggle need not be associated with gender at all. In fact, many premodern texts avoid gender in imagining "virtues" that matter. What David Aers identifies as William Langland's "organicism" in his late fourteenth-century master-piece, *Piers Plowman*, is just this sort of attempt to resist virtue's subversion.[92]

To be sure, Langland taps the tradition of feminized virtue at the end of Passus V in the B-Text; moreover, the debate between the four daughters of God in the B-Text's Passus XVIII is yet another variation on this artistic motif. Late in the poem, however, Langland turns away from feminized virtue: mining a naturalistic register, Langland figures the cardinal virtues—temperance, prudence, justice, and fortitude—as grains that Grace sows in the soul of mankind. In his effort to prevent virtue from becoming a flimsy covering for corruption, Langland invokes virtue's materiality, or its ability to suffuse all physical bodies. In this Langland is not alone, nor is his organicism a complete departure from what I have been calling traditional virtue ethics. Indeed, earlier Latin writers also use organic topoi to explain virtue's relation to divine agency and human autonomy. Hildegard of Bingen's twelfth-century *Ordo Virtutum*, which features sixteen feminized virtues singing to Anima, also imagines the virtues as the boughs of a tree rooted by the Patriarchs and Prophets ("Nos sumus radices et vos rami, / fructus viventis oculi").[93] The "tree of virtues" motif is part of a larger mnemonic structure that system-building philosophers employed to communicate the complexity of medieval virtue ethics.[94] We often think of medieval virtues as elaborately hierarchized, and it is true that medieval thinkers frequently used the tree of virtues to differentiate moral properties root and branch. Nevertheless, such depictions also unify virtue as a flourishing and dynamic system of connected excellences. These qualities grow from one another, and human excellence stems from divine power. In a thirteenth-century copy of the *Speculum Virginum*, the interconnection of virtues visually insists that moral goods are generative, material, and living (see fig. 1).

This motif does not fade away: in Additional MS 37049—the fifteenth-century Carthusian miscellany described as a "spiritual encyclopedia"—an English devotional poem "The Desert of Religion" uses the "tree of virtues" to show how goodness implanted by the divine grows within the human soul (see fig. 2).[95] As the early seventeenth-century *Two guides to a good life* (1604) insists, "The tree of vertue muste florish in euerie bra~ch, In which sence it

placuit· ut er ōfidatiōe peioris· grã uideat' melioris· Verũm ḡ adã atten
de in arce uirtioſe arborꝭ poſitũ· nouũ adã obtinẽ, puent' ſpatis ꝑnciꝑa
tũ· Deniꝗ· ſi ꝓſtantiꝯ detioꝛ· iðē ſi bonũ malo ꝯumꝑeris· ꝗ̄ in his emi
neat' ualent' īteliigꝭ· Collatis enim ꝗ̄uratiꝯ ōꝛioꝛ· luce clariꝯ patebit
eſtimatio melioꝛum·

FIGURE I. Tree of virtues in the Latin tradition, thirteenth century. Ms. W.72,
fol. 26ʳ. The Walters Art Museum, Baltimore.

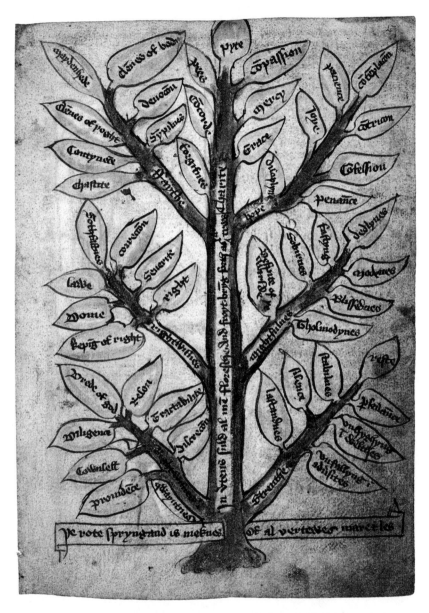

FIGURE 2. Tree of Virtues in vernacular tradition, fifteenth century, England. © The British Library Board. MS Additional 37049, 47ʳ.

will be as a shelter in time of neces|sitie, and a hauen of peace to the con|
science."[96] Poetic organicism enables vernacular writers to investigate the ethical implications of community norms in material terms. In *Piers Plowman*,
the corruption Langland imagines in the poem's grim conclusion is social.
Pride preys on the "Cristen peple," but in casting doubt on virtue's veracity,
"Wiþ swiche colours and queyntise comeþ Pride y-armed," Langland's poem
levies a broader critique against degraded cultural practices.[97] The erosion of
virtue arises from social habits that make moral excellence less substantial.
Through abuse, virtue becomes intangible. Ideally, though, Langland suggests that virtue has a palpable impact on the world. As Will's search for
Dowel affirms, virtues are not ethereal principles, but lived practices that rely
on material embodiment. The invocation of virtue's materialism in everyday
contexts was not unique to Langland; indeed, as this book shall detail, many
medieval and early modern writers sought to make virtue more substantial.

Moreover, Rosemond Tuve's still-powerful analysis demonstrates the importance of medieval representations of vices and virtues to early modern writers. She not only charts the numerous, overlapping classical and medieval
traditions that ground ideas about the virtues for Spenser, Lodge, and their
contemporaries. She also emphasizes the dynamic, responsive, and generative
fluorescence of the virtues as gifts from the Holy Ghost—invested by divine
Grace—as a response to the seven vices. In Tuve's words, in imagining the
virtues, "accommodation rather than rivalry or substitution" marked authors'
representations.[98] In the sixteenth and early seventeenth centuries, treatises on
the virtues and vices continued to be translated and reprinted. And, although
there were formal treatises that delineated the virtues in a schematic, hierarchical fashion, virtues nevertheless remain sites for creativity and combination.
Thomas Paynell's English rendering of *The ensamples of vertue and vice, gathered
oute of holye scripture*, originally compiled by the thirteenth-century Dominican
and Patriarch of Jerusalem, Nicolas Hanape (1561), uses biblical paraphrase to
guide readers through a series of exhortations to virtue and condemnations of
vice. With chapters including "Of the wisedome of wemen," as well as "Of the
pietye & compassion of wemen," Paynell's translation imagines virtues as
actions that actual women perform in their everyday environs.[99] Similarly, John
Larke's 1565 translation, *The booke of wysdome, otherwyse called, The flower of
vertue*, uses classical and Christian examples to demonstrate "howe a Man (or
a Woman) oughte to be adorned with vertues."[100]

Medieval representations shaped sixteenth- and seventeenth-century
notions of virtue and vice, but, and perhaps more importantly, renderings of

virtue that originate after 1500 frequently share with their earlier counterparts a conception of virtues as material, living, and, in many contexts, feminine.[101] This is not to say that writers from the sixteenth and early seventeenth centuries have the same religious outlook on virtue as writers from the late fourteenth and fifteenth centuries. On the contrary, Thomas Becon's daily guide, *The gouernaunce of vertue* (1566), cautions readers, "against the plucking away of thy trust and confi|dence from Christ and his merites, to put in the merites of other creatures, or in thine own good workes, or in the intercession of Saintes, or in sacrifice of the popish Masse."[102] The argument of this book acknowledges differences between medieval and early modern periods, but it also examines continuities that have hitherto been ignored. Above all, there is a concerted effort to make virtues matter in people's everyday lives. As a consequence, pastoral literatures often use organic figures of spiritual cultivation: *The Book of Vices and Virtues*, a fourteenth-century translation of the popular *Somme le Roi*, returns man and woman to a prelapsarian garden of spiritual growth where God grafts virtues into the individual soul.[103] The virtues God fosters, importantly, are imagined as making a substantial difference in the shared lives of fellow Christians. *The arbour of vertue* (1576), like *The vineyard of virtue* (1579), conceptualizes virtues as both natural and intertwined.[104]

The Positive Case: Feminine Virtue

As these examples demonstrate, premodern virtues are often represented as material. Viewing virtues this way, I propose, remakes what counts as ethical excellence, and also transforms what it means to be human. Imagining virtues as collective, generative, material, and open does not correspond with a notion of human subjectivity as individual, governing, intellectual, and closed. In fact, the fourth major criterion said to have caused virtue's demise—the prominence of the individual moral agent—stands in direct opposition to the conception of ethical excellence I investigate in the following chapters. Rather, and importantly for the argument that unfolds across this book, the model of human subjectivity that corresponds to this alternative formulation of virtue is historically associated with women: rooted in the body, connected to others, and involved in fostering, not governing, intimate relations that cross all boundaries of individual selfhood.

Unsurprisingly, therefore, women are often central to figuring material virtues. *The Digby Mary Magdalene*, a fifteenth-century saint's drama, cannily renders virtues as organic properties, which grow from the seeds Christ implants in the human soul.[105] Yet this organicism is overlaid by gendered allegory, which figures human submission through Mary's obedient response to Christ. Mary is embarrassed when she realizes her error, "I wentt ye had bin Simond the gardener," but Christ reassures her:

> So I am, forsothe, Mary;
> Mannys hartt is my gardin here.
> Therin I sow sedys of vertu all the yere;
> The fowle wedes and vicys, I reynd up by the rote.
> Whan that gardin is watteryd with teris clere,
> Than spring vertuus, and smelle full sote.[106]

Mary's reliance on Christ's power is a model for women and men alike, but her pliancy draws on the premodern belief in feminine passivity.

Accounts of ethics that rely on individual agency cast passivity in a wholly negative light. In yet another way, then, women are shut out of the conventional history of virtue ethics. Women's passivity was commonly assumed by foundational thinkers in this tradition, as Joan Cadden explains: "From Aristotle came the hierarchical formulation which represented females as consistently inferior and specifically cool, weak, and passive."[107] *The Generation of Animals* contains key passages linking women's passivity to their materiality, and thereby to their social inferiority: "By now it is plain that the contribution which the female makes to generation is the *matter* used therein. . . . The male provides the 'form' and the 'principle of the movement', the female provides the body, in other words, the material."[108] Female materiality made women passive, and this lack of agency distanced them from powers of governance—over self or others. Because women are limited by their materiality, furthermore, they are ideally submissive to the active powers of masculine governance.[109] In *Book to a Mother*, a fourteenth-century epistolary guide from clerical son to widowed mother, the speaker advises, "Also wommen, be ʒe soget to men" since women are unable to govern themselves.[110] Thomas Aquinas echoes Aristotle when he asserts women's lower status: "But the father, as the active partner, is a principle in a higher way than the mother, who supplies the passive or material element."[111]

Misogyny has long relied on just this kind of sexist appropriation of matter as inert, pliant, and passive. Yet, as Caroline Walker Bynum argues, "matter was not mere dead stuff": "Because it was understood to be that which changes, matter was threat and opportunity: a threat because it decays, an opportunity because change is manifestation of the new. Matter is the place where what was seems to depart, yet it is also the place where life can be born. Astonishing things erupt in it. It can renew itself . . . generate new matter . . . or return from decay to life in resurrection miracles."[112] Matter is where virtue might be realized, since matter is where powers of the divine take physical shape. Consequently, as this book demonstrates, it is through material virtues that women's actions might gain moral authority. In this book, I spend a lot of time detailing how women's actions—particularly those that might be taken to be passive in traditional accounts—assume ethical heft in different literary representations. Across the following chapters, however, I aim to show that material virtue is not confined to women. Most men experience subjectivity in ways similar to those I will trace as feminine: as vulnerable, as subject to others, as shaped by sources outside the self. Furthermore, there is an important tradition of putting women at the center of human experience, both in spiritual and secular writings.

When women are taken as examples for spiritual relations with the divine, their pliancy is meant to be a positive attribute that should be instructive to all. *A commemoration of the life and death of the right worshipfull and vertuous ladie; Dame Helen Branch (late wife to the right worshipfull Sir Iohn Branch Knight, sometime Lord Maior of the famous Citie of London) by whose godly and virtuous life, virgines are insinuated to virtue, wiues to faithfulnes, and widdowes to Christian contemplation, and charitable deuotion, &c.* (1594) praises its subject for her submission to God: "A godly life she always led, vprightly she did deale."[113] In other words, because virtue is frequently thought to be bestowed by a higher power, the receptivity of pious women becomes an ethical model for emulation. In such accounts passivity is not inertia, nor is it weakness; rather, it is a performance of compliance, of selflessness, and of receptivity that reorganizes human subjectivity. The fourteenth-century religious writers Richard Rolle and Walter Hilton certainly understood the significance of feminized receptivity, selflessness, and compliance for all spiritual subjects.[114] This is because virtues are endowed with agency and substance even in early renderings. To return briefly to Hildegard's *Ordo Virtutum*: when Anima turns to follow Diabolus, the sixteen feminized virtues not only sing to her, but they also take up her cause. According to Peter Dronke, the "Virtues [are] conceived not only as qualities within the human being but as creative forces in the cosmos, forces that fight on Anima's behalf."[115]

The virtues' martial might recalls their earliest allegorical dramatization, when Prudentius stages a pitched battle between feminized virtues and vices in his late fourth-century *Psychomachia*.[116] This contest is firmly located within the human psyche, but the qualities themselves maintain a nonhuman autonomy. Because such representations derive from allegory, scholars frequently assume these powers have little to do with women, their bodies, or their experiences. Yet, as Helen Cooper demonstrates, in personification allegory "a feminine personification invited development in female terms."[117] She further notes a difference in conceiving a certain quality—including a virtue—as having "an existence independent of the person that feels it; it is a state larger than one's self but in which one can participate."[118] Imagining feminized virtues as having an independent existence entails picturing women—many of whom look like contemporary elites—embodying different virtues, the powers of which reach beyond the conventionally drawn boundaries of the individual self. Medieval virtues could be understood as material and female, collective and positive; to dismiss the tradition of feminized virtues as purely figurative is to deliberately ignore the tangible influence these ideas exercised over premodern understandings of women's ethical action.

The refusal to credit a connection between figures of feminized virtue and women's ethical action discounts instances when actual women are praised for virtue. Anthony Gibson's *A Woman's Worth* (1599), like many treatises extolling women's virtues, is dedicated to the Countess of Southampton, along with named and unnamed ladies-in-waiting to Elizabeth I.[119] And, even if we are tempted to dismiss the numerous dedications that declare women's virtues in the sixteenth and early seventeenth centuries as opportunistic flattery on the part of favor-seeking authors, it is difficult to set aside the amazing collection devoted to the memory of Richard Crashaw's stepmother, Elizabeth Skinner Crashaw, after her untimely death in childbirth. *The honour of virtue* (1620), or a collation that includes funeral sermon, elegies, and epitaphs, insists that its subject combined "Wisdome with Vertue" and that "Beauty and vertue together dwelt in her faire Brest."[120] The ability for material virtues to affect the inner and outer lives of subjects bespeaks their positive connective powers. Material virtues link subjects to the world and to one another, as Thomas Dekker's *Pleasant Comedie of Old Fortunatus* (1600) confirms. In this play, the goddess Virtue seeks a land with a climate hospitable enough to replenish her withered tree. Because virtues are powers that thrive on connection, virtue's isolation dooms her to rootless wandering.[121]

About a century earlier, as Liza Blake directs us to notice, Henry Medwall's *Nature* (c. 1495) debates whether "virtues are understood . . . as
abstract and immaterial moral qualities, . . . [or] as properties of nature."[122]
When virtues are part of the natural world, they circulate between bodies,
growing and multiplying as a network of material excellences. When virtues
are imagined as material, they are not superficial, nor can they be worn
like a pleasing, and sometimes deceptive, garment. They grow organically,
connecting body and soul, human and divine, subject and community.
They remake more than the gender division that structures traditional virtue ethics. Because they render the body as a positive ethical endowment,
material virtues transform what it means to be human. They critique traditional virtue ethics for making the individual the ideal moral subject. They
also provide a new foundation for ethics, one based on openness and connection, not governance and domination. To put women at the center of
human experience is to prioritize another model of the human; it is to
develop a counter-ethics that critiques the individual, usually masculine,
agent whose actions express ethical qualities.

Individualist Virtue: Ophelia's Songs

In many of the literary representations traced in this book, material virtue
issues an important critique of individualist ethics. In Shakespeare's *Hamlet*,
it becomes troublingly apparent, women are relegated to supporting roles in
masculine shows of individual virtue. Shortly after Hamlet appears impaired,
Gertrude tells Ophelia,

> so shall I hope your virtues
> Will bring him to his wonted way again,
> To both your honours. (III.i.42–44)

Ophelia's recognized excellence is meant to return Hamlet to his former
habits, but instead, his public dissolution predicates her death. With her
breakdown, Ophelia shows the terrible consequences of the cultural logic
that insists women's virtue depends upon and complements that of men. *The
Flower of friendshippe* (1571) makes women's supplementary status explicit:
"hir husba~d['s] . . . face must be hir dayly looking glasse, wherein she ought
to be alwais prying, to sée when he is mery, when sad, when content, and

when discontent, wherto she must alwais frame hir own countenance."[123] Through its shocking futility, Ophelia's demise uncovers material virtue as a countertradition of ethics that contests the public excellence required by the heroic model of *virtus*.

It is not so important that Ophelia's madness upends Hamlet's claims to moral or mental soundness, though it does both. More crucially, Ophelia's break with reason uncovers an embodied excellence that calls into question the moral logic motivating Hamlet's personal pursuit of justice. Her bodily immediacy, to be clear, critiques Hamlet's virtue. Rather than focusing on Hamlet's failure to achieve virtue, my project works to explain why Ophelia's endurance is a model of virtue in and of itself. In doing so, I follow the groundbreaking argument of Mary Beth Rose, who traces the emergence of endurance-based heroism in sixteenth- and seventeenth-century England. As she contends, the ability to endure rather than exercise agency formulates a powerful model of heroism.[124] How Ophelia responds to others, not how she acts as an individual, founds her excellence. I differ from Rose, though, because I acknowledge the existence of endurance-heroism as a valued model of ethical action in the late Middle Ages. To attend to vernacular English literatures of the fourteenth century, including writings by John Gower, the *Pearl*-poet, Julian of Norwich, and William Langland, is to understand endurance as an important resource of power. Fifteenth-century writers not treated in this study, such as Thomas Hoccleve, Margery Kempe, and Nicholas Love, equally suggest that endurance is a multivalent expression of an influential ethics. Perhaps most strikingly and shockingly, the cycle drama, with its focus on the vulnerable "manhed" of Christ, makes enduring (rather than exercising) agency the basis of an incarnated excellence.[125]

Besides establishing the longer history of endurance-based ethics, this book also aims to locate the reasons why this material form of virtue emerged, and to identify why and when it was eclipsed. In this, I am instructed by the work of early modernists including Melissa Sanchez, James Kuzner, and Joseph Campana, all of whom trace the importance of vulnerability as a foundation for ethics in sixteenth- and seventeenth-century England.[126] While these studies focus on vulnerability as a virtue, I suggest that material virtue requires vulnerability. As the following chapters shall detail, material virtue is the ability to survive and thrive in response to the common conditions of physical embodiment. It consists of how we react to others' treatment—good or bad—and it is evident when we react to the solicitations, provocations, and even aggravations that arise in our everyday dealings with one another. It is not limited to suffering, but, as Chaucer's representation of Criseyde affirms, it also includes enchantment, inspiration, and love.[127] As Mark Miller argues, ethical virtue defies binary distinctions between agency and passivity.[128] Because material virtue relies on embodiment, it crosses the nonhuman/human divide. And, although it might arise from mistreatment, material virtue can reinscribe painful experiences in restorative ways. Ophelia's virtue critiques the conditions that precipitate her suffering, but it is also reparative, insofar as it includes an ever-present offer to connect with others. The material virtue Ophelia enacts—like that of other female characters studied across this book—enables subjects to remain open to the world. Because it acknowledges shared finitude between bodies, this form of virtue is not based on active mastery over docile matter. Julia Reinhardt Lupton differentiates between the "excellences practiced in civic humanism and those capacities that subsist in things, whether animal, vegetable, or mineral."[129] My interest is with the latter, but I suggest that these powers animate nonhuman and human bodies alike.

These virtues arise from embodiment, and they allow their practitioners to maintain their dignity even in circumstances that are beyond their control. When these virtues arise as a consequence of harms, they are not simply an expression of mourning or lamentation. Rather, the virtues I study also entail a critique of the conditions that produce them. What Jane Bennett calls "thing power" denotes a persisting ability to uncase the circumstances that make certain bodies marginal or disposable.[130] Elsewhere, Bennett argues for what she calls an "enchanted materialism," which acknowledges that "matter is animate without necessarily being animated by divine will or intent."[131] In the period I study, the common vibrancy of bodies is frequently thought to result from divine agency, but this does not mean that all bodies have a determinist telos. "Vertues" are freewheeling, and are central to what enables different bodies to join in ethical alliance. These virtues body forth the prevailing modes of governance in a way that includes critique. Their persistent power is a disruptive counter to the forms of public action approved by dominant social powers.

Across Shakespeare's *Hamlet*, an individualist model of virtue becomes increasingly powerful, but also increasingly problematic. This is due in part to Hamlet's performance of madness; when he kills Polonius, his claim to cloak calculated action under the cover of madness breaks down. Hamlet still purports to maintain his wits. Yet Hamlet's continued disrespect for Polonius drives Laertes into a moral cycle of vengeance that is not too far removed from that of the play's titular protagonist. More disturbing, however, is Ophelia's reaction to Hamlet's murder and mistreatment of her father. Ophelia is moved to madness by her former suitor's violence and disregard. But her break with reason, critics have observed, is not without rhyme. Ophelia's songs are popular street ballads. Putting such songs in the mouth of a madwoman, Mary Ellen Lamb points out, means that Shakespeare has erected a binary of elite/popular, male/female to establish Hamlet's superiority.[132] Theater gives him an arena in which to try out different moral outcomes before he takes action; through "the mousetrap" he might learn more about his uncle's guilt, and through his madness he might measure the culpability of others at the Danish court. By staging a course of justice, Hamlet means to maintain personal control over the moral consequences of his individual actions. *Hamlet*'s theatricality not only hails a form of subjectivity marked by inwardness; it also elaborates a model of virtue that makes the individual moral agent the principal mover in ethical life.

The content of the ballads Ophelia performs, however, invests her grief with a different kind of virtue. A betrayed lover's song, a dirge for a dead beloved, and a ballad of a maiden's downfall: through these songs, Ophelia delineates a visceral awareness of the harms she has suffered, so that her performance gives her dignity even as she becomes a spectacle of tragedy. Caralyn Bialo observes that Ophelia's songs allow her to inhabit female subject positions usually placed off-limits for elite women, such as herself. Ophelia bodies forth the voices of sexually aware, socially expendable women. As Bialo argues: "Her ballads foreground an embodied, presentational mode of performance that establishes a privileged rapport between Ophelia and the audience. Furthermore, Shakespeare takes advantage of the non-elite discourse of the ballad to stage Ophelia's madness as a gender-based critique of the Danish court. Shakespeare therefore exploits precisely those aspects of 'low' performance that the ballad shared with popular performance in order to produce the form and meaning of Ophelia's madness."[133] Ophelia does not go quietly. Rather, her physical immediacy critiques the social and ethical failures that have led to her madness. Hamlet's vengeance, though he might choreograph it to catch the conscience of Claudius, also entails Ophelia's reckless and heedless destruction.

Ophelia's death confirms what Polonius's murder had previously suggested: certain bodies are not just "ungrievable," to use Judith Butler's way of putting it, they are socially and ethically dispensable.[134] Laertes then Hamlet may jump into Ophelia's grave, but their theatrical mourning is simply part of the public masculine contest they wage against one another. When Ophelia makes herself visible—as broken, disheveled, and discarded—she uncovers a material virtue that stands in direct opposition to the public posturing of Hamlet then Laertes. Unlike Hamlet's madness, which is donned for social advantage, Ophelia's madness is a scandal that subjects the court's values to critical scrutiny. When Gertrude reports Ophelia's death, she paints a picture of a faithful maiden whose drowning was precipitated by her lover's desertion. While attempting to hang garlands of flowers on a willow, as abandoned lovers were proverbially said to do during this period, a branch breaks and Ophelia is drowned in the tangled weight of her garments. If her madness prevents her from preserving herself, her death also indicts Hamlet's use of Ophelia as an expendable prop in the revenge tragedy he plots against Claudius.

We might object that material virtue is unsurvivable, that Ophelia's excellence is predicated on her endurance of harm. In fact, because it arises from the materiality of the body, her virtue is in keeping with what the political theorist Bonnie Honig has recently termed "mortalist humanism," a species of posthumanism that derives ethics from vulnerability, not rationality.[135] Honig does not identify this trend to compliment it; indeed, for her, it is a departure from politics that she sees as problematic.[136] Yet Honig's critique, as well as the objection that material virtue is predicated, like so many stories of old, on the suffering of an abandoned woman, is directed at the wrong type of virtue. It is not virtues that matter that drag Ophelia under. Rather, these embodied excellences allow Ophelia to mine a discourse of femininity that admits, enables, and celebrates female sexuality and that, as Pamela Allen Brown convincingly shows, allows women to find solidarity through a common language of jest.[137] The prescriptive virtue that Hamlet extols, which he recommends to his mother when he advises her not to sleep with Claudius, causes Ophelia's destruction.

Matter and Discourse: Ophelia's Plants

Hamlet treats virtue as a superficial guise that might be donned, but Ophelia's demise attests to the complex intersection of matter and discourse in the making of women's excellence. Shakespeare's play, like the other premodern writings examined in this book, shows the fruitfulness of pursuing what Stacy Alaimo and Susan Hekman call a "material ethics": "A material ethics entails

. . . that we can compare the very real material consequences of ethical positions and draw conclusions from those comparisons. We can, for example, argue that the material consequences of one ethics is more conducive to human and nonhuman flourishing than that of another."[138] With his observation, "This nothing's more than matter" (IV.v.172), Laertes acknowledges that Ophelia achieves more than madness with her carefully gathered nonsense.

Besides the songs she sings, Ophelia presents a catalog of plants that give material substance to her virtue. These plants, scholars have noted, provide a rich commentary on her suffering. "There's rosemary, that's for remembrance. Pray, love, remember. And there is pansies; that's for thoughts. . . . There's fennel for you, and columbines. There's rue for you, and here's some for me. We may call it herb-grace o' Sundays. O, you must wear your rue with a difference. There's a daisy. I would give you some violets, but they withered all when my father died" (IV.v.173–74, 178–81). Rosemary and pansies focus the mind on remembrance of loss. Fennel and columbines signal flattery and infidelity. Rue symbolizes regret, sometimes repentance. The daisy was long associated with self-sacrifice in love on account of Alcestis; her belief in an unfaithful lover, however, also linked the plant to dissembling. Violets are signs of faithfulness, and their death is a rebuke to the Danish court and its prince. Taken together, the emblematic resonance of Ophelia's botanical offerings critiques Hamlet's betrayal and laments Polonius's murder. But these plants were also believed to have virtues that were not simply derived from their symbolic associations. Most of Ophelia's plants are herbs, and all were thought to have medicinal power during the early modern period. The "vertues" of each, as my earlier examples attest, exerted physical power over material bodies.

Rosemary was widely used to promote a clear head, and to ward off plague. In *The admirable vertue, property and operation of the quintessence of rosemary flowers* (1615), this multiuse plant "sheweth forth euidently her heauenly vertue."[139] Its practical potency, then, was attributed to sources greater than nature. Pansies were described as anti-inflammatory, and were credited with curing the falling sickness as well as convulsions. Fennel and columbines were both healing and poisonous. Like many of Ophelia's herbs, rue is connected to sexuality and reproduction: according to John Gerard's *Herball* (1597, 1633), it not only "expels the dead child and after|birth," it also "opens the matrix, and brings it into the right place."[140] And too, it serves as a "re|medie against the inflammation and swelling of the stones, proceeding of long abstinence from ve|nerie."[141] Its capacity to protect and renew bodies is more extensive, however, since rue was believed to be a powerful antidote against a variety of poisons: "[Rue] is a counterpoyson a|gainst deadly medicines or the poyson of Wolfs-bane, Ixia, Mushroms, or Tode-stooles, the biting of Serpents, stinging of Scorpions, spiders, bees, hornets, and wasps."[142] When she at last points to the daisy, Ophelia rounds out a bouquet with the power to heal as well as harm, protect as well as poison.

As Rebecca Laroche points out, the critical history of *Hamlet* has foreclosed the idea that Ophelia distributes actual plants during this distressing scene.[143] Doing so sidelines the material virtue that Ophelia enacts. If Ophelia shares these plants with Gertrude, Claudius, and Laertes, as Laroche argues, it is neither a neutral nor a symbolic act. I suggest that it is a practice of material ethics, a bodily virtue that allows Ophelia to protest the harms she undergoes. This form of material virtue, furthermore, enables Ophelia to warn those who have perpetrated the injuries she endures. In other words, the medicinal plants she offers provide a last chance for a reparative reconfiguration of the Danish court. Without change, the poison of so many unremedied wrongs will fester and spread. By noting the absence of violets in her gathering of plants—"I would give you some violets, but they withered all when my father died" (IV.v.181–82)—Ophelia denounces the loss of faithfulness that Polonius represented. She also affirms the difficulty of moral change, given that the beauty of violets was meant to instill ethical virtues in their beholders. As Gerard's *Herball* explains: "The re|creation of the minde which is taken hereby, cannot be but very good and honest: for they admo|nish and stir vp a man to that which is comely and honest; for floures through their beautie, variety of colour, and exquisite forme, do bring to a liberall and gentle manly minde, the remembrance of honestie, comelinesse, and all kindes of vertues."[144] Though beauty might exert as much force over bodies as violence, classifying Ophelia's performance as "a document in madness" (IV.v.175)—a scripted, disembodied record of her individual suffering— prevents her virtues from reaching those who witness her enacted woe.

This play's relentless focus on the individual prison of harms—the mental isolation that comes from suffering wrongs, which, not coincidentally, drives the eponymous protagonist throughout the play—means that Ophelia's virtues cannot circulate. She is cut off, stranded in a domain where virtue is viewed as a theatrical display of the discrete subject. To confine virtue within the definite bounds of the individual self makes that isolated self the only outlet for ethical action, the play affirms. And, as Ophelia (then Hamlet) demonstrates, cabining virtue in this fashion is (self)destructive. If *Hamlet* hails the modern subject, it also announces the erosion of "virtues that matter," those collective forms of ethical excellence nourished by the interaction, connection, and circulation of material bodies.[145] And, although scholars have amply demonstrated that earlier centuries had a robust concept of the individual, *Hamlet* signals a change in humanism, a move to make the atomistic individual the principal mover in ethical life.[146] No longer is goodness—human or otherwise—defined through connection, as Medwall's Man suggests it once was:

> So that I know / that creature no where
> Of whose vertue / I am not partyner
> I haue as hath / eche other element
> among other in thys world / a comen beyng
> wyth herbys and trees / contynuall noryshement
> that ys suffysant / to naturall lyuyng.[147]

On the contrary, the individual's ordering power divides material virtues, and the bodies they enliven, from one another.

Organization

In charting the importance of these embodied excellences, this study focuses on a period between periods: from ca. 1343 to ca. 1623, or an era that roughly encompasses the lives and works of Geoffrey Chaucer and William Shakespeare. From the surmised date of Chaucer's birth to the print release of Shakespeare's First-Folio, this "figure-centric" approach credits literature with making a tangible contribution to cultural understandings of virtue, gender, and embodiment. Vernacular poetic writers do not simply reflect the historical attitudes of their day. Rather, writers from Chaucer to Shakespeare share concerns over virtue's performative externality, or the reduction of ethical character to a set of gendered prescriptions. And, even if their opposition to rigid norms is driven largely by artistic concerns—since less scripted characters provide more moving narratives—taking a longer view of material virtue acknowledges the importance of poetic renderings of women's ethical action in premodern England. Writers including John Lydgate and Robert Henryson move beyond back-and-forth debates about women's ethical (in)capacities. Instead, Thomas Lodge and Edmund Spenser put women at the center of human experience, and by so doing, writers such as Osbern Bokenham, John Capgrave, and John Fletcher elaborate new forms of ethical action with the power to transform conceptions of the human itself.

This book considers medieval and early modern poets together because, from the late fourteenth to the early seventeenth century, writers continue to imagine the possibility of an ethics based on shared human vulnerability through the experiences of their female characters. The fact that such modes of ethical action were eclipsed is part of the history of humanism to which this book contributes. It is also part of the history of literature, which divides periods according to concerns that remain salient to modernity (individualism, nationalism, secularization, and so forth). Given that current scholars are interested in rethinking notions of the human, this book affirms that this concern has a history, which is inseparable from poetic reformulations of matter, virtue, and femininity between 1343 and 1623. For the posthumanist project to get off the ground, this book insists, scholars must investigate earlier attempts to shift the foundation of ethical life to the fact of our common finitude. Doing so will not only redraw the boundaries between medieval and early modern literary periods; it will also demonstrate the relevance of feminist questions to new materialisms and posthumanist ethics alike. Reimagining human centrality, it turns out, was something poets attempted during the centuries when classical humanism consolidated its cultural prestige.

This book has three parts. Part I, "Prescriptive Failures," investigates how retellings of Criseyde's demise structure a poetic debate over the potential for women's ethical action in a world dominated by masculine violence. Near the end of *Troilus and Criseyde*, Chaucer's heroine bewails her storied fate:

No good word, for thise bokes wol me shende.
O, rolled shal I ben on many a tonge! (V.1058–59)[148]

This is despite her manifest capacity for love, and the situational hostility that predicates her betrayal. As subsequent treatments by Lydgate and Henryson demonstrate, Criseyde remains conspicuously absent from exemplary catalogs of famous women because her vexing story disturbs prescriptive truisms about women's (in)fidelity. To tell her story is to uncover the cultural conditions of oppression that prevent women from fulfilling traditional expectations for women's virtue. Yet if early modern light and miscellaneous verse makes Cressid into a trashed heroine as punishment for her wanton refusal to validate social norms, Shakespeare returns to the scene of Cressida's ruin in order to construct a nonheroic model of material virtue based on endurance rather than conquest. Although Cressida is a prescriptive failure, her ability to maintain dignity in the face of extreme cultural contingency invents a new form of ethical action for premodern women.

Part II, "Grace, Enacted: Romance and Material Virtue," develops this model of ethical action by exploring women's ability to effect material change within cultural settings they do not control. My project turns to female saints' lives by Chaucer, Bokenham, and Capgrave to investigate the power of grace as it enables women's material virtue. Frequently counted among the virtues, grace becomes a conceptual and doctrinal fulcrum in the transition between the medieval and early modern periods. While admitting the restrictive elements of grace theology, my project also looks to premodern grace as a potential means of escape from customary conceptions of power and agency. When women are endowed with grace, either spiritual or social, action gathers around them that cannot be accounted for in the discourses that equate ethical power with the exercise of agency, control, or sovereignty. In early modern romances, including those by Lodge and Spenser, I investigate women's control over the graces with which they are endowed. Because these women are neither active nor passive, they contribute to a new form of material virtue in premodern England.

Part III, "Homely Virtues," examines women whose virtues are related to household structures. Many of these women are confined by domestic spaces, as the framing examples of Griselda from *The Clerk's Tale* or Katherina from *The Taming of the Shrew* demonstrate. As Griselda stories affirm, women gain gravity from performances of passivity that validate their suppressed strengths. Similarly, Katherina's radical abasement challenges the patriarchalism that increasingly imagines the household as a "little commonwealth" in late Tudor and early Stuart England. Other women go further. Maria from *The Woman's Prize* tames Petruchio by wielding the procreative power of the female body for transformative social change. Her labor, like that of earlier shrews, scandalously adopts the precepts circulated in household guides. As I shall suggest, when poets imagine a material mode of virtue, one based on yielding rather than wielding agency, they allow men *and* women to escape the restrictive expectations of individualist ethics.

This book concludes with a short chapter, "Legends of Good Women," because Chaucer's poem confronts a problem that all writings featured in this

study must address: the restriction of women's ethical action within a normative framework that privileges the most empowered strains of elite masculinity. In beginning this book with Shakespeare and ending it with Chaucer, I
mean to contest a teleological account of women's ethical action by showing
the shared affinities of writers working on the problem of women's excellence.
I also assess the difference literary representations can make to women's material virtues in my analysis of *The Legend of Good Women*: with the abandoned
cycle of wronged women, Chaucer draws attention to the limited ethical
framework within which women's virtues are counted as culturally legible. As
Chaucer's poem affirms, a heroic ethics harms all but the most elite masculine
subjects in service to an absolutist, individualist conception of virtue. Besides
identifying the ethical confinement of traditional *virtus*, Chaucer formulates
a new vision of humanity through his vulnerable yet steadfast heroines. If
Hamlet shifts the ground of ethical action to the particular subject, *The Legend of Good Women* affirms that material virtue, or the embodied ability to
withstand chaos, violence, and oppression, is a world-(re)making excellence
that affords equal benefits to women and men.

PART I

Prescriptive Failures

CHAPTER I

The Fragility of Virtue, from Chaucer to Lydgate

Then should no poet have the cause
Faire Creyseydes treuthe to blame,
Nor after this with ladyes falce
Remember Creseydes name;
Ne yet no mann his fickle dame
With Creseyd should upbraid,
Nor by examples bringe me in
Howe Troyolus was betrayde.
                    —William Fowler, "The Laste Epistle of Creseyd
                              to Troyalus" (ca. 1600)

Near the end of *Troilus and Criseyde*, Chaucer's heroine bewails the storied fate that awaits her:

Allas, of me, unto the worldes ende,
Shal neyther ben ywriten nor ysonge
No good word, for thise bokes wol me shende.
O, rolled shal I ben on many a tonge!
Thorughout the world my belle shal be ronge!
And wommen moost wol haten me of alle
Allas, that swich a cas me sholde falle! (V.1058–64)[1]

She is right of course, but not in the way Chaucer might have anticipated. In the vast accounts of Troy written in the twelfth and thirteenth centuries, the earlier verse *Roman de Troie* by Benoît de Sainte Maure and the later prose *Historia destructionis Troiae* by Guido delle Colonne, Criseyde's narrative formed part of a grand history of cultural demise that included stories of other ancient female worthies, including Medea, Helen, Cassandra, Penthesilea, Polixene, and Penelope. All these women—all but Criseyde—were also featured in exemplary collections of legendary heroines. Criseyde is the only literary heroine who is not included in those collections designed to shape cultural ideas about women's ethical action.

This chapter investigates Criseyde's absence from the "famous women" tradition that stretched from Homer to Hesiod, and from Giovanni Boccaccio to Christine de Pizan. Why was Troilus's beloved left out of collections that featured the virtues and vices of notable heroines? Could she be worse than Medea? More moving than Dido? In a word, yes. Criseyde is left out of exemplary catalogs because her story challenges prescriptive models of women's virtue. Criseyde's story does not have the exemplary power of Helen's, Lucrece's, or even Cleopatra's narrative. This is because Criseyde's story cannot be rendered as a set of moral directives that might be deployed to support heroic culture: her virtues emerge from a contingent collection of cultural factors, in the same way that her infidelity results from a specific confluence of tangible forces. Her virtue is material, living, and literary, assuming its contextual complexity only within the Troy Chaucer creates. Criseyde's virtue is specific, and it is wholly situated. It is neither abstract, nor symbolic. It depends on Criseyde's personal comportment, and it is degraded by her individual misfortunes. Criseyde's ethical qualities—good or bad—cannot be separated from the conditions of their production. As I shall argue, hers is a material virtue that challenges the prescriptive ideals circulated by the famous-women tradition.

In modeling *Troilus and Criseyde* on Boccaccio's *Il Filostrato*, which also represents the vulnerabilities that make erotic love into a potential source of human good, Chaucer imagines a model of virtue that is material, embodied, and living.[2] This form of virtue is fragile, but it has the capacity to refigure the human itself. The ground of shared vulnerability, which is intensified by the experience of love, allows Criseyde and Troilus to yield to one another. Yet this alternative vision of virtue falls apart in Chaucer's Troy. Troilus suffers, and even swoons, for Criseyde. Criseyde loses her breath, and even exchanges her heart, for Troilus. Nonetheless, their relationship never surmounts the disparities of power that distinguish gender and differentiate status in Trojan culture. Instead, Criseyde becomes a pawn traded between men in a contest over heroic stature. As a consequence, her vulnerability critiques traditional *virtus*, as well as prescriptive femininity's role in authenticating masculine worth. In accounting for Criseyde's conversion from widow to lover, Chaucer chronicles the shifts his heroine must accept to fulfill competing expectations for her character. More than a cultural double standard, I will show that Criseyde's alteration relates to the social contingency of ideal femininity prescribed for women in late medieval culture. Unlike other famous women, Criseyde cannot be incorporated into a classical narrative of *virtus*, but instead, as Chaucer's *Troilus and Criseyde* reveals, her suffering condemns an ethical life defined by masculine competition.

As Criseyde's betrayal affirms, all is not well in this mutable world. But while Chaucer reveals a rift between the values of the first and eighth spheres, John Lydgate more fully comprehends the social dimension of virtue ethics that destroys Criseyde's embodied excellence in his *Troy Book*. Most studies of Lydgate refer to Chaucer, but in this chapter I argue that we would better understand Chaucer with recourse to the monk of Bury. Unlike those accounts that take the fifteenth-century poet at his word, regarding him as a lowly imitator of his more masterful precursor, I claim that the *Troy Book* elucidates many of the social anxieties regarding women's potential for an alternative, embodied form of virtue.[3] This is not to say that Lydgate simplifies Chaucer, or that because Chaucer's presentation of Criseyde is more ambiguous, the earlier poet is somehow superior to Lydgate in poetic achievement.[4] It is to acknowledge, rather, that Lydgate can see the damage that a prescriptive model of femininity causes *in light of* Chaucer's poem.[5] If Chaucer's narrator is confounded by Criseyde's betrayal, Lydgate has a more confident grasp of the cultural norms that exalt and condemn women based on a shifting index of masculine achievement. As he translates his declared source, Guido delle Colonne's thirteenth-century Latin prose narrative, *Historia Destructionis Troiae*, Lydgate disavows the misogyny he faithfully transmits.[6] And though we might suspect Lydgate's apologetics, "Þat to translate it is ageyn my wille" (2.3558), the *Troy Book* acknowledges the foundational misogyny of heroic narratives, extending the critique of prescriptive femininity initiated by *Troilus and Criseyde*.[7]

Lydgate's innovation in the *Troy Book* amounts to a formal return. Using the broad historical framework of earlier Troy narratives, Lydgate includes accounts of those heroines who become narrative exempla for late medieval women.[8] From Medea and Helen to Penthisilea and Polyxena, Criseyde's story is nestled among other narratives of wartime betrayal. Moreover, because Lydgate refers his readers to Chaucer, it is as if his poem works in tandem with *Troilus and Criseyde*. So, if we think of Chaucer's poem as somehow incorporated within Lydgate's *Troy Book*, we can more clearly see the differences between Chaucer's representation of Criseyde's virtue and traditional accounts of feminine excellence. To be sure, the monk of Bury would likely have been pleased at the idea that his *Troy Book* had successfully integrated *Troilus and Criseyde*. I entertain this fantasy of poetic capture to assess the cultural alienation of Criseyde's material virtue. Reading Chaucer through Lydgate allows us to see Chaucer's focus on embodied endurance as the foundation of a new form of ethical excellence, but it also allows us to understand how that new model of material virtue is ruined, even discarded, in the effort to preserve and protect a heroic formulation of *virtus*.[9]

Following Alasdair MacIntyre, who observes the historical interdependence of social structure and moral theory, I will argue that poetic representations of Criseyde stage an ethical debate over the organization of the late medieval self.[10] Chaucer attempts to separate Criseyde from the prescriptive discourses shaping expectations for feminine excellence in late medieval England. By so doing, he makes room for material virtue, insofar as her adherence to principles, including pity and trust, are presented as a counter-tradition of ethics that might resist the valorization of aggression, domination, and transactional advantage—in short, the valorization of values that endorse and extend masculinist military achievement.[11] Her betrayal arises, I shall suggest, from the ethical flexibility required to survive the violence of war. Preserving a masculinist ethical ideal of subjectivity—the ideal of selfhood that ultimately elevates Troilus—necessitates Criseyde's infamous "slydinge." Lydgate's portrayal recognizes the social circumstances that produce Criseyde's mutable virtues. These conditions arise from an ethical system that favors elite men, whose social privilege ultimately derives from military success. As Lydgate makes clear, socially inflected virtues frequently validate masculine violence, rendering acts of aggression as feats of magnificence. Taken together, Chaucer and Lydgate critique the social construction of a heroic model of *virtus*.

This critique of heroic ethics is mobilized in contrast to a model of material virtue that is founded on enduring, not exercising, dominance. Importantly, I shall show, an endurance-based model of material virtue does not simply amount to an emphasis on women's suffering. Criseyde decides upon her love for Troilus in Book II of Chaucer's poem, and furthermore, as Lydgate's Polyxena demonstrates, women's mistreatment can uncover the ethical vacancy of a given society. And yet, as this chapter shall also acknowledge, sacrifice can be mandated for certain bodies in a way that separates those bodies from the moral choices that determine their suffering. Chaucer's Criseyde is ultimately confronted with the realization that her ethical bearing is not really up to her; as Pandarus makes clear, she is meant to conform herself to a code of heroic ethics that glorifies masculine action. Criseyde understands that she is culturally disposable, and accepts the flexible values required for her survival. As Lydgate affirms, heroic virtues foreclose women's ethical action except as it might function to support masculine fantasies (or nightmares) of empowerment. But to focus exclusively on women's socially prescribed virtues, Lydgate's Helen reveals, would be to miss the powerful intermingling of lay and religious discourse in the development of women's material virtues.[12] As this chapter will detail, Lydgate's famous women disclose an ethical rift between sacral and secular values; in turn, they reveal the disposability of feminine virtues constructed to consolidate heroic masculinity, and they ultimately show why his Criseyde, following Chaucer's, is destroyed.

Although he treats men's and women's virtues differently, Lydgate does not reduce the complexities of women's worth to a moral taxonomy mandated by ecclesiastical discourse; rather, like other writers of this period, Lydgate frequently adapts religious ideals to offer women protection from the masculinist values that make women socially expendable.[13] In his secular poetry Lydgate empowers female worthies, including those from pagan antiquity, using values derived from Christian ethics. Famous women from the classical tradition, conversely, elevate spiritual devotion to Mary in Lydgate's religious works. This intermingling of sacred and secular heroines reflects a larger trend: fifteenth-century female saints' lives, including Lydgate's, contribute to the prescriptive tradition that uses exemplary narratives to shape cultural expectations for feminine virtue.[14] Medieval conduct books include religious and secular examples of feminine excellence, and Christine de Pizan expands the genre of famous women by including pagan and Christian worthies within her city of ladies.[15] The

result for female saints' lives, according to Karen Winstead, is a greater
emphasis on "'transferable' qualities—courtesy, patience, diligence, humility, piety, charity—which would make the saints suitable models for laywomen as well as consecrated virgins."[16] Women from pagan antiquity are
also deployed, as Catherine Sanok claims of Christian female saints, to
teach readers that "feminine ethical practice is contingent on contemporary
social expectations."[17] But at least with Lydgate, historical contingency galvanizes a moral critique of fifteenth-century society. Lydgate's cross-valua-
tion of famous women affirms the lasting power of women's embodied
excellences, but he also emphasizes the precarity of those women—most
obviously Criseyde—whose entanglements in heroic competitions between
men alienate them from any pantheon of virtue.

Prescriptive Virtue: Lydgate's Helen

When Criseyde is reintegrated into the longer narrative tradition from which
she was taken—when she is viewed in relation to other women involved in
this ancient upheaval—the cultural contingency of women's virtue becomes
frighteningly clear. Lydgate makes no pretense of suggesting that women's
virtue is anything other than a cultural production. We might suspect he
does so to intensify the misogyny of his source, but Lydgate's wariness of
women's virtue uncovers the reasons why women become mutable, as well as
the awful consequences of female constancy in a culture where virtue is politi-
cally contingent. Far from trivial stuff, in the *Troy Book* the failure of a woman's virtue is an original myth galvanizing cultural destruction:

> O mortal harme, þat most is for to drede!
> A, fraude y-cast be sleiȝt of wommanhede,
> Of euery wo, gynnyng, crop, and rote! (2.3575–77)

Helen's desire is enflamed by the report of Paris's arrival, yet according to
Lydgate, the fateful meeting that dooms two nations could have been avoided
if Helen had only stayed home, like a good woman. In a series of questions
addressed to Helen, the poem lays a future of ruin at her door: "now, sey,
þou quene Eleyne, / What gost or spirit, allas, haþ mevid þe, / . . . / Oute of
þin house to gon among þe pres?" (2.3588–89, 3591). With his caution about
female mobility, Lydgate echoes the protective father in William Caxton's

translation of the late fourteenth-century conduct treatise, *The Book of the Knight of the Tower*, who warns his daughters about appearing at public events: "It is a grete perylle to alle good ladyes that haue their hertes ouer-moche set on the world ne be ouer desirous to goo to suche feestes / that they may kepe them honorably. The feestes and reuelles ben cause of whiche many good ladyes and gentyl women gete moche blame and noyse without cause."[18] The image of Helen as a homebody is ill-fitting, in part because the quotidian ideal of feminine virtue is so far removed from her heroic character. Indeed, Lydgate's fictive address would more fittingly be directed at an errant housewife:

> Whi were þou wery to liue at home in pes,
> And wentist out straungeris for to se,
> Takyng noon hed [vn-]to þin honeste? (2.3592–94)

Lydgate's worries echo prescriptive articulations of feminine virtue in behavioral guides for women, insofar as he treats Helen's ravishment as a catastrophic effect of a rather mundane misstep. The concerned husband in *Le Ménagier de Paris* sounds a similar alarm, connecting the petty desire to be seen in public to the deadly sin of vainglory. In modeling a confession for his young wife, le ménagier instructs her to seek forgiveness for "throwing large parties, decorating luxurious chambers, inviting high society to gather-ings."[19] In similar fashion, Helen is subjected to the continuum fallacy, viz., *if you leave your house, you will cause the destruction of all civilized society.* I suggest that Lydgate's treatment is deliberate, and that it reveals the strange-ness of women's conduct literature. When he chides Helen for her failure to "kepe at home þi boundis" (2.3601), Lydgate caricatures those who would condemn women for the very losses they suffer in aggrandizing narratives of masculine conquest. With its tonal incongruity, in fact, *Troy Book* uncovers the actual source of Helen's ruined virtue. Lydgate's poem may fault Helen for willful folly, but the *Troy Book* evinces equal awareness that the real danger she faces when she leaves the security of her domicile is other men. Compar-ing her to a "hare among [þe] houndis" (2.3602), Lydgate presents female ravishment as a surety of male privilege. *Of course* Paris will abduct Helen, but not simply because the story of these lovers is fatefully inscribed. As part of the militarist masculinity Lydgate recounts in order to reform, the male propensity to dominate vulnerable women is a cultural prerogative and a narrative given.[20]

And although the formulaic, somewhat fussy denigration of Helen's fidelity takes comic advantage of her unfortunate history, Lydgate iterates prescriptive codes of feminine virtue as a way of acknowledging her vulnerability. Hers is not the assured, wayward betrayal featured in earlier and later renderings of her character. In a war poem that expands beyond any solitary tale of doomed lovers, Helen of the *Troy Book* is surprisingly fragile. Lydgate's portrayal is in keeping with exemplary catalogs, which also present Helen as a figure divided against herself. As Christopher C. Baswell and Paul Beekman Taylor explain, this representation extends an antique rift concerning her character: Ovid portrays Helen as enchantingly beautiful in the *Heroides*, while Virgil depicts Helen as deceptively treacherous in the *Aeneid*.[21] Boccaccio's catalog of famous women, *De claris mulieribus* (1374), considers the totality of Helen's history, setting competing narratives of her character in sequence as a way of acknowledging the aporia of her heroic legacy. He begins by acknowledging her reputation for wantonness, for causing Troy's destruction through her wayward desires. But he also recognizes her superlative beauty, which captivated artists as well as heroes, as a generative, world-making power. She is accused of willful collusion in Troy's destruction, but she is also recognized as a hapless victim of Paris's ravishment. Her narrative ends with something of a blank, however, since Boccaccio remarks, "But I do not remember reading how long Helen lived afterwards, or what she did, or where she died."[22] If famous women are meant to offer models—to caution or to inspire—then Helen's narrative in Boccaccio's collection reveals a basic confusion over women's prescriptive virtue.

Was Helen a victim or an agent of devastating circumstance? Was she complicit with or resistant to impassioned catastrophe? According to Christine de Pizan's *Cité des Dames*, Helen was one of those women who "was gretely praysed aboue all other women of y^t lawe more for her good fortune than for ony other excellence."[23] There is a profound difference, at least in Christine's collection, between women who win fame through their exercise of excellence, and women who gain renown for their experience of history. Helen's passivity negates her legacy of treachery, but it also diminishes her heroic stature in Christine's city of secular and religious heroines. *Fame happens*, at least to women who endure historical circumstances beyond their control. Caught up in the sweep of events, Helen's riven character prevents her from becoming a positive actor in a catalog that recuperates women's powerful deeds. Elsewhere, in *The Book of the Knight of the Tower*, Helen is cited as an example of the dangers of masculine seduction. The wife's curt assessment of knights' promises, "but these wordes coste to them but lytyll to say for to gete the better and sooner the grace and goode wylle of theyr peramours," leads to an excursus upon the destructive powers of Venus, who counseled Paris to ravish Helen, and "was of al thys grete meschyf pryncipall cause."[24] Blaming Venus not only divests Helen (and Paris) of agency; more importantly, it attests to the corrupting dangers that erotic passion poses to good gentlewomen such as her daughters.

Probably the most crucial aspect of the wife's warning is its universality. Later the Knight's wife goes on to condemn deceptive men who victimize unsuspecting women; here, she cautions against worthy knights, those her husband characterizes as "more encouraged to excercyse hym self more ofte in armes / And taketh therfore better maner in al estates for to please vnto his lady or loue."[25] When she faults Venus for Helen's abduction, she erases the distinction between predatory and laudatory men. Any man, she claims, who says "theyr loue encourageth them to goo in vyages / And for to plese to them by state of armes" is dangerous to women.[26] She charges her daughters to maintain vigilant control over their circumstances, especially when they are confronted with supplications from noble admirers. And, though she might agree with her husband, who claims noble men are true in word as well as in deed, her wariness shows that women do not determine the social values that constitute feminine virtue in the late Middle Ages: "It is so as to me semeth / that euery woman / mayde / or wydowe / may wel bete her self with her owne staf."[27] Should a woman accept a noble suitor, or will she be blamed for lightness? Should a woman spurn a worthy admirer, or will she be condemned for haughtiness?

Helen's experience of ravishment in the *Troy Book* bears out the wife's warnings to her daughters in *The Book of the Knight of the Tower*, and validates Criseyde's fears over unguarded affection in *Troilus and Criseyde*. Though he claims to be a true lover, as soon as Lydgate's Paris leaves Venus's temple, he designs a plan of conquest that has nothing to do with fervent devotion. Helen is the priority spoil in an attack meant to avenge earlier Greek wrongs. Paris's design does not bespeak sincere affection, or even erotic fascination. As he explains, "ȝif þat we by manhood myȝt atteyn / To rauisch hir" (2.3788–89), the Trojans will collectively send a martial signal in a competitive struggle between equally matched, glorious foes. Any personal interest Paris might have in carrying Helen off is quickly converted to the tactical advantage of his people. As Menelaus's queen quickly realizes, Paris makes her captive in an imperial narrative of territorial conquest. Unsurprisingly, consent turns to grief when Helen realizes her fragile position. Showing her affiliation with suffering women from other heroic narratives, isolation, estrangement, and bewilderment separate her from willfulness, curiosity, and frivolity:

> [Eleyne] gan ful rewfully compleyne
> Hir vnkouþe lyf, to dwelle with straungers,
> Al dissolat among[es] prisoners,
> Fer sequestrid a-weye from hir contre,
> Solitarie in captiuite. (2.3902–6)

Her compliance with Paris is a sign of her broader conformity to a model of gender extolled in late medieval culture. No longer does she burn with passion for the dazzling warrior whose renown inspired her imagination. Instead, she yields to Paris because her gender makes her tractable to masculine command.

In a fascinating reversal of the poem's declared misogyny, Helen's assent offers another glimpse of the cultural expectations that define particular women according to standards of behavior that benefit men. When Lydgate's narrator reports that Paris meets no resistance from Helen, because "It sat hir nat, sche was so womanly" (2.3834), it is a tautological invocation of a kind of femininity so familiar that further exposition is unnecessary. Helen's heart already belongs to Paris, so she has less fear about yielding to him in this particular instance. But her willingness to leave her husband and homeland for the stunning warrior she encounters in Venus's temple is also predicated on a more general principle of submission, which the poem defines as a universally constitutive part of feminine character: "Sche can nat stryue, nor no woman scholde" (2.3839). Helen recognizes the binding power of this cultural expectation later, when Paris seeks to recall her from her misery, "it ne longeth vn-to womanhede / In straunge soille to stryuen or rebelle" (2.3968). Here, she adopts feminine submission as a pragmatic understanding of her strategic powerlessness, noting the uselessness of resistance, "namly þer, wher as hir querelle / Schal haue no fauour nor sustened be" (2.3968), thereby linking her actions to the vicissitudes of conquest. Any cultural standards for feminine behavior, she realizes, are connected to other, more immediate, social practices. The standards for feminine virtue, in other words, are posited as moral and universal, but emerge from the cultural and specific. That she finds herself the primary spoil in a power struggle between heroic cultures does not enable her to make her own ethical choices regarding her allegiance, her safety, or her fate.

Helen recognizes the circumstantial contingency that necessitates her submission, even as she embraces the epic suffering that elevates her pain. Once she recognizes her vulnerability as a captive, Helen's erotic passion does not drive her actions:

> Vn-to ȝour wil I may nat now with-seie;
> I am so bounde, þat I most obeie. (2.3961–62)

But after Paris tells Helen he will marry her, and presents himself to her as a more honorable and faithful husband than Menelaus, she embraces an elegaic relation to fortune in order to situate her ravishment within a grander design sanctioned by the gods. In a figural approximation of the situation that besets Henryson's Cresseid, Helen treats her fate as cosmic, not cultural. Rather than complain against unjust treatment, Helen overcomes her will to become Paris's obedient companion. Her response vests her pain with dignity despite her ethical confinement:

> But, sith goddis han as now ordeyned
> No bettre chaunce of hope vn-to me,
> I can no more—I mote it take at gre
> And humblely accepte also her sonde;
> For I am feble her power to withstonde.
> Wherfor, I schal ageyn my wil [now] stryue,
> Al-be for wo myn hert I fele ryue,
> For to concente and lowly to admitte
> Þilke þing [fro] whiche I may not flitte,
> Maugre my wil, of necessite,
> Fully to obeye what ȝe list do with me—
> It wil not helpe þauȝ I seide nay. (2.4060–71)

Through a struggle to match her inner convictions to external powers, Helen both exemplifies and problematizes women's virtue. The elegaic voice draws attention away from the social circumstances that precipitate her loss, but it also reveals a form of virtue that arises from the capacity to endure injustice. And, although James Simpson is correct to notice the ways the elegaic mode, "in which the unfulfilled lover turns away from public affairs," might have, as he argues, "produce[d] the Renaissance," he attends less to the transfer of agonized experience from women to men that marks the supposed rebirth of this poetic tradition.[28] Elegaic narratives of suffering, wherein a divided self is alienated from historical affairs, traditionally feature the sorrow of ill-fated women.[29] That they do so without seriously engaging the social contexts that might have given rise to women's misery is the terrible point of elegy, especially in a politicized environment that "offers no escape from the demands of ineluctable power."[30] Helen's strength is evident, but she must summon this terrific resolve to accommodate herself to enforced captivity and enjoined marriage.

And while Paris presents marriage as an immediate and miraculous salve for her suffering, his commitment cannot repair Helen's loss, since she mourns a more expansive set of familial connections than the loss of reputation that will follow her ravishment. Helen's sorrow at losing her friends and family—especially her husband, "For whos absence in rage furious, / Hir lif sche hateþ & curseþ eke fortune" (2.3914–15)—undermines Paris's attempt to rewrite his act of conquest as a glorified romance. Helen acts under compulsion, achieving a measure of heroic forbearance from the ability to withstand the injustice committed against her. This form of material virtue, which enables Helen to commit herself to a fine-grained domesticity, is quickly glossed over. In a passage unique to Lydgate, the poem associates Helen's conciliatory struggle with the usual habits of weepy women (2.4077–96). Women must cry themselves out, Lydgate muses, so that they can then be moved to follow masculine counsel:

> Þat þei can nat of sorwe make an ende,
> Til þei be leiser han y-wept her fulle. (2.4078–79)

Besides the tonal incongruity between Helen's difficult struggle to forfeit her familial connections and the poem's clichéd formulation of women's altered moods, by suggesting that Helen's transformation verifies the clerical adage, "For after stormys Phebus briʒter is" (2.4089), the poem attributes monitory wisdom to Paris's position. "And so be comfort & counseil of Parys" (2.4090), Helen is persuaded to dry her eyes and make better cheer. Without material virtue, the challenging narrative of Helen's captivity becomes a triumphant example of masculine influence.

By the end of the episode, Helen has reconciled herself to a life with Paris, not, it is worth noting, because she is "In hold distreyned and cap-tiuite" (2.3964), but because, for her as for other women, "Þer is no storme þat may lasten euere" (2.4086). Even if Lydgate gives voice to her formidable powers of endurance, and the domestic commitments that arise when she is allowed to articulate the ethical principles she embodies, Helen's mutation will not be recognized as a product of her agonized surrender, required by circumstance, and attended by suffering. And, while Lydgate's generalizations are not nearly as severe as Guido's, they successfully transform her into Paris's ruined beloved. Perhaps most terrible, however, is the fact that Helen is not allowed the autonomy that would make her ethically responsible for her unfortunate downfall. Although Cassandra identifies Helen as "causere of oure peyne" (2.4232), her catalog of fault is careful not to attribute these horrible events to Helen's doing. Instead, Helen's very presence works to effect the destruction Cassandra foretells, making Helen responsible, even if she does nothing, for Troy's doom. Helen is fully integrated into the story of Paris's conquest, but as an inert symbol of his violence. Helen marks the place of Paris's violence, serving as a negative reminder of his militarist aggression. Castigating Helen, then, is a way of condemning Paris without naming his wrong. Her lack of virtue signifies his, but Helen takes on the shame that results from Paris's ravishment.

Lydgate's account of Helen's despoiled virtue is important to my larger argument for two reasons: first, her fidelity shows that certain forms of ideal-ized behavior—even those lauded by prescriptive discourse—get erased because there is no ethical space for them in heroic culture; and second, her material virtue, which commits her to a notion of collective life that is mani-festly opposed to violence and oppression, is rendered irrelevant by military conquest. These are important elements of plot, which are familiar from classical narratives of women's betrayal in Virgil as in Ovid.[31] But the discur-sive unevenness of Helen's story is equally important to a consideration of Criseyde's material virtue from Chaucer to Shakespeare. The elegance of Helen's complaint, which captures the militarist conditions of her alien cap-tivity, is under- and overwritten by stock assessments of femininity. The prescriptive discourse of feminine virtue—which faults women for not stay-ing home, then reconciles them to translated circumstances of conquest—is riven by this palpable, heartbreaking performance. Helen is enjoined to be faithful to her husband, but when she laments her separation from Menelaus in terms so extreme that they threaten to overwhelm her very existence, she is assimilated within a series of clichés affirming women's emotional variance. If Helen's culture tells her to exemplify fidelity and obedience, her adherence to those values undermines the social practices of sexual alliance such values are meant to fortify. But of course, Helen's culture tells her no such thing: she is subjected to the evaluations of this discourse, but she is allowed no recourse to the values that might insulate her from violence, betrayal, or vulnerability. Medieval authors might situate her actions in relation to gendered expectations with social significance and moral valence, but characters within the narrative treat her commitments as fully expendable in service to grander heroic trajectories.

Material Virtue: Chaucer's Criseyde

In this way, Lydgate's Helen is remarkably similar to Chaucer's Criseyde. Taken together, Chaucer and Lydgate critique heroic society by showing how women's material virtues are suppressed in the interest of advancing and maintaining an ethical system that supports masculine domination. Of course, Criseyde's exchange exposes problems inherent to the values of heroic culture; yet the values that lead to this particular circumstance are manifest from the moment the poem initially presents its heroine. It might be difficult to consider Criseyde as a figure whose immutable virtues reflect those of the heroic community.[32] Indeed, I maintain that her story is excluded from the prescriptive tradition for this very reason. But at the outset of *Troilus and Criseyde*, she is presented as an emblem of the femininity that is esteemed in heroic culture:

> Among thise othere folk was Criseyda,
> In widewes habit blak; but natheles,
> Right as oure firste lettre is now an A,
> In beaute first so stood she, makeles.
> Hire goodly lokyng gladed al the prees.
> Nas nevere yet seyn thyng to ben preysed derre,
> Nor under cloude blak so bright a sterre. (I.169–75)

As Diane Vanner Steinburg points out, widow's weeds distinguish Criseyde, drawing Troilus's attention to her distinctive beauty as "the only woman among the crowd at the festival whose attire indicates sexual fidelity."[33]

By linking Criseyde's widowed status to her sexual desirability, Chaucer invokes the long tradition of admonitory literatures shaping proper conduct for widows, though he conspicuously distances his rendering of Criseyde from the discursive tradition on which he draws.[34] Chaucer certainly knew the stories of the sexually aware, single, independent woman: versions of the widow of Ephesus type were common in the medieval misogynist tradition, and inform his characterization of the Wife of Bath.[35] But he keeps such tales away from Criseyde, focusing instead on her perfected comportment. Her behavior, Chaucer makes a point of saying, implies specific virtues. With a single look,

> men myght in hire gesse
> Honour, estat, and wommanly noblesse. (I.286–87)

We might believe that Chaucer dismisses cultural skepticism about the lone woman to heighten the tragic irony of his narrative, since the image of a lascivious widow certainly doubles back to haunt Criseyde's characterization after her betrayal. I argue that Chaucer develops Criseyde's virtue to critique its cultural instability, but also to affirm its individual persistence. Rather than situate her as a product of social discourse, Chaucer vests Criseyde with an excellence that she generates, manages, and protects.[36] And while she is a product of social training (her adherence to prescriptive gender regulations is frequently noted in the poem), Criseyde's performance arises from the way she uses gendered norms to express her individual virtues.[37] Criseyde's virtues are individually embodied expressions of culturally recognized excellences, insofar as she enacts lauded principles in ways that attach them to the particularities of her character, as well as her experience.

With Criseyde, then, Chaucer explores the potential for women to take up prescriptive virtues in ways that might protect them from the material harms that heroic cultures often inflict against female bodies. If women make culturally favored virtues their own, in other words, can they become secure within heroic societies? At least initially, it appears that Criseyde gains cultural immunity from her ability to embody idealized femininity. When Criseyde is introduced, she is a morally genuine character who surpasses belittling gender typologies. Carolyn P. Collette convincingly argues that Criseyde is "much more complex, knowing, and aware than . . . more romanticized versions of Criseyde [that depict her] as lovely, timid, and indecisive."[38] Unlike Paris, who uses his ocular privilege to conquer Helen with a look in the *Troy Book*, Troilus is amazed to inaction by Criseyde's demure beauty. When Criseyde returns his gaze, furthermore, Chaucer highlights the individual power that might accrue to women's performances of gender ideals. Criseyde meets Troilus with a look that affirms her singular ability to enact a faultless femininity:

> To Troilus right wonder wel with alle
> Gan for to like hire mevynge and hire chere,
> Which somdel deignous was, for she let falle
> Hire look a lite aside in wich manere,
> Ascaunces, "What, may I nat stonden here?"
> And after that lokynge gan she lighte
> That nevere thoughte hym seen so good a syghte. (I.288–94)

Criseyde's magnificent appearance affirms her confidence and independence as an exemplar of virtues extolled within her community.

These qualities serve her well when Pandarus attempts to convert her from widow to lover. But it must also be noted that Pandarus aims to destroy Criseyde's virtue by fitting her ethical status to the superficial assessments of women's moral commitments circulating in medieval instructional discourse. His is a difficult task, as is clear when Pandarus encourages Criseyde to "Do wey youre book, rys up, and lat us daunce / And lat us don to May som observaunce" (II.111–12). For Criseyde, her reaction to Pandarus demonstrates, worthiness does not amount merely to good manners, or to an outward display of gestures socially favored for her gender. When Criseyde rejects her uncle's invitation, her response aligns her with a more extensive system of values, an embodied commitment that encompasses an entire way of being. Her protest, "Be ye mad? / Is that a widewes lif, so God yow save?" (II.113–14), does not simply indicate her knowledge of the cultural expectations for widows. Rather, her surprise at Pandarus's outlook demonstrates a profound loyalty to the social practices that express her moral bearing:

> It satte me wel bet ay in a cave
> To bidde and rede on holy seyntes lyves;
> Lat maydens gon to daunce, and yonge wyves. (II.117–19)

Criseyde knows her uncle seeks to manipulate her, for she understands the risks that an affair would pose to her virtue. Despite these dangers, across

Books II and III, Criseyde embraces the power to love as an embodied practice of excellence. In a protracted scene of reflection, she turns over the idea:

> And gan to caste and rollen up and down
> Withinne hire thought his excellent prowesse,
> And his estat, and also his renown,
> His wit, his shap, and ek his gentilesse;
> But moost hire favour was, for his distresse
> Was al for hire, and thought it was a routhe
> To sleen swich oon, if that he mente trouthe. (II.659–65)

When she claims the power to determine her affection—"I am myn owene
womman, wel at ese" (II.750)—she avows her commitment to love as a material enactment of fidelity, one that is moved by enchantment "Who yaf me
drynke?" (II.651). She does not merely reflect Troilus's desire. Rather, her
love arises from her favorable assessment of his character: "To telle in short,
hire liked al in-fere / His persoun, his aray, his look, his chere" (II.1266–67).
More famously, after his swoon, she presses him to perform as a fulfillment
of her amorous desire: "Is this a mannes game?" (III.1126). Her love becomes
the galvanizing force that enables Troilus's excellence:

> For whi she fond hym so discret in al,
> So secret, and of swich obëisaunce,
> That wel she felte he was to hire a wal
> Of stiel, and sheld from every displesaunce. (III.477–80)

By contrast, Pandarus seeks to deny Criseyde's control over her own
virtues. With his threat, "Wo worth the faire gemme vertulees!" (II.344), he
posits worthy love as a defining condition of virtuous femininity. If a gem-
stone's constitutive property is its "vertu," to use the idiom of late medieval
lapidaries, then a jewel without this natural quality would be worthless.[39]
Likewise, if a woman's essential characteristic is her virtue, to recall the terms
of late medieval behavioral manuals, then a lady without this inherent attribute would also be valueless.[40] Because Criseyde's love is meant to be inherent, Pandarus suggests that she has no control over her powers of affection.
Yet Criseyde maintains her powers of consent, as scholars have long noted.[41]
At the same time, she recognizes the cultural bind her uncle uses to compel

her consent. Caught between conflicting expectations for women's excellence, Criseyde laments her compromised position:

> Allas! I wolde han trusted, douteles,
> That if that I, thorugh my dysaventure,
> Hadde loved outher hym or Achilles,
> Ector, or any mannes creature,
> Ye nolde han had no mercy ne mesure
> On me, but alwey had me in repreve.
> This false world—allas!—who may it leve? (II.414–20)

Here, we see that Criseyde is guarded about the dangers that attend amorous attachment, but she is also subject to the argument, voiced by the Knight of the Tower, that honorable men merit the affection of virtuous women: "For in certayne me semeth that in good loue and trewe maye be but welthe and honour. . . . And also I tell yow that grete almesse it is whanne a lady or damoysell maketh a good knyght /eyther a good squyer."[42]

Criseyde's skepticism aligns her with those women who seek to control their virtue, and her love suggests that she seeks to exercise that excellence independently.[43] Chaucer develops this capacity for material virtue in his heroine, but he also shows how it is destroyed by external appraisal and prescriptive redescription. Virtue, Chaucer affirms, can be an expression of individual will, and therefore personal consent.[44] Yet it can also be a manifestation of collective expectations, and therefore cultural ideals. Neither should be exclusive, and the domination of one can destroy the other. Pandarus, quite simply, believes Criseyde's transformation is as simple as removing her veil; when he tells her to "Do wey youre barbe, and shew youre face bare" (II.110), he treats feminine modesty as an extrinsic condition that is exclusively social in its construction. But Criseyde harbors a deeper view of herself, regarding her fidelity to cultural signs as the expression of intrinsic principles that she enlivens. Pandarus views feminine modesty as constructed by sources beyond the self, while Criseyde sees it as animated by practices of the self. This conflict in values ultimately destroys Criseyde, but in ways that do not pass unnoticed in Chaucer's poem. Even as he recognizes women's potential for material virtue, Chaucer also reveals the heroic fantasies that subject women to external codes of virtuous conduct. Hector might declare, "We usen here no wommen for to selle" (IV.182), but since Troy's siege is caused and sustained by the traumatic exchange of women, he seems to be the only character who subscribes to this view.[45] Warriors value women as signs of conquest and dominance before they see them as icons of fidelity or forbearance. Their value is social more than moral, but this is *itself* an ethical stance that organizes the acts of heroic culture. Criseyde is asked to accept this rendering of her worth, and from there her actions follow. She changes out of necessities that are at once ethical and material, since the values of her culture lead to her physical translation.

With her final letter, Criseyde accepts an impoverished moral understanding of women's ethical action in a warrior's world:

> Come I wole; but yet in swich disjoynte
> I stonde as now that what yer or what day
> That this shal be, that kan I naught apoynte. (V.1618–20)

Taking up feminine virtue as an external posture, she avows her fidelity as an abstract absolute detached from the particularities of circumstance. One day she will return, but she does not have the power to say when that day will arrive. The shocking truth of this statement, including the stark recognition that she does not control her physical circumstances, is one of this poem's most disturbing instances of pathos. And, though this moment has long been on the horizon, Criseyde's feeble attempt to remain true to a hero—any hero, it turns out—threatens to evacuate the poem's entire ethical system. With her detached declarations of long-suffering fidelity, Criseyde reduces what might have been a system of ethical values to a code of social conduct. Here, decorum trumps virtue, for Criseyde obviously knows what she should say in a social situation requiring mannered delicacy. Criseyde changes her view of idealized femininity, moving from a moral to a social view of its significance. Even Criseyde seems to accept the fact that her identity will be taken up by others as a token of feminine frailty that will damage the moral standing of those following after her: "And wommen moost wol haten me of alle" (V.1062). Translated into the prescriptive discourse of feminine virtue, Criseyde suffers the loss of an ethical identity.

Destroyed Virtue: Lydgate's Criseyde

If Chaucer shows the loss of dignity that attends Criseyde's transformation, Lydgate investigates the circumstances that condition her betrayal. Unlike

Chaucer, Lydgate intensifies the moral stakes of his poem by considering cultural standards for feminine virtue. And if Lydgate's infusion of Helen's characterization with negative commentary from exemplary discourse is tonally incongruous, with Criseyde it registers the double bind she faces. Once again, though perhaps not so ridiculously, Lydgate references cultural ideals of femininity to clarify Criseyde's predicament. Contemplating suicide, Lydgate's Criseyde avows a deep commitment to Troilus, since that pairing represents a way of life for her. Similar to Helen, Criseyde recognizes the alien vulnerability she will face after her translation to the Greek camp:

> For how shulde I oute of Troye wende,
> He abide, and I to Grekis goon,
> Þer to dwelle amonge my cruel foon?
> Allas! allas! I, woful creature,
> Howe shulde I þer, in þe werre endure—
> I, wreche woman, but my silf allone,
> Amonge þe men of armys euerychon! (3.4146–52)

She loves Troilus, but she also anticipates her isolation in a hostile camp of warrior men.

By giving voice to Criseyde's alienation, Lydgate proposes a direct connection between virtue and circumstance. He does so, importantly, in a way that acknowledges the limitations women face in a milieu of prescriptive virtue. Paul Strohm convincingly demonstrates that Lydgate's focus on prudence as a practical mode of applied excellence promises to enable princes to overcome *fortuna* through the exercise of this robust virtue.[46] Yet, as Criseyde's example attests, Lydgate evinces equal awareness that mastering social exigency is inflected by gender as much as status. Lydgate does not obscure the social sources of Criseyde's betrayal; instead, he uses her demise to reveal the problematic consequences of feminine virtue's increasingly social character in the fifteenth century. Manuals for women often declare the benefits of prescribed virtue, but only in rare circumstances do they address women as embodied agents who might be able to manage their own moral lives. Lydgate is pessimistic about women's surety in the tenuous environment of Lancastrian England.[47] For Lydgate, only divine transcendence offers refuge from the shifting social alliances that might cause women harm, shame, or both. As a political force that allows agents to resist, even overcome, the vicissitudes of fortune, virtue is not available to women.

Across his poetry, Lydgate defines virtue for women differently than he does for men. The "Disguising at London" convenes the cardinal virtues—Dames Prudence, Righteousness, Fortitude, and Temperance—to configure virtue for the nation's rulers. Resistance to Fortune, here as elsewhere, is the responsibility of good governors.[48] Lydgate follows a long tradition of writers, including Plato, Cicero, Macrobius, Ambrose, Aquinas, and Dante, in associating the cardinal virtues with human exercises of sovereignty over self and state.[49] These moral, intellectual virtues were believed to be produced by sustained training of the soul, a *habitus* of excellence that the *fürstenspiegel* and *de casibus* traditions shored up through their exemplary renderings of historical figures.[50] Lydgate furthers their extension into a broader civic arena through the "Disguising at London," but he also follows a distinctive late medieval trend with this and his other civic spectacles. The four cardinal virtues are associated with the king's rule in a number of late medieval pageants and treatises, but the London Guildhall, rebuilt between 1411 and 1430 with statues of Discipline, Justice, Fortitude, and Temperance lining the porch doorway, affirms an enlarged association between the cardinal virtues and secular power in Lydgate's day.[51]

These virtues are figured as women, but women are notably absent from the governmental transactions these representations are deployed to solidify.[52] Only Katherine of Valois, wife of Henry V and mother of Henry VI, is repeatedly acknowledged as a participant in the realm of secular politics in Lydgate's poetry. As several poems attest, however, her role is attenuated at best.[53] She might suffer the contingencies of circumstance, but she does not have active recourse to the cardinal virtues in facing down Fortune's perils. The brief *ubi sunt* meditation, "That Now is Hay Some-Tyme Was Grase," reportedly written "at þe commandement of þe Quene Kateryn," lays stress on the world's "transmutacion," but offers no remedy against "thes chaungis all" in forwarding its relentless refrain.[54] Since the poem features the demise of fallen heroes and heroines, we might conclude that it offers a signal instance of what Maura B. Nolan characterizes as a "distinctly mixed aesthetic," which for her, like other critics interested in Lydgate's Ovidianism, "renders history in deeply ambivalent fashion, as both sexual and moral, providential and contingent, tragic and elegaic all at once."[55] A comparison between heroes and heroines, however, not only reveals two orders of virtue operative in Lydgate's understanding of a fortune-tossed world, but also calls for a more careful consideration of the gender dynamics at work in Lydgate's conception of cultural contingency.[56]

In accordance with Lydgate's theme, the Nine Worthies lose all manner of wealth and possession on account of Fortune's relentless wheel. Nevertheless, great earthly power is evident in the magnificent downfall of men including David, Hector, Arthur, and Charlemagne. They have conquered lands, amassed riches, and wielded government, and even if such ephemeral trophies are "now brought full base," their sources of loss bespeak their ability to shape the circumstances in which they lived.[57] The famous women, by contrast, have only one way of making it in the world, and that is but fleeting:

> Whilome full feyre was Polixene,
> So was Creseyde; so was Helene
> Dido also of Cartage quene,
> Whos beaute made many one pleyne;
> But dethe came laste and can dysteyne
> Their freshenes, and made them full base,
> Youre remembraunce let not disdeyne,
> That now is heye some tyme was gras.[58]

Women admired for famous deeds or unique qualities, namely Esther and Griselda, are connected to a host of legendary women through the influence their beauty confers. By treating women's beauty as superficial, Lydgate suggests that their control over worldly affairs is derivative, bestowed upon them by strong men. There is no distinction between women who were true or false, strong or weak, victims or victors. Across Lydgate's poetry, famous women are alienated from those contingencies of history that the cardinal virtues are so frequently summoned to contest in late medieval England.

This is not to say that Lydgate forecloses women's capacity for what I am exploring as material virtue across this book; as I aim to show, his critique of heroic virtue produces a conflicted, ultimately cynical, representation of Criseyde. Elsewhere, however, he suggests that women might develop embodied resources of excellence. To return briefly to his treatments of Queen Katherine, Lydgate suggests that her virtue is innate, mobilized in the secular realm of contemporary politics through an incarnational ability to certify the king's legitimacy.[59] At the end of the *Troy Book*, Katherine brings the hope of peace, for her marriage to Henry V will unite France and England in the Treaty of Troyes (1420):

hir gracious arryvaille
In-to þis lond shal so moche availle,

. . . .

Plente, welfare, & fulsom abundaunce,
Pes & quiete, boþe nyӡe and ferre. (5.3429–30, 3434–35)

After her husband's untimely death in 1422, Katherine's maternal presence
continued to legitimate the reign of the young Henry VI, so that in the late
1420s, when Lydgate is believed to have composed the *Mumming at Eltham*
for child king and queen mother, her status as the source of unity between
the kingdoms of England and France is an explicit theme.[60] Like other artists
of the era, Lydgate often depicts queenship with reference to the Virgin
Mary, positioning Katherine as a source of intercessory grace mediating
between powerful monarch and petitioning supplicant.[61] As J. Allan Mitchell
remarks with specific reference to the *Troy Book*, Katherine is sanctified for
political ends.[62] But her virtue does more than ensconce masculine power. As
Katherine's example demonstrates, Lydgate develops women's material virtue
as a means to protect women from political upheaval, and he does so using
terms derived from a sacral register.

With Queen Katherine the parallel between sacred and temporal power
is most available, but elsewhere Lydgate praises other women for virtues that
are embodied, which cannot be donned (or shed) like a garment or covering.
Equally important to my argument, Lydgate utilizes catalogs of famous
women to delineate the material virtues that protect women from martial
masculinity. This topos crops up over and over again. In "The Floure of
Courtesy," Lydgate enumerates feminine virtues by cataloging notable
women:

For good she is, lyke to Polycene,
And in fayrenesse to the quene Helayne,
Stedfast of herte as was Dorigene
And wyfely trouthe, if I shal not fayne,
In constaunce eke and faythe, she may attayne
To Cleopatre, and therto as secree
As was of Troye the whyte Antygone.[63]

Similarly, in "A Ballade, of Her that Hath all Virtues" he amasses laudable
qualities through a recitation of familiar names:

Wyfly trouthe with Penelope,
And with Gresylde parfyt pacyence,
Lyche Polixcene fayrely on to se,
Of bounte, beaute, having þexcellence
Of qweene Alceste, and al þe diligence
Of fayre Dydo, pryncesse of Cartage.[64]

Satirical treatments also employ famous women to expound feminine excellence. In "A Ballade on an Ale-Seller," the jaded speaker associates legendary women with the virtue of fidelity:

To trewe Grisilde I wil nat compare,
To Lucrece nor vnto Penelope;
Trew love in yow I trow is so ful rare.[65]

"Horns Away," a poem criticizing women's elaborate headdresses, features a speaker who claims that female worthies were adorned only with their societies' virtues, earning them praise among "Famous poetis of antyquyte."[66]

Lydgate's catalogs of famous women valorize forms of excellence that are antiheroic and traditionally feminized in male-dominated societies. Truth, fidelity, bounty, and most of all, beauty, are embodied features of womanly excellence. As such, they derive from modes of agency usually reserved for women. Qualities requiring exertion, such as diligence or patience, become negative exercises. Women's agency amounts to mercy, pity, and compassion. And, while these excellences certainly contribute to the construction of femininity as passive in the late Middle Ages and beyond, there is more to this rendering of women's virtues than its historical contribution to a shopworn distribution of agency according to a gender binary. This is because Lydgate imagines qualities mined from religious discourse as powers with the potential to protect women in heroic society. In his development of material virtue, however, he acknowledges the threat that cultural contingency poses to women's ability to exercise these qualities. The chaos, violence, and instability of secular politics—especially during war—frequently make embodied virtues practices of necessity as well as means to survival. Accordingly, Lydgate appears to sympathize with the plight of Queen Katherine, who entered into a clandestine marriage with Owen Tudor because parliament explicitly forbade her to rewed until after Henry VI reached the age of majority.[67] Her involvement in secular politics, it seems almost too obvious to say, was thoroughly sexualized, since her erotic relations were central to delineating and legitimating the royal succession. But if Lydgate advised the queen to compare her situation to that of another beautiful widow, "so was Creseyde," this is because he recognizes the unique dangers that contingency posed to virtuous women.[68]

The *Troy Book*'s representation of Criseyde, because it resituates Chaucer's doomed heroine within a broader theater of historical conflict, discloses the physical dangers that heroic ethics pose to women. Criseyde exemplifies her culture's values—indeed, she performs the social formulation of women's virtue to perfection—but by so doing, she shows how prescriptive femininities endanger, translate, and destroy virtuous women. Though it is prefaced by antifeminist outrage, "Þer is no fraude fully equipollent / To þe fraude and sleiȝty compassyng / Of a womman, nor like in worchynge" (3.4332–34), and hedged with Lydgatean apologetics, "Þus techeþ Guydo, God wot, & not I!—/ Þat haþ delyt to speke cursidly / Alwey of wommen þoruȝ-out al his bok" (3.4343–45), the source of Criseyde's betrayal is cultural, not personal, in the *Troy Book*. In a series of scenes punctuated by fierce battle, Diomede wins Troilus's horse, which he then sends to Criseyde, "Beseching hir þat she wolde it take / As for a gyfte of hir owne man" (3.4628–29). Her equivocal replies earn her the moniker "double Cresseyde" but they also reveal the feminized stance she must assume in relation to Diomede's aggressive suit.[69] Because he appeals to "verray pite and . . . wommanhede" (3.4639), her reaction is already scripted by his subservience. Criseyde knows her part, playing the generous beloved exactly as Diomede desires. To his messenger she replies:

> Ful wommanly bad hym repeire ageyn
> Vn-to his lord, & pleynly to hym seyn
> Þat she ne myȝt, of verray kynd[e]nesse,
> Of womanhede, nor of gentilnes,
> Refusen hym, platly, from hir grace. (3.4643–47)

She feels compelled to accept his gift, but not simply, it is worth emphasizing, because the dictates of feminine liberality mandate receptivity to masculine largesse.[70]

Rather, in a canny interweaving of social circumstance and cultural idealization, Criseyde reveals her exchange as the ultimate source of her generosity. She follows cultural expectations for femininity when she accepts Diomede's proffered kindness, for she explains that it would not behoove her to rebuff anyone "Þat was to hir, þere in straunge place, / So kynde fo[u]nde, and so counfortable / In euery þing, and so seruisable" (3.4648–50). Though she limns her acceptance with mannered courtesy, she is aware that her physical vulnerability subjects her to Diomede's desire. Even if she wishes to remain true to Troilus, she must affect interested availability, for she is bereft of protection in the Greek camp. When she makes Diomede happy, "He was recured of his peynes smerte" (3.4658), Criseyde secures her place in this newfound cultural situation. Anticipating Shakespeare by nearly two centuries, Lydgate reveals the futility of asking whether Criseyde retains inward fidelity to either lover. But unlike his source Guido, Lydgate does not insist that essential feminine mutability prevents Criseyde from maintaining resolute affection. Her complaint shows her emotional intensity (3.4138–52), and the sorrowful mutuality she achieves with Troilus affirms her capacity for reciprocal devotion (3.4159–90). Lydgate's expansion of the lovers' anguished parting, more than a dilation of Chaucerian material, gives Criseyde moral depth. Her ability to love with truth and woe, moreover, reveals the cultural necessity behind her precipitous shift to Diomede. Although she follows the mannered formulas prescribed for ideal femininity in late medieval England, her actions are at odds with her feelings.

It is possible, of course, that Criseyde experiences a change in affection. But since Lydgate represents that moment later (4.2130), the emphasis in the lovers' separation lies on Criseyde's change in loyalty, which says nothing about her love. Her virtue, her loyalty in particular, is shaped according to cultural ideals of heroic desire. As Criseyde's exchange indicates, heroic desire is intensely public, invested primarily in securing a warrior's social position. And, while Lydgate might have attributed shallow morality to any number of classical heroes, as Shakespeare will later go on to do, Lydgate refers his dismissal of prescriptive virtue to Criseyde alone. In an uncharacteristic departure from all sources, Lydgate figures Criseyde's ultimate betrayal as a choice motivated by her commitment to contemporary standards for feminine conduct:

> For leuere she had chaunge & variaunce
> Were founde in hir þanne lak of pite. (4.2172–73)

Criseyde's commitment is completely undermined, but Lydgate recognizes late medieval gender expectations as the primary source for her shifting affection:

As sittyng is to femynyte,
Of nature nat [to] be vengable,
For feith nor oþe, but raþer mercyable
Of mannys lyf stondyng in distresse. (4.2174–77)

Mercy has the power to associate human and divine compassion; with its feminization, however, its metaphysical gravity is flattened into a social nicety. Like other virtues practiced by women, mercy and pity become gestures of social decorum that attest to a woman's prized value within a system of patriarchal exchange. For Lydgate, Criseyde's pity is equivalent to her mutability, which, in this cultural context, is simply and merely related to a commodified system of cultural valuation. With an almost forced closure, "Her-of no more" (4.2178), Lydgate separates Criseyde from this story's infamous trajectory. We might conclude that Criseyde is securely settled in her new pairing, but whatever comes of the relationship with Diomede, her virtues are not the stuff of *any* legend. Using a reductive dismissal, the *Troy Book* denies Criseyde even the lasting power of a ruined reputation.

Sacrificial Virtue: Lydgate's Polyxena

Lydgate's Criseyde disappears, much like Shakespeare's heroine in *Troilus and Cressida*. And, while scholars have long critiqued the silence that bespeaks Cressida's alienation, Lydgate uses Criseyde's betrayal to condemn the mutability of values that leads to her destruction in his *Troy Book*. His dismissive condemnation, in fact, shows how communities of powerful men discard women whose utility for heroic culture is expended. Heroic culture ruins Criseyde, then suggests that her loss of virtue is a personal failure that arises from her tainted, feminized materiality. There is no acknowledgment that prescriptive femininities—good or bad—are products of heroic value systems. With his misogynist erasure of Criseyde's suffering, Lydgate looks forward to the treatment of later Cressids in sixteenth-century short verse. There, as I shall suggest in Chapter 2, Cressid circulates as a trashed heroine whose repeated punishment displaces masculine abuse. Lydgate's poetry, however, uncovers a fundamental incompatibility between Criseyde's virtue and her culture. Indeed, in another of his satirical poems, *Amor vincit omnia mentiris quod pecunia*, Lydgate recalls the failed love affair between Troilus and Criseyde as a signal instance of the world's instability, laying particular emphasis on the devaluation of truth in erotic relations governed by conditional change:

> Remembre Troye, of Troylus and Cres[e]ide,
> Eche in theyr tyme furthered to plesaunce;
> But what fille after longe or Troylus deyde?
> A false serpent of chaunge and variaunce
> Withouten any lengger attendaunce
> Put out Troylus, and set in Dyomede.[71]

Creseide is not responsible for the alteration of her amorous fortunes; instead, tumult of situation, characterized as "A false serpent of chaunge and variaunce," is invested with powerful, coherent agency, remaking cultures as well as lives, lives as well as loves.[72] Here again, Creseide disappears, marking the place of masculine betrayal in a fashion similar to that of Helen in the *Troy Book*.

And although the source of Creseide's ruin derives from masculine, militarist conquest—"set in Dyomede" (22)—the poem emphasizes variance as an agent of destruction, thereby treating contingency as an inevitable aspect of life in a martial society. In a move recalling the apocryphal Chaucerian poem, "Against Women Unconstant," Criseyde is equated with mutability.[73] The cynical ballad proclaims, "For ever in chaunging stant your sikernesse . . . If ye lese oon, ye can wel tweyn purchace," faulting Criseyde for her ability to shift circumstances to solidify survival, if not security.[74] Similarly, in the *Troy Book* Lydgate suggests that feminine virtues are tactical, deployed to manage contingency:

> Loo! what pite is in wommanhede,
> What mercy eke & benynge routhe—
> Þat newly can al her olde trouthe,
> Of nature, late slyppe a-syde
> Raþer þanne þei shulde se abide
> Any man in meschef for hir sake!
> Þe change is nat so redy for to make
> In Lombard Strete of crowne nor doket—
> Al paie is good, be so þe prente be set:
> Her lettre of chaunge doth no man abide! (4.2148–57)

The transactional opportunism of currency exchange overwrites the transcendent virtues motivating women's pity. Following as it does immediately after Criseyde's decision to love Diomede, this passage recasts her transformation as thoroughly and unabashedly calculating.

Instead of attributing Criseyde's virtues to a *politique* sense of necessity—the savvy ability to cultivate qualities needed to negotiate historical change—Lydgate condemns Chaucer's heroine by associating her with commodified trade. Despite Lydgate's clarity about the social basis of Criseyde's betrayal, his poetry does not make room for women's cultivation of the so-called political virtues, those cardinal virtues that allowed men to resist the vicissitudes of Fortune. Indeed, the *Troy Book*'s turn away from Criseyde reveals a normative assumption expressed more widely across Lydgate's poetry, namely, that women's virtues should be inherent and immutable, not cultivated and performative. The qualities Lydgate recommends, especially mercy and pity, are derived from the tradition of the *theological* virtues, or those virtues that were infused into the human soul by the power of the divine. Derived from Paul's letter to the Corinthians, religious writers had long considered these virtues—faith, hope, and charity—to be precious gifts from God: "And now there remain faith, hope, and charity, these three: but the greatest of these is charity."[75] Such virtues could not be earned or instilled by moral or behavioral training, for unlike the natural virtues of prudence, justice, temperance, or fortitude, they exist outside human capacity. As a revelation of human dependence upon divine power (*theos*), these qualities distinguished virtuous pagans from sanctified Christians.

Even a glance at Lydgate's religious poetry reveals a deep investment in the theological virtues, for again and again, with women as well as men, holiness is consequent upon the infused presence of faith, hope, and charity.[76] Across his poetry, however, both secular and sacred, Lydgate defines women's excellence using qualities derived from the theological virtues. This is clear from his renderings of feminine mercy and pity, two qualities explicitly modeled on the glorified virtues of the Virgin Mary. As was common in late medieval religious verse, Lydgate repeatedly emphasizes Mary's mediating pity, her compassionate mercy, for the penitent pleas of sinful humanity. The "Ballad at the Reverence of Our Lady, Qwene of Mercy," somewhat more interestingly, sets Mary's unwavering virtues against those of mortal women, whose pity for adoring lovers is inherently unstable by comparison. Mary provides the perfect model of feminine fidelity, though she is manifestly superior to those women whose virtues she might inspire:

All women surmountyng,
But she moost benynge be to me mercyable,
That is of pite the welle and eke the spryng.[77]

In "The Fyftene Ioyes of Oure Ladye," and in "Gaude Virgo Mater Christi," Mary is hailed as "Pryncesse of mercy," an address that connects her exalted sovereignty to her inherent excellence.[78]

As Lydgate's treatments of Helen and Criseyde attest, Mary's virtue offers a constant reminder of women's instability, since their qualities cannot remain constant in a world of violence. In prescriptive literatures, accordingly, women's exercises of these virtues are often explicitly connected to female models of holiness, particularly the Virgin Mary. As Kathleen Ashley observes, Mary was frequently extolled as a mirror for feminine conduct, despite the recognition that her virtues surpassed human capacity.[79] In *The Book of the Knight of the Tower*, Mary is offered as an example designed to fashion women's pity and charity, even though the gulf between perfection and imitation is powerfully underscored: "And therfore is here good ensample to euery good lady and to euery good woman how they may not be desmayed ne esmeruelled as they suffre ony mysease / seynge that the quene of heuen suffred in this world soo moche payne and dolour / Thenne oughte we wel to suffre and haue pacyence we that be poure synnars / & that deseruen more after our meryte / to receyue payne & euyll than good / And that by reason ought not to be spared in berynge dolours and trybulacions seynge that god spared not his moder."[80] Christine de Pizan also emphasizes the irresolvable distance between Mary and other heroines included in her City of Ladies, but she does so to underscore Mary's perfect humility and charity: "it please her of her grete makenesse to dwelle here alowe amon|ge them in theyr Cyte & congregacyon without hauynge them in dysdayne for the regarde of her hyghnesse towarde theyr lytelnesse."[81] By making Mary queen of womankind, Christine seeks to position the virtues of all female worthies underneath the sanctifying protection of Mary's divinity: "[all good women] beseche the mekely y^t thou abhorre not to dwelle amonge them by grace & pyte as theyr defende|resse / & protectryce / & keperayenst all ye assaultes of ŷ enemyes & of the worlde."[82]

For Lydgate, embodied virtues are reinscribed as social values unless they have a connection to sanctity. The embodied strengths of female endurance, as Lydgate demonstrates, are rendered faulty, mutable, and expendable by heroic culture's militarist violence. Though Helen is an innocent, she becomes an icon of cultural instability when she is incorporated into Paris's narrative of conquest. And if Criseyde does not make it into catalogs of famous women, it is because her story does not compare with those of other heroines, whose betrayals are overwritten by legends of masculine achievement. Lydgate's Polyxena shows why women need recourse to material virtue; yet with her example the *Troy Book* reveals the devastating consequences of cultural contingency for women's embodied excellences. Much like the traffic-in-women Lynn Shutters finds throughout the *Troy Book* (which in her insightful reading is connected to the marital arrangements between Henry V and Katherine of Valois), Polyxena's innocence is coopted to solidify bonds between powerful kingdoms.[83] Hecuba promises Achilles Polyxena's hand in marriage if he will secure peace, and though this arrangement is ultimately untenable for both parties, Achilles agrees to wed as an end to war. When no alliance is possible, however, Polyxena becomes a sacrificial spoil.

Many Greeks believe Polyxena's beauty is at fault for Achilles's death, for without his impassioned devotion to the lovely young maiden, the Greek champion would not have been lured into the deadly trap Hecuba had set for him. But Polyxena's death is not an act of spontaneous vengeance. Instead, her virtue is so spotless that Antenor and Aeneas are moved to pity, hiding Polyxena even while they slaughter Troy's nameless inhabitants. Following a consistent pattern of self-serving treachery, Calchas's false divination claims that Polyxena must be executed to assure the safe departure of the Greeks. The pronouncement, "By blood ageyn be made satisfaccioun" (4.6662), sends Achilles's son Pyrrhus into a murderous frenzy of paternal restitution. And, despite the pity she inspires among the Greek witnesses, Pyrrhus hacks Polyxena to pieces on his father's grave. Lydgate uses such brutality to elucidate the prudence he seeks to install in his patron, Henry V: Pyrrhus is a tyrant, bestial in the unregulated rage that drives him to shocking violence. Polyxena's material virtue, moreover, heightens the contrast between a militarist and domestic ethics, the latter of which is foreclosed again and again over the course of the *Troy Book*.

But what I would like to focus on here, in building to a concluding appraisal of feminine virtue's shifting status, is the futility of Polyxena's embodied excellence. Immediately before she is killed, Polyxena issues a moving lament, which powerfully indicts the cosmic, cultural, and personal circumstances that supposedly necessitate her death. Through her lengthy argument (118 lines—so long, ironically, that it guarantees its own erasure in critical discussion!), Polyxena asserts her virtue's stability, autonomy, and materiality. She is guiltless, "Clene of entent of þat I am accused! / And ȝit, allas! I may nat be excused" (4.6761–62), an innocent victim of Greek cruelty: "Out of youre herte, allas, pite is gon" (4.6785). Yet as she understands, the contingency of women's excellence is a cultural production, here imposed by the necessities of conquest. She might practice a perfected femininity, but she can do nothing to justify herself in the face of the warrior community's violence.[84] Contemplating her fruitless sacrifice, Polyxena expresses mournful, resentful awareness that social standards for women's idealization have limited, prevented, and decimated any life she might have led.

Unlike Helen or Criseyde, prescriptive femininity has little direct bearing on Polyxena's behavior in Lydgate's representation. Early on, her enduring beauty, which provides evidence of her devotion to her brother (Achilles first sees Polyxena while visiting Hector's tomb), suggests that she animates a set of values which stand quite apart from her wartime mistreatment. Calchas's sentence, with its sacrificial demand, severs this relation. If she survives, she will be forced "to be ladde oute of þis cite / Amonge straungeris to live in pouerte" (4.6819–20). Her ceremonial execution, moreover, will rewrite her beauty as the "orginal / Cause of [Achilles's] deth" (4.6664–65). Either alternative excludes Polyxena's desire to live a generative life of peace and vitality surrounded by family. It is not, to be clear, an appeal to a sacrificial ethics, the power and appeal of which Aranye Fradenburg has so convincingly detailed in late medieval culture.[85] Her sacrifice is not hers to make, but will become part of a masculinist narrative of revenge. After declaring her preference for unjust death over captive virtue, she warns later women about the perils that accompany heroic "aventure":

> And alle maidenes, remembreþ vp-on me
> To take exaumple how ȝe shal ȝow kepe
> And þat ye wolde a fewe teris wepe
> Whan þat ye þinke vppon Polycene,
> Þat was of age and of ȝeris grene
> Whan she was slayn by cruel auenture. (4.6840–45)

Considering her horrid sacrifice, women might wonder what kind of example Polyxena is meant to set, or how the disparity between her idealized life and her gratuitous death can possibly be reconciled.

What Lydgate's *Troy Book* shows above all, I submit, is that no such reconciliation is possible in the fraught world where virtues are prescribed to advance the interests of powerful men. No woman can inhabit material virtue in a manner sufficient to valorize the precarious conditions of her own existence. Later religious writers, quite famously Luther, will extend this unjustified condition to all manner of persons. But here, Lydgate settles this frailty of existence on women, especially those who must negotiate and forbear the treacheries of wartime politics. Polyxena is noticeably different from other infamous women: Helen and Criseyde falter on account of their feminized affections, opening themselves to erotic relations that exploit culturally favored ideals of women's submission. But Polyxena never stumbles in her virtue, not even over inherent contradictions in expectations for idealized femininity. She knows hers is a death "with-oute gilt at al" (4.6759), but she also knows feminine innocence is totally expendable depending on the cultural context. Her prayer for other women is instructive and terrifying, for when she implores the gods to send "euery maide better happe and grace" (4.6835), she underscores the fragility of feminine virtue in an ethical climate ruled by warring men.

Shifting Virtue

Polyxena's sacrificial futility, which results from a failed marital alliance, reveals women as the overwhelmed victims of this cultural, ultimately unethical practice. Lydgate expresses hope for the marriage between Henry and Katherine, but only two years later, Scott-Morgan Straker persuasively demonstrates, he expresses considerable concern over the dynastic coupling between Jacqueline of Hainault and Humphrey, Duke of Gloucester, in his purported epithalamium, "On Gloucester's Approaching Marriage."[86] Of course, the historical circumstances of 1422 were considerably altered from the promising possibilities of 1420; crucial to my concerns, however, is Lydgate's willingness to use famous women to show the circumstantial slippage between one set of cultural valuations and another. In short, Straker demonstrates, not all political alliances are equal, particularly since the union of Humphrey and Jacqueline threatened the peace between England and France solemnized through the wedding of Henry V and Katherine of Valois.[87] When he lauds Jacqueline's manifold virtues, Lydgate once again turns to the power of famous women to impart rarefied goods:

> Flouring in youþe lyke to Polixseene,
> Secree feythful as Dydo of Cartage,

Constant of hert lyche Ecuba þe qweene,
And as Lucresse in loue truwe and clene
. . . .
Feyre was Heleyne, liche as bookes telleþe,
And renommed as of seemlynesse.[88]

Detached from complex narrative contexts, each of these heroines has a doubled history, signifying more than her deictic invocation might superficially
imply. Lydgate might appear to praise Jacqueline, and might claim to extol
her marriage to Humphrey, but as Straker suggests, the vexed record of every
woman undermines the moral praise that the poem putatively offers: "The
remaining women to whom Jacqueline is compared all intensify conflict in
some way, usually at high personal cost."[89]

In Lydgate's poetry, prescriptive femininity is an unstable register of ethical values. This is not because the values are mutable, and it is not because
the women are changeable; rather, as Lydgate shows through his renderings
of famous heroines, it is because their ethical import can signify differently
in changed cultural circumstances. Social articulations of virtues must, as a
matter of necessity, change with their cultures. As a consequence, basing
virtue on social foundations alone, Lydgate shows over and over again, is not
merely insufficient, but is actually endangering to the women meant to
embody prized principles. The social expendability of prescriptive femininity,
recounted in bracing detail throughout his *Troy Book*, is most powerfully
expressed in religious poems that set the contingent virtues of famous women
against the transcendent excellence of the Virgin Mary. Powerful women
might frequently be compared to the queen of heaven, but as Lydgate demonstrates in his poem, "A Valentine to her that Excelleth All," famous worthies do not confer lasting values:

What shal I seyne of qweene Penelope?
Or in Grece of þe qweene Alceste?
Of Polixeene oþer of Medee?
Or of qweene Heleyne holden þe fayrest?
Lat hem farewell! and let her names rest!
My laydyes name þeyre renoun dooþe appalle
Whom I haue chose for she excellþe alle.[90]

Their deeds have already faded, but even the fame of these women will pass
away, for the basis of their virtues is itself transitory. Compared to Mary,

indeed, the worth of these women is as superficial as Lydgate's indexical invocation of their names.

Yet if we are tempted to condemn these individual women, Lydgate instead connects the ephemeral stature of famous heroines to the cultures that produced their worthiness. In the *Life of Our Lady*, Lydgate draws an explicit line between cultures and heroines:

> Late be, thow Grece, and speke not of Eleyn,
> Ne thow, Troy, of Yong Polexene,
> Ne Rome of Lucresse, with hir eyn tweyne,
> Ne thow, Cartage, of thy fresshe quene,
> Dido, that was so fayre some tyme to seen;
> Late be your boste, and take of hem noon hede
> Whose beaute fayleth as floure in frosty mede.[91]

With the fall of great societies comes the destruction of venerated heroines. And, although Lydgate once again invokes a series of notable female worthies to extol the permanence of Mary's virtues, the detrimental relation between women's virtue and social contingency is made witheringly obvious. If a woman's values emerge from her culture's ideals, such principles are only as permanent as the society itself. When Troy falls, in other words, Polixena's ethical value is also destroyed. As her narrative reveals, moreover, ethical ruin leads to actual harms. If women exemplify lauded cultural ideals, then they are exposed to damage—physical and emotional suffering—when those cultures are devastated.

Because cultures inevitably change, ethical values based upon social norms simply enshrine the prerogatives of the powerful. And, while Lydgate has long been characterized as a poet who promotes Lancastrian legitimacy, his investment in England's ruling elite is informed by a larger moral program of transcendent virtues.[92] It is because the Lancastrians identified themselves with the defense of religious truth, not because they asserted a militarist claim over the crown of France, that Lydgate extols their propensity for peaceful, harmonious, virtuous governance. As his civic productions make equally clear, Lydgate is committed to England's cultural abundance and domestic tranquility.[93] It is no coincidence, I believe, that the insecurity of his famous women points to a traumatic loss of social vitality and communal accord, those very values that Lydgate extols in his various forms of poetic address to England's governing powers. Helen, Criseyde, and Polyxena, not to mention a host of other famous women Lydgate invokes in the *Troy Book* and elsewhere, are notable for their lack of cultural security. Virtue's social production, though it might enable Criseyde to adapt herself to changed circumstances, is dangerous to women, especially during wartime. Without an immutable domain of reference, the values women embody, from familial attachments to communal associations, may be sacrificed in order to substantiate war's fundamental injuring function.[94] As Lydgate seems to understand, women's virtues remain vulnerable to cultural violence if they are not connected to grander, more lasting systems of excellence.

The next chapter pursues this material destruction of idealized femininity, since, as I shall suggest, Cresseid's demise in Robert Henryson's *Testament of Cresseid* intensifies a critique of socially inscribed virtue for its violence against those famous women it promises to immortalize.[95] Before turning to Henryson, however, I conclude by returning to Chaucer's Criseyde. With the translation of his heroine, Chaucer uncovers the dangers that heroic culture poses to vulnerable members, namely women. More troubling, perhaps, is that Criseyde's translation by Pandarus, by the parliament, and by the Greeks uncovers a shared human reluctance to protect qualities that emerge from enduring rather than exercising power. By privileging the virtues of violence—qualities including honor, courage, and bravery—heroic culture makes an ethical choice to expose women, along with the values they represent, to emotional and physical suffering. In a parallel with Lydgate's Polyxena, we might go so far as to say that Criseyde is sacrificed in order to make way for the articulation of heroic excellence that Troilus ultimately exemplifies.

At the very least, it is evident that Troilus's courage and bravery in battle subsume his devotion and fidelity in love. Criseyde's betrayal is the immediate cause of this shift in values, but her "slydinge of corage" (V.825) emerges directly from Troy's martial priorities. Chaucer's attempt to extol a form of human love that eclipses all other values is a failure, for it is obvious even to Troilus that military priorities win the day in the culture that entitles his noble, heroic virtues. Shakespeare's *Troilus and Cressida* will return to this heroic culture to pressure the idea that martial values are ethical virtues. In doing so, however, there is no assumption, as there is with Lydgate, that a divine register of virtues would stand in reparative relation to a human economy of values. Instead, following upon Henryson's harrowing production of Cresseid's material virtue, Shakespeare challenges the idea that human excellence is founded on wielding rather than yielding agency. This is not, it is important to say even here, to suggest that Shakespeare is somehow recuperating Chaucer's Criseyde. It is to suggest that Shakespeare departs from his contemporaries, returning to and extending a medieval interest in alternative modes of ethical action. Chaucer makes room for Criseyde's material virtue, showing her capacity for a type of ethical excellence that stands outside the heroic struggle for masculine achievement. Her virtue is made captive to *virtus*, but through her betrayal, Chaucer shows the ethical impoverishment that follows from basing an entire system of communal values on advancing the privileges and prerogatives of an elite few.

CHAPTER 2

The Matter of Virtue, from Henryson to Shakespeare

Whilome full feyre was Polixene,
So was Creseyde; so was Helene
Dido also of Cartage quene,
Whos beaute made many one pleyne;
But dethe came laste and can dysteyne
Their freshenes, and made them full base,
Youre remembraunce let not disdeyne,
That now is heye some tyme was gras.
—John Lydgate, "That Now is Hay Some-Tyme Was Grase"

The fifteenth-century scribe John Shirley rather famously claims that John Lydgate wrote his *ubi sunt* meditation "at þe commandement of þe Quene Kateryn," widow to Henry V and mother to Henry VI.[1] Yet if Criseyde is meant to capture the misfortunes of a culturally translated queen, early modern audiences would likely have regarded the comparison as scandalously misplaced. The reasons for divergent standards of poetic decorum are several, but with respect to Criseyde, they are collectively captured by the name "Chaucer." In 1561 John Stowe included a short ballad, "Against Women Unconstant," in his edition of Chaucer's *Works*.[2] Chaucer's ballad catalogs only negative qualities with its gathering of notable women:

Ye might be shryned for your brotelnesse
Bet than Dalyda, Creseyde or Candace,

For ever in chaunging stant your sikernesse;
That tache may no wight fro your herte arace. (15–18)

To be sure, satiric ballads frequently deride fickle mistresses. Chaucer's contribution is important, though, because it shows how short verse might recast
an established tradition. Criseyde's devastating betrayal might have warranted
thousands of lines to situate its fraught complexity in *Troilus and Criseyde*;
here, on the contrary, her conventional mutability can be rendered using just
a few pejorative associations.

    With this ballad, the entirety of Criseyde's experience is distilled to con-
demn feminine "newefangelnesse" (1). To compare Criseyde to a living
queen, as Lydgate appears to do in the fifteenth century, would be to criticize
that queen little more than a century later.[3] By the sixteenth century, Criseyde is nearly always a figure for vice. This shift, of course, is not prompted
by the inclusion of a minor satirical ballad, "Against Women Unconstant,"
in an early Elizabethan edition of Chaucer's *Works*. It is, rather, the result of
a grander poetic reworking, beginning with Robert Henryson's *Testament of
Cresseid*. As scholars are well aware, in 1532 William Thynne includes the
shocking story of Cresseid's demise in the first printed collection of Chaucer's
Works.[4] Henryson's poem is thought by many to be the primary culprit in
establishing what Gretchen Mieszkowski characterizes as her "traditional
position as a type of fickle woman."[5] This is despite the fact that the printed
page clearly announces Henryson's continuation of Chaucer's narrative:
"Thus endeth the fyfth and laste booke of Troylus: and here foloweth the
pyteful and dolorous testament of fayre Creseyde."[6] Nevertheless, it is equally
true that, for many early moderns, the details of Henryson's account were
incorporated within Criseyde's history, which continued to be attributed
exclusively to Chaucer.[7]

    The *Testament of Cresseid* has long played a central role in the critical
assessment of Chaucer's early modernization.[8] And while I harbor no wish to
disturb the scholarly focus on what Henryson did to Chaucer, in this chapter
I mean to expand it, in particular by examining what sixteenth-century versifiers did to Henryson.[9] Those scholars who have considered sixteenth-century
renderings of Criseyde have usually viewed Henryson's poem as a formative,
though perhaps misunderstood, source for the demise of Chaucer's heroine.[10]
Since the details of Henryson's account are included in many satiric portrayals, this analysis is basically, perhaps even trivially true: early modern depictions of Cressid as a wanton and a leper would not have been possible were

it not for the *Testament of Cresseid*. As this chapter demonstrates, many of
these portrayals offer something beyond simple proof of Henryson's influence, for they actively intervene in the history of Cressid's representation.
Sixteenth-century poetic treatments, though they may derive their details
from Henryson, provide distinctively new fashionings of Troilus's beloved.
Many of these portrayals are reductive, including Cressid as a defining
instance of the feminine perfidy under construction. Others are more
extended, recasting Cressid's infidelity as a premeditated performance of
feminine duplicity. All these renderings are punitive, insofar as Cressid
is explicitly—materially—held responsible for her betrayal. But none are
medieval, despite, or as this chapter will show, on account of their didacticism.

Instead, poetic remakings of Cressid form a vital part of the sixteenth-
century's growing corpus of prescriptive verse.[11] From George Turberville's
cutting dismissals, to Robert Greene's snide impersonation, Cressid's
betrayal assumes a social function independent of all prior instantiations.
In particular, the poetic circulation of Cressid is a direct departure from
Henryson, whose representation of his heroine's dissolution bears little
resemblance to the derisive, sometimes mocking, versions of her demise
featured in sixteenth-century verse references.[12] By reading Henryson's
Cresseid in tandem with later Cressids, this chapter includes Henryson
among those poets who invent a tradition of material virtue in a world of
ethical instability. Unlike Chaucer and Lydgate, who indict heroic culture
for the harms visited upon vulnerable women, Henryson represents the
emergence of women's virtue from conditions of material instability. The
body is where virtue happens in Henryson; it is not just a base site of
corruption but a positive ethical endowment. By contrast, Cresseid's poetic
proliferation in the sixteenth century disperses her narrative's ethical power.
As I argue in this chapter, her circulation as a prescriptive illustration makes
her not an exceptional heroine, but a common woman. Exchanged between
members of an enlarged audience, in sixteenth-century verse Henryson's
heroine "change[s] in filfth all [her] feminitie / And be with fleschelie lust
sa maculait" (80–81).[13]

When Shakespeare takes up this matter in *Troilus and Cressida*, he shows
more commonality with Henryson than with sixteenth-century versifiers. As
I shall suggest, Cressida's medieval legacy provides an important poetic backdrop for Shakespeare's play, but not because Shakespeare recovered Chaucer's
heroine from literary disgrace. Instead, Shakespeare continues an important

late medieval poetic tradition, which highlights the material consequences of prescriptive virtue for idealized women identified with prized social values. If Henryson suggests that virtue might result from the challenging conditions of material existence, Shakespeare shows how heroic culture belittles that virtue to preserve masculine dominance. Shakespeare's Cressida joins a poetic tradition of ethical resistance, which formulates an embodied example of women's virtue that exceeds and critiques premodern scripts of idealized femininity. Yet, as Cressida's corruption affirms, when women have no say over their excellence, their virtue is impoverished, if not altogether eradicated. To be "as false as Cressid," therefore, is to play the woman's part in an ethical theater of heroic values.[14] Through Cressida's precarious plight, Shakespeare's play counters a vast literature that erases women's ethical agency by cultivating a model of prescriptive virtue.

Making Virtue Matter in *The Testament of Cresseid*

Because it convenes a cosmological court that sentences Cresseid to suffer the ravages of leprosy, *The Testament of Cresseid* metes out the moral punishment deferred by earlier poets, exacting harsh penalties for the violation of virtue's prescriptive norms.[15] Some critics see Henryson's poem as a redemption narrative, and it is true that Henryson makes Cresseid the paragon of a kind of virtue, which accrues a form of dignity.[16] But this virtue, akin to that of Shakespeare's Cressida, emerges from a character's ability to endure material acts of cultural injustice. Henryson's poem asks what kinds of strengths might emerge from enduring the most punishing conditions of embodiment. If this book suggests that material virtue need not emerge from women's suffering, in Henryson's case the miseries of his heroine multiply to demonstrate the ethical powers of mortal finitude itself. Henryson's poem inflicts severe pain on Troilus's beloved, but this is not, as some have assumed, a vengeful gesture designed to destroy Cresseid. Rather, as I shall detail, Henryson pursues the logical outcomes of heroic ethics, representing what happens to women who are caught between warring elite men. Cresseid is not a betrayer, though she is certainly treated as one. That she is asked to bear moral responsibility for the mortal harms she suffers, to be sure, is one of this poem's most devastating disclosures. But Henryson also shows how Cresseid bears up under a comprehensive program of material deprivation.

Many readers fault Cresseid for her reactions to her punishment, but these analyses already assume her moral culpability. Despite readers' assertions to the contrary, Henryson's Cresseid is not punished for wantonness. She is treated badly for leaving Troilus, particularly since Henryson's Diomed is a canny seducer who seeks sexual conquest in his dealings with the Trojan prisoner. Cresseid falls pretty far before she finds refuge with her father, Calchus. It is no wonder, frankly, that Cresseid makes her formal complaint against the gods, the most moving lines of which capture her deep sense of abandonment, as well as her grave feeling of betrayal. Echoing Chaucer's initial description of Criseyde, Henryson's heroine mourns her loss:

> Ye gave me anis ane devine responsaill
> That I suld be the flour of luif in Troy;
> Now am I maid ane unworthie outwaill,
> And all in cair translatit is my joy. (127–30)

That the gods then descend from their spheres, collectively sentencing Cresseid to bear the punishment of leprosy, is not, or not exclusively, a disciplinary plot meant to mark feminine duplicity in the flesh.

Instead, Cresseid's punishment offers a complex critique of treating virtue as an externally imposed set of cultural expectations over which women have no control. As Cresseid's demise demonstrates, simple abjection is not enough to gratify the fantasies of heroic agency in which she is entangled. Rather, she must perform her submission in a style that validates its compulsion.[17] In other words, it is not enough to submit to a Trojan, and then a Greek, because in both cases Cresseid is otherwise bereft of protection. Instead, her submission must validate an ethical code that privileges heroic conquest. Each man must be worthy of her submission, but if either proves unworthy—and the logic of male competition is mutually exclusive—then she is the one to blame. This is despite the fact that she follows prescriptions for idealized femininity in her culture, and despite the fact that both heroes violate their promise to protect Cresseid as an expression of affection.

The famous complaint that follows, at least for many readers, marks a turning point for Cresseid.[18] Here begins Cresseid's inward journey, or the redemptive passage from vanity to humility that ultimately enables her to overcome physical suffering. By this reckoning, hers is no easy triumph.[19] Yet, unlike other poets, Henryson does not focus the complaint on Cresseid's interiority. As Denton Fox rightly notes, "[Cresseid] has, in a completely non-metaphorical sense, a pain caused by love which slays her and which can be seen in her hue; a seclusion from society; and sores that cannot be healed by any medicine."[20] Cresseid's complaint focuses on the physical conditions that cause her pain; even so, her complex *ubi sunt* meditation does not focus exclusively on her body's dissolution. Instead, she remembers those material surrounds that are now gone, from her plush bedchamber, to her lush garden. In a radical departure from earlier examples of the form, her sorrow extends to the tangible losses that condition her betrayal.[21]

For Cresseid, the material stuff of culture signifies her loss. While it is true that Cresseid is an abandoned lover, in the *Testament*'s spare account, Diomeid's rejection is the least of her troubles. As she retreads the paths of her memory, Cresseid's concerns run to a different place than the Greek camp. To the question, "Quhair is thy chalmer wantounlie besene" (416), or "Quhair is thy garding with thir greissis gay" (425), the answer is always *Troy*. And, although Troy's impending doom would not be lost on Henryson's later Scots audience, who certainly knew that the illustrious city would ultimately be burnt to a cinder, the difference between the city's vaunting greatness and Cresseid's lowly misery suggests that a breach in virtues, as much as walls, felled Troy. The radical externalization of her complaint registers this rift, for if Cresseid was "the flour and A per se" (78), then her decay signals the transience of those social values.

But the challenging outwardness of her complaint does more than indict Troy for its superficial adherence to transitory ideals of women's worth. Instead, she gains dignity from enduring harms that are not her doing, much less her fault. Like so many other elements of Henryson's poem, Cresseid's complaint attends to the tension between individual agency and cultural necessity. When Cresseid addresses the ladies of Troy and Greece, she identifies mutability of situation as the paramount peril to women who enjoy the exalted conditions of heroic culture. Importantly, and it is worth repeating, Cresseid focuses not on beauty's decay, but on the material consequences of social upheaval as the greatest danger to idealized women:

> O ladyis fair of Troy and Grece, attend
> My miserie, quhilk nane may comprehend,
> My frivoll fortoun, my infelicitie,
> My greit mischeif, quhilk na man can amend.
> Be war in tyme, approchis neir the end,

And in your mynd ane mirrour mak of me:
As I am now, peradventure that ye
For all your micht may cum to that same end,
Or ellis war, gif ony war may be. (452–60)

Unhappy happenstance, or the changing favor of fortune, is here presented
as an inevitable hazard of temporality itself. And, even if she is held responsible for her downfall, Cresseid argues that good fortune is no more a product
of moral worth than bad.

With her relentless focus on external infelicity, Cresseid connects the
sufferings of her body to the chaos of her universe. Her inwardness remains
inaccessible—she proclaims its utter incomprehensibility—but her body bears
punishment, nonetheless. Cresseid's complaint, therefore, is far more frightening than a personal meditation on vanities lost. Indeed, by cataloging the brutality of circumstance, she severs the connection between moral worth and
mortal punishment in heroic society. Her plight might befall any woman, she
warns, no matter how secure her idealized place might presently appear:

Exempill mak of me in your memour
. . . .
All welth in eird, away as wind it weiris;
Be war thairfoir, approchis neir your hour;
Fortoun is fikkill quhen scho beginnis and steiris. (465, 467–69)

If Cresseid seeks to evade blame, it is only insofar as she suggests that horrific
downfall is a common ending for elite women. Changes to the poetic complaint allow Henryson to contemplate not only what it means to be subjected
to unwarranted suffering, but also what it means to accept responsibility for
wrongs that might remain beyond one's volitional control. With Cresseid's
exteriorized suffering, the *Testament* writes an alternative account of the virtuous heroine, who accrues dignity from the ability to endure overwhelming
oppression.

Living at a leper hospital, and begging as the Trojan garrison passes,
Cresseid is a testament not just to fortune's fickleness, but also to society's
indifference. Troilus casts a glance near Cresseid's very spot, but she is so
changed that he passes "not witting quhat scho was" (497). The only thing
that gives him pause is her unsettling ability to return his look: "Than upon
him scho kest up baith hir ene" (498). Cresseid's ability to meet the gaze of

those who look down on her is a crucial moment, when Henryson's poem struggles to represent Cresseid's disturbing materiality. Viewed by her society as untouchable, Cresseid lives in a state of suspended animation, or what George Edmondson cannily interprets as, using Jacques Lacan's words, "the space between two deaths."[22] Because she is like a living corpse, she should remain unable to transfix passersby with the vivacity of her look. Her gaze is fundamentally unsettling because it is, like her, distressingly out of place. In reducing Cresseid to bare materiality, Henryson's poem invests her suffering with the power to undo gendered hierarchies of virtue in a culture that extols masculine violence. Indeed, what Derek Pearsall characterized as the "nonrecognition scene" is a tellingly missed encounter, a revealing instance of *méconnaissance* that figures larger social processes of ethical impoverishment.[23] Like Troilus, who gazes upon his beloved without recognizing her, most passersby see Cresseid without actually seeing her.

The miserable condition of the lepers evokes Troilus's pity, but the transformed reality she faces does not register. Instead, he converts the slightest shadow of recognition into an occasion for remembering the beautiful lover he carries within, not the ruined Cresseid who sits before him.[24] This misrecognition reveals two orders of virtue, which have different relations to cultural power, and even to material reality. Troilus conjures his own ethical reality, resurrecting Cresseid as a reflexive idealization that lifts him above war's degrading transactions. As Felicity Riddy observes, Cresseid's abjection is the consequence of Troilus's elevation.[25] Yet, unlike later poets, Henryson chronicles Cresseid's translation into a worthless object that remains ethically invisible under the masculinist gaze of heroic culture. Her devaluation arises, as Henryson's poem makes clear, from the shocking continuity of her conduct. She does not change her behavior, but the radical change in the context for her behavior remakes her character. In a way that Henryson's poem makes literal, changing one's place, even slightly, radically changes one's stars. This outcome is consonant with medieval cosmology, which also calibrated personal disposition according to physical location.[26] The four elements that founded humoral medicine (earth, air, fire, and water) were distinctively linked to the four cardinal directions (east, west, south, and north).[27] When Cresseid travels across the arc of her demise—from the Trojan city to the Greek camp to the leper house to the city walls—Henryson imbues material place with moral consequences.[28]

In Henryson's poem, Cresseid's movement ethically remakes her character. Even if her sexual availability in Troy galvanizes the agonies of ennobled masculine desire, it ultimately subjects her to the belittling exchanges of homosocial competition. Cresseid is not worth a fight, much less protection, if she does not enjoy love's favor. Her privilege as an object of desire, the planetary court affirms, relies on her fixed place in Troy. The cruel irony of Cupid's malevolence is not lost on Cresseid, for when she recalls the conditions of promise that perfected her beauty, she notes the loss of material security that precipitates her downfall. Those who see this poem as Christian are certainly right, then, to emphasize the shifting ethical register with which Cresseid must contend in her suffering. The human sphere of love is devalued, since war corrupts all bonds of human affection in this violent domain. Yet, despite the poem's willingness to show the fateful inconstancy of human love, the *Testament* offers no fulfilling, transcendent form of devotion—which derives from a higher sphere—to console Cresseid for the cosmic vengeance she endures. Unlike Chaucer's Troilus, who laughs at mortal follies from his exalted position, Henryson's Cresseid never gets beyond the material fracas of physical dissolution. She remains subject to the shifting motions of material change, buffeted by the variable progress of those heavenly bodies that constitute her world, and her person. Cresseid is transformed into a dissolute object as a means to assure Troilus's privileged position.[29]

Her degradation reveals the ethical mutability required of women in societies that promote heroic virtue. Yet, like Lacan's famous sardine can, whose uncanny glinting implies a thing-ish agency that defies possessive mastery, Cresseid's unclassifiable mattering—her placeless yet enduring existence as a ruined object—threatens to upend the structuring capacity of traditional virtue ethics.[30] Cresseid is materially objectified—she is trashed, disposable, yet uncanny—but this does not mean that her alternative model of material virtue reforms the cultural conditions her suffering exposes. Indeed, in a move that counters posthumanist attempts to realize Bruno Latour's "parliament of things" through a recognition of matter's liveliness, Cresseid's ethical impoverishment shows how one system of ethics might be actively suppressed to sustain an alternative. Cresseid gains dignity, even a kind of autonomy, from mattering in a place where she should not, from making visible the conditions of her cultural abjection. But Troilus never sees her, and despite her unnoticed agency, she never challenges his idealized fantasy of himself. As Henryson's Cresseid attests, individual agency, moral intelligibility, and even ethical identity do not always promote social equality. In Henryson as in Chaucer before him, parliaments operate according to notions of majority, minority, representation, and difference.

As a woman traded between enemy camps, and as a beloved condemned by divine assembly, Cresseid knows that the distributive agency of parliaments often settles destruction on a singular, radically other *thing*. As the destroyed thing ordering perceptions of human value—in Lacan's thinking, *das Ding*—Cresseid represents another model of ethical action, one that must constantly be misperceived in order to preserve the cultural ascendancy of heroic *virtus*.[31] Troilus's treatment of Cresseid demonstrates how a dominant model of ethics edges out, and actively subsumes, any alternatives. When Troilus casts down purse and ring, "And in the skirt of Cresseid doun can swak" (522), he honors his recollections of Cresseid's perfection in a gesture of spontaneous kindness that affirms his moral excellence. His generosity attests to a perfect combination of habituation and disposition, capturing the balance of performance and proclivity extolled as virtue in late medieval treatises.[32] Yet if Troilus fulfills the Aristotelian mean by exercising magnanimity in an unexpected context, then his generosity also attests to Troilus's privileged cultural position. His benevolence is nonchalant, a careless tribute to a source of excellence that remains immune to the leprous body he encounters. Rather than confront Cresseid, Troilus uses her ruined figure to preserve virtue as an ideal he remembers within himself.

Through Troilus's idealizing misrecognition, Henryson affirms the vital link between bodies and their virtues. Virtues belong to the bodies that generate them; they cannot be imposed from the outside, nor should they be appropriated by other bodies. That said, the remainder of Henryson's poem details how Cresseid's virtues get swept up in the narrative of Troilus's heroism. And, though critics have sought to pry apart her every utterance to discern her internal condition, Cresseid remains as elusive as her Chaucerian namesake. This is not to suggest that she evades blame; on the contrary, for those expecting a penitent display, Henryson's heroine is completely, if rather ostentatiously, gratifying. Once her benefactor is revealed, Cresseid performs a three-stanza litany of her former lover's manifold virtues, differentiating his worth using a constant refrain, "O fals Cresseid and trew knicht Troilus!" (546, 558, 560). Casting his virtue in universal terms, "Of all wemen protectour and defence" (556), allows her to assume full blame for their failed love:

My mynd in fleschelie foull affectioun
Was inclynit to lustis lecherous. (558–59)

By embracing these vices, she makes herself into a cautionary fable of human frailty: "Nane but my self as now I will accuse" (574). After Cresseid dies, Troilus writes her epitaph, and the poem makes her into a literary exemplum:

> Now worthie wemen, in this ballet schort,
> Maid for your worschip and instructioun,
> Of cheritie, I monische and exhort,
> Ming not your lufe with fals deceptioun:
> Beir in your mynd this schort conclusioun
> Of fair Cresseid, as I have said befoir.
> Sen scho is deid I speik of hir no moir. (610–16)

By enclosing Cresseid in a prescriptive tomb, Henryson's *Testament* enshrines Troilus's heroic virtue.

Even a narrative as sealed as this, however, cannot contain the troubling conditions of heroic virtue revealed by Cresseid's closing performance. Since Troilus's role in this poem is comparably minor—Henryson's story picks up after Cresseid's exchange, so there is only declarative evidence to support Troilus's devotion—her account of his fidelity is central to his virtuous reputation. But her final reckoning is transparently conventional, as well. Indeed, Cresseid's confessional recitation reveals the dependence of prescriptive virtue on visible modes of performance that gratify masculine fantasies of heroism. Once she is traded to the Greek camp, Henryson's heroine can only learn to suffer in a mode that consolidates Troilus's reputation for "trew lufe" (591). The pain she bears, however, constitutes a more embodied model of endurance than the sloganeered virtue she ascribes to Troilus. To see an analogous tension in Judith Butler's more recent work on precarity in a world of war, the suffering Cresseid undergoes "remain[s] proof of stubborn life, vulnerable, overwhelmed, [her] own and not [her] own, dispossessed, enraged, and perspicacious."[33] Through Cresseid's forbearance, Henryson at least acknowledges the struggle to maintain dignity in the face of overwhelming oppression. Indeed, her warning to lovers, "be war and tak gude heid about / Quhome that ye lufe, for quhome ye suffer paine" (561–62), could be directed to any number of virtuous heroines of the subsequent literary age.

Pieces of Cressid in Sixteenth-Century Short Verse

This is not to say, however, that later writers appreciated the degrading conditions of prescriptive virtue revealed by Henryson's poem. Although I am arguing for Henryson's contribution to a tradition of material virtue that unsettles heroic ethics, in the following century many writers adopt the *Testament*'s confessional display to justify Cresseid's disposable cultural status. We might say that Cresseid claims a kind of control over her situation, since her testament enables her to assert a type of authority over her demise.[34] Once she sets the terms of her blame, there is little more that anyone else can say about her, at least in Henryson's poem. Her dignity accrues from surviving the hostile motions of a tumultuous world. She endures extreme physical punishment, leaving the narrator only to conclude, "Sen scho is deid I speik of hir no moir" (616). Later writers speak of her all the time, although they do so not with the somber respect that might be afforded to Lucrece, Judith, or even a relatively unknown contemporary.[35] Usually Cressid is treated as a wanton, a trashy deceiver whose abuse of Troilus parallels the speaker's treatment at the hands of a faithless mistress. In the miscellany attributed to Thomas Proctor, *A gorgious gallery, of gallant inventions* (1578), a lover bewails his poor judgment, "My fayth alas I gaue, / To wight of Cressids kinde."[36] Another lover from the collection resolves, "Thy fawning flattering wordes, which now full falce I finde, / Perswades mee to content my selfe, and turne from Cressids kinde."[37] George Gascoigne's beleaguered speaker protests, "I found naught else but tricks of Cressides kinde, / Which playnly provde, that thou weart of hir bloud," and elsewhere characterizes his fickle mistress as "Cressides heir."[38] George Turberville composes an entire poem in which "The Louer in vtter despaire of his Ladies returne, in eche respect compares his estate with Troylus."[39]

In truth, it is difficult to capture the texture of this corpus, since as Hyder E. Rollins notes in his early survey, "from 1575–1585 poetical miscellanies, under fantastic and verbose titles, swarmed; and Cressid's name monotonously appears in them . . . as a fearful example."[40] The references to Cressid are so frequent, and are in so much agreement, that they begin to run together after a few instances. This is likely the point, as I will detail by returning to these largely unstudied poems. For these poets, the female body is a base source of moral corruption. Virtue cannot contain that corruption, but can serve at best as a pleasing veneer and at worst as a dangerous cover for women's duplicity. Women control their virtues, but they do so in order to humiliate, deceive, and destroy faithful men. As the signal instance of all these feminized vices, Cressid's corruption and duplicity become individually cultivated traits. Cressid's mutability is taken for granted in sixteenth-century verse, so that a ballad ascribed to Leonard Gibson, "to the tune of lightie loue," can knowingly announce, "It séemes by your doynges, that Cressed doth scoole ye, / Penelopeys vertues are cleane out of thought."[41] Similarly, a forlorn lover might confidently declare, "So Cressids crafte shall kepe the féeld, for to resound thy shame / Vlisses wife shall mate the sore, whose wifely troth doth shine."[42]

The foregoing occurrences underscore two aspects that are important to a consideration of material virtue as a counter to heroic *virtus* in the sixteenth century. First, as the contrast with Penelope is designed to show, Cressid is an exemplary figure who models a debased form of femininity; she demonstrates why women's virtue needs to be subject to masculine dominance. Second, as references to Cressid's kind, blood, or lineage attest—"But what? by kinde the Cat will hunt, / hir father did the like"—her sullied behavior supposedly arises from an inherent, physical, taint. This usually means Cressid cannot help herself, so that even if she is deliberate in her deceptions, Cressid is not fully in control of the damage she does to others, and ultimately to herself.[43] Unlike Henryson's Cresseid, who gains dignity from assuming blame for a situation beyond her power, Tudor Cressids are punished again and again, replaying Troilus's pain as a means to condemn feminine duplicity. We might say that later writers gleaned practically nothing from Henryson, except that vivid details from his *Testament* are central to the disciplinary reprisal of Cresseid's betrayal. Almost every poem features Cresseid's leprosy, and many also include her poverty. A frustrated lover in *A gorgious gallery* calls down his own curse:

> And all the sorte of those: that vse such craft I wish
> A speedy end, or lothsome life, to liue with Lasars dish.[44]

Elsewhere, a lover exhorts fidelity with an ominous reference:

> Can Cressid beare witnesse
> . . . .
> Whom Leprosy paynted
> And penury taynted.[45]

A complaint from Richard Edwards's *Paradise of daintie devises* (1585) magnifies Cressid's wrong, though it at least distributes the threat of her punishment between lovers:

I hope you will not be so false, as Cressed was to Troye:
For if I be vntrue, her Lazars death I wish,
And eke in thee if thou be false, her clapper and her dish.[46]

For these early moderns, leprosy is a causal consequence of Cressid's moral taint. In subsequent renditions of a single poem, Thomas Howell uses Cressid to solve the aporia that might be said to burden the entirety of Lydgate's secular verse. His early version, printed in 1570 as "The britlenesse of thinges mortall, and the trustinesse of Vertue," concludes with an exacting resolution:

All such as treadeth Cresids cursed steps,
Take heede therefore how you your youthes do spende,
For vice bringee plagues, and vertue happie ende.[47]

Amplifying Henryson's emphasis on matter as a source of change, Howell draws a blazon from Cressid's blighted condition:

Hir comly corpes that Troylus did delight
All puft with plages full lothsomly there lay:
Hir Azurde vaines, hir Cristall skinne so whight,
With Purple spots, was falne in great decay:
Hir wrinkled face once fayre doth fade away,
Thus she abode plagde in midst of this hir youth,
Was forst to beg for breaking of hir truth.[48]

Her dissolute living affirms the moral that becomes the pithy title of this poem's 1581 revision, "Ruine the rewarde of Vice."[49] Other poems cast Cressid's suffering as deserved punishment, which follows unproblematically from her conduct. If a mistress models her manner after Cressid's, then the most vicious curses are deserved, "I pray the Gods to plague thee, / as they did the dame of Troy."[50] Brooking no mitigating factors, corruption in feminine character is expressed by the diseased female body: "Whose slight falsed faith . . . Did bréed by plagues, her great and sore dis|tresse."[51]

These poems affirm Cressid's sullied reputation, as well as connections between contagion and society.[52] In the Middle Ages leprosy was a "disease of the soul," to recall Saul Brody's characterization, but by the sixteenth century its moral significance is determined by social expectations.[53] Accordingly, the deep linkage between moral disease and the social body—which Shakespeare explores with devastating acuity in his *Troilus and Cressida*—emerges within this poetic corpus. It does so not only on account of a growing sense of what Jonathan Gil Harris so cogently delineates as "the pathologization of foreign bodies as the enabling discursive condition for the globally connected nation-state."[54] Rather, the ethical status of Cressid's betrayal discloses a change in virtue ethics. Tudor versifiers justify Cressid's punishment via moralized standards of femininity that come exclusively from social sources.[55] Virtues derive from sources outside the self, but, and this is especially true for Tudor Cressids, these sources are explicitly secular, and overwhelmingly masculinist. Groups of men are frequently depicted as both witness to and judge of Cressid's guilt. The student compilation, *A poore knight his pallace of private pleasures*, literalizes the indictment against Cressid, for in this dream-allegory, Troilus brings a bill of complaint against Cressid in the court of Venus.[56] Elsewhere Cressid is described as she "that knew in loue no law," a charge that justifies her disease as warranted punishment in a social arena of erotic courtship.[57]

Troilus is frequently depicted as an ally of the young men who are imagined as readers of this body of verse. It is not just that Diomed displaces Troilus in Cressid's affections, though Gascoigne uses this triangulation of desire to articulate amorous loss:

> Some *Diomede* is crept into Dame *Cressides* hart:
> And trustie *Troylus* nowe is taught in vaine to playne his part.[58]

Readers should be outraged, but they should also beware: in many examples, Cressid intends harm, calculating her betrayal to inflict greater pain. To stay with Gascoigne, in "Dan Bartholomew his first Triumphe," the lover's musings weave together Cressid's duplicity and disease:

> Thy brother *Trolus* eke, that gemme of gentle deedes,
> To thinke howe he abused was, alas my heart it bleedes:
> . . . .
> Whom crafty *[C]resside* mockt to muche, yet fede him still with words.
> . . . .
> But this I knowe to well, and he to farre it felte,
> How *Diomede* undid his knots, & caught both brooch and belt,

And how she chose to change, and how she changed still,
And how she dyed leaper like, against hir lovers will.[59]

Cressid's cunning redoubles in the concluding poem to *Willobie his Auisa* (1594), for in "The praise of a contented mind," the narrator remarks, "Now foolish fancie was the cause, this Crysed did lament, / For when she had a faithful friend, she could not be content."[60] In Thomas Proctor's collection, *A gorgious gallery, of gallant inventions*, Cressid's downfall affirms the premise "that wemen choose to change."[61]

Following Cressid's example, wayward mistresses use the pretense of faithfulness to humiliate unsuspecting suitors; consequently, this body of verse more generally represents women's virtue as a cover for feminized vice.[62] As Proctor's speaker avers,

There is no one aliue, that nature euer made
That hath such giftes of vertues race, and such vntroth doth shade.[63]

To extend this idea, Tudor versifiers imagine Troilus as a cultural guarantor of masculine excellence. Men's virtue, modeled as it is on Troilus's many strengths, remains genuine: "To Troilus halfe so true / vnto his Creside was / As I to hir."[64] Medieval satirists set themselves apart from the feminine perfidy they observed, but early modern critiques assert a concomitant fidelity for the male lovers they compliment.[65] Cressid's unmaking certainly aids in this process, but her stark punishment also endangers it: the shrill vengeance of so many lovers threatens to topple the disciplinary apparatus that is supposed to warrant the graphic suffering of a lone woman.

Because Cressid takes on the moral sentence for all errant women, in other words, she might structurally assume the place of victim in a theater of cultural sacrifice. Her victimization is prevented, however, by an expansion of her culpability; in keeping with the "misfortunes of virtue," Cressid's virtue is faulty because it arises from individual foibles. She is not just at fault for a change in lovers, a change in cultures, or even a change in planetary alignments. As we see in earlier treatments, these occasions might befall any virtuous woman. The terror of such narratives, I have maintained, consists in the notion that any good woman might be subject to similar mutabilities. But not just any woman can fulfill Cressid's role in early modern verse: repeatedly, she captures the particular faults of all faithless women. She does so because the intentional, individual quality of Cressid's mutability is increasingly emphasized. On account of poems that charge Cressid with using "smyling baytes" and "fawning flattering wordes," her betrayal is situated as a deliberate product of feigned virtue.[66]

In a breathtaking exposé, George Whetstone destroys the last vestige of Cressid's innocence with his *Rocke of regard* (1576).[67] Divided into four sections, including an "arbour of vertue: wherein slaunder is highly punished, and vertuous ladies nad [*sic*] gentlewomen, worthily commended," the treatise aims to teach separate audiences of men and women how to practice virtue.[68] Part I, "The Castle of delight," is primarily directed at young men, for it contains a piece entitled, "Cressids complaint," wherein "the subtilties of a Courtisan discouered, may forwarne youth from the c[om]panie of inticing dames."[69] What Whetstone characterizes as "Cressids subtile prankes" are not merely part of a cultural classification, wherein "The vertuous praisde, the vicious here are blamde," for that would presume virtue and vice are easily distinguished.[70] Rather, this is the story of an individual downfall. The poem promises to recount "her beggerie after brauerie, her lothsome leprosie, after liuely beautie, her wretched age, after wanton youth, and her perpetuall infa|mie, after violent death," because the threat her example poses is still potent for early modern audiences.

Her extended story gives her moral complexity, but only so that she might be condemned as an extreme example of feminized vice: "[These] are worthy notes (for others heede) to be remembred."[71] As the argument continues, her ruined legacy is explained and extended: "And for as much as cressids heires in eue|ry corner liue, yea more cunning then Cressid her selfe, in wanton exercises, toyes, and inticements: to forewarne all men of such filthes, to persuade the infected, to fall from their follies, & to rayse a feare in dames vntainted to offend, I haue reported the subtile sleites, the leaud life and euill fortunes of a Courtisane, in Cressid: name, whom you may suppose, in tattered weedes, halfe hungerstarued, miserably arrayde, with scabs, leprosie, and mayngie, to complaine as followeth."[72] This description represents Cressid as an individualized emblem of feminine shame, yet as the poem's argument insists, she still lives among the youth of England, infecting unwary men and corrupting naive women. She should inspire fear, not pity, according to Whetstone. A common courtesan, Cressid's abjection is the ethical expression of cultural censure. When Cressid speaks, she addresses herself to what we might suppose would be a rather small number of women, those "ramping gyrles, which rage with wanton lust."[73] The poem's putative audience, however, is immediately enlarged. What happened to her could happen to others, Cressid insists, because her destruction derives from degraded personal habits that remain fashionable in early modern society.

Cressid's deceptions should frighten virtuous women, Whetstone insists, but hers is really a cautionary example directed to elite men. In fact, as soon as she confesses her "delight in chaunge," the poem shows how elite men become unwary victims of the many vices Cressid practices.[74] Using her shape-shifting powers to deceive, "I did intice, king Priams sonnes to loue," Cressid makes fools of even the best of men: "The wisest wits, were thus bewitcht by me."[75] Like a ravenous hawk, "When hunger pincht, on lustie youthes I prayd," Cressid is meant to terrify and repulse, to show young men the perils of calculating women.[76] Since her vice is so rife, we might suspect it would be hard to find a youth gullible enough to see her maneuvering as sincere: "I traind them on, with outward shew of grace."[77] Only Troilus is true enough to fill that role. His fawning naiveté could hardly be said to offer a credible model for elite lovers (although it might explain why Petruchio's spaniel is named "Troilus" in Shakespeare's *Taming of the Shrew*).[78] Unless, that is, Whetstone aims to present Cressid as the deliberate negation of prescriptive virtue rather than its circumstantial failure. As the poem proceeds, it is clear that Cressid's complaint is more concerned to situate her demise as a consequence of individual, intentional action. Cressid joys in the suffering she causes Troilus, "Yet cruell, I did smile to sée his smart," using false virtue to perform true vice: "In hart a fiend, in face and forme a Saint."[79] In her rendering, idealized femininity is a sham, a superficial role that allows Cressid to practice guile. Without the slightest remorse, Cressid transforms virtue into its opposite.

If masculine fidelity looks foolish, it is only because feminine constancy is a ruse. Whetstone promises to protect against virtue's collapse, exposing Cressid's wrongs as a means to preserve the potential for gendered excellence. Her extensive, extended punishment, however, enshrines cynicism over women's potential for virtue: Cressid's fate might befall any woman, because any woman might pass off vice under the cover of virtue. Virtue becomes an analytic wedge that pries apart women's motivations, centralizing feminine volition as the principal ethical basis for deciding women's virtue. Perhaps this should come as no surprise, since the will, as scholars including Bonnie Kent and Steven E. Ozment demonstrate, was probably the most hotly contested issue among late medieval and early modern moral theorists.[80] It should follow, therefore, as Lisa Freinkel and Kathryn Schwarz affirm, that questions of volition and virtue fascinated poets as much as they did Luther or Erasmus.[81] As I suggested in Chapter 1, the long-standing critical debate over Criseyde's consent demonstrates the difficulties involved in measuring virtue by intention, though a host of thinkers during this period suggest that volition determines virtue. Sixteenth-century Cressid poetry aims to head off the argument, convincingly elaborated by Schwarz, that women's virtue arises from their volition; or, rather, these poems aim to establish the fundamental corruption of women's will, thereby making women's willfulness a precursor to and guarantor of Cressid's physical destruction.[82]

These short poems aim to map Cressid's volition in advance, so that the question of her consent is already answered. She is a victim only of her own willfulness, which, in keeping with Laura Gowing's astute analysis, arises from the female body as a site of unlimited sexual appetite.[83] As Whetstone's Cressid recounts her demise, explaining how she first used "painting" to hide her marred visage, she purports to teach other women to avoid her example, "Some wild me learne, anew my A.B.C."[84] Yet her extended metaphor of innate predilection, "But as the Hawke to gad, which knowes the way, / Will hardly leaue, to cheake at carren crowes," pairs habit with instinct.[85] Action follows desire, or so her inability to turn from the predatory hunt would suggest. When she can no longer capture the best quarry, she continues, "On kytes I prayde, til I could partridge get."[86] Cressid's base consumption, "But I so long, on carren crowes did pray," has predictable consequences, for "poysoned bloud" expresses practiced vice:

> In seeking sport, my haire did shed in iest,
> A sorrie ioy to ceaselesse sorrowe plight,
> French feauers now, in me can take no rest,
> From bones to flesh, from flesh in open sight,
> With grinckcomes grease, beholde a monstrous wight,
> My louers olde, with (fawth) their browes doth bend,
> Of Cressids lust, loe here the lothsome end.[87]

Commanding causality, *The Rocke of Regarde* aligns individual intention, personal action, and material consequence. Cressid's grotesque punishment arises from individual corruption, in will as well as act. It is not complex, Whetstone insists: in a world without ethical contingency, all women should sign up "in Uertues band to fight."[88]

Yet, it should be remembered, the ethical simplicity of "Cressid's Complaint" is constructed by foreclosing the competing narrative of cultural production of which Whetstone's poetic collection is itself a vital part. In other words, Whetstone treats Cressid's vice as a personal admixture of disposition and intention, all the while denying that either factor is produced, and perhaps even reduced, by prescriptive writings such as his own. This is despite *The Rocke of Regard*'s overt didacticism. The rhetorical effect, then, is the suggestion that prescriptive models of feminine virtue are merely disseminated, not actually invented, by poetic collections. It is to invest individual women with sole agency over their performances of virtue or vice, but only so that women can be punished for the transgressions enumerated across this body of verse. Although these poems claim to promote women's virtue, functionally they make virtue a disguise for vice, effecting a transposition of ethical value that can never be clarified with anything but a disciplinary unveiling. Vice may appear as virtue, unless, that is, poets expose the ethical vacuity of women's excellence. A harsh penalty will be excised, Cressid's example shows, and the explanatory moral narrative will be written around it as a means to erase its conditional, cultural, emergence. A text such as Whetstone's, then, both grants and denies women's moral agency, using normative urgency to shape the ethical conditions of its cultural existence. Women determine their own ethical course, but lest their performance of virtue run into trouble, it must run along strictly delineated moral tracks. What might have derived from a literary reckoning with ethical complexity—Criseyde's betrayal—ends up warranting moralized cultural standards for women's behavior.

Because it insists that Cressid's conduct is common, held only in check by the disciplinary triple threat of penury, disease, and scorn, prescriptive verse diminishes women's potential for virtue in the sixteenth century. Cressid is often compared to famous worthies, but her behavior is strictly distinguished from that of Lucrece, Penelope, or Dido. It is as if these exalted figures are imported to show Cressid's lowliness, as is apparent from George Gasgoigne's cross-gendered invocation:

In colder cares are my conceipts consumd,
Than *Dido* felt when false *Aeneas* fled:
In farre more heat, than trusty *Troylus* fumde,
When craftie *Cressyde* dwelt with *Diomed*.[89]

Dido's pitiful sacrifice might capture the lover's suffering, but Troilus's pain surpasses Cressid's duplicity. As I discussed in the prior chapter, Chaucer and Lydgate also use famous women to structure women's virtue. Unlike their gatherings of female notables, early modern verse isolates Cressid as a debased example, like when George Turberville's lover says of his mistress:

> If she be one of Cresids crue
> and swarue hir former Hest,
> No Lucrece must I terme her then,
> for that were but a iest.[90]

Cressid does cultural work in these and similar passages, crystallizing the contemporary conditions of feminine perfidy for early modern audiences. Eve remains relevant as a foundational example, but the metaphysical dimension of her trespass against humanity is perhaps too grandiose to capture the type of feminine transgression Cressid represents for Tudor versifiers.

Cressid's circulation through sixteenth-century verse reveals the normative fashioning of women's virtue: her sordid history cautions against her brand of behavior, and sets aside the ethical questions her freighted narrative might raise. The thorough mapping of Cressid's moral condition—from volition to action, from action to penalty—settles any questions surrounding prescriptive virtue. If a mistress acts like Cressid, numerous poems insist, her moral backstory is already written. Recounting Cressid's ruin ossifies its contours, making her disease an inevitable consequence of feminine volition. Ultimately, then, by presenting Cressid's corruption as a foregone conclusion, these poets direct suspicion toward women's capacities for virtue more generally. Her frequent connection to early modern mistresses transforms Cressid into a cipher for contemporary feminine perfidy writ large. Her manners are a patchwork, derived from each poetic mistress she is invoked to admonish. Whetstone's extended poetic impersonation imagines Cressid as a woman who might yet entice young men with her cultivated wiles. In *A Crowne Garland of Goulden Roses* (1612), a beloved compares herself to a by-then familiar instance of feminine deception: "Thinkes thou I am such a one, as Cressida?"[91] Earlier, "Avisa, her last reply" protests, "I came not of dame Chrysides kind."[92]

Early modern women might be like Cressid, because Cressid is putatively fashioned to be like early modern women. In Robert Greene's *Euphues his Censure to Philautus* (1587), Cressid evinces the chatty vacuity of a pompous court lady: "*Cressida* tickled, a little with a selfe conceipt of hir owne wit, willing to let the Troians know the phrase of hir speech was as fayre as the fourme of his face, & that womens tounges perced as deepe as their eyes, interrupted *Vlisses* in his talke thus."[93] To be sure, all Greene's classical figures are drawn on a romantic model of early modern gentility, so that Hector and Achilles sound more like participants in aristocratic debate than principals in heroic conflict. *Penelope's Web*, likewise, presents a fiction of feminine community that reflects and models the virtuous pastimes of contemporary women. Because early modern exemplarity extolled the value of classical models for instilling virtuous conduct, the translation of these figures for wider consumption entailed their early modernization. Cressid might *stand in for* a lover's frivolous mistress, in the same way that Zenobia might *show up to* supper in Elyot's *Defense of Good Women* (1541).[94] Troilus's beloved plays the role of all mistresses at once. And, while these narratives morally encode the personal motives behind particular actions, Cressid's indexical circulation in popular verse reduces her example to a bit part in a cultural theater of prescriptive virtue.

Unguarded Virtue in Shakespeare's *Troilus and Cressida*

Shakespeare departs from the model of prescriptive virtue devised by poets of his era, extending to Cressida the potential to love beyond, or at least outside, the masculinist terms set by heroic *virtus*. Even so, as scholars have often remarked, it appears that Shakespeare's Cressida is fated to dishonesty, marked by the legendary history informing her name.[95] Considering the multitude of Cressids that populated Tudor accounts, it is difficult to imagine a different destiny for Troilus's beloved. When *Troilus and Cressida* was entered into the stationer's register in 1603, decades of scorn had been poured on Henryson's heroine. Time and again, she'd been found wanton and abandoned to penury and disease. The story was hardly worth telling, so familiar was Cressid's ruined disgrace. We might think it strange for Shakespeare to return to this story at all, since all its characters are impoverished by their cultural familiarity. Yet as critics have also observed, Shakespeare seems drawn to this plot because it has been thoroughly hashed over, because each of its prior iterations "reflect shifts in ethics, value, and nationalist ideology."[96] Shakespeare examines the rift between virtues and actions with heroes as well as heroines. Linda Charnes gamely captures the play's limiting referentiality, its purported "nostalgia . . . for the titular epic forefathers whose names its characters carry around their necks like placards."[97] The idealism surrounding Hector, Achilles, and the other warriors is peeled back, baring the transactional negotiation of identity formation as a collaborative process of collective enculturation.

But what of Cressida, whose identity is already distinguished by its lack of idealism in early modern accounts? It should come as no surprise that Cressida's character is a cultural production: sixteenth-century verse *all but advertises* the collaborative construction of her individual attributes, circulating the pieces of her character to affirm the normative reach of prescriptive femininity. Indeed, this is a moral world Cressida knows all too well, for she has long inhabited its shopworn generalizations. We might therefore suppose that Shakespeare would need to do precious little with his representation of Cressida, since the cynical treatment of her character in Tudor representation accords very neatly with the reductive ethos of *Troilus and Cressida*. Given that Troilus is now skeptical about the foundational stability of idealized femininity, "What's aught but as 'tis valued?" (II.ii.52), is his attitude not better suited to the courtesan guile often presumed in his mistress? The simplest answer to this question is "yes," insofar as Shakespeare reveals the aggrandizing masculinist ideology that idealized femininity serves. Categories of value, from transcendent virtue to trifling vice, are contingent upon the standards of meaning men negotiate, often through world-destroying violence:

> Helen must needs be fair,
> When with your blood you daily paint her thus. (I.i.89–90)

Many of the play's most gripping insights derive from a willingness to reveal the voyeuristic power men wield over prescribed identities. If Ulysses attempts to goad Achilles onto the battlefield using a scripted inflation of Ajax, the very idea of a private theater of impersonation, where Patroclus "pageants" the other warriors for Achilles's entertainment, attests to an audience's shaping influence over an actor's performed likeness (I.iii.142–84).

The play extends these precepts to all characters, affirming the shallow ethical underpinning for heroic *virtus* in martial and erotic settings alike. Rather than single out Cressida for castigation, this play shows heroic virtue's collapse. For some readers, this unburnished look at warrior society is hard to take, insofar as Cressida is clearly identified as a disposable piece of cultural trash that should be available to gratify immediate masculine desires.[98] When the play opens, Troilus is maddened by longing, frustrated that Cressida refuses to play the part of willing mistress so frequently attributed to her: "As she is stubborn-chaste against all suit" (I.i.93). Troilus struggles to abide courtship, in Pandarus's terms, to "tarry the grinding . . . the bolting . . . the leavening . . . the kneading, the making of the cake, the heating of the oven, and the baking . . . the cooling too, or ye may chance burn your lips" (I.i.15–24). There is nothing in Troilus's impatience, or Pandarus's counsel, to indicate romanticized attachment. Indeed, Cressida knows what Troilus asks of her, characterizing this affair by referencing Pandarus's part in it: "By the same token, you are a bawd" (I.ii.272). Early on, then, *Troilus and Cressida* uses the poetic familiarity of its female lead to condition its ethical terrain. If Troilus declares Cressida's beauty, "O, that her hand / In whose comparison all whites are ink, / Writing their own reproach" (I.i.52–53), he does so to disclose the consuming passion he seeks to satisfy. For him, there will be no retreat into an agonizing isolation, where the extent of his ardor can be explored through extended complaint. Rather, Troilus expects Cressida to surrender, since that is what women are supposed to do in a world that privileges heroic masculine desire.

In a departure from poems depicting her as wanton, Cressida at least attempts to position herself as a worthy beloved. When Pandarus recounts Troilus's virtues, "birth, beauty, good shape, discourse, manhood, / learning, gentleness, virtue, youth, liberality, and so / forth" (I.ii.244–46), Cressida dismisses the cultural composite of idealized qualities that would make up such a "minced man" (I.ii.247). With a pageant of legendary heroes, each of whom merits only passing comment in Pandarus's dumb show, the play emphasizes virtue's externality, its function as a social display. Because Troilus is excellent—which, it should be added, has nothing to do with his amorous affection—Cressida should surrender to his suit. Rather than yield to the presumed cultural privilege of heroic desire, Cressida resists Troilus's magnificence with a canny protectiveness: "Upon my back to defend my belly, upon my wit to defend my wiles, upon my secrecy to defend mine honesty, my mask to defend my beauty, and you to defend all these; and at all these wards I lie, at a thousand watches" (I.ii.251–55). Her virtue, as her defensive parrying with Pandarus affirms, would be compromised by ready capitulation: "Men prize the thing ungained more than it is" (I.ii.280). Even if she loves Troilus, virtue's social inscription transforms the expression of affection into a protracted negotiation, which very well might destroy the amorous attachment it is meant to secure. Indeed, virtue's social construction makes Cressida vulnerable to masculine fantasies, which, because they render her an abstraction, alienate her from the looks, gestures, and deeds she is expected to enact.

In this, Cressida is not alone, for Troilus equally feels the dislocation of prescriptive virtue. As Troilus demonstrates, the intensity of private affection is always secondary to its public performance. Troilus bemoans his inner turmoil as he reports his own campaign of polite pretending:

> I have, as when the sun doth light a-scorn,
> Buried this sigh in wrinkle of a smile;
> But sorrow that is couched in seeming gladness
> Is like that mirth fate turns to sudden sadness. (I.i.35–38)

With his tone-deaf replies, Pandarus reclaims Troilus from his private feelings, turning his erotic agony into a petty pastime that will fill the hours until he may consummate his sexual longing. Pandarus even collectivizes Troilus's appraisal of Cressida's beauty, hedging in Troilus's fixation with his own estimation:

> Well, she looked yesternight fairer than ever I
> saw her look, or any woman else. (I.i.30–31)

Troilus's annoyance registers the public compulsion of heroic virtue, because even in a moment of confidence he is unable to stake an individual claim to his affection for Cressida. If Troilus is pressured by virtue's exteriority, however, he is also privileged by it in a way that Cressida is not. No matter if Cressida is sincere in her love for Troilus, she knows his commitment, even in love, is a completely public affair. To be "'As true as Troilus'" means to perform values whose veracity derives from their complete transparency (III.ii.177). Troilus has no secrets, hence it is no surprise that in Act III Paris knows he sleeps at Cressida's house, despite the novelty of the affair to the lovers themselves.

Cressida, by contrast, is a desperately elusive character. While critics have traditionally read her faltering declarations of love as proleptic evidence of her mutability, such lines have a sincerity about them, a vulnerability that counters the empowering virtues of the warrior community:[99]

I love you now, but till now not so much
But I might master it. In faith, I lie;
My thoughts were like unbridled children, grown
Too headstrong for their mother. See, we fools!
Why have I blabbed? Who shall be true to us
When we are so unsecret to ourselves?—
But though I loved you well, I wooed you not;
And yet, good faith, I wished myself a man,
Or that we women had men's privilege
Of speaking first. Sweet, bid me hold my tongue,
For in this rapture I shall surely speak
The thing I shall repent. See, see, your silence,
Cunning in dumbness, from my weakness draws
My very soul of counsel from me! Stop my mouth. (III.ii.116–29)

Cressida does not control her emotions, but is overcome with a passion that compels her to act against her own best interests; with this confession she thwarts all prescribed expectations for feminine demureness—especially those that might protect women from predatory men.[100] Although it is undoubtedly true, as many critics maintain, that Cressida's famous declaration, "I have a kind of self resides with you, / But an unkind self that itself will leave / To be another's fool" (III.ii.143–45), writes duplicity into her very language, it is equally true that Cressida's faltering doubleness reveals the vulnerabilities involved in erotic desire. With her admission, "I speak I know not what," Cressida allows for a tentative, fragile, and wavering negotiation of affection, something Troilus's fully formed commitment forecloses (III.ii.146). Her unguarded love provides a startling contrast to the superficial showmanship of so many notable heroes.

Indeed, Cressida's love is Shakespeare's most powerful acknowledgment of her material virtues. While some might see her affection as debased, as corrupt, as disposable, Shakespeare suggests that Cressida is undone by a love that Troilus simply cannot experience. Troilus retains his "truth," yet it is hard to see the worth of that fidelity by the end of the play. Barbara Hodgdon astutely characterizes Troilus's attempt to assign this emptiness to Cressida by "assimilating her within a male system of desire and representation."[101] Troilus seeks to blame Cressida for the play's devaluation of heroism, and in a way, he is right in his assessment. However, Cressida challenges heroic virtue, not because she fails to remain faithful, but because she shows how

the warrior community relies on the belittling exchange of women. Cressida's
ethical power, by contrast, arises from her ability to love in the face of the
heroic struggles that require her debasement, her corruption, her disposability. Her love is discarded, and yet, Cressida's alienation continues to challenge the heroic *virtus* that trashes her ethical potential. To say the least,
Cressida's unmoored vulnerability remains disturbingly present in Shakespeare's play. As Melissa Sanchez remarks of other Shakespearean investigations of women's virtue, "The female body that can be contaminated against
its will . . . figures a body politic that may be similarly compromised by
abusive and violent rule."[102] And, though her own virtue is eclipsed, Cressida's devaluation crystallizes the play's larger critique of the masculinist values
that subtend heroic culture.

Cressida's insecure position in heroic culture means that she cannot produce a performance of virtue that maintains consistency, or even coherence.
Much of the play's second half consists of her construction under the gaze of
the Greek warriors, whose skepticism about the worth of femininity is pronounced even before she is traded to their camp.[103] Prior to her exchange,
however, Cressida is equally suspected, and equally misunderstood. In their
parting, Troilus is full of justifications, but Cressida is full of questions: "Have
the gods envy? . . . And is it true that I must go from Troy? . . . What, and
from Troilus too? . . . Is't possible? . . . I must, then, to the Grecians?" (IV.iv.27,
29, 31, 33, 54). After Troilus answers her queries with appeals to necessity and
destiny, she understands the role she must assume: "A woeful Cressida 'mongst
the merry Greeks!" (IV.iv.55). Her impatience with Troilus's petitions for her
constancy is a warranted reaction to the scripted separation her lover enacts. As
Cressida recognizes, Troilus is not only playing goodbye in this scene; rather,
he casts her in the role of fragile partner so that he might make a more impressive showing of his dedication. Compared to the magnificent fidelity Troilus
declares, Cressida cannot help but be feeble. When he urges her again, "But
yet, be true," he affirms his superior virtues by cataloging the faults of his
authenticity: "I cannot sing . . . nor sweeten talk, / Nor play at subtle games—
fair virtues all . . . Whiles others fish with craft for great opinion, / I with great
truth catch mere simplicity" (IV.iv.73, 84, 85–86, 102–3).

Troilus presents his virtue as transparent, devoid of display, but Cressida
is as aware as anyone that she is undone by her lover's active inaction.
Although she is willing to disavow her father to remain with Troilus, Cressida's commitment is disregarded except as it might be observed from a distance. She becomes an icon of virtue, but the magnitude of that image

quickly overshadows her love. No one, least of all Troilus, appreciates her brave protest:

> I have forgot my father.
> I know no touch of consanguinity;
> No kin, no love, no blood, no soul so near me
> As the sweet Troilus. O you gods divine,
> Make Cressid's name the very crown of falsehood
> If ever she leave Troilus! Time, force and death,
> Do to this body what extremes you can;
> But the strong base and building of my love
> Is as the very centre of the earth,
> Drawing all things to it. I'll go in and weep—(IV.ii.97–106)

Indeed, her willingness to throw herself away for Troilus is displaced— quickly, tidily, and permanently—with her exchange for Antenor.

In other words, her material virtue has no bearing on Troilus's character. She makes no claims on him besides the "truth" he vows in their parting (which, not coincidentally, is a quality he already professes as a fundamental part of himself). Her arrival at the Greek camp underscores her isolation, emotionally and physically, for when the Greeks kiss Cressida in common, she can only act the part of war trophy. The expressiveness Ulysses condemns, "There's language in her eye, her cheek, her lip, / Nay, her foot speaks" (IV.v.56–57), suggests Cressida's continued awareness of the differences between her prescribed role and her personal feelings. As the play unfolds, however, that personal part of her is lost.[104] Her final scene, which locates Cressida in a veritable arena of masculine spectatorship, displays the nightmare of feminine vice supposedly lurking beneath all women's performances of virtue. Even so, the spectacle of her infidelity also shows the failure of heroic virtue ethics. Troilus is moved to disbelief when he sees Cressida's teasing appeals to Diomede, "Rather think this not Cressid" (V.ii.139), but he shows no awareness that the "secretly open" posture that she assumes with Diomede is exactly the role he wanted her to take on when he initially appealed for her love (V.ii.26). Rather, Troilus expects Cressida to suffer for her pledged affection, refusing Diomede's attention, even protection, as a visible sign of her fidelity.

That Cressida does not suffer for Troilus, following this logic, might be her most damning condemnation of his behavior. She rehearses the coyness of courtship once more, replaying virtuous deferral in a scene suggesting the indifference of, or really the manifest lack of distinction between, heroic lovers. Nonetheless, if we are not surprised when Cressida acts in a manner that prompts Ulysses to impugn her honesty, we should be, since we have seen her sincerity in her dealings with Troilus. In her amorous wrangling with Diomede, it is worth emphasizing, Cressida remains familiar enough only to be scandalous. There is a pathetic consistency about Cressida's uncertain exchange. Once again, we hear her express her faulty devotion to Troilus; once again, she admits her lack of control over her amorous attachment:

> You look upon that sleeve? Behold it well
> He loved me—O false wench!—Give't me again. (V.ii.72–73)

She loves Troilus, but she knows she is not in control of her erotic availability. According to the men's commentary, however, Cressida's dithering results from her ethical mutability alone:

> A proof of strength she could not publish more,
> Unless she said, "My mind is now turned whore." (V.ii.119–20)

Within the male community, Cressida is written off as an emblem of the failed ideals that started and sustained all this war. Or, as Florio learns in Robert Greene's *Mamillia* (1583), a faithless lover is a "kite [. . .] of Cressids kind."[105]

Still, Cressida remains one of the greatest victims of this war, a reality that Shakespeare does not shy away from in his rendering of this affair. Cressida's haunting question to Diomede, "What would you have me do?" (V.ii.25), is not rhetorical. She cannot refuse Diomede, since he can come to her father's tent whenever he likes. She has every reason to play along with his seduction, her final scene affirms, since doing so at least maintains the pretense of courtship. Diomede's temperamental violence remains just beneath the surface of the courtly game he plays with Cressida: "Fo, fo! Adieu. You palter" (V.ii.50). And, while Diomede's manner is different, Cressida is a trophy for Diomede in the same way she was for Troilus, a spoil of war meant to confer meaning upon the conquest these men perform. That she cannot ennoble their enterprise is more a condemnation of their violence than her virtue. Cressida might fail to live up to the truth Troilus invests in her, but his refusal, finally, to see her explanation as anything more than "mere words, no matter from the heart" (V.iii.107), affirms her alienation within heroic discourse. She promises to be an honest lover, but when she faces the truth of her situation, she can only be "as false as Cressid" (III.ii.191).

Conclusion: Cressid's Ruined Virtues

The trouble with prescriptive virtue, Cressid's ruined legacy affirms, is that it is predicated on doubleness. The rift between inner principle and outer behavior, however, is especially damaging to women's material virtue. Cressid appears only as a throwaway in the cultural literatures that seek to construct models of women's virtue using true and false examples. Instead, Troilus becomes a stand-in for ethical loss, insofar as later writers use his fidelity to signal the moral destruction wrought by feminine inconstancy.[106] In a telling pairing, Thomas Feylde sets Troilus alongside Griselda in a poem that simply but firmly emphasizes Cressid's cultural erasure as a model of feminine experience.[107] Cressid's ruined virtues are not worth remembering, except perhaps in a piecemeal reckoning of punitive social morality. And, although Troilus might grieve Cresseid's demise at the end of Henryson's *Testament of Cresseid*, his epitaph makes her life into an abstract admonition, which covers over the suffering she endured as a consequence of his idealism:

> Lo, fair ladyis, Cresseid of Troy the toun,
> Sumtyme countit the flour of womanheid,
> Under this stane, lait lipper, lyis deid. (607–9)[108]

Because *Troilus and Cressida* shows this moment of alienation without seeking to bury it under prescriptive appeals, Shakespeare's heroine materializes a dignity that remains outside transactions of honor, of conquest, or, most importantly, of heroic *virtus* in early modern England.

PART II

Grace, Enacted: Romance and Material Virtue

CHAPTER 3

Virtue's Grace: Custance
and Other Daughters

MED, s.v. "constaunce" (n.) 1. (a) Stability of character, steadfastness of purpose; also, self-possession, composure, equanimity; (b) faithfulness, loyalty. 2. Fortitude or patience under adverse circumstances, in bearing affliction, etc. 3. Stability, immobility.

Chaucer's Custance has long been identified with a form of virtue that has made her "so strange a creature" (II.700). John A. Yunck emphasizes her enmeshment within a medieval structure of Christian transcendence: "[Custance] is a vehicle for the providential theme and a vessel of divine grace. In herself and for herself—as character, that is—she is nothing."[1] According to Alfred David, Custance's moral perfection renders her story "not so much of a good woman as of the womanly virtue she personifies."[2] To be identified with virtue is to become an abstraction—a "vehicle" or a "vessel"—whose meaning remains external. Custance never takes up the values she carries, even when, in Eugene Clasby's analysis, she is supposed to transmit humanity's excellence.[3] By reading Custance as an abstract figure, these critics attempt to account for Custance's status as, in David Raybin's words, the "consummate outsider."[4] Such critical assessments have earned Custance few feminist sympathizers. In her memorable indictment, Sheila Delany argues that Custance is not even a believable person, but "an agglomeration of virtues."[5] For Delany, like those critics who emphasize the tale's transcendent spirituality, virtue's exteriority hollows out ethical action.

In what follows, I take issue with this view of Custance's virtue. It is true that virtues instilled by divine grace are imagined as extrinsic resources of excellence. Yet Chaucer also offers a glimpse of an alternate ecology of women's virtue, one that uses nonhuman networks to resist the vulnerabilities that physical embodiment entails. Through Custance's trials, Chaucer imagines a material virtue founded on endurance and receptivity, and mobilized through nonhuman encounters. Her congress with the sea, as much as her contact with Saracens or Northumbrians, makes Custance a crucial albeit unique actant in her saga.[6] This is not passivity. In fact, Jill Mann argues quite persuasively that the tale calls into question "a simplistic opposition between 'active' and 'passive.'"[7] As I shall suggest, ethical action gathers around Custance in a fashion that undoes the passive/active binary traditionally used to distinguish human performances of virtue. Her life *causes* ethical action, though she is distanced from the happenings—good and bad—that accumulate on account of her presence. As I contend, Custance's story challenges the model of virtue that vests moral action in a bounded, enabled, (self-) cultivating subject. Rather than dismiss Custance's curious in/action as a symptom of the tale's antifeminism, I suggest that it is part of a broader rethinking of virtue ethics, one that founds human excellence on modes of agency that are typical for women during the late Middle Ages.

Custance's material virtue, her ability to catalyze ethical change, involves her in customarily insuperable networks of territory, family, and religion. Her entailment produces suffering, and it demands resilience, forbearance, and steadfastness. Constancy, a relentless openness to the world's contingencies that includes both peril and promise, is the excellence this form of ethical action requires. As the fourteenth-century *Book of Vices and Virtues* describes it: "Þis is þe vertue þat m[a]keþ þe herte as steadfast and tristy to God as a tour þat is founded vpon þe harde roche and as a tree þat is roted harde in good erþe, þat shakeþ ne boweþ for no wynde þat may come ne blowe, þat is to seie for non auenture þat may come, good ne euele."[8] Instead of focusing on action wielded by a singular agent, this form of ethical change is brought about by a collaboration of myriad and varied forces, human and divine, spiritual and material. It is networked, and proceeds through relational, reciprocal, enrichment. Because it is a genre that relies on a rich spiritual network, female hagiography deeply influences Custance's narrative.[9] Besides late medieval women's saints' lives, I also turn to the fifteenth-century "Empress of Rome" frescoes in Eton College Chapel to elucidate Custance's material virtue. Together these representations of women's ethical action clarify the communal and antisocial aspects of material virtue that emerge from Custance's saga. Custance is not a virgin martyr, it is worth emphasizing, and her ultimate isolation from any network of virtue accounts for this tale's problematic conclusion.

True Virtue and Female Hagiography

The thought that virtues are connected was common by Chaucer's day. Virtues as multiple, as joined, and as commonly enriching derives from Aristotle's claim in *The Nicomachean Ethics* that "true virtue cannot be acquired without prudence."[10] In other words, one virtue—specifically prudence—is necessary for others. Medieval thinkers took up the idea of "true virtue" over many centuries in a rich and complex philosophical discourse that yielded mostly agreement. In the thirteenth century, Thomas Aquinas marshaled earlier statements by Ambrose, Augustine, and Gregory to establish consensus on the virtues' interconnection.[11] Later vernacular treatments designed for lay audiences also joined different orders of virtues. For instance, the fifteenth-century *Jacob's Well* imagines the theological virtues of faith, hope, and charity as a rope woven from distinct threads, "threfold to-gedere in on."[12] Because they are directly responsive to vicious actions, the remedial virtues—those powers that combat the seven deadly sins—are also imagined as unified, as the *Instructions for Parish Priests* indicates.[13] Similarly, in introducing the cardinal and theological virtues, *The Lay Folks Catechism* figures the virtues as forces that connect Christians to God and to each other:

> Of whilk seuen the thre first, that er heued thewes,
> Teches us how to haue us unto god almighten
> And the four techis us swa for to lyf
> Bathe onentes our self and our euen-cristen
> That it be bathe likand to god and to man.[14]

Virtues establish a moral relation between God and the human soul, but also between individuals and the larger community. They link inside to outside, self to other, and human to nonhuman in a shared Christian ecology.

Hagiography is the medieval genre that best captures the importance of true virtue in the Middle Ages. These narratives establish a pantheon of holy martyrs, an integrated community of excellence that protects the living. Virgin martyrs' lives are meant to offer spiritual guidance to a broad set of believers, but this does not mean that they are abstract.[15] In fact, recent assessments observe the historical specificity of the genre.[16] Of particular interest for my argument, Katherine J. Lewis, Karen Winstead, and Catherine Sanok attend to the overlaps between female martyr legends and conduct manuals for women.[17] This intersection suggests that we should not immediately think of medieval virtues as unchanging abstractions that compromise the subject's capacities for ethical action; rather, it indicates that medieval virtues were thought of as embodied, enlivened properties that might be shared or transferred. Networks of virtue included the living and the dead, the holy and the pious; women were joined by a common veneration of ethical ideals that were remembered through everyday behavior. If female saints were offered as models of feminine conduct, then their excellence—while it might "not [have been] meant to mirror 'real' life"—was nevertheless understood as actionably connected to actual women by the late Middle Ages.[18]

By the 1400s, in both visual and textual representations, virgin martyrs appeared to be remarkably similar to contemporary laywomen.[19] In Karen Winstead's words, later legends "represent the virgin martyrs as refined gentlewomen rather than triumphant viragos."[20] Katherine J. Lewis argues that the frequent appearance of female saints' lives in household miscellanies of the late Middle Ages indicates the likely use of these texts for behavioral guidance in family domains.[21] Although the events described in female saints' lives are far removed from the happenings of late medieval life, they cleared ground for women's ethical action in late medieval England. Because they imagine women's capacities for ethical action as lively, embodied, and enabled, they provide a crucial underpinning for material virtue as Chaucer imagines it in *The Man of Law's Tale*.[22] Virgin martyr legends include a socially enabled form of ethical action that is forceful and effective. This form of virtue is responsive to social conditions, but it is represented as arising from God's singular power. It is transcendent, but it is not otherworldly. In his Custance saga Chaucer takes a hagiographical model of virtue and investigates its potential as a source of power for women who are subject to Christian imperialism's masculinist transactions.

Virtue and Deference

Late medieval hagiography shapes Custance's narrative, but her excellence does not amount to Christian piety alone. Instead, she mixes qualities from body and spirit, sacred and secular:

In hire is heigh beautee, withtoute pride,
Yowthe, withoute grenehede or folye;
To alle hire werkes vertu is hir gyde;
Humblenesse hath slayn in hire al tirannye.
She is mirour of alle cureteisye;
Hir herte is verray chambre of hoolynesse,
Hir hand, ministre of fredam for almesse. (II.162–68)

She is exceptional, "Nas nevere swich another as is shee" (II.159), and even
shows potential for rule, "And wolde she were of al Europe the queene"
(II.161). But she faces a common problem: "Wommen are born to thraldom
and penance, / And to been under mannes governance" (II.286–87). Her
excellence is diminished by the inferiority that patriarchal imperialism
demands. Accordingly, Custance's marriage is a colonizing measure (II.233–
41), aptly described by Kathleen Davis as an attempt to "increase the jurisdiction of 'Christes lawe.' "[23] For this scheme to work, a daughter must yield to
paternal command, as Custance herself recognizes:

Allas, unto the Barbre nacioun
I moste anoon, syn that it is youre wille. (II.281–82)

Such obedience does not vitiate Custance's virtue, but, in a model directly
borrowed from female saints' lives, her vulnerability produces ethical change.
    Like the virgin martyrs of the late Middle Ages, Custance is able to stand
her ground in moments of oppression. She develops an elaborate rhetoric of
victimization that she deploys against the Emperor. By deploying her weakness to powerful effect, Custance resembles the virgin martyrs of Chaucer's
era.[24] The Auchinleck St. Margaret, part of an early fourteenth-century miscellany compiled for elite secular readers, features a heroine who is by turns
bold and lowly. Margaret evinces great verbal audacity when she refuses the
tyrant Olibrius's sexual advances:

"Þine wicke redes" sche seyd,
"Y do out of my þouȝt.
Y take me to Jhesu Crist
Þat wiþ hondes me wrouȝt."[25]

Elsewhere, her daring is offset by a cradling strategy, one that locates her
agency as a product of God's action: though she defeats the dragon, Margaret's triumph is ultimately credited to divine power.

Margaret's strength remains evident when she resists those worldly forces that would disrupt her devotion to Christ. Yet, when Margaret faces a solitary spiritual struggle, she must rely on powers of divinity external to herself. Although the dragon "tobrast" after it devours Margaret, this miracle is not of the maiden's making:

> Slayn is þe d[r]agoun
> Þurth vertu of þe rode.[26]

As the ultimate contact relic, the cross is suffused with divinity, and because Margaret takes up this object as a symbol of her faith, its powers—its virtues—are conferred upon the young maiden.[27] Virtue that transfers by connection, which requires alternating acts of brashness and meekness, is the model of excellence imagined in the Auchinleck *St. Margaret*. Given this manuscript's mixture of spiritual and secular materials, including its outstanding collection of Middle English verse romances, the Auchinleck *St. Margaret* generates a conception of material virtue that includes all members of a late medieval household—women as well as men. Yet, because the particulars of their struggles are drawn uniquely from women's experiences, virgin martyrs like Saint Margaret continue to shape expectations for feminine excellence. That Margaret is a protector of women in childbirth, for instance, physically connects the saint to the majority of laywomen. As Wendy Larsen demonstrates, moreover, women's widespread participation in the cult of Saint Margaret preserved certain elements of her legend—namely, her ingestion by the dragon—that various clerics found dubious.[28] With her intrepid reliance, the Auchinleck *St. Margaret* outlines the tension between autonomy and dependency required to sustain a more embodied form of women's virtue by Chaucer's day.

This balance, importantly, is shaped by a confluence of outside sources, earthly and divine. Margaret gains her Christian faith from her nurse, Azie, who makes sure the young maiden "was sett to boke" as part of a long program of training.[29] This is not a new feature that signals a suppression, or that reimagines sources of women's virtue in later virgin martyr legends. In the late thirteenth-century *South English Legendary*'s legend of Christina, the maiden's father attempts to dissuade his daughter from her professed Christianity with a countereducational program,

> Ne þat noþing bote hore false godes · ne come in hure þoȝte
> Maumes of riche golde inou · and of preciouse stone.[30]

Despite his constant attempts to divert his daughter, Christina's forbearance is sustained by her complete dependence on divine might:

> Louerd he[o] sede ȝif it is þi wille · ne let me noȝt ȝute deie
> Ac ssewe on me here þi miȝte · þat þis fok mowe iseo
> Þat þou ert alone Louerd · and non oþer ne may be[o].[31]

In earlier and later examples, female saints' lives locate power in sources outside the self; they do so, crucially, in scenarios of spiritual contest. When virgin martyrs face challenges that arise from social associations, they embody the material virtues entailed by their privileged relationships with Christian divinity.

Fathers and Daughters

Of equal importance, fathers who try to render their daughters' virtues as static extensions of their prescriptive governance are depicted as corrupt tyrants across this genre. Such narratives issue a direct challenge to the Emperor's designs in Chaucer's *Man of Law's Tale*. According to late medieval female saints' lives, a virtuous father respects his daughter's propensity for virtue by fostering her membership in broader networks of excellence. This is the case even in non-Christian contexts. For instance, in John Capgrave's fifteenth-century *Life of St. Katherine*, the maiden's extensive learning in the liberal arts—which results from a wide-ranging program of collaborative instruction—leads to a life of natural virtue destined for holy sanctity:

> There was nevyr wrong founde in that may.
> The cors of hir governauns was evyr so clene,
> Bothe pryvy and aperte; at every asay,
> Stedfast and stable was evyr this qwene.
> Sche was a very seynt, truly as I wene,
> Thow sche were not baptized.[32]

From the earliest age, Katherine's "norture" exemplifies the Aristotelian idea that virtue develops as a result of constant guidance and deliberate practice. Katherine is fostered by an ethical habitus that promotes her innate goodness, yet the collectivized training she receives also affirms her father's virtuous governance.

As a righteous heathen, the Emperor is afforded high praise in Capgrave's extended account:

A goode man was he, this is the grounde:
Meke as a mayde, manful at nede,
Stable and stedfast evyrmore i-founde;
Strong man of hand, douty man of dede,
Helper of hem that to him hade nede;
Wrong thinges tho wroute he nevere,
Petous of spiryt and mercyful was he evere.

Pees wold he put debate evyr above;
That vertu cleymyd he only to himselve.
Alle his noble werkys onto pees and love
Were mad as mete as ex onto helve.
Among all the lordes that men dyd thoo delve
He was most worthy and eke most wys.
Synne hated he hertly, harlatrye and vycis.[33]

Capgrave's Emperor is responsible for finding suitable women to tend Katherine, and when she is "set to book," tutored by the finest minds near and far, her involved education is credited to her father's generosity and diligence:

Hir fader, that sche schuld lern these artes alle,
This nobyll lady, his owyn douter dere,
Ded mak a paleyse large and ryalle
In whech he wold that sche schuld lere.[34]

Unlike other pagan fathers, whose early educational programs are designed to enforce strict obedience to paternal authority, Katherine's father allows her to develop those "innate" virtues that lead her to Christianity.

When he represents the Emperor as a model of pagan excellence, therefore, Capgrave redefines paternal virtue. A father should at once be central to and distant from the production of his daughter's excellence, an ideal fulfilled by Capgrave's Emperor when he turns Katherine over to her schoolmasters:

Hir fadyr the kyng seldom wold hir se:
Onto these clerkes he hath hir thus take.[35]

Fittingly, when it extols early training, *The Book of the Knight of the Tower* invokes Saint Katherine's virtuous example in the chapter, "How men oughte to sette and put theyr children to scole."[36] While it ultimately legitimates paternal authority, this model of education is designed to foster a woman's ethical excellence through her enmeshment within shared networks of embodied virtue. This does not confine Katherine within an abstract system of static values; instead, it gives her access to powerful reserves of moral excellence that enhance her personal capacities. If Custance's will is evacuated by the imperial designs her father pursues, Katherine's is fostered by the extensive training her father arranges. Katherine's father puts her to school, but her desire already runs that way:

> Sumtyme to hir mayster wold sche sey nay—
> Whan he bad hir play, sche wold sit stylle.
> To stody and goodenes inclined was hir wylle.[37]

Because it allows her to cultivate excellences that are commonly prized within a larger community, Katherine becomes more ethically enabled as a result of educational training.

Capgrave's *Life of St. Katherine* features a benevolent patriarch, but the Emperor Costus's natural virtue is a rarity in late medieval virgin martyr legends. In *The Life of St. Christine*, Bokenham separates earthly and heavenly fathers. When the young virgin refuses to recant her adopted Christian faith, her pagan father has Christine's maidens beheaded and his daughter beaten. Her mother urges Christine to adopt an attitude of obedience, appealing to her maternity, "þat I / Ten monethis þe bare in my body," to compel her daughter's submission.[38] Instead, Christine declares her fidelity to a non-lineal, holy family:

> "But þou þan travuaylist," quod she, "in veyn,
> To clepe me doughtyr, & lesyst þi labour;
> For þis I wyl þou know in wurdys pleyn
> My name I haue of cryst my creatour.
> He is my fadir, he is modir also,
> Wych me hath clepyd to heuenly cheualrye.
> . . . .
> Wherefore go hens, & labour nomore.
> Clepe me not doughtyr; here I þe forsake."[39]

Although Bokenham's Saint Margaret is cherished by her father, and fostered by her nurse, the young virgin ultimately renounces this paternal bond as a gesture of devotion to Christ:

> Behold me, lord, wych am the only
> Doughtyr of my fader, and he hath me
> For the forsakyn, and so hym haue y.
> Hens aftyr wil thou my fadyr be![40]

She cannot obey two fathers, even if both are virtuous. In these popular legends, paternal masculinity fails to nourish women's material virtue.

Sources Outside the Self

Virgin martyrs are independent from worldly forces, but they depend on divinity for their force in the world. Capgrave's Saint Katherine is not free to direct herself however she pleases. Notwithstanding her social privilege and learned authority, Katherine is subject to spiritual demands that are similar to those pressed upon other virgin martyrs. Consequently, her manner is like that of other holy maidens in the genre: Katherine is fierce and enabled in social interactions, gentle and submissive during spiritual encounters. She is strong, then subdued. Her manner defies binary classifications of bold or meek, pliant or daring. On account of her education, Katherine has the discretion to see the truth of Christianity, as well as the strength to defend her convictions following her conversion. She is autonomous, yet because her power is not self-generated, her *Life* undermines the meaning of that term as modern thinkers understand it. According to the political theorist Amy Allen, autonomy involves "the capacity for critical reflection" as well as "the capacity for deliberate self-transformation."[41] Katherine might be able to give a rational account of her conversion, but she would never claim that power as a personal resource.

As a consequence, Katherine's holy espousal is simultaneously presented as her choice *and* as God's will. In an effort to avoid the sort of dynastic marriage that befalls Chaucer's Custance, Katherine tells her mother and counselors she will only marry a husband who meets the strict set of criteria she devises. Unfolding an eight-stanza catalog, Katherine "dyscryve[s] myn husbond whom I wyll hafe."[42] Later, when Mary conveys Christ's suit, his qualities fulfill Katherine's professed desires in every detail. Yet if Christ is portrayed as a husband fashioned according to Katherine's will, this is rather obviously a feint. Because Christ satisfies every condition of Katherine's superlative description, her marital consent is moot. She has the rationality and independence to generate an idealized account, but that simply means she has the power and intelligence to apprehend Christ's spousal perfection. As Capgrave's *Life* presents it, Katherine has *already agreed* to marry Christ once she describes her ideal husband. The intellect and composure that make Katherine one of the most popular saints in late medieval England bind her to Christianity's irresistible perfection in Capgrave's *Life*.[43] Because Katherine's natural excellence is cultivated, Christian virtue inevitably claims her.

From the outset, then, Katherine's virtue is never fully her own. Before Katherine is named, Capgrave emphasizes the directing power of divine providence over the young virgin's life:

> For God to Himselfe this mayden had i-chose
> As for His owyn spouse and for His wyffe dere.[44]

Similarly, many heroines from Osbern Bokenham's fifteenth-century *Legendys of hooly wummen* are depicted as willing the choice God has already ordained for them. In his *Life of Christine*, for instance, the maiden's propensity for sanctity is inherent, and stands at odds with her pagan heritage:

> But lych as oftyn off a full scharp thorn
> Flouris spryngyn fayre and delycious,
> And off foull erthe grouyth good korn,
> Gold eek and siluyre ant stonys precious,
> So off these hethene folk and vicyous,
> Wych in ydolatrie here lyfe dyde fyne,
> A mayde both fayre and eke gracious
> Was born, whos name thei clepyd Cristyne.[45]

Christine's excellence is elemental, which means that it grows organically from the instilled goodness of sovereign divinity. Inborn virtue of this type does not depend on traditional notions of volition or potency. Instead, the nested agency of virgin martyrs allows Capgrave or Bokenham to acknowledge the insignificance of human power in contrast to the might of divine providence.

Though virgin martyrs withstand a panoply of harms, their vitae demolish all claims to self-creation or reflexive cultivation. They do so, it should be added, in specific devotional contexts, which model surrender to God's omnipotence for all audiences. This submission does not diminish the transformative capacities of virgin martyrs in social situations; on the contrary, their complete reliance on divine power makes female saints invincible in their dealings with all manner of masculine tyranny. With respect to women's ethical action, virgin martyrs present a model of virtue that troubles any easy divide between activity and passivity, autonomy and dependence. The maiden's volition might already belong to Christ, but the primary ability to give herself, what Jocelyn Wogan Browne calls a virgin martyr's "dotality," is an important enabling factor that distinguishes her ethical action in subsequent trials.[46] In sum, the female martyr retains a hold over her own volition, even in surrender. Her power in secular contexts, as a consequence, is magnified and extended. Because ultimate authority is vested in God, whose relation to goodness is absolute, a maiden's submission becomes an enriching source of spiritual and social excellence.

The virtues a father might instill are not necessary for Christian conversion; at best they serve as a stopover on the moral route guaranteeing a maiden's sanctity. At worst they pose a threat to a daughter's holiness, and must be jettisoned as part of her new affiliation. With startling finality—"Farwell Arystotyll"—Katherine declares her independence from the philosophical tradition that enabled her to see the truth of Christianity.[47] Even in Capgrave's favorable assessment, an ideal father promotes God's power over his own dynastic prerogatives. This is the case regardless of whether the father is pagan or Christian. Even so, as Chaucer's *Man of Law's Tale* demonstrates, a father could just as easily exploit Christianity for his own lineal purposes. The expansionist campaign the Emperor hopes to realize using Custance's marriage is justified on religious grounds.[48] Nonetheless, when the Emperor treats Custance's virtue as an inanimate extension of his own power, Chaucer allies him with those unreasonable fathers who use daughters to enhance their political power. As I shall suggest in the next section, the tale's *anti*-imperialism critiques those institutions—social and religious—that use militarist violence to suppress the lively power of women's material virtues.

Imperialism That Doesn't Work

In her indispensable analysis of English romance, "Magic That Doesn't Work," Helen Cooper observes what might at first glance seem like an anomaly: magic is useless, and ultimately must be sidelined, in the tradition known for supernatural occurrence.[49] In the The Man of Law's Tale, imperialism works in parallel fashion: designed to uncover the heroine's fragility in a hostile environment, the Emperor's militarist designs threaten to devastate the narrative's exemplary pathos.[50] Rather than figuring Custance as a willing sacrifice in a fantasy of paternal empowerment, she appears more as an overwhelmed casualty of patriarchal aggression. On account of Custance's self-abasing acceptance, "I, wrecche womman, no fors though I spille!" (II.285), the cold machinery of arranged marriage resembles a tyrannical engine of virgin martyrdom. Rather than furthering the Emperor's sinister designs, the tale curtails an absolutist fantasy of paternal empowerment.[51] The combination of exogamy and empire is supposed to provide an outlet for paternal desire that prevents incest. This structure's continued reliance on the suffering female body, so it would seem, is sanctified by the Christian ethics of self-sacrifice with which Custance is identified. As an unchanging ethical constant, virtue should enable Custance to accept her fate; when she surrenders volition, she can endure extreme emotional suffering. If she neither complains nor resists, Custance's virtue naturalizes its own exploitation. This is what is supposed to happen in The Man of Law's Tale, and it is what happens in romances that treat a daughter's innocence as a mark of masculine empowerment.

Yet, in Chaucer's Custance saga, the Emperor's stultifying view of virtue thwarts his expansionist designs. As part of the tale's Orientalist estrangement of the East, Custance's marriage is designed to achieve a powerful alliance, but it is never intended to form a unified dynasty reaching from Rome to Syria. In particular, Custance is never supposed to be assimilated into the Sultan's lineage. Instead, she is meant to transmit a direct copy of her father's virtues without the slightest alteration. This stasis is imagined in terms that are equally physical and ethical, and it hinges on virtue's multiplicity in the late Middle Ages. Since "vertu" was also a term of humoral medicine in Middle English, physiology and morality are elided in racialized demarcations of religious distinction. The King of Tars, which also appears in the Auchinleck MS (beginning nine leaves before St. Margaret, discussed earlier in this chapter), is famous for its insistence that religious admixture causes physical monstrosity. The union of Christian and Muslim generates a formless lump of living flesh; only the redeeming power of Christian virtue—which is imagined in explicitly material terms—can convert this amorphous mass into a human infant. After the Sultan's idols fail to provide healing, he tells his Christian wife:

> Now dame, ichil do bi þi lore,
> ჳif þat y may se bifore
> Þi God is of swiche miჳt,
> Wiþ ani vertu þat he can,
> Make it fourmed after a man
> Wiþ liif & limes ariჳt.
> Alle mi godes ichil forsake,
> & to Ihesu, þi Lord, me take,
> As ich am gentil kniჳt.[52]

Here as elsewhere, Christianity enlivens material substances, spreading active virtues through the bodies it perfects. The elemental vitality of Christian divinity stands in contrast to the bare stasis of pagan idols, whose lifeless forms reflect worshippers' barren desires.

Rather than allow for the alterations that virtue initiates in other scenes of conversion, the Emperor expects Custance to remain faithful in her transmission of paternal, Christian, imperial power:

> And in encrees of Cristes lawe deere,
> They been acorded, so as ye shal heere. (II.237–38)

Custance is an agent of conversion, and on account of this power—this virtue—she will never be changed herself. In this expectation, the Emperor is like those non-Christian women whose investments in lineal sovereignty attempt to render virtue inert and unvarying. The salient difference is not between Christian and Muslim, or between Christian and pagan; instead, it is between two views of virtue. Like the Emperor, the Sultaness treats virtue as a static inheritance that might be preserved through the deliberate, sometimes violent, management of offspring:

> The Sowdan and Christen everichone
> Been al tohewe and stiked at the bord. (II.429–30)

Later on, Donegild objects to the marriage between Custance and Alla because she seeks to prevent alterations to her son's lineage:

> Hir thoughte a despit that he sholde take
> So strange a creature unto his make. (II.699–700)

In her forged letter, Donegild plays not only on fears of physical admixture; when she claims Custance "delivered was / Of so horrible a feendly creature" (II.750–51), and suggests that this monstrous birth was realized by "charmes or by sorcerie" (II.755), she also references a late medieval belief that virtue—carried by stones, herbs, or charms—enlivens unthinkable bodies. In linking the Emperor with tyrannical, irrational, villainous women, the tale challenges his efforts to suppress virtue's inherent dynamism.

In a dubious trade-off, then, base misogyny furthers anti-imperialist critique. Elsewhere, the tale opens relational circuits that undercut the Emperor's militarist Christianity and confound rigid gender distinctions. The Sultan's ready conversion does not signal his effeminate submission to the Emperor's aggressive demands; instead, it endorses material virtues that originate outside the self. Custance's virtue is catching, but this is not because her qualities are uniquely her own. On the contrary, this story figures virtues as external powers that transfer between bodies, remaking subjects through transformative moments of unsettling contact.[53] It might be trivially true, therefore, to observe that Custance's wandering is the most effective catalyst of conversion in the tale. To note this here, however, is to distinguish between evangelist and imperialist modes of Christian virtue. The Emperor's attempt to consolidate a Christian empire is predicated on colonizing territory. But the presumptive universalism of Roman Christianity means that all domains already fall under its totalized authority. Following this logic, conquest becomes a strategy of preservation, of patrolling and enforcing values that are understood to be preexistent and unchangeable. This form of Christianity assumes virtue's immutability, and it is a religious and military failure in *The Man of Law's Tale*. Because it aims to suppress virtue's vitality, imperialism doesn't work, and actually must be sidelined in order to prevent the erosion of Christian authority it is meant to enlarge.

After her wedding turns into a massacre, Custance is set adrift in the rudderless boat that visually marks her surrender to the external power of divine providence.[54] Yet, I suggest, her wandering makes her more than an abstract figuration, which features God steering the ship of the human soul.

It connects her to other circuits of virtue, but it also provides a further critique of imperialist masculinity. Custance's story recalls that of Mary Magdalen, who, as I shall discuss in more detail later in this chapter, was imagined in many medieval accounts as drifting seaward before she evangelized southern Gaul.[55] But it also captures women's fragility in patrilineal transactions they neither direct nor command. Custance has no control over her fate, yet she is less endangered than when she lived out the Emperor's desires. Although Custance once again traverses dangerous waters to an unknown land where she will marry a foreign ruler, the passage is less troubled. This is, of course, because she travels to Northumbria, recognizable as *pre-England* on account of its exceptionalism.[56] Arriving in a place where she is a stranger, speaking "A maner Latyn corrupt" (II.519), Custance cannot be identified with the Emperor's expansionist designs.[57] Itinerant and vulnerable, she is without nation, family, or language.[58]

Custance is less endangered because material virtues direct her contact with others. Custance's only means of communication, her dealings with Hermengyld affirm, is via an embodied form of shared excellence. In her groundbreaking assessment, Elizabeth Robertson underscores Custance's "'elvyssh'" power, or what she argues is a form of "secular sanctity" that achieves nonviolent conversion despite Custance's lack of direct action.[59] This power, with its ability to connect bodies across divides that are temporal, spatial, cultural, and spiritual, is Chaucer's most expansive rendering of material virtue's transformative potential. Once she arrives in Northumbria, Custance enacts the qualities she was earlier assigned:

> She was so diligent, withouten slouthe,
> To serve and plesen everich in that place
> That alle hir loven that looken in hir face. (II.530–32)

As it happens, the Sultan is attracted to Custance on identical grounds as later converts:

> Thise marchantz han hym toold of dame Custance,
> So greet noblesse in ernest, ceriously. (II.184–85)

Since it appeals to Muslim and pagan alike, we might suppose Chaucer creates a form of material virtue that *exceeds* religion.

As Hermengyld's devotion attests, this model of excellence also surpasses, and potentially confounds, gendered forms of erotic possession. Through its ability to forge an affective, nonfamilial bond between women, "But Hermengyld loved hire right as hir lyf" (II.535), the material liveliness of women's virtue promises to demolish all structures that limit or partition desire. All edifices except one, that is. Though Custance claims to have lost her identity, "She seyde she was so mazed in the see / That she forgat hir mynde" (II.526–27), her material virtue invigorates the authority of her heavenly Father: "God liste to shewe his wonderful myracle / In hire" (II.477–78). What I have been elaborating as virtue's vivacious and unsettling relationality is revealed as God's providential power. Viewed within a structure of providence, Custance's ability to catalyze ethical change looks less like active virtue and more like passive stasis. Similar to magic, providence has the potential to outsource virtue, to diminish individual achievement by attributing its cause to a power higher and other than the subject. And, even more than imperialism, providence insists that all change is vitalized from without. As a consequence, the providential subject is at risk of becoming a helpless pawn, which is how many critics have traditionally read Custance's position.

This is true if providence functions as a framework—a rigid structure that determines all ethical life—rather than a network—a shifting association that assembles specific moral pathways that lead to particular ends that only God can anticipate. As Ingrid Nelson explains, "Medieval representations of providence offer a detailed articulation of the ways in which human agency is subject to forces outside of the individual's control."[60] Gerald Morgan, discussing Chaucer's amplification of providence in his Custance saga, rightly notes that, for Aquinas, "providence [is] the idea of things ordained to an end pre-existing in the divine mind."[61] God's foresight does not, however, erase human will or negate human action. In its most ideal iterations, providence works as a network that relies on shared virtues to bring about ethical transformation in particular circumstances. By functioning as channels of ethical connection, virtues create a living bond between God and man. Consequently, God's plan is not actualized without the cooperation, even the collaboration, of chosen subjects. This is not to say that providence carries no restrictive elements. In *The Man of Law's Tale*, providence ultimately divides Custance from human associations, including those that enable women's ethical action. On this point, the difference between Chaucer's narrative and female hagiography is instructive: virgin martyrs whose suffering achieves singularity are never completely alone. Margaret faces the dragon on her own, and Barbara is locked in a tower, but the very logic of female saints' lives integrates these maidens into a network of sanctity that extends beyond the boundaries of the individual.

Networked Virtue

The network of virgin martyrs is more than a spiritual community of iconic saints; it is a living association constituted from devoted bodies. As a number of scholars have detailed, women were deeply involved in the production and consumption of female martyrs' legends in the late Middle Ages.[62] Whether as patrons, owners, or audiences, fifteenth-century women actively participated in the culture that generated and sustained these narratives.[63] Bokenham's *Legends of hooly wummen* relates its composition to six contemporary laywomen: Isabel Bourchier, Katherine Denston, Agatha Flegge, Katherine Howard, Isabel Hunt, and Elizabeth de Vere.[64] As Catherine Sanok observes, Bokenham is notable because he creates a "fiction of feminine community" that credits contemporary laywomen as direct sources of his narratives.[65] By invoking these specific women, Bokenham creates "a doubled image that points to a larger audience of women joined—like the women depicted in the legends—in their devotion to female saints."[66] Isabel Bourchier, Isabel Hunt, and Elizabeth Vere, three of the powerful East Anglian women Bokenham addresses, certainly never expected their daily experiences to resemble the physical and spiritual trials undergone by Saints Elizabeth, Dorothy, and Mary Magdalen. Their access to this model of female sanctity relies on the persistence of virtues across radical differences in temporal and political circumstances. This persistence is not abstract; it is tangible, quickened by the lived excellence of successive generations of virtuous women.

According to Eamon Duffy, late medieval laywomen saw venerated saints "not so much [as] a model to imitate, something most of them never dreamt of doing, but rather [as] a source of power to be tapped."[67] To see female saints as inimitable might imply a less potent or intimate form of congress between virtuous women. Yet, in contrast to the continual separations of Custance's narrative, late medieval virgin martyr legends institute a network of holiness that defends and enables contemporary women.[68] These martyrs protect the actions of laywomen, valorizing the behavior of later women by virtue of their suffering, endurance, dignity, and bravery. Women such as Katherine Howard, Katherine Denston, or Agatha Flegge do not have to imitate their namesake martyrs, since the intercession of these and other powerful female saints includes them within a community of sanctifying grace. When John Lydgate names Anne, Lady March, as the patroness responsible for his *Legend of St. Margaret*, he also lauds her example to those "Noble princesses and ladyes of estate, And gentilwomen lower of degre" who are encouraged to "calle to your aduocate / Seynte Margarete, gemme of chastite."[69] Women who make female saints available, those who are a living reminder of the acts of virgin martyrs, are more than stock imitators of an original model of feminine virtue. They continue to participate in these virtues, vitalizing and renewing them through their shared participation in the composition and circulation of virgin martyr legends.

Just as female saints depend on contemporary women to bring forth their animate virtues, so do contemporary women rely on virgin martyrs to make room for their enacted excellences. A culture of women and books, as Carol Meale, Felicity Riddy, and Rebecca Krug have demonstrated, is authorized by the holiness that female hagiography promotes.[70] The fifteenth-century laywoman Margery Kempe justifies her peripatetic spirituality by crediting it to the guidance of female saints: "sumtyme Seynt Mary Mawdelyn, Seynt Kateryne, Seynt Margaret, er what seyt in Heuyn þat sche cowed thynke on thorw þe wil & sufferawns of God, þei spokyn to þe vndirstondyng of hir sowle, & enformyd hir how sche xulde louyn God & how sche xulde best plesyn hym."[71] These activities might be prohibitively transgressive without female saints' earlier departures from established norms. Moreover, without the dynamic examples offered by virgin martyrs, the virtues of late medieval laywomen might remain incomprehensible. For instance, *The Book of the Knight of the Tower* mobilizes its advice concerning charity with the example that female saints provide: "And at thexample of [the Virgin Mary] dyd saynt Elizabeth / saynte Lucye / saynt Cecylle and many other holy laydyes / which were so charitable that they gaf to the poure & Indygent the most parte of theyr reuenues / As reherced is playnly in theyr legendes."[72] As these accounts suggest, female saints were valuable for their ability to serve as spiritual protectors who inspire and shield the actions of later women.

This fortification extends to other narratives, including another analogue to Chaucer's Custance story. The exquisite frescoes in Eton College Chapel, which were completed in the 1480s, and were uncovered in 1847 after they had been whitewashed in 1560, feature a version of the "Empress of Rome" narrative on the lower panels of the south wall.[73] The frescoes depict a queen who is falsely accused (of adultery then murder), condemned to the sea, succored by the Virgin Mary, and revealed as a powerful healer. Rather than reconcile with the Emperor, the Empress decides to enter a monastery as a conclusion to her trials. Nancy B. Black details many differences between this story and Chaucer's *Man of Law's Tale*, but here I emphasize a final point of distinction, which is the Empress of Rome's continued connection to a network of female sanctity.[74] The panels are surrounded by a series of female martyrs: Saint Katherine, Saint Barbara, Saint Apollonia, an unidentified saint, Saint Ursula, Saint Dorothy, Saint Lucy (?), Saint Juliana, and Saint Winifred (see fig. 3).[75]

On account of this arrangement, powerful saints surround each narrative segment. The tranquility of these figures, which, as M. R. James and E. W. Tristram remark, are clearly painted "to produce the effect of carved reliefs," diverges from the bustling activity inside each panel.[76] The painting in which the Empress is falsely charged with adultery is filled with motion: in the foreground, the Emperor prepares to strike off her head, but in the background, we see that he has changed his mind, and that he simply has the Empress taken away to meet her death at another's hands (see fig. 4). Similarly, after the Empress is rescued by a nameless lord and becomes nurse to his infant son, her betrayal unfolds in panels that use juxtaposed spaces to convey tumultuous violence: first, the lord's villainous brother prepares to cut the child's throat (see fig. 5); then, the Empress is ushered into exile on a perilous ship after being accused of the crime (see fig. 6). By contrast, the virgin martyrs offer a calming majesty that suggests providential control over the turbulent events on display.

Structuring this story with reference to a series of virgin martyrs also establishes a shared experience among women. The Virgin Mary comforts and protects the Empress in the same fashion as she did other female saints. The concluding panel, in which the Empress decides to enter a monastery (see fig. 7), does not just use female saints to render one woman's experiences comprehensible with reference to an unchanging set of intangible virtues; instead, it joins women through a common set of material excellences that are expanded through different enactments. The Eton Chapel frescoes, by detailing the Empress's ability to heal her accusers (both of whom contract leprosy after accosting her), figure virtue as a restorative power that overcomes slander, betrayal, and assault. The wrongs the Empress overcomes are social, and prominent in the late fifteenth-century English women's lives. In fact, scholars such as Sheila Delany, Catherine Sanok, and Carol Hilles read late medieval female saints' lives, in particular Bokenham's legendary, as a response to the upheavals

FIGURE 3. Panels depicting the "Empress of Rome" story are surrounded by a series of female saints. Frescoes at Eton College, fifteenth century, Historic England Archive, FF91_00225.

FIGURE 4. The Empress as she is about to be beheaded. Frescoes at Eton
College, fifteenth century, Historic England Archive, FF91_00227.

FIGURE 5. The Empress falsely accused of killing a child. Frescoes at Eton
College, fifteenth century, Historic England Archive, BB91_06833.

of late fifteenth-century English politics.[77] Similarly, virgin martyrs in the Eton
frescoes remain relevant to contemporary social harms because their responses
to suffering provide sources of power and comfort in shifting political domains.
The paintings were completed during the most tumultuous years of the Wars
of the Roses; between 1479 and 1487 England was ruled by Edward IV, Edward
V, Richard III, then Henry VII. Despite these political upheavals, the virgin
martyrs ensure political tranquility even in a domain where elite women are
constantly endangered.[78] Indeed, the Empress's transformation recalls the eventual triumphs of the virgin martyrs in a fashion that renews the virtues of both.
Within this interwoven sequence, virgin martyrs and elite women are drawn
together, figuring a unified model of material virtue that can withstand the
vicissitudes of time, place, and ethical enmeshment.

FIGURE 6. The Empress set adrift in a rudderless boat, then succored
by the Virgin Mary. Frescoes at Eton College, fifteenth century, Historic
England Archive, FF91_00229.

FIGURE 7. The Empress enters a monastery. Frescoes at Eton College, fifteenth century, Historic England Archive, FF91_00231.

Saving Grace

Like the Empress figured in the Eton frescoes, Custance builds a small but
vital network of relational virtue. Because Hermengyld loves Custance, and
because the Constable sees the miraculous fruit of his wife's conversion (in
the puzzling "blinde Britoun" encounter, II.561), material virtue intertwines
them in an association invigorated by God's power. In this and the following
conversions, Custance does not preach, or take more than a secondary role
in the transformations her presence inspires. Instead, her faultless example
opens a space for religious conversion. And, although Hermengyld becomes
receptive to Christianity on account of her love for Custance, this connection
leads to a more momentous intervention: "Jhesu hath converted thurgh his
grace" (II.538). Yet, as Hermengyld's grisly death attests, this is not a bloodless
relationship of holiness. It is, rather, a grace-based model of divine authority,
one that alienates Custance from more extensive spiritual and social networks. Grace as an instilled source of external virtue was a constant of medieval ethical writings, as I shall discuss in the following section. In the late
Middle Ages, let me acknowledge now, grace theology took a disaggregating
turn that affects Chaucer's representation of Custance's ethical action. In an
astute reading of Augustinianism in late fourteenth-century thought, James
Goldstein identifies *The Man of Law's Tale* as an important locus for Chaucer's considerations of "the relation between human and divine agency in the
free will's cooperation or resistance to grace."[79]

As she is moved across water and lands, Goldstein argues, Custance's volition is ever more irrelevant, which means her virtue—animate
or otherwise—is increasingly isolated as a product of divine power.[80] To be
sure, God's grace takes priority in a series of extreme displays. If Satan is
dismayed when he "Saugh of Custance al hire perfeccioun" (II.583), his con-
niving provides the ultimate opportunity to demonstrate providential control. Custance is endangered, just as Hermengyld is sacrificed, to show God's
ultimate authority over human affairs. When the knight accuses Custance of
cutting Hermengyld's throat, the physical evidence, "the blody knyf by dame
Custance" (II.601), leaves Custance defenseless. She is helpless to gainsay the
charge against her:

> Allas, what myghte she seye?
> For verray wo hir wit was al aweye. (II.608–9)

Unlike late medieval virgin martyrs, who are emboldened by divine grace during moments of social duress, Custance is utterly speechless. Only her embodied virtue, with its powerful ability to *move others*, indicates her innocence.[81] Alla pities Custance on account of her evident excellence:

> The kynges herte of pitee gan agryse,
> Whan he saugh so beninge a creature
> Falle in disese and in mysaventure. (II.614–16)

The people, too, sorrow for Custance, "For they han seyn hire evere so virtuous" (II.624). Her apparent goodness is not a product of cultivation, but emerges from God's control.

Once again, Custance's material virtue makes way for the transformative power of Christian grace. Observers might pity her exposure to harm, "Allas! Custance, thou hast no champioun, / Ne fighte kanstow noght, so weylaway!" (II.631–32), but her jeopardy assures God's triumph. The moving spectacle of Custance's vulnerability even reaches out to contemporary women, since, in one of the tale's many apostrophes, women are called on to imagine themselves in Custance's position:

> O queenes, lyvynge in prosperitee,
> Duchesses, and ye ladyes everichone,
> Haveth som routhe on hire adversitee!
> An Emperoures doghter stant allone;
> She hath no wight to whom to make hir mone.
> O blood roial, that stondest in this drede,
> Fer been thy freendes at thy grete nede! (II.652–58)

Women are meant to be moved by Custance's precarity, because lineage and alliance are useless defenses against this order of danger. In a miraculous show of divine agency, a disembodied voice acquits Custance of all wrong:

> Thou hast desclaundred, giltelees,
> *The doghter of hooly chirche* in heigh presence;
> Thus hastou doon, and yet holde I my pees! (II.674–76, emphasis added)

This wondrous incident identifies Custance as the exalted offspring of a Christian Father, the prized daughter of a force greater than any human network of material virtue.

Accordingly, Alla's marriage to Custance is devised by no human will, motivated by no human desire:

> And after this Jhesus, of his mercy,
> Made Alla wedden ful solempnely
> This hooly mayden, that is so bright and sheene;
> And thus hath *Crist ymaad Custance a queene.* (II.690–93, emphasis
> added)

Custance's reformed nuptials follow divine providence, superseding all human arrangements of politics or ethics.[82] As a consequence, Custance is cut off from the networks of virtue that might sustain and extend her ethical influence. Chaucer represents Custance as God's creation, *His daughter.* Accordingly, Custance does not marry Alla on account of affection, desire, or any form of passion. Just as equally, Alla is moved by Custance's virtue alone. As a will-free union, theirs is a marriage that privileges the father-daughter bond between Custance and God. A spiritual connection to the divine, to put it another way, disaggregates human networks of virtue, circulating all excellence between the subject and God. Of course, numerous female saints disassociate themselves from familial and social networks; yet there is no sense that Custance will ever occupy a place within a pantheon of female worthies.

Instead, Custance's connection to God takes precedence over all other moral relations. Her marriage to Alla is a sanctified means to Christian progeny, since, as Geraldine Heng observes, "motherhood, not wifehood, is the point of this marital union."[83] It is no surprise that Custance prays to Mary, for like the mother of God, she is involved in a spiritual union that supplants human connections:

> Thow glorie of wommanhede, thow fair may,
> Thow haven of refut, brighte sterre of day,
> Rewe on my child. (II.851–53)

It matters little if Custance is daughter *and* mother in a family romance that transgresses the sanctified boundaries separating heaven and earth. Alla's role is minimized, but Custance's renewed exile ends up renovating the patriarchal family. When Custance is returned to the shifting seas, the family becomes a union headed by God. In this, the tale recognizes the harms that men frequently perpetuate against women and the children they foster. Custance indicts what she believes is Alla's cruelty in a sorrowful lament that affirms her maternal strength: "O litel child . . . Why wil thyn harde fader han thee spilt?" (II.855, 857). Doubting God's design, however, is utterly foreclosed: "He that me kepte fro the false blame . . . He kan me kepe from harm and eek fro shame" (II.827, 829). Custance may not understand divine workings, "althogh I se noght how" (II.830), yet her task is to accept God's providence.

Custance's willing surrender recalls the legendary history of Mary Magdalen, who, in Caxton's translation of Jacobus Voragine's *Legenda aurea*, is "put in to a shyppe in the see wythout ony ta|kyl or rother / for to be drowned."[84] In following the story recounted in *The Golden Legend*, Bokenham similarly credits Mary Magdalen's powers of conversion to sources beyond the self:

> These alle to-gedyr & many anoþir
> Of crystene men, by the cruel decre
> Of iewys, with-owte sterne or rothyr
> In a shyp were set up-on þe se
> To þat entent þei dynklyd shuld be;
> But as goddys prouydence hem dede gye
> Alle saf to Marsilye þei dede applye.[85]

Instead of exhibiting Custance's helpless passivity, Chaucer uses the transformative power of externalized divinity to distance Custance from the lineal entanglements of traditional family structures. When she yields herself to an unknown fate, Custance declares her undivided loyalty: "Farewel, housbonde routhelees!" (II.863). In this way, the construction of a providential family expands Custance's material virtue through nonhuman circuits: "dryvynge ay / Somtyme west, and somtyme north and south, / And somtyme est, ful many a wery day" (II.947–49). Her trials detach her from all worldly powers, since, absented from father and husband, she drifts "Fyve yeer and moore, as liked Cristes sonde" (II.901). By floating free of human associations, she gains a strength the tale likens to the biblical heroism of David as he defeated Goliath, or Judith as she overcame Holofernes.

Unlike earlier virgin martyrs, and notwithstanding the tale's comparison to other biblical heroes, Custance's power does not result from a heroic

exercise of agency against a stronger opponent. Instead, it is a power of
endurance that derives from without:

> That right as God spirit of vigour sente
> To hem and saved hem out of meschance,
> So sente he myght and vigour to Custance. (II.943–45)

Indeed, Mary only "make[s] an ende of al hir hevynesse" (II.952) once Custance's constancy is established. After she washes ashore "under an hethen
castel" (II.904), she must fend off the sexual aggression of a wicked steward,
who "seyde he sholde / Hir lemman be, wher-so she wolde or nolde" (II.916–
17). Custance's sadness, her tears, and even "hir struglyng wel and myghtily"
cannot save her from violation (II.921), as the tale acknowledges in its affirmation of women's sexual vulnerability in late medieval society. Lest anyone
wonder, "How may this wayke womman han this strengthe / Hire to defende
agayn this renegat?" (II.932–33), the tale is careful to dramatize the rapist's
demise as a miraculous occurrence, noting that he "fil over bord al sodeynly"
(II.922), crediting her safety to divine intervention: "And thus hath Crist
unwemmed kept Custance" (II.924). Custance is strong, but as the tale labors
to demonstrate, that power comes from without, "Wel may men seen, it nas
but Goddes grace" (II.938).

Inhuman Grace

Custance is endowed with God's grace, a magnificent agency that makes material virtue into an ethically invincible cultural endowment. This autonomy, it
must be observed, is specific and strange at once. In theological terms, grace is
capable of renovating the individual soul, in part because it is connected to
medieval understandings of virtue. As Richard Cross explains, "During the
Middle Ages, a doctrine of grace developed that either identifies grace as a kind
of virtue, or at least understands grace in a way highly analogous to virtue.
Viewed in this way, grace is a kind of additional remedy for the various kinds
of weakness introduced by original sin."[86] For Augustine, grace perfects the
fallen will, and is therefore necessary for virtue.[87] Richard Rolle's fourteenth-
century English psalter captures the moral tractability that grace enables: "Crist
and his lufere spekis bath in a voice, for thai ere ane thurgh grace and confour-
mynge of will."[88] For my purposes, grace is important because it locates a

condition of dependency at the heart of ethical action. For many prominent thinkers, the ability to accept God's grace relies on God's preeminent power. To put it another way, humans cannot act alone, but may only respond to God's summons, or, if we prefer to think in more hospitable terms, to God's invitation.[89] Aquinas uses Aristotelian physics to suggest that God moves man's soul internally, though he also claims that the human soul contributes to grace's actualization.[90] By his account, humans are always somewhat estranged from their ethical capacities, insofar as an external power exerts a form of control that directs and even produces moral actions. This does not mean that humans are no longer morally responsible, since medieval thinkers also developed a robust notion of free will.[91] While some later medieval thinkers conflated grace and charity—arguing that charity perfected the rational will—grace was still widely understood as an external power, as is evident in Reginald Pecock's fifteenth-century vernacular effort to reconcile the capacity of human reason with the authority of church doctrine: "Þis grace muste nedis be freeli ȝouun fro god, and may not be bouȝt neier in fullist maner worþili deserued . . . and ellis it were no grace."[92]

Theologians of the period developed elaborate and far-reaching theories of grace. The point I take from these involved debates is not nuanced, however: medieval grace has a profound impact on ethical agency, so much so that humans conform more closely to what modern philosophers describe as moral patients rather than moral agents.[93] In modern philosophy, differentiating moral agents and moral patients provides a means to distinguish between those whose rationality makes them morally responsible for their actions and those whose lack of mental adroitness prevents them from giving an account of their conduct. Humans/animals, adults/children, men/women: the ethical stature of moral agents depends on their actions, while the ethical standing of moral patients relies on their treatment. Do you act virtuously? Or are you treated unjustly? By suggesting that the boundaries of the human are determined by the first question (and by implying that the second question is merely a corollary of the first), modern ethical theory reinforces the ideal of the autonomous, self-determining subject. This is despite the fact that contemporary thinkers have increasingly sought to shift the grounds of ethics, frequently by engaging with the nineteenth-century philosopher Jeremy Bentham's provocative questions about the status of nonhuman animals:

> The day has been, I grieve to say in many places it is not yet past,
> in which the greater part of the species, under the denomination of

slaves, have been treated by the law exactly upon the same footing as, in England for example, the inferior races of animals are still. The day *may* come, when the rest of the animal creation may acquire those rights which never could have been withholden from them but by the hand of tyranny. The French have already discovered that the blackness of the skin is no reason why a human being should be abandoned without redress to the caprice of a tormentor. . . . What else is it that should trace the insuperable line? Is it the faculty of reason, or, perhaps, the faculty of discourse? But a full-grown horse or dog is beyond comparison a more rational, as well as a more conversable animal, than an infant of a day, or a week, or even a month, old. But suppose the case were otherwise, what would it avail? the question is not, Can they *reason*? nor, Can they *talk*? but, Can they *suffer*?[94]

I cite this passage at length because Bentham is acutely aware that humanity is historically contingent, and reliant upon ethical norms that are socially inflected.

Nevertheless, when the modern philosopher Martha Nussbaum develops a "capabilities approach" to justice that extends "human" rights to animals and the disabled, she retains an investment in maintaining the distinct human subject even though she proceeds from the Aristotelian assumption that man's social and political nature precludes a strong individualist emphasis on independence.[95] Likewise, Alasdair MacIntyre, who relies heavily on Thomas Aquinas's moral theory in his *Dependent Rational Animals*, approaches Bentham's provocations from a perspective that sees discrete human action—even as that might be reimagined as structured by acknowledged dependency—as a transhistorically valid foundation for ethical life.[96] This might simply be the purview of contemporary ethics, which adopts the eternal now to consider what makes the best life and to ponder how we should live it. As John Marenbon observes, "we make the text we study, whenever it was written, into a piece of philosophy now."[97] The eternal now should not presuppose the eternal individual, however. In his attempt to recover medieval philosophy from the history of ideas, Marenbon is also quick to emphasize the work of translation—a careful elucidation of the historical particularity of specific philosophical conversations—required to bring philosophical writings from earlier periods to bear on modern problems.[98] With Marenbon's intervention in mind, I suggest that medieval

ethics, like contemporary posthumanist theory, emphasizes common vulnerability; both modes of thought, moreover, open a space to reimagine the
human based on an ethics of what Cary Wolfe calls our "shared finitude"
with "fellow creatures."[99]

Unlike later adaptations of early thought, medieval ethics is not definitive in its assignment of moral agency to the individual; instead, it ensconces
a hybrid form of ethical action that makes the independent, rational subject
less crisply distinct from all designated Others. The workings of divine grace
shift attention from conduct to treatment as the basis for medieval virtue. No
longer does a person's behavior provide the foundation for moral judgment;
instead, a person's treatment reveals her ethical standing. In a departure from
ethical theories that make determining right and wrong the province of moral
agents alone, medieval notions of grace outsource ethical capacity in a fashion
that leaves intact the responsibility of moral patients. By attending to a person's *reaction to ethical treatment*, including but not limited to that person's
response to God's influence, medieval grace diminishes the self-cultivating
ethical subject. Late medieval vernacular literatures show this difference in
emphasis very distinctly. Although Mary Magdalen is cast adrift in the sea,
her robust *response* to hardship—her enthusiastic ministry to the pagan
strangers she encounters in southern Gaul—actualizes her moral power. Neither is she weak because she accepts Christ's redemption. Rather, and in a
fashion that is meant to guide others, her submission reveals that she is strong
enough to accept her fundamental dependence on divine grace. As one of the
most popular legends of divine transformation in the Middle Ages, Mary
Magdalen's story accords with medieval grace, which, in its most theological
dimension, Jean Porter explains, "brings about virtue in the soul . . . through
the exercise of free will in cooperation with God's grace."[100]

Equally important, medieval grace enfolds moral action within a network
of cooperation. Through its dispensation of grace, *The Life of St. Mary Magdalene* dispatches any logic that sees a single agent acting upon another. Mary
Magdalen becomes a miraculous protector, but her power does not derive
from an individual capacity she generates within herself. Rather, one of the
central episodes in *The Golden Legend*'s version of her *Life*, wherein Mary
Magdalen restores a mother and child left for dead on a barren island, is a
gathering of action that confounds distinctions of time, space, and the subject. Even though she remains in Marseilles, Mary Magdalen provides nour-
ishment to the lost child for two years and revives the dead mother after her
husband returns from a pilgrimage. When Saint Peter comforts the forlorn

prince for the loss of his heir and wife, he explains that Mary Magdalen's power derives from a source mightier than herself: "And be thou not heuy / Yf thy wyf slepe / And the lytil chyld rest with her For our lord is almyghty for to gyue to whom he wyl / and to take awaye that he hath gyuen / and to restablisshe and gyue agayn that he hath taken."[101] Saint Peter and Mary Magdalen are part of a cooperative network that connects Jerusalem, Rome, and Marseilles. By working together, they enact Christ's divinity on earth. The Magdalen performs mighty miracles, but the virtue she materializes is wrought by divine grace.

As such, grace forges bonds between the living and the dead, the human and the nonhuman. Like the account captured in *The Life of Mary Magdalene*, the Eton frescoes feature a noblewoman stranded on a rocky outcrop (see fig. 8). Yet, in this version of the Empress of Rome narrative, the Virgin Mary is the source of miraculous preservation. The Virgin gives the Empress a marvelous herb that transforms the exiled queen into a formidable healer, forging a connection between all orders—human and divine, organic and inorganic—as a product of divine grace. Notwithstanding its barren desolation, the Empress's exile emphasizes the vibrant interconnection of all God's creation. Here, stone yields plant in a miraculous moral ecology. In *The Man of Law's Tale*, more mundanely, perhaps, a watery grave breeds a renewed family. In Chaucer's story grace reconfigures the patriarchal family in a way that makes room for women's ethical action. With God firmly positioned as her sole source of strength, Custance has sufficient independence to reestablish human bonds. Earlier, the tale compares Custance to a doomed prisoner:

> Have ye nat seyn somtyme a pale face,
> Among a prees, of hym that hath be lad
> Toward his deeth, wher as hym gat no grace. (II.645–47)

Because Custance is filled with God's power—because she is a protected member of a providential family—she remains free from the patrilineal manipulations of men.

The Senator's answer to the query regarding Maurice's origins, "A mooder he hath, but fader hath he noon / That I of woot" (II.1020–21), suggests the continued irrelevance of earthly paternity. Equally, though, his encomium to Custance's perfection specifies the estranged conditions of her excellence:

Figure 8. The Empress stranded on a rock, preserved by the Virgin Mary. Frescoes at Eton College, fifteenth century, Historic England Archive, FF91_00229 (detail).

"But God woot," quod this senatour also,
"So vertuous a lyvere in my lyf
Ne saugh I nevere as she, ne herde of mo,
Of worldly wommen, mayde, ne of wyf.
I dar wel seyn hir hadde levere a knyf
Thurghout hir brest, than ben a womman wikke;
There is no man koude brynge hire to that prikke." (II.1023–29)

Her material virtue puts her out of any man's governance, but Custance's power is both derived from and directed toward others. To protect her son, Custance passes through the world unknown, living as an anonymous wanderer defended only by the virtues God's grace vitalizes. With her father, Custance assumes a deliberate obscurity, only revealing herself once her familial independence is secure.[102] Prostrating herself before the Emperor, Custance issues something of a challenge: if the ruler is once again to become her father, he must accept those things she has done without his guidance or consent.

Custance has been living beyond the Emperor's governance, but he must reconcile himself to her decisions. Though she begs for clemency, her powerful address recalls a pathetic history, one that simultaneously nullifies and restores the Emperor's authority:

"Fader," quod she, "youre yonge child Custance
Is now ful clene out of youre remembrance.
I am youre doghter Custance," quod she,
"That whilom ye han sent unto Surrye.
It am I, fader, that in the salte see
Was put allone and dampned for to dye.
Now goode fader, mercy I yow crye!
Sende me namoore unto noon hethenesse,
But thonketh my lord heere of his kyndenesse." (II.1105–13)

It is hard to imagine a statement that is more assertive *and* submissive at once. Custance reinscribes her past, erasing childish weakness to announce filial authority. She underscores her father's wrong, repudiating his control by recalling her sojourn to Syria as an endangered passage of rudderless drifting. Earlier, Custance praised God's protection, but when she confronts the Emperor, she characterizes the sea voyage as a death sentence. And, although she asks for her father's mercy, her request allows her to direct her father: he should never send her away again, but he should also be thankful that Custance's marital arrangements were successful.

The distance Custance establishes as a condition of her renewed familial immersion reveals what I would characterize as grace's inhuman character. Her material virtue does not depend on the Emperor's recognition, acceptance, or agreement. Crucially, it is not contractual. Rather, Custance's connections to others—including her husband, Alla, her son Maurice, and her father, the Emperor—depend on God alone. Although it separates her from networks of virtue that link human and divine communities, Custance's spiritual isolation is beneficial for its ability to release her from the social strictures of patriarchal control featured in late medieval romance as well as hagiography. Nonetheless, because Custance depends exclusively on God's power, what I am calling her autonomy is really an exhaustive form of reliance. And, to be sure, an alienating distance is lodged at the heart of Custance's relationship with God. There is no reciprocity between her and the divine; neither does God recognize her worth through the affordances of protection Christ provides. Medieval grace is fully nonrecognitive, to the extent that there is no accounting for the divine's dispensations. Late medieval thinkers including Duns Scotus, William of Ockham, and Gabriel Biel, insisted that the preeminence of divine will meant human actions—those that might be taken to signal ethical goods—did not merit salvation, and only counted as virtue because God chose to accept them as such.[103] God chooses those whom he favors, and when he bestows such grace, as Custance's narrative demonstrates, human effort merely affirms human weakness. Christ preserves Custance, and there is very explicitly nothing she can do to merit her treatment.

A Familiar Passivity

I rehearse the radically antisocial conditions of medieval grace theology to account for the conclusion of *The Man of Law's Tale*, which is outlandish in its very familiarity.[104] In her sturdy "you're welcome" moment, Custance opens then closes a crucial doorway to an expanded feminist ethics. When she confronts her father, Custance reveals and conceals women's power: she demonstrates her strength even as she reinstates the Emperor's authority. Through Custance's story, Chaucer valorizes a form of material virtue that gathers moral resources from outside the self. Even if a woman does not enact ethical change as a discrete exercise of individual agency, her excellence still may precipitate important shifts in the ethical life she shares with others. Despite Custance's ability to convert those whom she meets, and notwith-standing the spiritual friendship she achieves with Hermengyld, in the end she takes up a more limited form of social *and* moral autonomy. When Custance reintroduces herself to the Emperor, she points to Alla as if he is the source of her safety and legitimacy: "But thonketh my lord heere of his kyndenesse" (II.1113). Following their reunion, moreover, Alla's kingdom becomes the province of Custance's virtue:

> This kyng Alla, whan he his tyme say,
> With his Custance, his hooly wyf so sweete,
> To Engelond been they come the righte way,
> Wher as they lyve in joye and in quiete. (II.1128–31)

Through her submission, Custance's virtue becomes a territory protected by a benevolent masculine power. God might be the head of Custance's family, but Alla reproduces divine paternity in human society. I conclude this chap-ter by considering why Custance would reinsert herself within the very patri-archal structures her constancy challenges.

The major reason, I propose, is the alienation inherent to late medieval theorizations of grace. As the brief account above demonstrates, divine grace functions outside all networks of human control. Virgin martyrs, because they enjoy a special dispensation of divine grace, stand apart from society. Their gruesome deaths, moreover, affirm the inhuman character of grace, in the first place because they endure punishment that exceeds all imagined limits of mortal suffering.[105] Their grisly treatment, however, also discloses another of grace's inhuman aspects, one that sheds light on Custance's volun-tary reentry into familial life. Recipients of God's grace are afforded a distinc-tion so exceptional that in saints' lives they become an affront to their societies. To be sure, martyrs defy social and religious norms, facing down tyrants and performing public miracles. But their extreme punishments, which exceed political efficacy and outdo religious zeal, suggest that martyrs are made inhuman by the unique moral status that grace confers. On account of their relation to grace, martyrs threaten human society, whether it is pagan or Christian, tolerant or tyrannous.

For this reason, virgin martyrs are usually regarded as models for inspiration, not imitation. What happens, though, when grace becomes a central element of all Christian experience? Writing in the early fifth century, Augustine imagined grace as God's gift to a Christian population with a fragile hold on cultural legitimacy.[106] In the late fourteenth century, likewise, John Wyclif prioritized grace as part his push for religious reform.[107] Grace protects spiritual renegades; in a more troubling consequence, it also sets recipients apart from their less-favored neighbors. Grace was doctrinally crucial for nearly a millennium; yet, as grace gained prominence as the organizing principle for religious experience, its antisocial aspects became problematic. Social organizations—including family and polity—exert no claim over recipients of grace. They are spiritual as well as cultural aliens, whose special autonomy poses a direct threat to governmental and religious institutions. In Custance's case, her family is organized in relation to God alone. Nevertheless, even though she directs the conditions of these relations, she resubmits herself to familial norms. She does so, I suggest, because grace must be socialized in order to minimize the challenge it poses to communal formations. Custance is no martyr, but the alienating threat she poses is evident when Donegild contracts her death in Northumberland (Donegild calls her an "elf" and insists that her offspring is monstrous, II.745). There as elsewhere, Custance's status as "so strange a creature" (II.700) signals the radical distance that accompanies divine grace.

If grace is to become a more universal feature of spiritual experience, its recipients must successfully integrate themselves into their societies. No longer are they meant to be martyrs, whose spectacular sacrifice unravels or reweaves the social fabric; rather, those who enjoy God's grace are supposed to transform communal formations through their voluntary participation in those limiting structures. When Custance reimmerses herself in the family, this is because the family is reconstituted.[108] Indeed, by means of God's grace, patriarchy is remade but not discarded. At the close of Chaucer's *Man of Law's Tale*, the hierarchical family is renewed outside militarist institutions of masculinist aggression.[109] The Emperor's dominion over Rome is downplayed. As it is reported, Custance could be any holy pilgrim visiting the city:

To Rome is come this hooly creature,
And fyndeth hire freendes hoole and sounde;
Now is she scaped al hire aventure. (II.1149–51)

The Roman Church's involvement with her paternal reconciliation is also handled very lightly:

> In vertu and in hooly almus-dede
> They lyven alle, and never asonder wende;
> Til deeth departeth hem, this lyf they lede. (II.1156–58)

The emphasis of the tale's conclusion, as its redeployed nuptial language reveals, is the union between father and daughter that Christian grace enables.

Replaying the earlier scene of recognition, Custance returns to her father in a submissive reintegration sanctified by God:

> And whan that she hir fader hath yfounde,
> Doun on hir knees falleth she to grounde;
> Wepynge for tendrenesse in herte blithe
> She heryeth God an hundred thousand sithe. (II.1152–55)

Whether she yields to God or the father is irrelevant. In fact, blurring the distinction between heaven and earth is this encounter's very purpose. Here, God's grace is socially generative in ways that obscure the alienating dispensation of divine favor. To make grace social, in other words, is to emphasize the bond—not the gulf—between humanity and divinity. Those late medieval theologians identified with the *via moderna*, for instance, Gabriel Biel, whose Scotist and Occamist views influenced sixteenth-century reformist thinking, placed emphasis on humankind's *pactum* with God.[110] This covenant recognizes the preeminence of God's will, but also insists that God's righteousness and consistency guarantee that those who make an effort at practicing virtue will be rewarded with salvific grace. Although man can never "earn" virtue, God will honor man's efforts as a consequence of His eminent benevolence.

Through Custance's trials, Chaucer uncovers the radical social capacity of divine grace; nevertheless, he diminishes its unsettling impact by reconciling Custance with a reformist model of the patriarchal family. While Custance no longer has to suffer violence or uncertainty, her grace becomes social, to the extent that her reappearance expands the Emperor's lineage in a fashion that is far more efficacious than military conquest. By the end of *The Man of Law's Tale*, Custance occupies a secure position. Unlike the virgin martyrs, she does not dismantle the institutions that oppress her; instead, she remakes patriarchal imperialism to ensure her own safety and choice. Her fate is less gruesome than theirs, but the tale hardly provides a guide for the overthrow of masculinist exploitation. Even so, the tale's acknowledgment that women precipitate ethical change in circumstances they do not control offers a significant reappraisal of women's virtue. Indeed, Chaucer's Custance narrative complicates the idea that ethical agency comes exclusively from within; by so doing, *The Man of Law's Tale* disputes the notion that material virtue is always a performative accomplishment of the individual subject. Indeed, Custance does more than enact God's commands as a holy puppet. Rather, how she reacts to divine treatment—her response to the bestowal of divine grace—achieves important moral change in the tale. Earlier in this chapter, I sketched theologians' emphasis on divinity's preeminence in the dispensation and operation of grace. This is not to say, however, that human action had no moral value whatsoever. In particular, how the favored subject responded to grace remained central to formulating a theory that accommodated divine choice and human action.

Importantly, in her trials Custance manifests a continued effort to cooperate with God's providential workings. The struggle to conform to the designs of divinity is not just an internal process. Nor is it a superficial enactment. It issues spiritual demands, such as endurance and steadfastness, that aggregate into the embodied virtue of constancy. But it also yields social results, including a critique of imperial Christianity and a renovation of the patriarchal family. In crucial ways, then, Custance is similar to the virgin martyrs whose stories modeled expectations for women's excellence in the late Middle Ages. Because Chaucer's version of her story grapples with the individual's responses to grace, it also dovetails with many of the concerns that later conduct books address. With respect to the argument I elaborate across this book, the socialization of grace that occurs in *The Man of Law's Tale* is crucial for considering the potentially *positive* role conduct manuals play in the centuries following Chaucer's. I have argued that the prescriptive virtue found in behavioral guides suppresses women's ability to create their own moral lives. Yet conduct books need not be prescriptive; because they ultimately rely on women to put certain ethical ideals into practice, they can create space for women's material virtues. As premodern writings on grace reveal, virtues might derive from sources beyond the subject, but these powers amount to nothing if the subject does not enact them.

For this reason, a social ideal of grace is crucial to courtesy manuals and conduct books. As Jonathan Nicholls explains, human courtesy was said to provide a channel for divine grace, forging a connection between human and divine which, I maintain, enables women's ethical action.[111] Caxton undertakes his translation of *The Book of the Knight of the Tower*, he says more than once, "atte contemplacion of her good grace," viz., to recognize the model virtue of "that noble lady which hath brouȝt forth many noble & fayr douȝters which hath ben vertuously nourisshed & lerned."[112] Like Chaucer, writers and translators of conduct books imagine the powerful impact of women's grace on social relations. Women might be receptive to social ideals they did not construct; furthermore, they might rely on a notion of grace to enact the excellences extolled by their communities. The important difference, or the factor that makes such virtues material, is the ability for women to use their embodied experiences to bring such qualities to bear on everyday encounters. To take up such virtues in a fashion that renders them material, I should say now, requires deliberation, knowledge, and volition. Even if a woman depends on external powers for her virtues, she must take up such potentialities in a fashion that is decidedly active. Custance decides to surrender; she actively pursues dependence upon the divine. She knows what she is doing. Material virtue depends upon the body, but it also requires thought, as I shall detail.

In the next chapter, I shall address the ways that women's behavioral training allows them to wield the individual graces with which they are culturally endowed. By showing the dangers that accompany women's unthinking virtue—the harms that accrue when women do not direct their graces with intelligence—poets including Thomas Lodge and Edmund Spenser, create worlds where women's ethical excellence becomes something more lively and substantive than a masculine province of governance. This chapter continues to consider the ethical stature of daughters, particularly as the paternal production of their virtue is entangled within the plot structures of imperial romance. As I shall detail, later writers imagine grace as a socially empowering behavioral cultivation. This reformulation is evident in the fifteenth-century satirical poem, "Why I Can't Be a Nun," which features a daughter who petitions for divine grace in a fashion that affirms her receptivity and submission:

Lorde God, that alle vertu hast
. . . .
For thowgh my fadyr and alle my kyn
Forsake me thus in necessite,

Yyt I hope suche grace to wyn
That owre Lord Ihesu wolle resceyve me.[113]

The maiden's family would like her to join a nunnery, but she rejects the many corruptions of religious enclosure to follow the teachings of "Dame Experience." This poem affirms that women's virtue cannot be cultivated by others, or enclosed to protect its purity. Instead, as Lodge and Spenser also show in the following century, women's virtue requires the ethical discernment that embodied experience provides.

CHAPTER 4

Virtue's Knowledge in Lodge and Spenser

The rarer action is / In virtue than in vengeance.
—Prospero, *The Tempest*, V.i.27–28 (1616)

Oh I moste miserable! To what place shall I flie? To whom shall I
haue recourse? Of whom els, or in what place shall I from henceforth
aske succour, helpe, and comforte? Truely beeyng so poorely ap-
parelled as I am, and euill intreated bothe of gods and men; and in
this wise disdained and abandoned, euen almoste to my beyng cherished, or imbrased of none, it were farre better for me to bee a blocke,
then a goddesse.
—Virtue, *A pretie pithie Dialogue betwene Mercurie & Vertue* (1579)

In the concluding dialogue of Thomas Salter's *Mirrhor of Modestie* (1579), Vertue's despair prompts her to wish for an insentient passivity.[1] Yet, even in a
monitory treatise like Salter's, which tightly circumscribes women's conduct,
feminine passivity stands at odds with women's virtue. Because virtue is a species of action, as Shakespeare's Prospero acknowledges, a good woman cannot
be an inert "blocke." Rather, it takes a great deal of effort to enact the obedience, compliance, and submission that culturally counted as feminine passivity
in premodern England. What we see in the works of several sixteenth-century
poets, though, is a growing sense that these efforts, despite their putative social
advantages, are ethically objectionable. A number of authors begin to ask what
happens when a woman follows all the social prescriptions for feminine passivity as it was culturally recognized in Elizabethan England. In Thomas Lodge's

A Margarite of America (1596), called a "horror novella" for its gruesome departure from the restorative marital conclusions of traditional romance, the results are not pretty.[2]

With violence that is almost comically shocking, Lodge's romance recounts the frightful story of a stupid girl. Margarita is so naive, so sincere, and so *doomed*, it is something of a relief when the brutal Arsadachus runs her through with a rapier in response to her final profession of devotion. The greatest wonder is that Margarita lives as long as she does: indeed, we might marvel as she manages to travel to the court of Cusco disguised as a lowly shepherdess, accompanied only by her trusty maid, Fawnia.[3] All her efforts are directed at submission, yet, as I argue, Margarita indicts women's culturally cultivated passivity. Margarita meets favored standards for women's virtue as they are articulated in early modern behavioral discourse; nevertheless, Lodge suggests that she is a source of degeneracy, not excellence. Because she suffers from a dearth of ethical intelligence, in fact, Margarita's pliancy furthers the story's escalating violence. In Lodge, as elsewhere, virtue must be galvanized by knowledge; it cannot consist in bodily practices alone. Consequently, Lodge's romance challenges those prescriptive femininities that manage female materiality by denying women's capacities for moral discretion. An emphasis on virtue's knowledge does not devalue material virtue, however. It is true that material virtue, which includes the body's vulnerability in efforts to withstand the world's contingencies, is impossible in *both* the Old and the New World, according to Lodge. Yet Lodge's critique of *any* model of ethical excellence that evacuates moral discretion is crucial for elaborating a material virtue that includes mental capacities in an understanding of embodied ethical life.

Just because virtue is material does not mean it is simply or merely physical. Rather, Margarita's lack of moral knowledge reveals the dangers of a model of virtue founded on bodily comportment alone. With this chapter I mean to specify the ways in which the ethical excellence I have elaborated across this study makes room for women's moral knowledge. While thinking through the intellectual aspects of material virtue is critical to the larger argument of this book, Lodge's insistence on virtue's knowledge is also central to the ethical world-making project of Spenser's *Faerie Queene*. Critics have long acknowledged that Spenser devises an embodied model of ethical virtue.[4] In his brilliant recent study of the 1590 *Faerie Queene*, Joseph Campana extends this established precept to found a new ethics of masculinity: "What is at stake . . . is the question of whether poetry can or should contribute to the project of creating an invulnerable, heroic, rational, masculine citizen (resistant to compromising incitements of pain, pleasure, bodily sensation, and affect) on whom a nation might be founded. And if not, what should be the work of poetry if not to posit the fundamental vulnerability of the flesh as a new ground for ethics?"[5] This goes for the "gentleman or noble person," so famous from Spenser's "Letter to Ralegh."[6] But I suggest that it also pertains to women's ethical action. The good women who populate Faerieland are not just ideas; instead, they enact ethical values in a world where their virtues are lively, embodied, and material. As Campana observes, Spenser addresses matter's negative gendered associations, forging an ethics of vulnerability that remakes martial masculinity.[7] To do so, I will suggest, Spenser formulates a model of material virtue that acknowledges women's ethical intelligence.

Like Lodge, Spenser uses feminine endangerment to criticize masculine violence. But across Faerieland, ethical knowledge enables women to navigate the material contingencies of courtly society despite the fact that they do not control those social domains. This is not a martial form of female power, though Spenser imagines this possibility in his capacious world, too. Britomart can fend for herself, since she wears armor that represents, among other things, a legacy of feminine excellence enabling heroic autonomy.[8] Functioning as a counter to Lodge's critique, Spenser's *Faerie Queene* imagines material virtue as an embodied ability to manage physical vulnerability using ethical knowledge. It does so via a character who is constantly subject to abstraction, and relentlessly beset by materiality: Florimell, or "the fairest Dame aliue" (III.i.18.8). In thinking of beauty not just as an ethical concept, but also as an active, intellectual, and embodied virtue, Spenser confronts the prescriptive tradition that would reduce women's excellence to external codes of bodily conduct. Indeed, when beauty is doubled through False Florimell, Spenser insists upon the importance of women's ethical knowledge. The thing that distinguishes true and false beauty, in other words, is Florimell's moral discretion, which manifests itself through her physical suffering for Marinell.

For Spenser, women's virtue is a unified practice of body and mind, matter and spirit, intellect and substance. In fleeing from all male admirers in her quest to find Marinell, Florimell develops beauty as an embodied virtue, called "true" beauty in the Platonist tradition.[9] The form of true beauty Spenser elaborates does not make virtuous women into helpless icons, who are moved about like playing pieces in a divinely ordained game of providential grace. Instead, Florimell's struggles bespeak the need for women's ethical intelligence in a world riven by physical contingency. Yet grace remains central to Florimell's beauty. As a social reflection of ordered divinity, grace coordinates Florimell's mental and physical capacities, ultimately defending against suspicions of beauty's deceptive duality. Through grace, Florimell directs her own desires: she loves Marinell, and, like other heroic characters in the poem, she withstands a series of physical challenges to demonstrate her amorous commitment. To a degree that differentiates her from Spenser's knights, Florimell's physical vulnerability leaves her continuously open to the vissicitudes of worldly change. In fact, as the creation of False Florimell affirms, materializing beauty as a living, thinking virtue will never completely dispel the dangers that threaten Florimell across Faerieland. At the end of the day, Florimell's ability to avoid such perils demonstrates the integration of knowledge and endurance that characterizes Spenser's formulation of material virtue.

Dumb Virtue

It seems almost unfair, or potentially even mean-spirited, to linger too long over Margarita's lack of ethical intelligence in Lodge's colonial romance. Yet, before turning to Spenser, it is important to compass the powerful critique of early modern femininity that *A Margarite* issues. Like Una from Spenser's *Faerie Queene*, Margarita subdues violence in others. For instance, when Margarita encounters a vicious lion, who devours her maid Fawnia because "she had tasted too much of fleshly love" (186), the wild beast is immediately tamed, licking Margarita's hands and putting his head in her lap as a gesture of deference. Given the prominence of this motif in Spenser's *Faerie Queene*, Lodge links his Margarita to Spenser's Una. She is a rare gem of femininity, hailed for her fidelity, chastity, and simplicity: "Ah, Margarita, so faire, as none so faire, more vertuous then vertue her selfe . . . being the mirror of beauty, and even the miracle of constancie" (151). She exemplifies the feminized ideal of passive virtue, yet the qualities that sustain Margarita ultimately lead to her destruction. Pitted against Arsadachus's thoroughly dissembled virtues, Margarita never stands a chance. Indeed, in this old-world-meets-new-world debacle, Lodge explores shifting ethical systems. Arsadachus is thought by many to be modeled directly on the "new" virtues articulated by Machiavelli and Castiglione, while Margarita is visibly aligned with an older pearl-cult of values newly revived for the Elizabethan court.[10] What does it mean that new slaughters old in this arena of vice, not virtue?

In accordance with those readings that look to Lodge's disastrous experiences with English imperialism as a survivor of Thomas Cavendish's doomed second voyage to South America, including his bitter disenchantment with colonial exploration recorded in the dedicatory epistles to *A Margarite* itself, the New World is imagined as a dystopian territory, where an unbroken tradition of European virtue is wantonly exploited and brutally destroyed.[11] As heir to the Incan kingdom of Cusco, Arsadachus's failed union with Margarita, only daughter of the European Emperor of Musco, affirms a fundamental ethical incompatibility between worlds.[12] Lodge's New World is a racialized territory that grows corruption, but Margarita abets violence in Cusco. Indeed, Margarita is virtuous to a fault, so that she never questions her betrothed, even when he enlists her in a conspiracy that precipitates an honest man's death. Her love for Arsadachus, which he renounces in the very poems he sends to her, prevents her from perceiving his many outrages. She believes love is a condition of the eye, yet as a consequence, she is morally blind:

> Margarita (poore princesse) thinking all that golde which glistered; the stone pretious, by reason of his faire foile; the water shallowe, by reason of his milde silence, trusted so long, until she perished in her trust, wholy ignorant that love is like the sea-starre, which whatsoever it toucheth it burneth: for knowing the resolution of her father, the conclusion of her nobilitie, she beganne to straine her thoughts to the highest reach, fancying every motion, wincke, becke, and action of the Cuscan Prince, in such sort as that (assisted by the vertuous, constant, and unspotted simplicitie of her nature) she seemed not to suspect whatever she saw, nor to count it wrong, however shee endured. (72–73)

She remains loyal to the end, but Margarita's lack of ethical distinction means that her virtue is empty, if not debased.

Through Margarita's destruction, Lodge's romance affirms that virtue is not passive. Furthermore, it involves more than purity, truth, or love. And, finally, it requires more than power, agency, or independence. Virtue necessitates ethical intelligence, a faculty of moral discernment that distinguishes one's excellences as one's own. This intelligence is not abstract, ethereal, or theoretical; it is material, enabling a fully embodied ethical habitus. As I shall detail, this intelligence is connected to the social power of grace, or the coordinated exercise of body and mind, acumen and beauty. The moral insight so disastrously absent in Lodge's Margarita criticizes the femininity favored in prescriptive discourse for women, as Juan Luis Vives's influential advice affirms: "It becometh nat a mayde to talke / where her father and mother be in communication / about her maryage: but to leaue all that care and charge holly unto them: whiche loue her as well as her selfe dothe. And lette her thynke that her father and mother / wyll prouide no lesse diligently for her / than she wolde for herselfe: but moche better / by the reason they haue more experience & wysedome."[13] In advisory articulations of idealized femininity, women must pretend that they do not have a say over their virtues as a way of displaying those very qualities. Yet, by asking women to act like they do not have the knowledge to direct their conduct toward different ethical goods, monitory discourse erases women's virtue exactly where it should garner respect.

Margarita is a woman who cannot defend herself, but this helpless passivity is an undesirable condition in Lodge. At the moment of her death, after she has been gored, and after she knows Arsadachus has split and disemboweled his mistress, torn the unfortunate beloved's heart with his teeth, and dashed out the brains of his bastard son, "the poore princesse even when death beganne to arrest her, pursued him" (200). Margarita's lack of self-knowledge, particularly her self-gratifying fantasy of Arsadachus's virtue, is fatally dangerous. Writers of advice texts for women recognized the peril of predatory men, but in reaction, many simply advised greater isolation for the unknowing innocent: "Principally bycause as ofte as a mayde goth forth amonge people / so often she cometh in iugement and extreme perell of her beautie / honeste / demureness / witte, shamfastnes / and vertue."[14] In the 1598 English translation of Giovanni Michele Bruto's treatise, *The Necessarie, Fit & Convenient Education of a Young Gentlewoman*, seclusion is justified with reference to reductive ethical assumptions about feminine character: "A wise father will neuer take example, nor assure himselfe that a / young gentlewoman *by nature weake & feeble*, will shew themselues audacious in publicke Theaters & common spectacles, to dispute for the glorie and pre-nemenence of learning."[15] Salter compares daughters to "thynges that are reasonlesse," specifically plants, that "by wantyng the continuall care and diligence, that is necessarie for them, are seen to lacke their naturall force and vertue, and finallie become wilde."[16]

Margarita's exaggerated innocence cautions against just this sort of behavioral overtraining, because foolhardiness as comprehensive as hers can only be achieved as the result of deliberate cultivation. Moreover, as Lodge's romance makes explicit, the social training that stunts Margarita's ethical judgment is drawn directly from a colonialist register. In a still-influential argument, Peter Stallybrass recognizes how early modern texts with little connection to imperial expansion are invested in patriarchal fantasies of the female body: "Woman's body could be both symbolic map of the 'civilized' and the dangerous terrain that had to be colonized."[17] With Lodge, in what was possibly the first English text written *in* the New World, possessive desire culminates in a quivering heap of bloody violence.[18] Not only does Margarita's misguided love lead her to abandon her sheltered existence, but her unwavering virtues also render her a defenseless victim in this brave new world. On the one hand, therefore, *A Margarite* counters skepticism regarding women's virtue—Margarita proves that women who appear to be chaste, silent, and obedient are genuine in those manifestations—but this grim romance also affirms the shallow value of these qualities. Yet in Lodge, as in conduct books, this pristine purity is represented as a product of regulatory cultivation. With the gory pileup that concludes *A Margarite of America*, colonial violence and masculine regulation are equated. As this colonial romance insists, a woman's virtue can be true yet empty.

In a striking devaluation, Margarita enacts prescriptive femininity, but she is helpless to navigate the dangerous moral terrain of Lodge's romance.[19] To focus only on bodily discipline is to deny that the body needs thought to function. It is to suggest that weaker bodies must be directed by fitter minds—making women's bodies into territories controlled, cultivated, and patrolled by men. To figure territory using a feminized body, or so the habits of early modern cartographers would indicate, is to conquer that body through the process of mapping itself. This practice can suggest the body's regal impenetrability or its sensual permeability (see figs. 9 and 10). The most shocking feature of Walter Ralegh's famous solicitation near the close of *The discoverie of Guiana* (1595) is his explicit acknowledgment that the unspoiled innocence of feminized terrain becomes available for masculine conquest: "To conclude, Guiana is a Countrey that hath yet her Maydenhead, neuer sackt, turned, nor wrought, the face of the earth hath not beene torne, nor the vertue and salt of the soyle spent."[20] Perhaps due to his own disillusionment with colonial expansion, Lodge focuses unflattering attention on men's

FIGURE 9. Europe depicted as a virgin queen, Heinrich Bunting, *Europa Prima
Pars Terrae In Forma Virginis* (1582). Wikimedia commons,
Bunting, *Europa*, 1582.

territorial governance of feminized bodies. *A Margarite* directly challenges
a recurrently articulated cultural assumption, that masculine regulation is
beneficial to women on account of their vulnerability. Geoffrey Fenton's
translation of Jean Talpin insists that a virtuous woman cannot get along on
her own since she is "a brickle glasse, which, as if you touch unto but with
your least finger, it is enough to make it fall and breake."[21] In forwarding his
argument for women's education, Richard Mulcaster also appeals to their
fragility: "And therefore [women are] charilie to be cared for, bearing a iewell
of such worth, in a vessell of such weaknesse."[22] Yet, as colonialist discourse
emphasizes, feminine vulnerability does not prompt masculine benevolence.
Through Margarita's unthinking virtue, Lodge uncovers not a benign form
of governance that protects women, but a species of predatory violence that
subtends their social conditioning.

FIGURE 10. America depicted as a sensual, sexually available woman. Jan van
der Straet (artist), Théodore Galle (engraver), "America," ca. 1580. New York
Public Library Digital Collections.

Knowing Virtue

The anticolonial critique structuring *A Margarite of America* uncovers the
importance of ethical knowledge to material virtue. This dimension of material virtue becomes thinkable, I contend, during the reign of a powerful
female sovereign. With the accession of Elizabeth I, material virtue becomes
an embodied ethics that acknowledges women's intelligence. Having a
learned, savvy woman on the throne provided a material model of thinking
excellence. For some, of course, this was no virtue. As a number of scholars
have demonstrated, Elizabeth I's expansive, frequently eroticized authority is
a prolific yet productive source of gendered anxiety for a host of courtier-
poets.[23] But rather than see the "virgin queen's" sovereignty only in sexualized
terms, as producing the "threat of dishonorable effeminization," in Louis

Montrose's words, I suggest that we view the expressed admiration of those seeking favor outside an eroticized domain.[24] Elizabeth I also renders virtue a practice of intelligence; indeed, she makes virtue matter because of her ability to evince the lively intellect required of moral excellence. Accordingly, when Theodor Agrippa d'Aubigne writes a letter to his daughters advising them on appropriate femininity, Elizabeth I furnishes a living model of exquisite learning and exemplary prudence: "She replied in one day to eight ambassadors in the languages appropriate to them. But the most praiseworthy part of this soul blessed of God has been the practice of her theory, for she has so well put to use her *Ethics* and *Politics* that she has held the ship of her kingdom steady for forty years in the midst of a very troubled sea and in a tempestuous age."[25] As something of an enacted Aristotle, Elizabeth I enlivens a virtuous *habitus* that vests women with more than eroticized powers.

For Edmund Spenser, seeking to instruct readers in "vertuous and gentle discipline" (LR), Elizabeth I's intellectual power is morally generative.[26] Within *The Faerie Queene*, the singularity of the female sovereign's virtue does not diminish its value as a general ideal.[27] Rather, by means of "mirrours more then one" (III.proem.5.6), excellence multiplies, enabling Gloriana to unify an expansive kingdom where virtue takes on multiple dimensions, connecting physical, mental, and spiritual aspects. In its address to Elizabeth I, Spenser's poem presents its model of representation as privative, unable to capture the queen's manifold virtues.[28] Recalling the legendary painter Zeuxis, who combined isolated features from living women to suggest Helen's unworldly beauty, Spenser deploys a menagerie of virtuous women to indicate a grander totality of feminine excellence:

> But liuing art may not least part expresse,
> Nor life-resembling pencil it can paint,
> All were it *Zeuxis* or *Praxiteles*:
> His daedale hand would faile, and greatly faint,
> And her perfections with his error taint.
> Ne Poets wit, that passeth Painter farre
> In picturing the parts of beautie daint,
> So hard a workmanship auenture darre,
> For fear through want of words her excellence to marre.
> (III.proem.2.1–9).

Each reflection is partial from the queen's encompassed perspective, yet from any other point of view, the quantity of virtue's exemplars is materially increased. For a general audience, then, the proem to Book III emphasizes the multiplicity of excellence contained within "my Soueraines brest, / And form'd so liuely in each perfect part" (III.proem.1.5–6).

This plenitude works to materialize virtue in a specific fashion. When the proem directs itself to ladies, it must confront the tension between Elizabeth I's realized and idealized virtue. Because Elizabeth I perfectly exemplifies chastity, she is a model for women:

> That to all Ladies, which haue it profest,
> Need but behold the portraict of her hart,
> If pourtrayed it might be by any liuing art. (III.proem.1.7–9)

The queen's perfection frustrates representation.[29] Yet, rather than exhausting figural resources, the queen's presence engenders abundance in *others*. She is the seat of virtue's multitude, and that status is not up for grabs in Spenser's poem: instead, her living example serves as a guarantor for other women's excellence. To totalize the queen's virtue without risking its perfection, then, is to proliferate examples of virtuous women. We should not, therefore, treat Spenser's female worthies as imperfect copies, each of whom directs scrutiny, possibly skepticism, to the values identified with Elizabeth I. Rather, with the backing of a lauded queen, whose invisibility affirms her impassibility, Spenser sets about the task of fashioning a habitable model of material virtue for other women.

As Britomart's quest affirms, moreover, there is more to virtue than its outward aspects. Were chastity a practice of the body alone, Britomart's struggle would be resolved before she sets forth. Her ability to fell all foes is beset by a more unwieldy series of challenges to her chief virtue.[30] In a move that recalls Augustine's famous distinction, Spenser treats chastity as an integrated virtue of mind and body.[31] From rescuing Amoret, to fighting Radigund, Britomart must develop chastity to include mental as well as physical excellence. Her flourishing ultimately relies on the development of chastity as an intelligent virtue. Thus, with its female knight, taken together with its invisible queen, *The Faerie Queene* addresses Lodge's critique of feminine virtue, investing women's excellence with mental acuity in a fashion that prevents the suffering and degradation that befalls the titular heroine of *A Margarite of America*. This is not to say that female endangerment is absent throughout Spenser's poem. By way of those wandering, roving women scattered throughout Faerieland, Spenser's poem navigates the cultural fragilities of women's many virtues. Florimell, often thought of as true beauty in Spenser's Neoplatonic poetic framework, captures the dangers that threaten those animate worthies who must make their way in a hostile world. As I will argue in the remainder of this chapter, her doubled narrative shows why women's ethical action must be galvanized by an embodied intelligence.

True Beauty

It is one thing to elevate the queen by lauding her "true glorious type" (I.proem.4.7). It is quite another to align women with true beauty as a means to elaborate their material virtue. Although feminine beauty is frequently said to reflect the "Maiesty of the creator," as *The excellency of good women* claims, it is also vulnerable by definition, as Barnabe Rich goes on to acknowledge.[32] This is because beauty can always be doubled—its inside and outside can be divided—frequently as preparation for reducing its quality to an external manifestation. In Thomas Tuke's diatribe against cosmetics, for instance, beauty is confined to the surface, thereby distancing it from divine grace: "beware lest this borrowed grace bring yee not into disgrace both with God and his children, and that the counterfetting of forme doe not deforme you."[33] Tuke's speakers assume women's beauty is without interiority, or that superficial beauty defines any accompanying inwardness:

> SHeis a creature, that had need to be twice defined; for she is not that she seemes. And though shee bee the creature of God, as she is a woman, yet is she her owne creatrisse, as a picture. Indeed a plaine woman is but halfe a painted woman, who is both a substantiue and an adiec|tiue, and yet not of the neuter gender: but a feminine as well consorting with a masculiue, as Iuie with an Ash. She loues grace so well, that she will rather die, then lacke it. There is no truth with her to fauour, no blessing to beautie, no conscience to contentment. A good face is her god: and her cheeke well died, is the idoll, she doth so much adore. Too much loue of beau|tie, hath wrought her to loue painting: and her loue of painting hath transformed her into a picture.[34]

Antifeminist satire had long condemned women's artifice as a pleasing cover meant to hide latent corruption; Spenser utilizes this fearful visuality with his representation of Duessa in Book I. Notwithstanding negative treatments, feminine beauty also achieves otherworldly greatness in early modern writings on account of its associations with exalted grace. Spenser is equally invested in this aesthetic connection, describing Una's "angels face / [Which] As the great eye of heauen shyned bright, / And made a sunshine in the shadie place; / Did neuer mortall eye behold such heauenly grace" (I.iii.4.6–9).

Beauty is rendered an enlivened, embodied virtue by its association with grace in *The Faerie Queene*. As Spenser acknowledges, grace has a coextensive resonance in the early modern period, revealing excellence between body and mind in a Christian Platonist tradition.[35] Related to beauty, insofar as it marks a symmetrical arrangement of proportional qualities, grace brings all traits into alignment even in the most secular articulations. Ruth Kelso paraphrases Neoplatonist thinker Francesco India thus: "[Grace is] a certain external splendor of reason and a certain becoming nimbleness in actions, which are born of the good disposition of the body and mind together, and which signifies perfect beauty."[36] For many writers, the social and spiritual capacities of grace are intertwined as a superlative form of beauty: for instance, in William Averell's *Dyall for dainty darlings* (1584), the ideal woman prays for grace, and is subsequently extolled as "gouerned by grace" in her everyday comportment.[37] To emphasize the queen's status as God's vehicle of ordained action, Thomas Bentley's *Monument of matrones* includes descriptions of Elizabeth I as "fairest a|mong women; most full of beautie and maiestie."[38] When he hails Elizabeth as "Mirrour of grace and Maiestie diuine" (I.proem.iv.2), Spenser presents feminized beauty as a manifestation of divine grace embodied in the sovereign.

A lytell treatyse of the beaute of women (1525) extends this empowering idealism to women more generally: "beaute with bonte assembled in a place / Gyue demonstrance of an especyall grace."[39] Vives prefaces his discussion of beauty with a catalog of women's animate virtues:

> I suppose it be shewed playnly inough / y^t chastite is as the quene of vertues in a woman / and that .ij. inseparable companyons euer folowe hit / and that of shamefastnes commeth sobrenes / of whiche .ij. commeth all the other sorte of vertues longyng vnto wome~, demurenes / measure / frugalite / scarsite / diligence in house / cure of deuotion / mekenes / . . . Beholde the image of honestie drawen in picture / whiche is so goodly & so excellent of beautie / that if

hit coulde be sene with oure corporalle eies / as Plato sayth in the
boke called phedo / hit wolde take folkes wonderously with the loue
of it selfe. Nor no beautie dothe so enamour our eies / and taketh
and holdeth / as honestie shulde bothe take and lede with her / if
she were opened and she wedde vnto vs.[40]

Even so, because beauty and grace are mutually entailed, and because these
conditions are not identical, doubleness continues to trouble beauty's ethical
status. With the thread of the two Florimells, Spenser draws out the ethical
implications of beauty's inner and outer dimensions.[41]

Instead of diminishing the moral status of women's beauty, Florimell's
doubled ordeal shows that beauty has intelligence, which might stand outside
the aggrandizing designs of interested beholders. This is despite the fact that
Florimell's flight has traditionally been regarded with critical skepticism.
That she runs from all pursuers, Arthur in particular, is problematic for many
of the poem's readers.[42] Had she stopped running, so the story goes, the
difference between the purposes of her pursuers—between the gallant Arthur
and the frenzied Forester—would have become manifest.[43] Her inability to
distinguish between men, A. C. Hamilton avers, affirms her status as physical
beauty, which other scholars have taken to be unworthy of Britomart's lofty,
heterosexual interests ("[She] Ne reckt of Ladies Loue" [III.i.19.3]).[44] Indeed,
Britomart's indifference encourages critical disrespect, since "[Britomart]
Would not so lightly follow beauties chace" (III.i.19.2).[45] Though her initial
appearance is dazzling, "All as a blazing starre" (III.i.16.5), Florimell is often
regarded as little more than a superficial manifestation: beauty's worldly
shade. My argument largely sidesteps this critical debate, since beauty in a
Platonized tradition is regarded as a test to its viewers. As Kenneth Borris
remarks, "beauty in general affects its perceiver largely in accord with what
she or he brings to that vision."[46] I call attention to Florimell's lack of critical
stature because it is her presumed scarcity of intelligence that founds these
belittling assessments. Ethical intelligence has long been denied to Florimell.
Yet, in running Florimell only appears to lack reason. Florimell loves
Marinell, but scholars more frequently judge Florimell according to the
regard or disregard of those who behold her beauty.

This tendency is an interpretive shortcoming, I submit, because it
ignores beauty's autonomy in Platonist theorizations.[47] If beauty is elusive,
this might have precious little to do with her beholders. In accordance with
Platonist thought, Spenser's beauty remains independent from those who

view her.[48] Furthermore, as part of the project to vest women with a virtue that connects excellence of mind and body, *The Faerie Queene* endows Florimell with autonomous desires, which she refuses to surrender no matter who is breathing down her neck. This is not a sign of Spenser's anti-Neoplatonism, as Jerome S. Dees and Patrick Cheney suggest. Instead, I suggest that interpretations of Florimell are frequently not Platonist *enough*: to privilege beauty's beholders they ignore beauty's ethical intelligence. Platonized beauty has the power to disturb, revise, or refine ethical commonplaces. Accordingly, Spenser's Florimell affirms beauty's ability to take us outside ourselves, beyond what Iris Murdoch describes in *The Sovereignty of Good* as "an anxious, usually self-preoccupied, often falsifying *veil* which partially conceals the world."[49] The process of encountering beauty, Elaine Scarry argues in *On Beauty and Being Just*, almost inevitably enlightens us to the experience of being wrong, for we nearly always misperceive our relation to beauty on account of narcissistic fantasies.[50] This misprision is central to Spenser's account, since every man who sees Florimell regards her only in relation to gratifying fictions of possession. Through Florimell's suffering, the violent fantasies of masculine desire are exposed to foundational critique. More importantly, through Florimell's love for Marinell, Spenser imagines an embodied form of beauty, one that valorizes women's ethical agency, intelligence, and independence.

Heroic Reflections

The independent intelligence of Platonized beauty is not immediately perceptible. Rather, in a host of early modern writings, the reflective capacities of feminine beauty are commandeered to establish masculine splendor.[51] As Stephen Greenblatt has reaffirmed, in many early modern representations, beauty's facial featurelessness emphasizes abstract qualities of radiance, symmetry, and harmony.[52] This supposed blankness enables masculine gratification. Because they are presumed to organize feminine existence, men are positioned as feminine beauty's originating power. In Baldassare Castiglione's *Courtyer* (trans. Hoby, 1561), Guiliano de Medici remarks on the project of fashioning the ideal lady that will occupy the participants: "I shall speake of this exellent woman, as I woulde haue her. And whan I haue facioned her after my minde, and can afterwarde gete none other, I will take her as mine owne, after the example of Pigmalion."[53] If the Platonism of Castiglione's guide insists that "beautie is alwayes good," it also treats women's beauty as a quality that reflects and inspires men's performances of an elevated masculinity.[54] More pointedly, Edmund Tilney's marital debate, *The Flower of Friendship* (1571), defines a woman's gender position as narrowly reflective: "hir husba~d, whose face must be hir dayly looking glasse, wherein she ought to be alwais prying, to sée when he is mery, when sad, when content, and when discontent, wherto she must alwais frame hir own countenance."[55] These treatments use the Platonized tradition of beauty to make women into mirrors of masculine desire.

The blankness, even vacancy, required to sustain this asymmetry derives from a vision of Platonized beauty distorted to enforce masculine supremacy. Marsilio Ficino, whose commentaries and translations influenced a host of sixteenth-century Platonists, if not Spenser himself, sees beauty as "nothing other than the splendour of the highest good, shining in those things perceived by the eyes, ears, and mind."[56] Elsewhere, he speaks of beauty's ability to move others, but this description renders beauty inert, a luminous ornament to be collected by active contemplation.[57] Florimell's initial appearance is in keeping with this objective idealization. When she whizzes through the narrative scene, her features index a universalized feminine perfection:

> All suddenly out of the thickest brush
> Vpon a milk-white Palfrey all alone,
> A goodly Ladie did foreby them rush,
> Whose face did seeme as cleare as Christall stone,
> And eke through feare as white as whales bone:
> Her garments were wrought of beaten gold,
> And all her steed with tinsell trappings shone
> Which fled so fast, that nothing mote him hold,
> And scare them leasure gaue, her passing to behold. (III.i.15).

We might see why Florimell's onlookers confuse her for a figure whose immutable beauty provides an idealized site for masculine achievement. Her appearance is impressive, "At sight whereof the people stand aghast" (III.i.16.7), because she gratifies the fantasy that feminine beauty is a static mirror for masculine worth.

Vulnerable and afraid, Florimell looks like the fragile feminine ideal, a perfected woman who needs to be protected by a noble man's martial acts.

Sheila Cavanaugh recognizes the contradiction inherent in this form of masculine desire, which allows "women to be held up as icons needing protection, even though they are endangered by the same knights."[58] To return to the *Courtyer*, there Cesare Gonzaga relates masculine excellence to idealized femininity: "Do you not see that of all comelye exercises and whiche delite the worlde, the cause is to be referred to no earthlye thynge, but to women?"[59] Accordingly, Marie Buncombe points to Florimell's similarity to Castiglione's ideal lady to account for her harried fragility.[60] Castiglione expects Platonism to be actionable, insofar as he expects women to be fashioned according to immutable ideals of beauty, which are organized to reflect masculine excellence. As a consequence, there is no room for beauty's independence, much less intelligence. In the context of this Platonized tradition, then, it makes sense that Arthur and Guyon see Florimell as "Most goodly meede," since whoever saves "the fairest Dame aliue" will establish his superlative quality in Faerieland (III.i.18.8). What the knights who chase Florimell do not know is that the beautiful maiden has already dedicated herself to another. When Florimell hears that Marinell has been injured in his flight with the disguised Britomart, she leaves Gloriana's court in order to aid the knight she loves.

Florimell is not a static object of masculine fascination; rather, with her animated excellence, her quest reveals beauty's trials in a world consumed with superficial markers of women's virtue. Florimell does not get far in her quest to find her beloved before she becomes quarry for the predatory masculine gaze. She makes no distinction between true and false intentions, leveling masculine desire in a way that has been something of a challenge for those seeking to reconcile her response to a consolidated chivalric ideology. Lauren Silberman's insightful reading of the poem's visual erotics focuses attention on the aggression latent even in Arthur's pursuit.[61] Florimell's beauty reminds Arthur of Gloriana's virtue, and it is the exchange fantasy, "Oft did he wish, that Lady faire mote bee / His Faery Queene . . . Or that his Faery Queene were such, as shee," that causes him to suffer "sad sorrow, and disdaine / Of his hard hap, did vexe his noble brest" (III.iv.54.6–8, 2–3). Arthur wishes Gloriana were Florimell, or that Florimell were Gloriana. If beauty is a featureless void, a perfect emptiness that reflects the desires of its beholder, then beautiful women are potentially interchangeable in a visual economy of masculine desire. Florimell's flight undermines this fantasy, in the first instance by stripping away the distinction between true and false forms of masculine pursuit. More crucially, Florimell disrupts this fantasy of feminine exchangeability by pursuing her own desire, by following her *own quest*.

The idea that Florimell might have her own wants, which might exist independently from masculine desire, is apparently unfathomable, and not just to Arthur. Every man who sees her reacts according to form. Arthur's experience remains the exemplary ideal, since his response to Florimell is the most elevated version of a model of masculine desire based on feminine reflection, which necessarily entails physical possession. Spenser introduces women's powers of discretion into this economy of desire, beauty, and excellence, however, as the dwarf explains when he characterizes the kind of reward Arthur should expect for his service to Florimell:

So may ye gaine to you full great renowme,
Of all good Ladies through the world so wide,
And haply in her hart find the highest rowme,
Of whom ye seek to be most magnifide:
At least eternall meed shall you abide. (III.v.11.1–5)

He forecloses the possibility of physical reward by telling Arthur that aid to Florimell might elevate his place in Gloriana's affections, for he would be known among all virtuous ladies as a worthy knight. Arthur would be gratified, but the generative source of his excellence would not be his own self-extolling fantasies.

A more universal set of principles, which beautiful women recognize outside the desires of great men, secures the "eternal meed" his deeds will garner. This is because the good ladies of Faerieland are not flat mirrors of masculine desire. Instead, they hew to a more elevated standard of excellence, which even the poem's most idealized knight, Arthur, must be reminded to exemplify. The poem's code of values is heroic and martial, but idealized women play a constitutive role in ordering the embodied virtues of this fanta-sized domain. Beauty, like so many other sources of good in *The Faerie Queene*, is an active quality, whose material power surpasses all heroic fantasies of aggression or possession. By acknowledging beauty's agency, Faerieland's landscape adjusts the masculine perspective: just as the frenzied Forester mistakes his relation to Florimell's radiance, the befuddled Arthur misperceives his connection to beauty's splendor. These moments of misrecognition recur throughout the Florimells thread, but through them Spenser does not just critique martial masculinity, he also makes room for women's ethical intelligence.

Beauty's Desire

Beauty's stature is not a given in Spenser's *Faerie Queene*. This virtue must achieve coherence as the result of a prolonged, concrete struggle. As Florimell's ordeal affirms, even if an excellence is afforded theoretical independence, its embodied performance is hardly guaranteed. By insisting on virtuous femininity's dependence, *The Instruction of a Christen Woman* demonstrates just how far women have to go if their beauty is to confer strength: "For nothing is more tender / than is the fame and estimation of women / nor nothynge more in daunger of wronge: in so moche that hit hath be sayde / and nat without a cause / to hange by a copwebbe."[62] Florimell's beauty is not a settled virtue before she sets out; rather, she earns this virtue through her embodied efforts. Like other heroic characters, Florimell has to accrue the ethical knowledge that will allow her to achieve her virtue, as well as her desire. Through Florimell's flight, Spenser suggests that beauty is an intellectual and physical endowment.

In the case of Florimell, however, her need of ethical intelligence is frequently treated as a fault. Readers often observe the fact that she lacks the power to guide herself.[63] In the first instance, she is drawn to "A little cottage, built of stickes and reedes" (III.vii.6.2), but in truth Florimell lands herself at the hovel of a crafty witch and her adoring yet boorish son. For some, Florimell's inability to perceive danger in this context, taken together with her earlier flight from Arthur, validates pronouncements against women's ethical discernment in early modern discourse.[64] To take Florimell as a paragon of women's virtues, by this logic, is to designate the weakness of such qualities outside a rarefied theoretical domain. She cannot take care of herself, because she does not have the judgment to differentiate between good and bad (men). It is true that Florimell cannot distinguish between various perils, but instead of casting this naivete as a fault, Spenser represents feminine beauty's struggle to gain independent moral knowledge. Her struggle, not coincidentally, critiques early modern social expectations for women's passivity. If beauty's virtue is fragile, if its exemplar is trusting and gullible, this ethical impoverishment derives directly from the social practices that make women dependent on men for protection.

Not only are women trained to be helpless, but men retain the cultural prerogative to exploit their beauty for personal gratification. Beauty's trials have nothing to do with Florimell's determination, constancy, or resolve. Nor do they have much to do with her initiation, except as her growing cultural knowledge might deepen the moral significance of her enacted commitments. Her experience has the potential to ruin beauty, of course. Martha Nussbaum, discussing the noble death of Polyxena in Euripides's *Hecuba*, makes a startling claim about the inverse relation between experience and virtue: "In the tragedies of Euripides it frequently seems that the good die young. This, however, is not the result of special divine malevolence. It is because if they had not died young they would in all likelihood not have remained good. To live on is to make contact in some way at some time with the possibility of betrayal. . . . But the encounter with betrayal brings a risk of defilement: the risk of ceasing to look at the world with the child's free and generous looks; of ceasing, in the Euripidean way, to be good."[65] With Florimell's flight, Spenser details beauty's experience of betrayal. She gains knowledge of the ethical shortcomings of her environment, since, as Florimell's riven trial demonstrates, the system of values that would justify women's submission with a promise of masculine protection is evacuated by men's practices. This experience—her experiential knowledge of masculine aggression—does not corrupt her virtue. On the contrary, that Florimell survives her suffering without surrendering her virtue is a testament to women's excellence in a world continuously beset by violent contingency.

Although Florimell knows and seeks her desire (she loves Marinell), she must survive a long ordeal before others recognize this stubborn verity. If beauty inspires love, as philosophical accounts affirm, it also prompts idolatry, violation, and destruction.[66] These latter elements, Spenser demonstrates, define feminine beauty in terms of masculine gratification. Notwithstanding worth, intention, or action, beauty's grace—its culturally mandated favor— attaches Florimell to the men who admire her. It quickly becomes clear, however, that some forms of adoration should be beneath beauty's notice. The witch's son is too abashed (and too thick) to articulate his longing, so he conducts his courtship by means of proffered tokens:

> Oft from the forrest wildings he did bring,
> Whose sides empurpled were with smiling red,
> And oft young birds, which he had taught to sing
> His mistresse prayses, sweetly caroled,
> Girlonds of flowres sometimes for her faire hed
> He fine would dight; sometimes the squirell wild
> He brought to her in bands, as conquered
> To be her thrall, his fellow seruant vild;

All which, she of him tooke with countenance meeke and mild.
    (III.vii.17)

Despite the absurdities of his offerings, Florimell is beholden to her devotee.
When she flees, she faces violence: the witch seeks to avenge her son's pain
by sending the spotted beast, "That feeds on womens flesh, as others feede
on gras" to devour her (III.vii.22.9). The witch's instructions reveal Florimell's trespass against the boorish son's supplications, for she tells the beast
it might "deuour[. . .] . . . her beauties *scornefull* grace" (III.vii.23.5), emphasis
added). Beauty's failure to gratify the beholder issues a supposed warrant for
its violation.

Rather than blame Florimell for the son's besotted idolatry, Spenser
imagines beauty's degradation as a product of viewers' belittling fantasies.
Florimell avoids the spotted beast by jumping into the boat of a sleeping
fisherman, but when he wakes, Florimell finds herself in even greater danger.
When he sees "that blazing beauties beame" (III.viii.22.5), he is awakened to
a violent passion: "The sight whereof in his congealed flesh, / Infixt such
secret sting of greedy lust, / That the drie withered stocke it gan refresh"
(III.viii.25.1–3). Florimell can mount only a meager defense against the old
man's attack. It is only because Proteus hears her cries that beauty is saved
from violation. Unlike her other pursuers, Proteus understands that Florimell
must be won, even if he holds her within his bower. Physical possession does
not amount to amorous conquest. After he takes Florimell back to his watery
abode, Proteus commences upon an extended, expansive program of seduction. With his shape-shifting powers, Proteus endeavors to become Florimell's desire. Whatever Florimell wants, Proteus will become. And, though
he initially fails to impress her "With flattering words . . . [and] faire gifts
t'allure her sight" (III.viii.38.6–7), Proteus does not waver in his attempts to
capture Florimell's erotic imagination:

Sometimes he boasted, that a God he hight:
But she a mortall creature loved best:
Then he would make himself a mortall wight;
But then she said she lov'd none, but a Faerie knight.
    (III.viii.39.6–9)

Florimell might resemble a stony mistress, who has "sealed vp her brest"
against the supplications of a beseeching lover (III.viii.39.5), but, notably, she
does not refuse desire.[67]

In reply, Florimell details the contours of her longing, rebuffing Proteus by elaborating her love's specificity. Proteus attempts to impersonate her beloved, but since each iteration enumerates a particular quality, every instantiation fails to capture the totality of Florimell's affection. With her precise parries, Florimell avows the constancy of her love. Once it is clear that Florimell refuses to surrender, to give up her particular attachment to Marinell, Proteus becomes as menacing as the old man who sought to ravage her beauty:

> With harder meanes he cast her to subdew,
> And with sharpe threates her often did assaile." (III.viii.40.7–8)

Florimell proves beauty's truth, but she is nearly destroyed as a consequence. Unlike critics who interpret Florimell's trials as an initiation, whether sexual, social, or spiritual, I read Spenser's attention to beauty's suffering as a judgment on those who would degrade her excellence.[68] It is not that Florimell is unaffected by these attacks. Rather, in a departure from a Platonic ideal, which resists a world of contingent change by cultivating a contemplative domain of transcendent values, Spenser leaves true beauty open to experiential risk. Perhaps realizing, in Martha Nussbaum's words, "that there is in fact a loss in value whenever the risks involved in specifically human virtue are closed off," Spenser treats Florimell as a woman whose virtue might develop through her realization that she lives in a domain where her beauty subjects her to masculine violence.[69] Instead of protecting beauty as a rarefied idea, Spenser imagines Florimell as a flesh-and-blood woman whose vulnerability might demonstrate her material virtues. Florimell's steadfast devotion to Marinell, in fact, realizes Nussbaum's articulation of Aristotelian virtue: "There is a beauty in the willingness to love someone in the face of love's instability and worldliness."[70] By opening beauty to the ravages of contingency, Spenser offers a positive account of women's embodied excellence, one that emerges in response to the ethical betrayals of others.

Case in point: the sea god's menacing turn encapsulates the presumptive control masculine desire exercises over feminine beauty, as well as the violence that subtends this relation of dominance. Proteus understands the independence of Florimell's affection; yet, like the witch's doltish son, he refuses to recognize its intellectual settlement. Her desire, Proteus believes, should be responsive to his seduction, notwithstanding Florimell's attachment to Marinell. Limned with threats, his blandishments ultimately promise bare subjection. Because Proteus knows Florimell fosters independent desires, he seeks to bring her under his erotic control, whether by charm or by force. Proteus does not assume Florimell is a featureless mirror for masculine desire, but he seeks to transform her into one by means of his shape-shifting seduction. He works to erase her desire, to reproduce her as a blank totality of his own longing. Consequently, when he fails to conform Florimell to a self-gratifying fantasy, Proteus does not simply relent:

> To dreadfull shapes he did himselfe transforme,
> Now like a Gyant, now like to a feend,
> Then like a Centaure, then like to a storme,
> Raging within the waues: thereby he weend
> Her will to win vnto his wished end.
> But when with feare, nor fauour, nor with all
> He else could doe, he saw himselfe esteemd,
> Downe in a Dongeon deepe he let her fall,
> And threatned there to make her his eternall thrall. (III.viii.41)

Proteus sees his efforts are useless, yet, in response, he ratchets up the level of menace, punishing Florimell on account of what he regards as her rebellious forbearance.

Spenser lauds Florimell's steadfast endurance, mining a register of sanctity to class her among love's martyrs:

> Eternall thraldome was to her more liefe,
> Then losse of chastitie, or change of loue
> Die had she rather in tormenting griefe,
> Then any should of falsenesse her reproue,
> Or looseness, that she lightly did remoue.
> Most vertuous virgin, glory be thy meed,
> And crowne of heauenly praise with Saints above,
> Where most sweet hymmes of this thy famous deed
> Are still emongst them song, that far my rymes exceed. (III.viii.42)

If Florimell becomes a saint, she is also an embodied model for emulation. Heaven might record her glory with celestial praise, but Spenser's poetry offers a more humble, albeit more immediate, form of elevation. Mourning beauty's predicament, Spenser expresses poetic devotion to Florimell's suffering, notwithstanding what he calls his "feeble Muse" (III.viii.43.2). His efforts "Shall be t'aduance thy goodly chastitee, / And to enroll thy memorable name, / In th' heart of euery honourable Dame" (III.viii.43.3–5). Women's commemoration, as this stanza's logic discloses, will shadow her heavenly reward. To magnify Florimell, therefore, Spenser moves beyond a Platonist ladder of metaphysical signification. As women remember Florimell, they translate reverence into endeavor, forming a living apostrophe that verifies beauty's truth: "That they thy vertuos deedes may imitate, / And be partakers of thy endlesse fame" (III.viii.43.6–7).

Beauty Redoubled

Spenser does not, however, suggest that a network of women will enliven beauty's excellence. Unlike the circuits of female community that I detail in Chapter 3 with my discussion of late medieval female saints' lives, Florimell is cut off from other notable women. Immediately after he represents her beauty as an ideal shared between good women, Spenser unceremoniously dispatches beauty:

> It yrkes me, leaue thee in this wofull state,
> To tell of *Satyrane*, where I him left of late. (III.viii.43.8–9)

Although she is not dead, Spenser leaves Florimell to rot in Proteus's bower for fifteen cantos. Florimell is as good as dead, and she would perhaps be better off were she actually dead. This is because, as the poem's readers know in ways its characters cannot, Florimell's beauty is already subject to degradation in Faerieland. While Britomart and Amoret explore circuits of desire that might be mutually nourishing, and while Scudamour details Amoret's emergence from a community of feminized excellence in the Temple of Venus (she is surrounded by Womanhood, Shamefastness, Cheerfulness, Modesty, Courtesy, and Obedience), Florimell languishes as a captive in Book IV. It would be hard for other women to realize Florimell's virtue, to put it another way, because no one knows she is missing from Spenser's poetic landscape. As soon as she flees from the witch's son, the maternal hag fashions a false double of Florimell, a simulacrum composed of wire and snow, animated by a malevolent male sprite.[71] As long as

False Florimell circulates, the meaning of Florimell's beauty is subject to contention and revision.

Indeed, when Spenser leaves Florimell under the sea, he offers a negative assessment of Faerieland's ethical topography. Harried and pursued, worshipped and threatened, beauty can find no unassailed abode. The universal response to beauty is a desire for possession, revealing the invested ethics of masculine service in this poetic terrain.[72] If Platonist thought defined love as a desire for beauty, the range of men Florimell encounters demonstrates the myriad ways in which this desire can be warped to support a self-gratifying ethos. In *The courtiers academie* (1598), Annibale Romei claims that beauty's connection to proportion inspires only measured love.[73] Likewise, in the English translation of Tommaso Buoni's *Problemes of Beauty* (1618), Buoni claims that "Loue being the moderator of al affections, it should seeme to build her neast in those that are Beautifull.[74] In Faerieland, as Snowy Florimell's creation discloses, love inspired by beauty is a petty species of selfish projection. From the moment of her creation, the doubled dame reveals ethical weakness, divulging the shallow fantasies that equate to normative authority in courtly culture. Robert W. Tate calls False Flormell "an 'anima-ideal,' a social construct of femininity that men project . . . upon women."[75]

It is no surprise that the rube son adores False Florimell, for the snowy double performs beauty in an exact reflection of his longing: "Him long she so with shadowes entertained" (III.viii.10.8). Though False Florimell is made for the son's delight, the unheroic lover quickly yields Snowy Florimell to the first knight who challenges him for her hand:

The fearefull Chorle durst not gainesay, nor dooe,
But trembling stood, and yielded him the pray. (III.viii.13.1–2)

Quite predictably, the knight who takes False Florimell as an ornament signifying his prowess is Braggadoccio. Empty beauty decorates empty heroism until the pair encounters other knights in their travels about Faerieland. Spenser entangles other knights in False Florimell's thread, leveling masculine pursuit in a fashion that once again dissolves distinctions between noble and base admirers. Because False Florimell muddles the ethical distinction between knights' responses, it is evident that masculine desire should not be the generative source of beauty's excellence. Rather, snowy beauty's expansive circulation affirms the necessity of women's independent ethical intelligence. Her animation by a male sprite means that False Florimell is a masculinist illusion of idealized feminine beauty. Accordingly, she changes hands readily, bestowing favor on each knight who wins her in a martial contest between men. She does not know the difference between men, but her extreme dependence makes her powers of recognition moot, anyhow. Because she is an exact reflection of each man who beholds her, she cares very little about who might hold her at any given moment.

Rather than reinforcing homosocial desire, False Florimell's easy virtue threatens to evacuate the ethical system of achievement upon which knights base their claims to valor, to service, or to chivalric identity. To prevent a chaotic melee, Satyrane devises a tournament at which Florimell's lost girdle will be a reward for the fairest dame, who will become meed for the most valiant knight.[76] The contest is a mockery before it begins, since Paridell and Blandamour (Snowy Florimell's latest contenders) unite "Gainst all those knights, as their professed fone, / That chaleng'd ought in *Florimell*, saue they alone" (IV.ii.28.8–9). Were the absurdity of *sharing* Florimell not apparent enough, the following stanza differentiates selfish alliance, "spred with golden foyle, / That vnder it hidde hate and hollow guyle" (IV.ii.29.4–5), from true friendship, "For vertue is the band, that bindeth harts most sure" (IV.ii.29.9). Knights with a claim to Snowy Florimell are eager for the contest to begin, since each warrior nurses his individual smart from losing the glorious maiden. It should be clear that False Florimell would favor anyone, but each knight remembers the self-aggrandizing fantasy her presence consolidated. Individual desires are submerged, however, by the tournament's broader moral organization. Divvied up according to declared preferences— the knights of maidenhood vs. the knights of friendship—the contest casts elite violence as an ethical contest. And, though the fairest maiden is promised to the strongest knight, this ordered display of heroic prowess is removed from beauty's trials. As Florimell suffers the fisherman's sordid attack, the poem stipulates the uselessness of grandiose heroism: Satyrane, Calidore, or other knights plighted to her cause might level kingdoms to protect Florimell, "But sith that none of all her knights is nye," we are called to observe "how the heauens of voluntary grace, / And soueraine fauour towards chastity, / Doe succour send to her distressed cace" (III.viii.29.1, 2–4). Because "So much high God doth innocence embrace" (III.viii.29.5), and not because knights honor her with their might, Florimell's virtue remains inviolate.

Although her purity remains intact, Florimell retains a barren virtue. Like an enshrined relic, beauty is lost to action but preserved for reverence. The former sign of her power, Florimell's girdle, becomes a portable talisman that formalizes beauty's reflection of masculine desire. Or, at least, this is the explicit promise of "The controuerse of beauties soueraine grace" (IV.v.2.3). Book IV's pageant of lovelies is scandalized, however, when Britomart refuses False Florimell, "For that strange Dame, whose beauties wonderment / She lesse esteem'd, then th'others vertuous gouernment" (IV.v.20.8–9). Britomart prefers Amoret, the only woman who can fasten the cestus, a golden belt once worn by the chaste Venus and passed along to the actual Florimell once the goddess "vsd her looser sport" (IV.v.3.9). For many readers, False Florimell's inability to wear the girdle signals a lack of chastity. But other beauties at the tournament also fail to attach the belt, and chaste Florimell surrenders this marker when she is chased by the spotted beast. In an apparent crux of the poem, False Florimell later wears the belt that will not fasten during this competition.[77] When Artegall sets the genuine Florimell beside her fabricated double, the snowy maiden melts:

> Ne of that goodly hew remayned ought,
> But th'emptie girdle, which about her wast was wrought.
>   (V.iii.24.8–9)

Instead of providing a belittling commentary on all of femininity (women are loose), the cestus denotes the difference between virtue's disciplinary and empowering capacities. Because it marks fidelity as a bodily practice, the cestus may bind even False Florimell to her most faithful lover.[78] In fact, because it is merely physical, Snowy Florimell's commitment shows that treating virtue as a disciplinary practice works to subvert ethical truth.

Disciplinary virtue disrupts the ethical identities it is meant to guarantee. The failed beauty pageant prompts a heroic breakdown, with every knight vying to capture Snowy Florimell's attentions. To waylay violence, they place her in the middle of the martial retinue:

> Then, when she long had lookt vpon each one,
> As though she wished to haue pleasd them all,
> At last to Braggadochio self alone
> She came of her accord, in spight of all his fone. (IV.v.26.6–9)

Not only does Snowy Florimell choose, but William Oram notices her ability to settle upon the knight "whose worth most closely approximates her own."[79] False beauty is a good match for false heroism, and the girdle signifies the fidelity, albeit superficial, that binds lady and knight. Of this pairing, Rebecca Yearling rightly observes, "They show only a basic fidelity to their first choice of partner, and if such a union can be described as 'chaste,' then the value of chastity in itself is brought seriously into question."[80] False Florimell does more, then, than critique the narcissism of heroic display; her exact replication of fidelity threatens to reduce all virtues to surface, socially occasioned, qualities. The problem with False Florimell's choice is that it calls into question the truth of any professed ethical commitment, including Florimell's love for Marinell.

Mechanical Beauty, Mechanical Virtue

On account of its ethical vacuity, this moment provides insight into Spenser's development of virtue as, in Harry Berger's words, "a sustained process of control that can never stop."[81] Virtue's active, shaping capacity is about more than rote observance of a set of bodily rules. As a consequence, Spenser's *Faerie Queene* is crucial to understanding material virtue as an alternative to traditional *virtus*. Material virtue as Spenser elaborates it contains an important mental dimension that is realized through bodily practice. It is not superficial, but withstands struggle, betrayal, and endangerment. I suggest that this model of virtue is revolutionary for thinking about women's ethical action, for it makes explicit the need for women to exercise intellectual control over their moral choices, even in worlds where their social power is circumscribed. Nevertheless, it is important to observe that this model of virtue, what I am calling "material virtue" to mark its distinctiveness in premodern culture, is not alien to modern ethics, where it might more simply be called "true virtue." In fact, the most recent treatments of virtue ethics, those that take into account the importance of the body's vulnerabilities in their thinking about the viability of achieving an ethical habitus, have much in common with Spenser's formulation of material virtue. While Alasdair MacIntyre insists on an acknowledgment of dependency that connects us to other (non)human bodies, Phillipa Foot argues that "moral defect is a form of natural defect," insisting that our flourishing as a species is tied to natural practices of ethical excellence.[82]

The moral philosopher Julia Annas describes virtue by means of a skill analogy, but she insists that a developed excellence requires more than a repetitive physical performance: "The intelligence displayed in an expert tennis player's strategy, for example, has come from practice and habituation, but it is not mindlessly repetitive."[83] Because her argument is Aristotelian in its foundation, Annas's formulation is relevant to beauty's doubled legend in *The Faerie Queene*. Even as it draws on Platonized notions of beauty, through its power to "ennobleth the person doubtlesse," the Florimells thread explores the material possibilities of this philosophical idealism.[84] Rather than posit a rarefied ladder of beauty's perfection, upon which all materialized instantiations inevitably stumble, False Florimell exposes the problems attendant upon elevating an ideal that is anything other than an enlivened, embodied, and thinking excellence.[85] While Spenser derives beauty from a Platonized register, he thinks through its potential using Aristotelian concepts of virtue. It is this thinking about materiality as enlivened, as embodied, as thinking, that reveals Snowy Florimell's debased ethical status. Consonant with early modern accounts, Snowy Florimell represents *mechanical* virtue, an outward show that is more dangerous for its counterfeit performance. Because Snowy Florimell mimics her "true" counterpart, which puts the possibility of beauty's truth within scare quotes, her existence emphasizes the dangers of a model of virtue that is dependent and reflective. Although his remarks are meant to condemn cosmetics, Philip Stubbes captures the problem False Florimell poses to beauty when he exclaims, "whereby it cometh to pass that one can scarsly know who is a noble woman, who is an honourable, or worshipful Woman, from them of the meaner sorte."[86]

Throughout this episode, no one can tell the difference between true and false beauty. Everyone at the tournament believes the snowy Florimell is the *real* Florimell, assuming, of course, that this distinction can be said to remain meaningful in any fashion. In fact, I suggest that the bright line differentiating genuine virtue from its pretended copy disappears when its verity is determined using an external register. The doubts raised over Florimell's chastity, caused we might think by False Florimell's inability to fasten the girdle, have always been present, and are intensified to the point of exposure by the snowy maiden's ability to wear the cestus.[87] Because beauty is an excellence haunted by its false simulation, its intellectual aspect is significant for thinking about the ways in which women embody virtues.[88] When False Florimell chooses Braggadocio, she affirms the problems that arise when beauty is powerful, independent, but lacking in moral discretion. Beauty's sovereign agency is frequently imagined as its principal threat in early modern discourse. The anonymous *Here foloweth a lytell treatyse of the beaute of women* (1525) seeks to defuse the potential dangers of a woman's beauty with the insistence:

Beaulte is lost in woman outerely
Yf she haue thys of very condycyon
As to regarde or loke dyspyteously
For that is the manner of the lyon.[89]

Not only might beauty's exemplar have desires, and not only might those
desires be independent; what Snowy Florimell affirms, causing great discord
in the chivalric community, is that beauty's desires might be malevolent,
deployed to deceive or possibly even humiliate the vulnerable beholder.

In the nightmare scenario, beauty might empower the beloved against a
helpless devotee. This threat arises from a masculinist suppression of beauty's
moral knowledge, even though this ethical evacuation is designed to gratify a
masculinist desire for beauty's physical possession. This is the danger that
Spenser's beauty presents, and it remains unchallenged in some modern ethical accounts. In the familiar structure of courtly love, which posits a knight's
service to an exalted lady, the capricious demands of an "inhuman partner"
affirm the lover's identity through masochistic denial. Jacques Lacan incorpo-
rates this logic into psychoanalysis when he distances the courtly lady from
material excellence: "The Lady is never characterized for any of her real,
concrete virtues, for her wisdom, her prudence, or even her competence. If
she is described as wise, it is only because she embodies an immaterial wisdom
or because she represents its functions more than she exercises them. On the
contrary, she is as arbitrary as possible in the tests she imposes on her servant."[90] In Slavoj Žižek's reading of Lacan, the lady is "a kind of automaton,
a machine which utters meaningless demands at random."[91] Rather than serving as blank surfaces that reflect masculine achievement, ladies endowed with
beauty's majesty transform their lovers into diminished simulations of their
own empty demands. The ethical assumption underpinning this relationship,
which poststructuralist accounts, notably, leave undisturbed, is that the
beloved object is an alien site of moldering emptiness. In this, psychoanalysis
sounds very much like the premodern conduct discourse that Spenser challenges with his tale of the two Florimells. To purge the exalted object of its
vacuous agency, women were constantly advised to avoid artifice, ornament,
or adornment, since natural beauty was morally and aesthetically privileged
in early modern renderings.

Snowy Florimell uncovers the empty power of the beautiful beloved, but
Florimell challenges the courtly logic that vests this amorous structure with
social prestige. Although each knight who sees Florimell wishes to possess

her, to position her beauty as a narcissistic reflection of individual excellence, she is not a meaningless void who galvanizes the self-centering fantasies of her beholders. Rather, the abundance of Florimell's desire confounds the twinned cultural ideals of feminine passivity and receptivity. She leaves Gloriana's court because she commands her own character. Furthermore, Florimell knows what she wants, and she never falters in her quest to find Marinell. Florimell might fail to gratify her viewers, but beauty's plenitude is ultimately far less disruptive to heroic ethics than its hollowness. This is not to say, however, that Spenser provides unencumbered moral ground for beauty's intelligibility. By setting Snowy Florimell loose on the chivalric community, beauty's power is diminished. That emptiness is scripted by early modern prescriptive writings for women. To say that virtuous women enflesh God's ideal of beauty, as Giovanni Michele Bruto claims of prized daughters, is potentially to declare beauty's inherent emptiness. Because it remains a mimetic rendering of divine excellence, women's beauty remains mired in staining matter.[92] This suspicion would be inevitable were we to assume that beauty's excellence is mechanical, registered only as an external condition of embodiment.[93]

This skepticism ignores the mental aspect of material virtue, which, for beauty, consists of an animating intelligence that unifies body and mind in perfect proportion. In *Problemes of Beauty*, Buoni claims that "*Beauty* is a cleare signe . . . of a faire (that is) of a vertuous minde."[94] In a more speculative vein, Henricus Cornelius Agrippa, writing a Platonist defense of women, *A treatise of the nobilitie and excellencye of woman kynde* (trans. 1542), upholds the Virgin Mary as the ideal of beauty, since her "fayre beautie the sonne and moone wo~der at, from whose moste fayre visage, so great clere|nes of beautie, with chastitie and holynes dyd shyne, that although she moued the myndes, and lyke|wyse the eies of all men, yet for al that, no mortall man at any tyme, was allured or inticed by her beu|tie, ones to thynke amysse."[95] To regard beauty as virtue is to behold divine grace in human form, as Anthony Gibson remarks in his translation called, *A Woman's Worth* (1599): "Womens beauty then is aboue all else most maruellous: It is the excellencie of the Diuine workemanship, or rather the chiefest thing of his hea|uenly labour: It is the modell, not onely of thinges that beautifie the world, but the very especiall of all formes: It is the table of the celestiall powers: the gadge of natures all|iance with the world, and the onelie mirrour of perfect Ideaes."[96] The animating power that connects these powers with flawless measure, theorists insist, is a beautiful woman's mental command. Naivete and stupidity are as dangerous as enmity and duplicity, since beauty's favor—its bestowed grace—relies on robust powers of moral discernment.[97] If False Florimell affirms the dangers of mechanical virtue, the superficial adherence to cultural prescriptions as an externalized code of discipline, it is only with her re-emergence that Florimell makes beauty an exercise of embodied intelligence.

Intelligent Beauty

Locked away in Proteus's bower, Florimell resembles "dead" virtue, which Buoni claims "seemeth to be a dead *Beauty* in a liue body."[98] Florimell is independent and intelligent, but her virtue is meaningless in seclusion.[99] Without Marinell, as her simulacrum's successful circulation affirms, Florimell's beauty is lost. Her recovery requires the reformation of heroic masculinity, but Marinell's love also remakes beauty into an animate virtue distinguished by its mental autonomy. This reciprocal refashioning scrambles traditional notions of agency and passivity, autonomy and reliance, that distinguish gender roles in early modern courtship. By characterizing Marinell as the flinty beloved of her affections, Florimell laments her rocky imprisonment in Proteus's bower. Her oblique address, however, reshapes Marinell's relation to beauty:

> Though vaine I see my sorrowes to vnfold,
> And count my cares, when none is nigh to heare,
> Yet hoping griefe may lessen being told,
> I will them tell though vnto no man neare. (IV.xii.6.1–4)

Love for Marinell defines Florimell; indeed, the generative power of the poetic complaint allows Florimell to define herself against the resistance of Marinell's "hard rocky heart . . . [which is] hardned more with [her] aboundant teares" (IV.xii.7.3, 5). As it does with so many courtly lovers, Florimell's long-suffering stabilizes and authenticates the boundaries of her self.

Yet if Florimell's erotic deferral establishes beauty's integrity, it also confines her excellence to a limited domain of self-affirming suffering. Spenser is not satisfied simply to reverse the polarity of courtly adoration, whereby women might be enabled to pine after an impossible beloved. Rather, he shows the bankruptcy of this erotic structure through Florimell's suffering. Beauty is true but isolated, without any meaningful connection outside the ossified contours of its formal perfection. Her complaint is meant for herself alone; Florimell remains unaware that Marinell overhears her sorrow when he attends the watery nuptials of Thames and Medway. Crucially, however, her agonized devotion radically challenges Marinell's identity, but not because Florimell's desire conforms to a traditional model of courtly affection.[100] Through the plenitude of Florimell's desire, Marinell sees how he looks to another. Importantly, however, this is not a reflective encounter, since it is not driven by vision. By moving the scene of erotic reformation from the visual to the aural, Spenser explores what Elaine Scarry characterizes as beauty's ability to provide "a more capacious regard for the world."[101] Hearing reforms erotic contact, principally by admitting that seduction is an amorous transformation that requires discretion as much as reaction.

Whatever Marinell thought of himself, and however he sought to actualize that vision, Florimell's appraisal takes him by surprise. Through hearing, love of beauty simply happens to Marinell, insofar as he is able to gain a fuller sense of himself without the struggle that Leo Bersani locates in a sexual economy bounded and arranged by visually demarcated oppositions.[102] As this encounter demonstrates, hearing is an accidental penetration that emphasizes the body's porousness, its constant openness to others.[103] This is not deliberate listening, for Marinell does not reach out to comprehend another. Even so, he is unable to close himself off from Florimell, for once he overhears her woeful meditation, he is enraptured by her account of him.[104] As Florimell rehearses her sorrow, beauty becomes *resonant* in the terms unfurled by Jean-Luc Nancy: "Resonance is at once that of a body that is sonorous for itself and resonance of sonority in a listening body that, itself, resounds as it listens."[105] Beauty is not an external, bounded entity that can be admired or possessed. It permeates and refashions according to an internal intimacy of reciprocal vibration.

Through its resonance, Florimell's portrayal of Marinell fulfills one of beauty's crucial functions in later philosophical accounts: her unbounded investment in him, to use Iris Murdoch's conceptualization of beauty's active role in fostering human good, gives him the opportunity for "unselfing," since beauty "invites unpossessive contemplation and resists absorption into the selfish dream life of consciousness."[106] Beauty can show us the world denuded of our selfish, self-shrouding fantasies. It can provide a more expansive notion of self simply because it can shake us free from the limiting fantasies of identity we have created. These ideals, countless knights demonstrate, are impoverished by their conformity to culturally privileged categories (active/passive, true/false, good/bad, real/sham). Florimell's version of Marinell, of course, is also a product of fantasy. That he is imagined by another, however, is a fact in the world that can change his conception of selfhood, moving Marinell beyond masculinist immuring fantasies. For Spenser, the idea that beauty can expand our consciousness, to return to Murdoch, "in the direction of unselfishness" is central to active, enlivened excellence, since, as she maintains, such a notion "is to be connected with virtue."[107]

To recognize that virtue is not merely a disciplinary apparatus of social regulation is also vital to the more inclusive notion of material excellence pursued across this book. Marinell is carried outside himself, for as he realizes when he hears Florimell's pain, his desire for erotic imperviousness has disfigured the core identity he sought to preserve. Florimell is equally transformed, since Marinell's affection actualizes the principles of amorous fidelity she sought to perform. His love gives credence to her truth, authenticating the beauty she struggles to enact throughout the poem. Nevertheless, her character is never completely freed from the specter of beauty's falsehood; Snowy Florimell melts, yet the possibility remains that false and true beauty are merely melded together in an uneasy, unstable admixture. As Braggadocio's outlandish self-promotion demonstrates, at any moment Florimell could once again be viewed as a trophy installed to aggrandize her beloved's accomplishments. Artegall, notably, is the only onlooker who suspects that Braggadocio's beauty is just a "fayre Franion" (V.iii.22.7), a conjured masculinist illusion made up to look like a genuine woman. But even the knight of Justice is powerless to see through False Florimell's empty pretense with moral certainty. From just looking, Artegall is unable to distinguish between true and false Florimell, for in truth, there is no visible distinction to perceive. With Florimell's splitting, true and false are forever suspended, held in a permanent tension that cannot be resolved by the ethical regard of beauty's beholders.

Fostered by Grace

Snowy Florimell's disappearance does not dispel the problems of beauty, settling its relation to virtue by affirming the "real" Florimell's truth. This is not a fault, but a vital element of the material virtue Spenser seeks to nourish in his poem's audiences. Unlike accounts that render virtue as the infusion

of a reordering power, or those that treat virtue as the practice of a cultivated
strength, *The Faerie Queene* situates virtue where performance meets dependence, where habitus includes grace. Virtue must be active and autonomous,
intelligent and deliberate. But its sources are external as much as internal.
When the bases of this form of virtue are purely social—completely reliant
on norms of value negotiated by powerful members of the community—they
merely naturalize dominance. To retreat into one's self as a protective,
immuring province is to occupy a barren terrain of alienating fantasy, as the
sufferings of Florimell and Marinell show in alternating narrative sequences.
Following Patricia Parker, who suggests the fantasy of (self-)possession is at
odds with the vision of the human that Spenser conceives, I suggest that the
Florimells thread imagines the human as open, liable to disperse but able to
reconvene.[108] The lone performance of virtue is not just vulnerable; it is also
inconceivable, especially considering Spenser's Protestant ethics. While *The
Faerie Queene*'s Aristotelian structure encourages the development of an ethical habitus, that natural capacity for practiced virtue is ultimately dependent
on divine grace.

Spenser is steadfast in the insistence that material virtue is a product of
divine grace.[109] Yet, in a departure from the theological tradition that saw
grace as the basis for *all virtue*, Spenser is not bothered to foreground *caritas*
as the unifying virtue differentiating Christian from natural human good.[110]
Neither is he exercised to insist on total human incapacity.[111] Just as grace is
infused, so virtue is embodied. By melding the sacred and social meanings of
grace, Spenser renders virtue as a power that is divine and human at once.[112]
In so doing, Spenser clears ground for a virtue that is material, natural,
infused, and intellectual. At least in Faerieland, a materialized virtue enacts
grace, reforming chivalric ideals according to a divinely appointed ethical
system ruled in perfect proportion by a beautiful queen. The poem's Elizabethan *logos* relies on human action but is enabled by divine favor. On
account of its complex interweaving of virtue and grace, its nuanced combination of infused favor and materialized good, *The Faerie Queene* generates
an ethical world where women's excellence is vitally important to the consolidation of a virtuous Christian kingdom. Florimell's history further affirms
the intermingling of inner and outer, physical and mental, material and spiritual, in the formulation of beauty as an embodied excellence that captures
the social and divine dimensions of grace:

> There *Florimell* in her first ages flowre
> Was fostered by those *Graces*, (as they say). (IV.v.5.7–8)

Because the Graces are cast in their classical role as handmaidens to a chaste
Venus, they extend a rich legacy of feminine excellence to Florimell.[113] Spenser's virtue is part of a network, an interconnected system of bodies that
refuses to vest excellence in the isolated subject. As their dance atop Mount
Acidale in Book VI indicates, the Graces are crucial to Spenser's ethics of
courtesy.[114] The scholars Kathleen Williams and Lila Gellar have further
emphasized the Graces' importance to the synthesis of classical and Christian
ideals.[115] Yet, as Gellar observes, "Spenser's usage of the Three Graces as
'types' of Christian grace lies easily within the tradition of the allegorization
of classic mythology."[116] My interest is less in asserting a direct link than in
attending to the intermingling of classical and Christian excellence in this
distinctively feminized vision of embodied excellence.

The hundred maidens who dance around the graces are described as
"lilly white," and are all identified as minor Graces who attend upon Venus
(VI.x.11.8, 21.6). The three central Graces, to focus only on their significance
in the Greek and Roman ethical tradition, signify liberality, a bounty of
gifts.[117] For later Platonists, in particular Marsilio Ficino, beauty derives from
the three graces, through harmony in sound, beauty in color and form, and
intelligence and eloquence.[118] In Calidore's vision their influence is vast,
"These three on men all gracious gifts bestow" (VI.x.23.1), establishing a
connection between bounty and power in a domain where "all the complements of curtesie" are paramount (VI.x.23.6). The fourth Grace, around
whom all others dance, is not an exalted queen; rather, in keeping with the
pastoral tableau animated by Colin Clout's piping, she is a maiden of humble
birth: "Yet was she certes but a countrey lasse" (VI.x.25.8). Her centrality
signals her excellence, "as a precious gemme" (VI.x.12.7), but it also makes
virtue material and spiritual at once:

> Aboue all other lasses beare the bell,
> Ne lesse in vertue that beseemes her well,
> Doth she exceede the rest of all her race,
> For which the Graces that here wont to dwell,
> Haue for more honor brought her to this place,
> And graced her so much to be another Grace. (VI.x.26.4–9)

> Another Grace she well deserues to be,
> In whom so many Graces gathered are,
> Excelling much the meane of her degree;
> Diuine resemblaunce, beauty soueraigne rare,

Firme Chastity, that spight ne blemish dare;
Al which she with such courtesie doth grace,
That all her peres cannot with her compare,
But quite are dimmed, when she is in place. (VI.x.27.1–8)

If women are endowed with certain gifts, their virtue emerges from the active
ways in which they inhabit those infused qualities. Rather than see grace as a
debilitating evacuation of feminine agency, or a domineering exercise of eroticized sovereignty, the dance interweaves action and reliance to furnish a
fuller picture of women's potential for embodied excellence.[119]

Here, Spenser assembles an expansive society of virtuous femininity,
where social and ethical ideals are unified through a harmonious dance. The
space of movement, as well as the dance itself, glorifies communal values. It
also establishes ethical terrain where the shaping influence of women's ethical
excellence can be culturally recognized. The ground reverberates with the
maidens' dance, and the circling harmony of the beautiful ladies interweaves
idealized qualities. This is no theoretical investiture of women's power.
Rather, as David Lee Miller remarks, "The dance has a certain weight, a
bodily reality."[120] Unlike courtly love traditions, where women's grace is cited
as a formal motivation for masculine action, these women bestow tangible
gifts with ethical discernment. Their favors bequeath advantages upon their
recipients, connecting social and moral grace in a comprehensive pedagogical
program: "They teach vs, how to each degree and kynde / We should our
selues demeane" (VI.x.23.7–8). They cannot be compelled to confer favor,
"none can them bring in place, / But whom they of them selues list so to
grace" (VI.x.20.4–5), but exercise their own judgment in bestowing gifts.
Such absolute independence recalls God's grace, which was an unmerited
grant of divinity in reformist thought.[121] In the sacred tradition, as it is during
the dance on Mount Acidale, grace is a source of bounty, not scarcity.[122]
Calidore's vision distances women's excellence from the emptiness or vindic-
tiveness that might otherwise characterize feminized grace in courtly fictions.

The Knowledge of Material Virtue

The robust physical virtue of the Graces, importantly, generates Florimell's
beauty. If true beauty initially appears to be fragile, chased as much as chaste,
it is because Florimell's world is not accommodating to women's embodied

excellence. Her naivete, furthermore, reveals the need for women's ethical knowledge, or the deliberate cultivation of moral judgment as a vital component of material virtue. It is not, however, that Florimell simply needs to learn the difference between male service and menace. As I have argued, the poem suggests that there is no difference between true and false masculinities as long as women's power—intellectual as well as physical—is lacking. Through the thread of the two Florimells, Spenser reshapes the masculine chivalric subject, thereby remaking Faerieland's ethical terrain. Not only does Marinell understand Florimell's autonomy; he gains respect for her judgment as he hears her mournful complaint. These elements—independence and intelligence—are fostered by the dance of the Graces, which illuminates Spenser's vision of virtue as a substantive form of harmonious action in a world warped by violent contingency.

When Calidore appears, however, the Graces vanish. Colin identifies Calidore "As thou vnhappy, which them thence did chace" (VI.x.20.2), once again linking knights to beauty's pursuit. Spenser creates a material domain of cultural intelligibility for material virtue, but this enlivened, harmonious vision is rarefied and fleeting. The following chapters will not dispatch this contingency; indeed, one of *The Faerie Queene*'s most enduring insights concerns the unsettling persistence of mutability. If False Florimell melts, it does not mean that beauty will always be perceived as true. The specter of virtue's duplicity remains, but this uncertainty heightens rather than diminishes the value of those moments and spaces in which particular instances of embodied excellence become intelligible. Spenser may be unable to dispel cultural instability (the Blatant Beast can merely be muzzled), but moral resolve emerges in moments that might otherwise prompt despair. Material virtue imagined as intelligent perseverance offers an important endorsement of women's excellence. Rather than identifying women with worlds, Spenser recognizes women's ability to shape, govern, or navigate realms that are inhabited by a host of others. Gloriana unifies the virtues in Faerieland, but such qualities are the product of feminine governance as an embodied practice. Because Florimell navigates Faerieland's ethical terrain on her own, she materializes virtue as an enacted ideal of social and spiritual grace.

In this respect, Spenser differs from other authors treated in this study, to the extent that he remakes a world in an attempt to make room for women's material virtues. It is only with *A Margarite*'s Philenia that Lodge explores the possibility of virtue that might remake the patriarchal territories of colonial romance. Though Philenia dies rather than suffer sexual violation, she has a perceptive wariness and a steadfast strength that makes her attractive and dangerous to Arsadachus. Philenia realizes a comprehensive form of excellence, which is mental as well as physical, habituated as well as infused: "Beside hir education, which was excellent, hir virtues such as equalled excellence, hir beuty so rare as exceeded both" (57). Her manifold goods are rewarded with genuine affection from the noble Muscovan courtier Minecius, but Philenia and her betrothed also become prey on account of her superlative virtue. And, though Arsadachus fails to ravish Philenia, her virtue is rendered moot by his attack. She is clever enough to understand that Arsadachus is behind the assault: "Ah Cuscan prince though thy face is shadowed, I knowe thee by these follies, though thy raiments are changed, I judge thee by thy rashness" (88). She can do nothing, however, to fend off his aggression.

Philenia is a model of embodied excellence, but her perfection is conceptual, not material. Recalling those virtuous maidens from prescriptive literatures, Philenia dies to keep her virtue intact. For instance, in Castiglione's *Courtyer*, a virtuous woman expires to avoid revealing her love: "And in this resolued determination the seelie soule van|quished with moste cruell affliction, and wexed through longe passion verie feint, at the three yeeres ende, died. Rather woulde she forgoo her contentacions and pleasu|res so much longed for, finally her lief [*sic*], then her honestie."[123] Similarly, Lodge imagines a marriage of fatality, which might be romantic were it not predicated on Philenia's sacrifice: "At last *Minecius* lacking blood, *Philenia* breath, both of them entangled arme in arme, fell downe dead, leaving the memorie of their vertues to be eternized in all ages" (91). If Minecius dies from his wounds, Philenia dies because her virtue is impossible, as hopeless as it is helpless, without masculine protection.

Unlike Spenser, who allows Florimell to materialize excellence according to terms she struggles to establish, Lodge ultimately treats women's virtue as a masculine production. Indeed, the rapid destruction of virtue's most able model—Philenia is one of Arsadachus's first victims—advances *A Margarite of America*'s narrative priority: the reform of masculine governance. To this end, her death occasions Arsinous's program of learning and revenge. Before her death, Arsinous dedicated himself to shaping his daughter's virtues: "deere wert thou unto me, who hast cost me many broken sleepes to bring thee up, many carefull thoughts to bestow thee, more fatherly teares to prevent thy overthrow" (92). After her death, Arsinous seeks redress: "wo is me that am carefull to publish my paines, and negligent to seeke remedy . . . ah,

Arsinous weepe not her that may not be recalled with teares, but seeke to revenge her; shew thy selfe rather fatherly in act, then effeminate in teares" (92). The father's dark magic is a direct result of Philenia's destruction. The tomb of doomed lovers becomes a memorial to lost values: *"Vertue is dead, and here she is enshrined, /. . ./ Beautie is dead, and here is faith assigned, /. . ./ Pitie was dead when tyranny first slew them"* (93). Lodge has scant problem asserting equivalence between the female body and a prized territory. Masculine management and protection lead to the active flourishing of a carefully cultivated feminized terrain. It would take years, and a few more doomed expeditions, before Shakespeare's Prospero in *The Tempest* drowns the book of patriarchal spells, and with it those territorial fantasies that render Philenia's virtue as a sacrificial power in Lodge's *A Margarite of America*.

PART III

Homely Virtues

CHAPTER 5

Shrewish Virtue, from Chaucer
to Shakespeare

Silence is a vertue, marie tis a dumbe vertue: I loue vertue that speakes, and has a long tongue like a belweather, to leade other vertues after.

—Dekker, Chettle, and Haughton, *The Pleasant Comodie of Patient Grissil*, I.ii.292–94

For patience she will prove a second Grissel.

—Shakespeare, *The Taming of the Shrew*, II.i.284

This chapter traces the emergence of material virtue in the shrew dramas by William Shakespeare and John Fletcher. The boisterous, brawling shrew became a stock character in sixteenth- and seventeenth-century comic literatures, yet one sort of shrew plot develops a model of material virtue that valorizes women's ethical action.[1] Perhaps surprisingly, this strain of shrew literature is related to Griselda stories of this period. Chaucer forges this connection with *The Clerk's Tale* and *Envoy*: after delineating the virtues of his patient wife, the Clerk concludes with a comic contrast. When he claims "Grisilde is deed, and eek hire pacience, / And bothe atones buryed in Ytaille" (IV.1177), the Clerk forever yokes patient and unruly wives. Nodding to "the Wyves love of Bathe" in his *Envoy*, the Clerk urges "archewyves" to throw off domestic obedience and strive against masculine governance (IV.1170, 1195).[2] With this conclusion, the Clerk does more than ridicule wifely patience; importantly, he establishes Griselda's story as a shrew-taming story. Later patient-wife fables extend this connection, since English Griselda narratives feature the kind of woman shrew-taming stories promise to produce: selfless, long-suffering, unstirred. And, because Griselda's virtue is independent, these tales provide an important backdrop for considering women's embodied excellence in the shrew dramas by William Shakespeare and John Fletcher. Read in the context of premodern patient-wife stories, *The Taming of the Shrew* (ca. 1590–94) and *The Woman's Prize, or the Tamer Tam'd* (ca. 1610) elaborate a model of embodied virtue based not on taming others, but on withstanding the suffering that goes along with everyday subjection.

Griselda narratives are important to understanding this quotidian, embodied excellence, since they provide the cultural scripts that determine wifely virtue in this period. These stories reveal what Petruchio wants from taming, but they also provide insight into why he gets something beyond any wager with Katherina's and then with Maria's transformation. Griselda stories articulate a different model of virtue, one that is based on enduring rather than exercising agency. Early modern shrew dramas take up and extend this ethical reformulation. In Shakespeare, Petruchio seeks to play shrew off virtue, binarizing feminine identity in a fashion he can control. Yet, when Katherina inhabits the cultural ideal of wifely submission circulated in early modern marriage manuals, she collapses one feminine category into the other. Fletcher's Petruchio inverts this very logic, but his Maria topples it once again: when she turns tamer, she utilizes the powers of the shrew to establish her virtue. The alewives' insurrection lasts only as long as it takes Maria to institute a program that will recover her husband from domestic tyranny. In very different ways, these tales entertain the possibility of a material virtue that arises from patience and obeisance, not domination and direction. Fletcher takes up this model of virtue for all members of the household, imagining a model of ethical subjectivity based on yielding (not wielding) domestic control.

Before turning to later shrew dramas, this chapter analyzes English Griselda narratives to challenge the idea that patient-wife plots feature passive women.[3] English Griseldas are as industrious as they are independent, otherwise they could not survive the trials their husbands devise for them. This survival invalidates the notion that the obedience of English Griseldas indicates moral or physical weakness.[4] Patient wives hazard their bodies to maintain their cherished principles, which are not ethically deficient. In tracing the strengths of premodern Griseldas, this chapter also contests the view that wifely submission reinforces masculine authority.[5] In every case, this is scandalously untrue. Rather, stories of wifely patience show that a woman's deference must appear to be the product of masculine regulation for it to valorize male authority. If a woman takes on subjection voluntarily, such abasement undermines her husband's claims to control. In the larger context of this book, Griselda stories articulate a model of material virtue that is based on modes of agency traditionally associated with women, including patience, humility, steadfastness, and submission. As various patient-wife narratives affirm, when husbands yield rather than wield agency, a model of material virtue emerges that is physically connected and mutually sustaining.

Later shrew plays develop and validate this kind of embodied excellence. In fact, Shakespeare's *Taming of the Shrew* departs from the traditional shrew genre by connecting it, as Carolyn E. Brown astutely details, to the Griselda tradition.[6] In suggesting that these two stories have been intertwined at least since Chaucer, I take a longer view of the relationship between shrews and virtues in premodern England. Doing so focuses attention on the ways that virtue and shrew might fruitfully be viewed as contiguous rather than opposi-tional categories of ethical identity.[7] When these identities are set beside rather than against one another, virtue might arise from shrewishness, and shrewishness might enable virtue.[8] In other words, material virtues might simply recognize shrews' strengths, including forcefulness, intelligence, and independence. As I shall detail, Shakespeare's folio-*Shrew* invests Katherina with this sort of moral distinction immediately before the play's close. Her strength of character is re-presented in a fashion that makes her behavior consonant with early modern ideals for wifely behavior. She is a shrew whose virtue becomes intelligible, in other words. When this happens, masculine dominance cannot be sustained as an ethically enabling cultural fiction.

Importantly, then, Katherina's material virtue creates as well as critiques: she uncases Petruchio's household tyranny, but she also bodies forth a new ethical subjectivity for women as well as men. Fletcher dramatizes what Shakespeare belatedly reveals. When he restages the classic shrew-taming plot in his *Woman's Prize, or The Tamer Tam'd*, material virtue is elaborated as a counter to the heroic model of *virtus* that relies on the masculine exercise of dominance over self and others. Katherina's suffering uncases Petruchio's domestic tyranny in *The Taming of the Shrew*, but when Maria upends Petruchio's household authority in *The Tamer Tam'd*, the play affirms that an ethics based on (masculine) dominance also has deleterious consequences for the men who are supposed to uphold those cultural ideals. Petruchio is reduced to tyranny by his harried, nearly frenzied attempts to establish his dominance. Fletcher flips the script, yet when Maria becomes tamer, she enacts a material form of virtue that remakes the gender categories of the premodern household for both partners. Not only does she show that women may exercise rationality, she demonstrates the common benefits of an ethics predicated on yielding to others. She surrenders to Petruchio, but only after he concedes the domestic power with which he is culturally invested. In imagining a more mutually constitutive household, one in which the categories of husband and wife suspend rather than enforce gender's power asymmetries, Fletcher's play answers Shakespeare's *Taming of the Shrew* by creating a space where the material virtues of partners might be collectively realized.

Premodern Griseldas

Household Politics

The Pleasant Comodie of Patient Grissil by Thomas Dekker, Henry Chettle, and William Haughton—written ca. 1599 and performed by the Admiral's Men ca. 1600—adds a comic subplot that explicitly links women's virtue to shrew taming. The brawling Welsh widow Gwenthyan counters Griselda's example, as the Marquess Gwalter exclaims:

> Oh my deare *Grissill*, how much different
> Art thou to this curst spirit here, I see
> My *Grissils* vertues shine. (IV.iii.156–58)[9]

As the play unfolds, Gwenthyan frames her resistance against her husband, the comically exasperated Welshman Sir Owen, as a reaction against Griselda's radical model of wifely patience: "*Grissill*? no, no, no, no, her shall not, mag *Gwenthyan* such ninny pobbie foole as Grissill" (III.ii.202). Not only does Gwenthyan's rebellion warrant masculine authority over the household, but her critique also diminishes Grissil's virtue. She does not recognize Grissil's strength, or her independence. Indeed, Gwenthyan acts as if Grissil is Gwalter's pawn, a docile puppet who is subject to a marriage contract that requires Chaucer's Griselda, as Walter puts it, "To al my lust, and that I frely may, / As me best thynketh, do yow laugh or smerte, / And nevere ye to grucche it, nyght ne day? / And eek whan I sey 'ye,' ne sey nat 'nay' " (IV.352–55). Gwenthyan treats Grissil as if she has no agency, autonomy, or virtue.

Yet her response does not match the play's representation of Grissil. It is not just that Grissil's virtue is established outside the domain of the Marquess Gwalter's desire, though it is. In this play, like most English versions, Grissil does not vow submission to her husband as a precondition of marriage. Later renditions handle the marital agreement very differently, so much so that Griselda's pledge is altogether absent in the ballad version of her story, which is thought to have been in circulation in the second half of the sixteenth century and was included in the second part of Thomas Deloney's *Garland of Good Will* (1593, 1631). John Phillip's *Plaie of Pacient Grissell* (ca. 1565), a moral interlude whose songs later circulated as independent ballads, requires no promise, though it does include a strong articulation of Griselda's deference.[10] Yet even here, when she declares, "Sith it hath pleasd you louinge Lord, to fix your loue on mee / Faith, Loue, and obedience due, I yelde here unto thee" (744–45), her obedience becomes just that—a strong articulation of her individual ethical commitment. This is not a compulsory form of subservience, since it derives from Grissell, not Gautier. Such alterations to this narrative, I mean to show, illuminate political dimensions of the premodern household that are also at work in shrew-taming plots of the period. Viviana Comensoli argues that English Griselda stories after Chaucer shift from allegory "to the human dimension of the marriage."[11] I suggest that this "human dimension" gives Griselda more ethical autonomy, and creates a new model of material virtue that challenges the masculinist absolutism of the early modern household.

In later English accounts, only the prose chapbook of 1619 makes Grisel's obedience obligatory. The Marquesse issues his demand using explicitly political language: "If your heart afford a willing entertainment to the motion, and your vertue a constancy to this resolution, not to repine a my pleasure in any thing, nor presume on contradiction, when I determine to command. For as amongst good souldiers, they must simply obey without disputing the businesse: so must vertuous wives dutifully consent withoute reproofe, or the least contraction of a brow."[12] Striking a parallel with military service, the Marquesse burdens Grisel to withstand hardship without question. Despite the fact that she agrees to this extensive prerequisite, the Marquesse is amazed when Grisel keeps her promise not to gainsay his authority after he demands the murder of their children. He supposes his demand is impossible, but not because it would be ethically problematic. Rather, in the closest English analogue to Chaucer, the Marquesse expects his lowly wife to fail as a political subject.[13] That she does not affirms her ethical grit.

Other early modern Griselda narratives endorse feminine autonomy. Deloney's ballad goes further than others, making Grissel's ethical and political standing mutually dependent. Grissel's plight is explicitly political, insofar as the Marquesse's grumbling subjects are the genuine cause of her ordeal:

> Many envied her therefore,
> Because she was of Parents poor,
> And 'twixt her Lord and she great strife did rise.[14]

The people's negative reaction to her social elevation, in other words, prompts the Marquesse to subject her to the series of trials she undergoes. It is not that the Marquesse oppresses his poor wife; the ballad notes that "most dearly, Tenderly, and intirely, / Lovd [her] as his Life."[15] In a gesture that the ballad presents as affection, he plans to use Grissel's demonstrated strength to dispatch her critics: "Minding in Secret, For to try her patient Heart / Therby her Foes to Disgrace."[16] She will prove her worth by displaying her mettle, which means that Grissel's embodied virtue will give her political standing. There is no sense that Grissel should have no power, or that her submission provides an index of her husband's control. Instead, by enduring great suffering, Grissel gains political legitimacy. It is only when he describes what will happen to her reputation that the Marquesse asserts any kind of claim over Grissel:

> Now blush for Shame,
> And honour virtuous Life;
> The Chronicles of lasting Fame,
> Shall ever more extol the Name
> of patient GRISSEL,
> My most constant wife.[17]

The Marquesse expects to gain stature from her excellence, but here too, he seems to acknowledge that Grissel's virtue will eclipse his own.

The Plaie of Pacient Grissell also outsources the cause of Grissell's trials, but in Phillip's moral interlude it is the allegorized vice figure, Politic Persuasion, who prompts Gautier to test his wife's patience. In establishing Grissell's excellence, the play articulates an emerging household politics that allows for and depends upon women's excellence. Not only do Gautier and Grissell sing a duet that expresses their compatibility as partners; the entire play, as Lee Bliss contends, showcases emerging early modern doctrines of the English household.[18] Bliss charts the interlude's heavy emphasis on children's obedience: while tending her parents, for instance, Grissell tells children to "Flye selfwill" (599).[19] Evidently she carries this disposition into marriage. As wives were promised, Grissell finds harmonious concord with Gautier because she enters their marital compact with a willing mind.[20] Later, once Gautier demands the deaths of her children and banishes her from court, she still bears her trials "with willinge minde" (1566). Phillip establishes companionate marriage as, in the words of Jeremy Taylor's marriage sermon (1653), "a school and an exercise of virtue."[21]

This does not mean that Grissell is passive, or complicit. Grissell embraces her trials as a "crosse, that [God] to me had sent" (1551), but she also critiques Gautier's conduct as morally unjust:

My Daughter reft from tender Paps, alas my wofull paine,
And caussellie by Tyrants fearce, with bloodie sword thus slaine."
　(1199–1200)

As she comes to terms with the deaths of her children, she indicts the social inequity that demands their sacrifice: "As my sweete Babes at Tirants heast, haue died on blooddy knife" (1514). And, though she might accept her husband's claim that the commons demanded the murder of her children, when she begs Gautier to kill her, "To swaige their raige, & win thee grace: spare not thy faithful wife" (1515), she recognizes her husband's power to oppose or gratify his subjects' ferocious desires. When Gautier declares his political impotence, "such is my haples state" (1128), he more accurately describes Grissell's helpless position. While the play shows she has little room to resist, there is no sense that Grissell is morally unaware of, or ethically complicit in, the evils committed against her children.

Rather, accusations of tyranny involve Phillip's interlude in a broader cultural conversation about the limits of male power in the early modern English household. As Kathleen McLuskie points out, most critical attention to the early modern Griselda story "turns on how far Grissil's patience exemplifies the ideal advocated by the writers of Puritan handbooks on marriage."[22] But the story's resonance with early modern domestic literatures has more to say about men's roles than has been acknowledged. Between 1599 and 1608, as Comensoli suggests, a series of "patient-wife plays" dramatized the challenges of marriage, especially those that are prompted by men's abuse of domestic authority.[23] Seeing the household as a "little Commonwealth," as John Dod and Robert Cleaver famously put it, analogized house and state in a fashion that also had serious consequences for men's ethical subjectivity.[24] The order of the house, as Thomas Smith notes, bespoke the order of the state.[25] Husbands had very distinct responsibilities in the marital handbooks that mandated wifely patience. William Whately made a general injunction: "It is one part of an householder's duty to provide for them of his household."[26] And importantly, William Gouge set down seventy-six "Husbands particular duties," observing, "If he abuse his authoritie, he turneth the edge and point of his sword amisse: in stead of holding it ouer his wife for her protection, he turneth it into her bowels to her destruction."[27] Lena Cowen Orlin observes that "in the oeconomic tracts of this period, the authority of the householder is never evoked without allusion to the manifold consequences of good or bad execution of those responsibilities."[28] Men could fail to live up to their prescribed roles, using patriarchal privilege to practice disorderly abuse.[29]

Without question, across different versions of the Griselda story, the Marquis fails to uphold the responsibilities that supposedly warranted his dominance. Traditional shrew literatures blame women for overturning domestic order, but *Pacient Grissell* challenges this misogynist commonplace. Indeed, this play, like other Griselda plots of the period, provides a trenchant commentary on the limits of masculine governance. In Phillip, notably, much of this commentary is provided by women. Despite the fact that Gautier is guided by counselors including Reason and Fidence, these interior powers prove useless against the vice's persuasions. Rather, as Pamela Allen Brown points out, a "shrew" furnishes the play's most searing moral critiques. The Nurse delivers scathing attacks against Gautier, negatively comparing his conduct to that of ferocious beasts: "The Tyger . . . The rauenous ramping Lion . . . The sauaidge Beare . . . Then sith that beastes which reason want, ther proper ones defend, / Much more should man, which wisdom hath for his own flesh contend" (1141, 1143, 1144, 1147–48). Brown sees a contrast between the Nurse's conduct and Grissell's, so much so that "Phillip makes the nurse a substitute for Grissill as a mother and a model for Grissill as a Christian."[30] Yet I suggest that the women's arguments form a continuum, insofar as they both recognize Gautier's failure to defend his children against the demands of the commons as a moral evil. Both women, in other words, point to the Marquis's abuse of absolutist marriage.

Though Grissell does not attack her husband in the same fashion as the Nurse, when Grissell reminds her husband of her reluctance to marry, she catalogs the wrongs his choice has settled upon her:

> I thought that twixt my vacant plight, and neadfull indigence,
> Thy rych estate, and Lordly rule, deseruinge reuerence,
> Might no comparisson be made, and therfore as unmeete,
> I dempt my selfe within thy roofe to place or set my feete,
> Yet dyd thine honor noble Lord, elekt me for thy mate,
> The gretter ruth the more my paine, and most unhappie Fate
> Fyrst both my babes dysmembred are, the sworde their flesh hath torne
> . . . .
> Which pacientlie I wofull wife, of women all forlorne,
> Will byde and beare laffinge my fooe, fond Fortune all to skorne.
>   (1554–60, 1562–63)

In accepting her fate as it benefits her husband, Grissell calls attention to Gautier's failure to protect his family. She does not beg for her children's lives, but she does call attention to their father's predatory relationship to those with less power.

The Nurse gives direct voice to the idea that Gautier is an unnatural patriarch:

> O cruell father, O most intollorable case
> In the brest of this *Marquis* Nature hath no place. (1448–49)

His conduct, she notes by returning to her analogy with wild beasts, runs against the duties that fathers were meant to perform:

> The Lionis her whelpes, doth earnestly tender,
> The Bear to her young ons in loue is not slender. (1456–57)

When the Nurse decries Gautier's beastly behavior, "But thou to thy owne flesh art father unkynde" (1458), her outrage voices a common attitude. The

Nurse's outlook, I maintain, runs cognate to Grissell's. She does not de-
nounce her husband's behavior, but Grissell calls attention to Gautier's fail-
ure to protect anyone but himself from his subjects' murderous demands.[31]
The Nurse, moreover, does not see Grissell's response as morally deficient.
Rather, when she reviles Gautier's cruelty, she counts Grissell as one of the
Marquis's victims: "I mourne thee poore Grissill, thy hap I lament" (1468).
And, though she wonders at Grissell's ability to withstand Gautier's sentence,
"But thou in this case art meruellous pacient" (1469), she does not condemn
Grissell's behavior. Instead, she sees it as her duty to extend kindness to her
mistress: "To court I will haste mee, to comfort thee all that maye bee" (1470).
This is not, it should be added, because her office requires such service.
Indeed, the Nurse remains determined to call out wrong where she sees it
being perpetrated: "But to crye out on the *Marquis* I will not delaye mee"
(1471). With the addition of the Nurse, *Pacient Grissell* creates a crucial confederacy between different sorts of women. Grissell and the Nurse are joined
in their stance against Gautier's self-indulgent violence, and, though they
bear up against patriarchal injustice in different ways, the play suggests that
both women are on the side of material virtue, which withstands harms
inflicted by the powerful.

In fact, Phillip gives very little play to the stereotype of women's unruliness. It is no accident that Politic Persuasion introduces the figure of the
shrew into Phillips's interlude. In trying to scare Gautier away from marriage,
the vice claims: "Sayth the good man, I haue such a shrewe to my wyfe"
(188). When Gautier details the virtues he seeks in a spouse, Politick Persuasion unfolds common characterizations of the unruly wife familiar from early
modern shrew literatures:

> But moast wyues are so knappish and cutted now,
> That they will be knowen to beare rule I saie to you,
> . . . .
> Sume of them I tell you will be stoberne and unkynde,
> Denye them of ther willes and then ye mar all,
> Ye shall see what there after is like for to fall,
> Ether brauling, saulyng, sknappinge, or snarringe,
> Ther tounges shall not cease but alwaies be iarringe. (401–2, 423–27)

His digression on women's household disruption is flatly dismissed by Reason and Fidence, who discount his claims as unrealistic and antifeminist.

Gautier also seems unwilling to compass these views, though he follows the vice's advice to test Grissell anyhow. Given this disconnect between Gautier's motives and actions, the play explores the conditions that might turn a loving husband into a cruel tyrant. These conditions, I suggest, derive from the pressures of traditional *virtus*, or the expectation that masculine excellence relies on the governance, regulation, and domination of vulnerable others.

Shortly after he marries Grissell, Gautier sings a song that praises his wife's manifold virtues:

> I Liue in ioyfull iollytie,
> With my true loue and Ladye deare:
> To mee shee gyueth loyaltie,
> For Uertuous acts shee hath no peare:
> So true, so iust, in worde and deed,
> I maye her trust, in time of need. (969–74)

Although his alteration is abrupt, *Pacient Grissell* faults Politic Persuasion for Gautier's transformation.[32] Politic Persuasion works on Gautier's fears, particularly those anxieties that attend a man's public role as husband and father. It is no small irony that in trying to be seen as absolute head of his household, Gautier subjects his wife and children to destruction. But this is what Politic Persuasion convinces Gautier to do. When Politic Persuasion urges Gautier, "It is time now to playe the man, and not a symple sheepe" (1583), the play acknowledges the social pressures men faced to display their household authority by subjecting their wives to a variety of emotional and physical ordeals.[33] Rather than making Gautier's motive what Cyrus Hoy terms a "dark fascination," as it is with earlier versions of the story, Phillip reveals the cause of the Marquis's transformation as masculine anxiety over public governance of the household.[34]

In Phillip as elsewhere, the Marquis degrades his authority by demeaning his wife. Indeed, versions of the Griselda story with very different views of the Marquis affirm that a husband's unrelenting desire to try his wife's patience undermines the masculine control it is deployed to demonstrate. In the drama by Dekker, Chettle, and Haughton, when others deride her husband Grissil defends him, as wives were instructed to do:

> A tyrant, no he's mercy euen her selfe,
> Iustice in triumph rides in his two eyes,
> Take heede how thou prophanest high deityes." (IV.ii.173–75)

Grissil shows her perfect obedience, but she also reveals how unworthy Gwalter is of her unyielding virtue. Conversely, in the 1619 prose chapbook, her reference to her husband as "soveraigne" potentially suggests that he abuses her deference.[35] In every instance, the asymmetry between the Marquis's power and Griselda's humility undoes masculine authority. As Catherine Belsey recognizes, Griselda stories involve a "paradox for patriarchy": "Marriage as the story defines it is entirely absolutist, but the moral superiority of the wife calls into question the justice of the absolutism."[36]

Labor, Virtue, and Marriage

Premodern Griselda stories afford women's ethical action an unexpected degree of ethical heft. They take seriously women's capacities for excellence by investing Griselda with a material virtue that derives from the labors of her body. These labors, it should be noted, cannot be reduced to childbearing alone. If the water-carrying of Chaucer's Griselda seems insignificant, later authors amplify her care for the household, as well as the daily work she performs to sustain her family. She is found spinning in the ballad version of her tale, and in the 1619 prose chapbook she is occupied with sheep-tending when the Marquis approaches her. Phillip adds an ailing mother, whose demise provides an occasion for Grissell to illustrate her dedicated service to her parents:

> Come on deare mother stay on my shoulder let us depart this place,
> You shall want nothinge to comfort you with all. (338–39)

In *Patient Grissil*, Dekker, Chettle, and Haughton develop an elaborate taxonomy of work, which involves all members of the family in the daily struggle to maintain household solvency. As Janiculo explains to this version's invented son, the poor scholar Laureo, the family is held together through its virtuous distribution of material labor:

> Come sit by me: while I worke to get bread,
> And *Grissill* spin vs yearne to cloath our backs,
> Thou shalt reade doctrine to vs for the soule. (I.ii.164–66)

Later the sage-servant Babulo complains that Laureo does not join in the family's work practices—instead, he tells stories of foreign wonders that derive only from books—but no one ever questions Grissil's contribution to the sustenance of this household.[37]

In fact, as Ann Rosalind Jones and Peter Stallybrass observe in their analysis of the heroine's (re)clothing in *Patient Grissil*, the physical sign of Grissil's labor is maintained in a fashion that supersedes its function as a tool of marital repression.[38] While Gwalter displays Grissil's pitcher and russet gown as part of his putative taming program, these reminders of her past life invest Grissil with a material virtue that undermines the Marquis's claim to control. Even after she is arrayed in finery, poverty distances her from the values of Gwalter's court, so when he taunts her with her former lowliness, "*Grissill* looke heere, this gowne is vnlike to this?" (III.i.85), he merely reveals his distance from her humility. As Kathleen McLuskie recognizes, the play "affirms a connection between poverty and integrity."[39] Because Grissil can always return to work, as she does when she is exiled to her family's modest lodgings, the Marquis undermines both his moral and social authority.

In the 1619 prose chapbook version of this tale, Griselda's return to poverty makes the Marquis's subjects hate him: "Onely shee got the hand of him in the opinion of the people, who by this beganne to whisper against his unkindnes, that had married so vertuous a woman, and bereaved her of two children; so that if they were slaine, it was a murther, if otherwise, it was unkindnesse. For though shee were poore Janicolas daughter by birth, yet she might come from heaven for her vertue, and was sure to go thither for her piety."[40] This version follows *The Clerk's Tale*, which charts the demise in Walter's favor that his treatment of Griselda precipitates:

> For which, where as his peple therbifore
> Hadde loved hym wel, the sclaundre of his diffame
> Made hem that they hym hatede therfore. (IV.729–31)

Although in Dekker, Chettle, and Haughton's play Gwalter uses the fiction of his subjects' complaints as a pretense to justify the children's murder, Grissil's banishment, and his remarriage, the depravity of his exertions provides a neat contrast with the meekness of hers.

Later English versions expose the Marquis's corruption by amplifying Griselda's intimate bond with her children. This connection is founded on the labors of the maternal body. *Patient Grissil*, by Dekker, Chettle, and Haughton, offers a series of shocking scenes that magnify the horror of Gwalter's demand for child-sacrifice. In this play Grissil plainly loves her twins. She coddles them, but in a protracted separation, the play also catalogs the emotional agonies she suffers when they are taken away from her, "Must I not kisse my babes: Must I not touch them?" (IV.i.100). Her pain is equally physical:

> I pray thee let them suck, I am most meete
> To play their Nurse: theyle smile and say tis sweet,
> Which streames from hence, if thou dost beare them hence,
> My angrie breasts will swell, and as mine eyes
> Lets fall salt drops, with these white Necter teares,
> They will be mixt: this sweet will then be brine,
> Theyle crie, Ile chide and say the sin is thine. (IV.i.129–35)

While Gwalter stands aside and weeps at this display, "My cheekes doe glow with shame to heere her speake" (IV.i.153), his continued desire to test seems downright perverse in light of Grissil's abject suffering. Felicity Dunworth characterizes the play's focus on Grissil's lactation as the "involuntary nature of maternal love," a power that threatens her role as devoted and submissive wife to Walter.[41] Tellingly, when she is turned out of the court, her judgment of her children's plight, "Thus tyranny oppresseth innocence" (IV.i.191), issues a withering critique of her husband's conduct.

Like Gwalter, the play is unsatisfied with a single display of maternal anguish. This is not because *Patient Grissil* is obsessed with the spectacle of a woman's suffering, however. Instead, the play remains interested in affirming the virtues of Grissil's domestic work. After Grissil is allowed to take her children into exile with her, Gwalter sends his men to fetch the twins to their supposed deaths. Delivery of the formal decree interrupts a tender domestic scene, one in which Grissil's father, brother, and servant labor to provide comfort for the babies. This humble household is without status or means, but the affection its members share is presented as more genuine than the self-serving love the Marquis expresses for his family. As the servant Babulo arranges a cradle, Griselda's father Janiculo soothes the twins with a sweet song:

> *Sleepe pretty wantons doe not cry,*
> *And I will sing a lullabie.* (IV.ii.101–2)

The contrast with Gwalter's lack of care is unmistakable. His only role in this scene is a self-centering attempt to entrap his wife in a scene of betrayal.

While disguised as a basket-maker, he casts aspersions on his own conduct in inflammatory terms: "The *Marquesse* is a tyrant and does wrong" (IV.ii.170). With this charge, Gwalter expresses concern only to justify his superiority in marriage. Grissil's selfless defense of her husband, by contrast, marks the difference in rank that hierarchical marriage imposes on partners. That this power asymmetry produces monstrous ethical consequences is *Patient Grissil's* unambiguous point.

Gwalter's labor, unlike Grissil's, is ethically barren. Besides the fact that it relies on dominating another, it merely preserves Gwalter's superior status. As Edward Pechter notes, it is a patent ploy to assuage Gwalter's insecurity.[42] It creates nothing that was not already existent; before Gwalter's taming efforts ensued, the Marquess was already superior, and Grissil was already virtuous. In fact, given the independence of her excellence, we might wonder if marriage to Gwalter endangers Grissil's virtues. When she defends him, for instance, Grissil verges on moral blindness. As a means of defense, Dekker, Chettle, and Haughton invest Grissil with insight into her husband's doings. Grissil does not unthinkingly excuse Gwalter; instead, at different moments she expresses awareness that her ordeals might be contrivances designed to test her virtues. These contrivances, the play insists, arise from the evils of hierarchical marriage. When her children are initially taken from her, Grissil tries to make sense of her predicament:

> For my soule tels me, that my honoured Lord,
> Does but to trie poore *Grissils* constancie,
> Hees full of mercie, iustice, full of love. (IV.i.150–52)

Later, when their doom is formally sealed, she comforts herself, once again using a politicized idiom that uncovers the power difference between herself and her husband:

> Thou dost but iest:
> I know thou must not rob me, tis to try
> If I loue them: no, no, heere I read,
> That which strikes blinde mine eyes, makes my heart bleede,
> Farewell, farewell, deare soules, adue adue,
> Your father sendes and I must part from you,
> I must oh God I must, must is for Kings,
> And loe obedience, for loe vnderlings. (IV.ii.136–43)

Grissil faces her helplessness—her utter inability to resist Gwalter's decree—by assigning him a motive other than cruelty and an aim other than violence.

That Grissil believes her husband might test her loyalty by pretending to kill their children exposes the senselessness of absolutist masculinity.[43] That she is right in her supposition—her husband really does try her constancy by staging a seemingly unthinkable sacrifice—indicts hierarchical marriage as an institution of moral corruption. Belsey points out that "Walter, with no grounds for his trial of her virtue, cannot easily be seen as her moral superior. . . . In offering a model of absolutist marriage the story challenges the very foundations of marital absolutism."[44] Since the play shows that husbands commonly had outsized control over their families, so much so that they might murder their children with impunity (or pretend to do so for their own satisfaction), we might rightly suspect Grissil's greatest moral fault is in marrying at all. With the addition of the comic subplot involving Gwalter's sister Julia and her failed suitors, moreover, *Patient Grissil* is direct in its critique of the masculinist bias inherent in premodern marriage. As she watches her brother proceed with the perverse labor of testing his supposedly beloved wife, Julia expresses her skepticism about marriage, and its cultural sanction of women's abuse: "*Grissils* patience . . . make[s] me heere to defie that Ape *Cupid*" (IV.iii.217).

While Julia provides another source of criticism of Gwalter's behavior—"Vex not poore *Grissill* more, alas her heart. . . . You doe her wrong" (IV.iii.235, 239)—the bumbling brawls her suitors undertake to impress her (and each other) comically show the indignities that formalized familial coupling imposes on men as well as women. After Julia says, "I loue not to serue mistris *Venus*," her disappointed suitor Farneze replies, "Then, I perceiue you meane to leade apes in hell" (II.i.255–56, 57). Rather than be bullied into courtship, Julia devises a nimble counterreading of this maxim as a means to bolster her rejection: "That spitefull prouerbe was proclaim'd against them that are married vpon earth, for to be married is to liue in a kinde of hell" (II.i.258–59). By marking marriage as a "combat," a "battaile," and "a kinde of fauourable terrible warre" (II.i.273, 274, 275), Julia suggests that partners' excellences are impoverished by marriage's institutionalized inequities. It is not just belittling to women; the pursuit of marital dominance equally degrades men. Her choice to remain single at the end of the play offers an alternative role for "mayden batchelers, and virgin maydens, those that liue in that freedome and loue it, those that know the war of mariage and hate it" (V.ii.279–81). After watching Gwalter torment Grissil to establish their happy marriage, Julia concludes that women *and* men are diminished by absolutist marriage.

Gwalter works to uphold the hierarchy valorized in early modern marriage discourse, but that labor, which principally involves taming Grissil, looks corrupt. In voicing skepticism about this view of marriage, Julia's role recalls that of Chaucer's Clerk, whose commentary also condemns Walter's testing:

> He hadde assayed hir ynogh bifore,
> And foond hir evere good; what neded it
> Hir for to tempte, and alwey moore and moore,
> Though som men preise it for a subtil wit?
> But as for me, I seye that yvele it sit
> To assaye a wyf whan that it is no nede,
> And putten hir in angwyssh and in drede. (IV.456–62)

Other narratives follow Chaucer in presenting marriage as male labor. For instance, Deloney's ballad depicts marriage as the Marquis's principal responsibility: he chooses Grissel for her beauty and virtue, and the popular song commends him for his good judgment. This is not unlike Chaucer's Walter, who is acclaimed for his marriage choice: "the peple hym heelde / A prudent man" (IV.426–27).

Taming Griselda

Most wives do not accept the submission absolutist marriage requires. In fact, the 1619 prose chapbook includes an extended digression that details wives' transgressions: (1) they seek superiority over husbands; (2) they desire liberty of movement. This text gets completely distracted by women's putative unruliness:

> What a filthinesse is it to a generous spirit, to have a woman so
> presumptuous as to take an account of her husband's actions and
> businesse? Wherein many times they are so peremptory, that I have
> scene them enter the rooms of privacy, where secret businesses of
> strangers have been imparted, and were to be discussed, nor hath

this been done with a lovely insinuation, or cunning excuse of
longing, or willingness to be instructed, or other pretty inducements
to permission, but with a high commanding voice, and impudent
assurances of their owne worth: yea, I have knowne them breake
open letters before they came to their husbands' overlooking, and
have wondred even at souldiers themselves, that would give way to
such indecency. Againe, to be counter-checked in this wilfulnes,
what clamours have beene raised! what tumults and discomforts
occasioned! that instead of awful obedience and delightsome affabil-
ity, they have burst out into outragiousnes, commanded teares of
mischeife, and threatned suspicious revenges. But let them soile
themselves in the filthinesse of this humour never so much. I say
plainely, that though their husbands were fooles by nature, yet is it
not befitting for a wife to discover the same, or over-rule in forren
affaires, I meane matters which concerne them not: for there is no
great man so weake but hath councell and supportation of inferior
officers, nor mean man so sottish but hath friends or servants in the
dispatch of his businesse. Secondly, concerning the desire of liberty:
oh, hellish device of the divell, and fearefull custome both of France
and England! I hope he that knowes the fashions of the East, of
Muscovy, Spain, Italy, and the Mores, understands that no married
wife goes abroad but to honorable purposes; and it is an introduction to death to salute any stranger, or be seene in private conference. For, in true understanding, what businesse should any man
have with my wife three houres together in private? or why, without
my leave, and that upon good grounds, should shee wander in pub-
like? I speake not to overthrow noble societies, generous entertainment, familiar invitations, curteous behaviour, charitable welcomes,
honest recreations, or peradventure, the imparting of private businesse; but meerly against foppish wantonesse, idle talke, suspicious
meetings, damnable play-hunting, disorderly gaming, unbefitting
exercises, and in a word, all such things as tend to obscenity and
wickednes; in which (say what women can), if there be not a moder-
ation by nature, there must be an inforcement by judgement; & that
woman that will not be ruled by good councell must be over-ruled
by better example,—of which, this now in hand (of Lady Grisel) is
a mirror, and transparent chrystall to manifest true vertue, and
wifely duty indeed; and so I come to the wonder of her obedience.[45]

I quote this passage at length to show its extreme preoccupation with wifely misbehavior. The contrast with its Grisel is meant to be clear, but the rambling, exclamatory, and disciplinary diatribe diverts attention, rendering its Grisel an unreal chimera.

The narrative goes on to report Grisel's triumph over adversity, but the digression on real wives calls the possibility of her excellence into question. Grisel is just a fable, a mirror that shows the deficiencies of living women. Never mind the strength and steadfastness she displays in regaining her dignity and her family. The 1619 prose chapbook suggests a story like this one could never actually happen. Despite its critique of masculinist bias in premodern marriage, Dekker, Chettle, and Haughton's *Patient Grissil* does much the same thing with its titular protagonist. Its shrew subplot, which grounds Gwalter's claim that he tames Grissil, diminishes the power of its patient-wife narrative. Most basically, the play's racist deployment of Sir Owen's and Dame Gwenthyan's incomprehensible Welsh reduces their constant squabbling to comic absurdity:

> —*Gwenthyan: En herawgh Ee? Me grauat the Legatee, athlan oth*
> *pendee, adroh ornymee on dictar en hecar Ee.* [Striking me? I'll
> scratch your eyes of your head for turning on me in anger.]
> —*Onophrio:* Doth she threaten you, *Sir Owen?* binde her to the
> peace.
> —*Sir Owen:* By Cod is threaten her indeed: her saies shee'll scradge
> out Sir *Owens* eyes, and her frowne vpon her, a pogs on her nailes.
> (IV.iii.151–55)[46]

There is no serious import to their strife; or, rather, Gwenthyan's scolding is presented as petty and mindlessly destructive. When she rips up a bond worth five thousand ducats, she shows her disregard for her husband's financial standing: "Goe loog . . . ile haue her willes and desires, ile teadge her pridle her Lady" (III.ii.269–70). Later, Gwenthyan demonstrates her indifference to Sir Owen's social stature when she gives away all the provisions needed to host a feast for the Marquesse Gwalter: "Ile tedge her pridle her Lady againe, her cozen *Marquesse* shall eate no pread and meate heere, and her Ladie *Gwenthians* will goe in tags and rags, and like peggar to vexe and chafe sir *Owen*, see you now?" (IV.iii.72–75). Gwenthyan's rebellion is a reaction to Grissil's mistreatment—"And I were *Grissill*, I would pull her eyes out"

(V.ii.19–20)—yet her critique is undermined because the play depicts her shrewishness as absurd.

More disturbing, Gwenthyan's rebellion valorizes Gwalter's testing of Griselda. Not only does her resistance suggest a parallel between taming plots—as if what the Marquess does to Grissil is comically unserious—but she also appears to agree that Gwalter's testing achieves transformation. After Grissil is restored, the Marquess claims that timing is key to his taming:

> I tride my *Grissils* patience when twas greene,
> Like a young Osier [willow], and I moulded it
> Like waxe to all impressions: married men
> That long to tame their wiues must curbe them in,
> Before they need a bridle, then they'll prooue
> All *Grissils* full of patience, full of loue. (V.ii.238–43)

Were Sir Owen to try to tame Gwenthyan, she would snap like reeds that have been allowed to dry with no tending or shaping. Exasperated, Sir Owen threatens violence or abandonment as his only means of recourse against his headstrong wife. Yet the play does not endorse the masculine violence of traditional shrew taming, for, as Julia remarks, "That were a shame eyther to run away from a woman, or to strike her" (V.ii.254). With another nod to domestic manuals of the day, the play insists that men are degraded by domestic brawling. Instead, as the Marquess's example demonstrates, women should be tamed through emotional not physical hardship.

In fact, the power of Gwalter's taming reverberates, transforming Gwenthyan from shrew to virtue through the mere spectacle of his achievement: "Cozen *Marquesse*, cozen *Julia*, Lawrds and Laties all, it shall not need: as her cozen [the Marquess] has tryed *Grissill*, so *Gwenthian* has Sir *Owen*" (V.ii.261–63). Once Gwenthyan understands the outcome of the Marquess's taming, in other words, she vows to be ruled by Sir Owen: "but sir *Owen* shal be her head, and is sorry has anger her head and mag it ake" (V.ii.265–66). Gwalter's rational governance makes up for Sir Owen's foolish threats. Her reconciliation with her husband, most importantly, makes Grissil's patience a product of masculine regulation. Tellingly, Grissil is silenced at the end of this play, upstaged by Sir Owen's newfound ability to valorize himself: "*Grissil* is weary: pray let sir *Owen* speag. *Grissill* is patient, and her cozen is patient, therefore is speage for two" (V.ii.297–98). The lesson Sir Owen learns from the Marquess Gwalter is ultimately quite simple: a man legitimizes his authority by speaking for a woman, ideally his wife. This teaching is exhaustively showcased throughout the play's final act, in which Gwalter carefully choreographs the events leading to Grissil's restitution.

In a final tableau of testing, the Marquess directs Grissil to assist him in wedding his new bride. She will crown her, as well as place the ring on her finger. Importantly, however, Gwalter manages Grissil's gestures of deference:

> Marquess: *Grissill* place you this crowne vpon her head,
> Put these imbrodered slippers on her feete.
> Tis well, deliuer me your wedding ring,
> Circle her finger with it, now stand by,
> Art thou content with all?
> Grissil: Content with all.
> Marquess: My Bride is Crown'd. (V.ii.113–19)

By arranging her submission, Gwalter ensures that Grissil's patience becomes a sign of his power more than her virtue. Grissil is reduced to near silence by Gwalter's maneuvering, but Sir Owen's and Gwenthyan's comic commentary on her behavior also serves to diminish her display.[47] When Sir Owen exclaims, "*Gwenthians* there's wiues, there's patient wiues," and she replies, "Fuh fuh is fooles, *Tawsone*, is arrant pobie fooles" (V.ii.111, 112), their back-and-forth leaves no room to see signs of strength in Grissil's gestures. In this context her submission is a compulsory surrender to an external power. She has no chance to show strength of character, since she registers her assent by echoing her husband's very words: "Content with all" (V.ii.118). If Chaucer's Clerk sees Echo as a protoshrew, who "holdeth no silence, / But evere answereth at the countretaille" (IV.1189–90), Dekker, Chettle, and Haughton return to the Ovidian resonance of this story, in which Echo is bound only to repeat and endorse what Narcissus says.[48] Because Grissil merely reiterates Gwalter's words, her material virtue is theatrically suppressed.

Griselda Untamed

Grissil's restricted position is quite a departure from earlier in the play, when her performance of passivity outstrips Gwalter's claim to control. Shortly after the Marquess develops his desire to try his wife's patience, he taunts her with her former poverty. Her reply is self-authorizing, "Poore *Grissill* is not proud of these attires" (II.ii.68), as Gwalter recognizes: "Spite of my soule sheele triumph ouer mee" (II.ii.76). The subsequent performance of deference he demands—he requires her to pick up his glove, then to tie his man's shoe—provides further occasions for Grissil's self-articulation. Though she abases herself, when she does so she claims a dignity that the Marquess cannot deny:

> Tis but my duetie: if youle haue me stoope
> Euen to your meanest groome my Lord ile stoope. (II.ii.81–82)[49]

Her lowliness is not compulsory, but is a place she claims as her own. Dekker, Chettle, and Haughton acknowledge Grissil's material virtues, even though they limit those same powers near the play's close. Far more instrumentally, the 1619 prose chapbook, in an introductory tag that, of course, might have been appended by a savvy publisher, limits Grisel's virtues by privileging the story's "how-to" utility: "How Maides By Her Example In Their Good Behaviour May Marrie Rich Husbands; And Likewise Wives By Their Patience And Obedience May Gaine Much Glorie." Virtue is here a means to social advancement. Confining Griselda's virtue is nothing new. Chaucer's Clerk circumscribes the power of her example with the casual dismissal,

> It were ful hard to fynde nowadayes
> In al a toun Grisildis thre or two. (IV.1164–65)

By contrast, the popular ballad refuses to restrict Grissell's virtue, but instead details her ability to withstand adversity with dignity and strength. The Marquis does not divest her of power; rather, "Her Velvet Gown / Most patiently she stripd off."[50] Phillip's moral interlude also maintains Griselda's ethical stature. This is due in part to the allegorical structure of the *Play of Pacient Grissell*: because different moral qualities are afforded speaking parts, the virtues that protect Grissell are actually separate characters. When her father, Janicle, laments their wretched condition after Grissell is banished, she points to her guardian virtues, Pacience and Constancye, and recommends that her father pledge loyalty to these same figures. There is no suggestion that these virtues arise from her contact with Gautier. Grissell sings a song of thanks to God for her virtues. Similarly, she views her trials as providential, administered by God to test her devotional strength. Gautier is diminished in her account, since he is just a tool that God uses to prove Grissell's spiritual election. Her virtues are embodied weapons that assure her success:

> Pacience is the Buckler wherwith I contend,
> And Constancie in combat, stayeth mee upright,
> These so arme mee, that I can not be vanquisht in fight. (1905–7)

Grissell's martial patience immediately comes to the fore. When Gautier weds his daughter, the Marquis asks Grissell to appraise his new bride. After cataloging the maiden's perfections, Phillip's Grissell makes her famous charge against Gautier:

> But harke my Lord, what I saye to thee agayne,
> Take heed thou pricke her not, with the Needles of disdayne:
> As thou hast done the other, for shee hath bin brought up dayntelie,
> And peraduenture can not take the matter so pacientlie. (1933–36)

Grissell acknowledges her own virtue, and the autonomy with which it invests her. Like Chaucer's Griselda, she points to her own toughness to cast doubt on her husband's behavior. Gautier's acknowledgment, "Oh Grissill, thy Vertues I must commend" (1937), affirms the independence of her excellence. Phillip's play has a greater appreciation for Grissell's material virtues, but this validation evidences greater anxiety surrounding men's exercises of authority as an index of their moral fitness, or their *virtus*.

By the end of the century, Dekker, Chettle, and Haughton rework Grissil's virtues to affirm Gwalter's household authority.[51] Other appearances of the Griselda story in England suggest that her virtues were granted more substance earlier in the Tudor period. The now-lost *De patientia Griseldis*, by Ralph Radcliffe, written between 1546 and 1552, is thought to be a play that extols the virtue of patience in the face of oppression.[52] Given the ability of the Griselda story to be adapted to promote a woman's strengths in the face of adversity, it is fitting that in 1558 William Forrest, chaplain to Queen Mary, wrote *The History of Grisild the Second* to laud the virtues of the late Catherine of Aragon.[53] By casting Henry as the tyrant Walter, Forrest depicts Catherine as a grieving mother who persevered in the face of injustices done to her dignity and her person. Although the tale is a heavily topical allegory, Forrest claims to draw plain parallels:

So clokedlye vnder darke couerture?
We haue not walked in this Historye,?
But that the readers may vndrestande sure?
The meane of oure mentioned memorye,?
Not fygured as by Alligorye,?
But this sayde *Grysilde*, playnlye to defyne,?
Is playnlye ment the goode Queene *Catharyne*.[54]

Earlier in the sixteenth century, the Griselda story was imagined to elaborate the injustices done to a virtuous queen, since, as Ursula Potter points
out, the lauded humanist, educator, and counselor to Catherine, Juan Luis
Vives, also draws a parallel between Griselda and Catherine in his Latin
grammar exercises (1539): "The fall of Griselda, which John Boccaccio wrote
so aptly and skilfully; but my master has decided to add a true story to this
fiction, which excels the story of Griselda, viz., that of Godelina of Flanders
and the English Queen Catharine of Aragon."[55] In fact, on account of the
Griselda story's portability, particularly its ability to critique Henry VIII's
abuse of subsequent long-suffering queens, Potter sees a parallel between Forrest's narrative and Phillip's interlude, arguing that the latter—entered in
the stationer's register after Elizabeth I took the throne—commemorates the
suffering of the new queen's wronged mother, Anne Boleyn.[56] As she argues,
"For Phillip, writing when Elizabeth was still new to the throne . . . promoting the virtues of the mother bestows legitimacy on the daughter."[57] The
political valence of Phillip's play has stirred considerable critical debate. What
seems clear, regardless of the play's topical connections, is that the figure of
the shrew does not provide the same ideological wedge that it does in later
English Griselda fables.[58]

    This is not to say that the shrew figure is altogether absent. As I men-
tioned earlier, Phillip's vice figure, Politick Persuasion, seeks to undermine
Gautier's confidence in Grissell with a series of misogynist denigrations of
women. Yet, when this happens in Phillip, the Marquis defends Grissell's
innate capacity for ethical excellence:

But my ellected mate God knowes, with vice will not procead,
She will obserue a modest meane, hir vertues shall increase,
All hatfull hate in hyr shall end, she loueth perfyt peace,
She feareth God, she dreads his name, she leades a Godly life,
And dayly sekes for to subdue, contensyon and strife,

She will as dutie byndes, hir spoused mate obaye,
From husbaudes heastes at no time she for any cause will straye.
　(388–95)

Phillip's interlude rehearses common antifeminist saws against women's ethical stature through Politic Persuasion's sexist diatribes, but it quickly and firmly dismisses such stereotypes as pernicious fictions. In Reason's words, "This talke from a mind malliscyous doth proceade / Therfore cease this vaine clatter" (416–17). The only moment when shrew and virtue are opposed in Phillip's interlude is when Politic Persuasion finds himself astonished by Grissell's ethical distinction as it compares with everyday Griseldas:

Therbe a number liuing that Grissills haue to name,
But yet very shrewishe by naturall dispocisyon,
Ther maners assuredly far differ from the same. (1618–20)

Because this comparison comes from a designated vice character, it serves to enhance, not diminish, the power of Phillip's patient wife.

Playing off Virtue in Shakespeare's *Taming of the Shrew*

Shuffling Subjects

The brawling shrew is not imagined as patient virtue's matched opposite in Phillip's moral interlude. Instead, the shrew is a gender stereotype that is staged in order to be dispatched in this midcentury drama. *The Play of Patient Grissell* establishes distance between shrew and virtue, but later renderings of the Griselda narrative bring these figures together. By the time *The Comedy of Patient Grissil* was performed in 1600, these femininities had dramatically limited one another. If we are surprised that Dekker, Chettle, and Haughton would imagine Grissel and Gwenthyan as a countered couple, we should not be. There is evidence that this play was written to compete with the success of Shakespeare's *Taming of the Shrew* (ca. 1590–94), since Dekker, Chettle, and Haughton composed their play for the Admiral's Men, rival company to the Lord Chamberlain's Men.[59] And, although it is clear that *The Taming of the Shrew* did not invent the theatrical doubling of virtue and shrew, the play could not function without coupling these femininities. Katherina could not be assigned the part of shrew, she understands in frustration, were Bianca not appointed the role of virtue.

Playing shrew off virtue, as Shakespeare's play illustrates, secures masculine dominance. It does so in a way that offers women no material control over the identities that define them. When Shakespeare's play begins, Katherina's lack of virtue is fixed by the men who appraise her character. Before she even speaks, Gremio refuses Baptista's invitation to court Katherina, claiming that "to cart her" would be a more appropriate response to Katherina's "rough" manner (I.i.55).[60] Bianca's virtue is also an identity settled by common masculine accord. Her prized worth can only be established, importantly, in contrast with Katherina's assigned shrewishness. Tranio calls attention to Katherina's conduct, thinking her a humorous spectacle "stark mad or wonderful forward" (I.i.69), but his exclamation only prompts Lucentio to remark on Bianca's contrasting demeanor:

> But in the other's silence do I see,
> Maid's mild behavior and sobriety. (I.i.70–71)

Bianca conforms to a model of virtue prescribed by men; not surprisingly, therefore, she is treated with admiration. Katherina, by contrast, is called "froward" and is provoked to anger. One can imagine the tables turning on these women: if Bianca were labeled a "fiend of hell" (I.i.88), or were treated with the disrespect shown to Katherina, Lucentio's description of her as "mild" might also need revision.

Petruchio seeks to gain advantage in this domain by treating both categories of feminine identity—shrew and virtue—as artificial constructs that men impose on women to further masculine schemes of self-advancement. When Gremio expresses incredulity at Petruchio's determination, asking, "But will you woo this wildcat? (I.ii.195), Petruchio delivers an oration that hierarchizes disruption, relegating the strife a chiding wife can produce to the private, domestic, and trivial domain of the household, a place any empowered husband can manage:

> Think you a little din can daunt mine ears?
> Have I not in my time heard lions roar?
> . . . .
> And do you tell me of a woman's tongue,
> That gives not half so great a blow to hear

As will a chestnut in a farmer's fire?
Tush, tush! Fear boys with bugs. (I.ii.198–99, 206–9)

Petruchio takes up shrew-taming as a rhetorical exercise, which, more radically than early modern Griselda stories, depends upon instituting absolute
masculine control.[61] To succeed, Petruchio has to deny Katherina's investment in the virtue with which he works to associate her. While he attempts
to redefine her as virtue, then, this is a prescriptive, explicitly nonmaterial
virtue that stands opposed to the ethical excellence studied across this book.

The feminine virtue that Paduan men seek, as reactions to both Bianca
and Katherina attest, is an empty form of obedience that facilitates male
competition. Like the normative virtues recommended for women in prescriptive literatures, this kind of excellence is wholly determined by men.[62]
Before Petruchio meets Katherina, he attempts to redefine her according to
this kind of disembodied excellence. He seeks "Katharina, fair and virtuous,"
a designation Baptista refuses to recognize, replying, "I have a daughter, sir,
called Katherina" (II.i.43). After Petruchio lists the traits he expects to find
in a wife (beauty, modesty, mildness), Baptista discourages Petruchio, believ-
ing that his daughter Katherina cannot gratify such wishes: "She is not for
your turn, the more my grief" (II.i.63). In response, Petruchio reclassifies
Katherina's worth in the community, telling Baptista that gaining Katherina's
love "is nothing" (II.i.130), countering her defiance with his confidence: "I
am as peremptory as she proud-minded" (II.i.131). With this move, he affirms
that the virtue he desires is an ethical category that Katherina cannot control.
Petruchio must teach others to read Katherina in the way that he does, but
in order to transform their perspectives, he must teach Katherina to read
herself according to his desires. She must accede, in other words, to the
ethical outsourcing of her character.

Petruchio convinces Katherina by offering her a social position confer-
ring dignity, not abuse. Or, as Leah S. Marcus puts it, "She also earns the
right to be treated like a gentlewoman rather than a hoyden."[63] To recreate
Katherina as virtue, Petruchio promises to change the material conditions of
her life without recourse to bodily taming. Scholars who study domestic
literatures of the period frequently emphasize the ways in which cucking,
carting, bridling, and beating all become part of a comprehensive program to
curb wifely insurrection through physical violence.[64] Linda Boose is certainly
right to argue that these practices color the play, though, of course, they

do so only indirectly.[65] Early on, Katherina's conduct recalls the raucous physicality of shrewishness. At the beginning of Act II, she interrogates a bound Bianca, and to her sister's entreaties to be released, she reacts with violence. Later, she responds to the instruction of the disguised Hortensio by breaking a lute over his head, refusing to be ruled by his advice, even in a field that requires training. Finally, when she meets Petruchio, their verbal sparring becomes physical when she "tries" his gentle status. Katherina meets verbal provocation with physical force. By common consent, Katherina is a shrew in need of taming, but Petruchio counters shared Paduan wisdom when he answers her anger with words, not blows. As Emily Detmer argues, Petruchio performs masculine dominance through physical restraint.[66]

Importantly for my purposes, Petruchio's restraint resists the traditional association of shrewishness with the disorderly (female) body. Before it was gendered feminine, the term "shrew" signaled an elementary imbalance of the physical body.[67] If the body's materiality (its humors and passions) remained ungoverned, an ill temperament caused the violence, disorder, and unruliness associated with shrewishness. In the Middle Ages, therefore, men as well as women could be shrews.[68] Shrews are everywhere in monitory literatures, but probably the most famous example comes from Chaucer. We might think of the Wife of Bath's habit of berating her husbands with the epithet, "olde dotard shrewe!" (III.291), as ironic, but if Chaucer means to mark her unruliness through her combative language, he does so by taking advantage of the gendered bivalence of shrew in medieval usage. By contrast, the early modern feminization of "shrew" forged an essential connection between women, embodiment, and insurrection.[69] As Katherine A. Sirluck explains, "women were commonly considered to be emblematic of disorder in general, as they were claimed to be governed by passion, to have irrepressible appetites, unstable minds, and inadequate reason."[70] When Petruchio denies this link, he suggests that there might be another way of viewing Katherina's actions.[71] Women's embodied action need not amount to shrewishness; instead, it might be ethical, even virtuous. Other men in Padua treat feminine shrewishness as essential, as a fundamental intransigence that derives from the female body. Rather than insist that she needs to be ruled because of this traditional misogynist association, Petruchio treats Katherina's shrewishness as a responsive condition that might be altered with the changed circumstances that his courtship promises to inaugurate.[72] Katherina might not act like a shrew, in sum, were she not treated as one.

Identity's performative basis, however, is something Petruchio aims to
direct to his own benefit. It is not meant to free Katherina, or to recognize
that her protests are warranted complaints against mistreatment. Instead,
Petruchio seeks to redistribute terms of femininity without changing the categories. In this, he seeks to make Katherina's virtue an exclusively masculine
production. His strategy looks ingenious compared to that of other tamers,
but it is fully consonant with a recognized masculine desire to transform
feminine identity using rhetorical persuasion alone.[73] As *A forme of Christian
policy* puts it: "Seeing a wife is giuen in discipline and correction to her
husband, and that she is neyther meare sauage, nor desperate intractable
(which though she were, yet men make tame both Lions and Tygers) it were
good first to vse doctrine as well by him selfe as others hir parentes and
nearest kinred, and bringing her to the conference of sermons, to leaue
vnproued no gentle, easie or friendly meane, that may further her conuer-
sion."[74] Instead of joining the Bianca chase, in which Bianca corresponds
directly to feminine virtue, Petruchio deconstructs categories of femininity,
insisting that the female subjects who occupy the positions of shrewish and
virtuous woman are interchangeable. To do so, he renders ethical identities
superficial, treating virtue like an external covering that he will require Katherina to wear.[75]

As Wayne Rebhorn makes clear, Petruchio seeks to install himself in the
position of *rhetor*, a man able to manipulate the linguistic figures shaping
identity in order to fashion his own.[76] His masculinity rests on a crucial
circularity: he can control himself by controlling a woman, so he can control
a woman by controlling himself. As Coppèlia Kahn remarks, "it is Kate's
submission to him that makes Petruchio a man."[77] There is no room for
Katherina to inhabit a virtue that is concrete and corporeal. Importantly, her
ethical identity is her husband's creation, not her own.[78] Separating Katherina's femininity from materiality, while it might work to free her from associations between women and shrews, is an ultimate loss. This is because, as I
have observed across this book, "vertues" also had physical valence during
this period. Losing the body means losing a source of potential excellence. In
fact, submerging the animate animality denoted by the community designa-
tor, "shrew," as J. A. Shea and Paul Yachnin argue, separates Katherina from
a material resource of vitality that renders her, in their words, a "wondrously
articulate and commanding public woman."[79] Since Edward Topsell characterizes his aim in *The historie of foure-footed beastes* (1607) as "*Describing the
true and liuely figure of euery beast, with a discourse of their . . . vertues (both*

naturall and medicinall)," it is clear that in premodern England, shrews were believed to have their own unique virtues. These powers are not positive in Topsell's account, though he does allow that the shrew "is feared of al."[80]

To sever Katherina's connection to her incorporated virtues is to vest Petruchio with full control over her character. Petruchio pursues just this sort of marital absolutism, which was promoted by domestic literatures of the day. Edmund Tilney describes the process by which a husband gains total control over all aspects of his wife's existence: "The wise man maye not be contented onely with the Spouses virginitie, but by little and lyttle must gently procure that he maye also steale a|way hir priuate will, and appetite, so that of two bodies there may be made one one|lye heart."[81] Outward conformity is not enough. As Tilney all but admits, bodily virtues work in tandem with intellectual and spiritual resources of excellence. To part one from the others, to suggest that virtues—inner and outer, mental and physical, spiritual and bodily—might be split from one another, is to diminish materiality's importance to an embodied ethics. We might suppose that a dematerialized ethics would be freeing, since revealing the flimsiness of the virtue/shrew binary would weaken its organizing power. There is nothing essential that tethers Katherina to shrewishness, just as there is nothing fundamental that ties Bianca to virtuousness. Katherina's complaint, "Her silence flouts me" (II.i.29), recognizes that the quiet submission Bianca performs associates Katherina with the stereotype of brawling shrew.

To outfit Katherina according to his ideal of wifely virtue, Petruchio treats shrewishness as a superficial display that has little to do with what he insists is Katherina's essential goodness. He tells Baptista, Gremio, and Tranio that *they* have misjudged Katherina, that her shrewishness is just an act, "for policy / For she's not forward, but modest as the dove" (II.i.289–90). When Katherina tells him that she would be hanged before she would marry him, he claims that his apparent failure is also a public performance:

'Tis bargained twixt us twain, being alone,
That she shall still be curst in company. (II.i.302–3)

Katherina only *acts like* a shrew; she *really is* virtuous. Petruchio asserts the detachable nature of feminine categories, only to claim the ability to perceive the identities named by those categories. Through this move, Petruchio claims exclusive mastery over Katherina's character. He gets to decide if she fits the shrew position, which denies the power of those who have hitherto determined her ethical status.[82]

The play charts Petruchio's ability to unmake and remake Katherina according to his own desires. As part of this process, he destabilizes her status through his own performance of unruliness: "By this reckoning [Petruchio] is more shrew than she" (IV.i.61). Because his behavior on their wedding day threatens to make Katherina look like a fool, her anger finally appears to be a warranted reaction to mistreatment. She has protested Baptista's decision to marry her off to Petruchio throughout the play, but it is only when Petruchio becomes deliberately disheveled that her complaints are afforded a persuasive eloquence:

> No shame but mine. I must, forsooth, be forced
> To give my hand opposed against my heart
> Unto a mad-brain rudesby full of spleen,
> Who wooed in haste and means to wed at leisure. (III.ii.8–11)

Behavior that has been described as shrewish is now understood as justified, as Baptista's reaction to Katherina's complaint attests:

> For such an injury would vex a very saint,
> Much more a shrew of thy impatient humor. (III.ii.28–29)

Because her harms are on display, Katherina's protest affirms that shrew is a name she is asked to bear only in relation to her submissive sister. In a pattern that is repeated, Petruchio proves that Katherina is not a shrew by making her suffer. Once again, his method is adapted directly from Griselda stories, although here the motive for his testing is clearly presented as reformative.

Like the Marquis in Griselda stories, Petruchio is ruthless in his treatment of Katherina. Petruchio relishes the power of his role as oppressor, employing sociopolitical terms to express his method of domination: "Thus have I politicly begun my reign" (IV.i.176). He takes up the house and state analogy circulated by domestic manuals, recreating Katherina's virtue as an absolutist discipline with explicitly material consequences. Katherina *must* calm him, or humor him, in order to get food, sleep, or peace. She cannot act like a shrew if she wants to survive. Before he ever returns to Padua, Petruchio declares his method a success:

This is a way to kill a wife with kindness;
And thus I'll curb her mad and headstrong humor.
He that knows better how to tame a shrew,
Now let him speak. 'Tis charity to show. (IV.i.196–99)

Lest his audience think that Katherina seems pathetic, or perhaps begin to
doubt the need for such a program, Petruchio reinvokes the identity he supposedly works to eliminate. Katherina will always *be* a shrew, but under
Petruchio's guidance she will be unable to *act* as one. Petruchio, therefore,
declares Katherina's essential shrewishness in order to establish his authority.

Just as he does earlier, Petruchio privileges himself as being able to see
through the fiction of identity. In Dekker, Chettle, and Haughton's *Patient
Grissil*, Gwalter claims to have tamed Grissil through similar means, but in
that play there is no discernible difference in the wifely protagonist's behavior. Grissil is patient before and after she meets the Marquis. What about
here? If Katherina no longer appears to be a shrew, Petruchio would have
audiences believe that such transformation is wrought only through his disciplinary agency. But is this true? Does Katherina's behavior change as a consequence of Petruchio's ordeals? Undoubtedly it does, and in a fashion that
shows the damaging consequences of the Griselda story in early modern
England. In a series of increasingly radical trials, Katherina's every move is
coordinated as a product of Petruchio's will. When she asks Grumio for
meat, we are led to believe, she does so only because Petruchio has humbled
her. It is true that Katherina is not accustomed to such subservience, as her
plea for food makes explicit:

But I, who never knew how to entreat,
Nor never needed that I should entreat,
Am starved for meat, giddy for lack of sleep,
With oaths kept waking, and with brawling fed. (IV.iii.7–10)

Her begging does not show her lack of humility, but rather reveals the
extreme conditions of subservience entailed by Petruchio's rendering of feminine virtue.

Enacting Passivity

By means of his "taming-school" (IV.ii.55, 56), Petruchio achieves the fantasy
of masculine authority circulated by Griselda stories: he is at the center of

Katherina's being, which means that each expression of her identity reflects his comprehensive power. Katherina's every move is Petruchio's. Griselda narratives usually condemn this fantasy, but this is because, as Shakespeare's *Taming of the Shrew* affirms, it is both undesirable *and* impossible. To insist that a woman's identity is a masculine production without leaving room for her to inhabit that position is to destroy that very identity, as feminist reactions to this play have revealed.[83] The prescriptive virtue Petruchio fashions for Katherina is unsustainable because it is unsurvivable. While isolated at Petruchio's house, Katherina reveals the impossibility of remaining virtuous, attesting to the fact that complete passivity would lead to self-annihilation.[84]

Disturbingly, though, when she beats Grumio because he "feed'st [her] with the very name of meat!" (IV.iii.32), she justifies Petruchio's claim that such treatment is necessary to enforce compliance. Any gesture that is not generated or directed by Petruchio confines Katherina further. Katherina is right back in the predicament that plagued her at the beginning of the play, but this time her body becomes a material register of the ethical category that defines her.[85]

Petruchio does not beat Katherina, but he does abuse her. Since Petruchio acts "under name of perfect love" (IV.iii.12), Katherina is unable to argue against Petruchio's cruelty. Any active resistance to his regulation would demonstrate its necessity. Her only defense is verbal protest, but Petruchio denies even her ability to express her own desires by treating her like a child who must be tended. By infantilizing Katherina, he once again subscribes to early modern domestic ideology, since, in the words of Vives, "For all though there be one made of two / yet the woman is as doughter unto her husbande / and of nature more weaker."[86] Joel Fineman expresses this idea in a more modern idiom: "In ways which are so traditional that they might be called proverbial, Shakespeare's *Taming of the Shrew* assumes—it turns out to make no difference whether it does ironically—that the language of woman is at odds with the order and authority of man."[87] Katherina articulates her own expectations for virtue, claiming that she wants clothing that signifies her worth in the culture:

> This doth fit the time,
> And gentlewomen wear such caps as these. (IV.iii.69–70)

But Petruchio separates her from such a designation, telling her that she may have the cap she wants *when* she becomes gentle. Petruchio determines *whether* she meets expectations for virtue; until she meets *his* standards of

wifely obedience, she cannot wear signs denoting excellence. During his taming rituals, Petruchio makes no room for Katherina to practice the active
obedience early modern Griseldas assume.

Katherina has no room to develop an enlivened model of material virtue;
every complaint she makes justifies Petruchio's domination. Katherina can "tell
the anger of [her] heart" (IV.iii.77); she can speak until her heart breaks. But
such displays of resistance will only validate the authority Petruchio seeks to
exert over her. Petruchio's taming, therefore, denies any investment she might
have in her own identity. Katherina's predicament shows that enacting passivity
is not enough; her submission must appear as a product of Petruchio's direction. Because Petruchio is in full charge of her femininity, Katherina is in a
dangerous position. Without another woman against whom to measure her
conduct, Katherina's every move demonstrates her agency, which separates her
in increasingly extreme ways from the basic necessities of existence. She cannot
get sustenance unless she returns to the community that originally labeled her
shrew. But Petruchio will not allow her to return to Padua until her agency
appears to derive from his particular will.

Hortensio, after witnessing Petruchio's tirade over Katherina's attire, incredulously remarks, "Why, so this gallant will command the sun"
(IV.iii.192); but the façade of absolute control is exactly what Petruchio hopes
to achieve. Until she agrees that the sun is the moon, Katherina will get no
relief from Petruchio's confining domination. When she resists his claim to
absolute authority, saying "I know it is the sun that shines so bright" (IV.v.5),
Hortensio cautions her, "Say as he says, or we shall never go" (IV.v.11),
expressing the pragmatic operation of the prescriptive virtue Katherina must
enact. She must not seem to affirm anything that Petruchio does not first
sanction. He must appear in control of her agency for her conduct to pass as
virtuous. Unlike early modern Griseldas, whose submission is a product of
personal autonomy, Katherina is Petruchio's creature. Thus, even if she
knows he is wrong, she must express agreement to achieve her own desires:

> But the sun it is not, when you say it is not,
> And the moon changes even as your mind.
> What you will have it named, even that it is,
> And so it shall be for Katherine. (IV.v.19–22)

She now no longer wishes to speak her heart's anger; she just wants to get to
Padua to escape the prison in which her husband has kept her since her
wedding day.

Petruchio allows Katherina to exercise her discretion only when she enacts the guise of virtue he specifies. In her isolated resistance, every gesture becomes one of self-destruction because her actions cannot qualify as submissive. As John Fletcher's answer play makes clear, the model of virtue that Petruchio prescribes, because it allows Katherina no agency outside his own, cannot stand. At the outset of *The Woman's Prize*, Katherina is dead. As I shall suggest near the end of this chapter, this is purposeful: Petruchio's household tyranny, which becomes legible in Shakespeare's *Taming of the Shrew*, is the subject of Fletcher's entire play. In Shakespeare's folio-*Shrew* it is only the company of other women that gives Katherina room to breathe; around her peers she gains a kind of agency, because her performance of feminine submission distinguishes her virtue as a product of her husband's sanction. When she finally gets back to Padua, however, those from whom she was removed on her wedding day act as if Katherina remains a shrew, reading her agency only through the interpretive mastery they have hitherto exercised over her character. The widow speaks this assumption in her address to Katherina, asserting her own virtue in relation to Katherina's supposed shrewishness. Like Gwenthyan in Dekker, Chettle, and Haughton's *Patient Grissel*, the widow demonstrates the ways in which women limit one another by deploying classifications of femininity from prescriptive discourse. The widow reads Katherina's agency narrowly, only as it confirms the model of femininity Padua imposes:

> Your husband, being troubled with a shrew,
> Measures my husband's sorrow by his woe. (V.ii.28–29)

Rather than offering Katherina a way out of the prison of her identity, the return to Padua marks a return to the same old binary system of classification. Even so, here we see the importance of Amy L. Smith's claim, that "Kate reiterates the [marriage] manuals with a difference."[88] This time it is Katherina who will set a new standard for virtue, and it is her agency, which paradoxically demonstrates her submission, that illustrates the supposed failures of the other women. Same as it ever was, the standards for virtue are removed from the interests of the women expected to perform them. As the widow and Bianca make clear during the first round of the contest, the demands made of them are part of a masculine game that should not really concern them. Bianca is busy—she does not want to trouble herself to humor her husband's frivolous command. The widow's reply is even more on point:

"She says you have some goodly jest in hand" (V.ii.95). Only Katherina, who has been trained to display her agency as the product of Petruchio's power, comes on command. She appears as an agent of Petruchio's will, which makes her conduct count as submissive despite its competitive bent. She is unlike the other wives, and her virtue defines their conduct as inappropriate. Katherina marks the difference between shrew and virtue, simultaneously ranking women and men in this game of patriarchal status.

Categorizations of gender and rank are rearranged in the play's closing scene, but these distinctions are reinforced by their continued ability to mark difference within the community. Cloaking feminine agency in the right garb determines cultural differences between women and men. Petruchio uses Katherina to silence the protest of the other women, preventing their critique—"Fie, what a foolish duty call you this?" (V.ii.129)—from taking hold. Petruchio orders Katherina to "tell these headstrong women / What duty they do owe their lords and husbands" (V.ii.134–35) as a display of his authority and as a performance of her submission. Katherina's apparent transformation has been rightly connected to cultural practices of wife-beating and social coercion, thereby conforming the play's ideologies to early modern notions of wifely subservience.[89] Petruchio's taming program is derived directly from early modern household manuals, which recommend a program of emotional violence that inflicts physical suffering. But, and this returns us to Griselda legends of the era, something goes awry with Petruchio's efforts. He is not able to maintain control over Katherina's virtue because her submission does not remain a product of Petruchio's masculine direction. Because she takes up a stance of radical obedience, she cultivates a material virtue that eludes Petruchio's control.

Playing A-Part

With Katherina's confounding final turn, *The Taming of the Shrew* thwarts Petruchio's desire to cultivate feminine virtue as a product of masculine agency. In the play's longest speech, Katherina delineates the components of wifely virtue circulating in early modern England:

Fie, fie! Unknit that threatening, unkind brow
And dart not scornful glances from those eyes
To wound thy lord, thy king, thy governor.

It blots thy beauty as frosts do bite the meads,
Confounds thy fame as whirlwinds shake fair buds,
And in no sense is meet or amiable.
A woman moved is like a fountain troubled,
Muddy, ill-seeming, thick, bereft of beauty;
And while it is so, none so dry or thirsty
Will deign to sip or touch one drop of it.
Thy husband is thy lord, thy life, thy keeper,
Thy head, thy sovereign; one that cares for thee,
And for thy maintenance, commits his body
To painful labor both by sea and land,
To watch the night in storms, the day in cold,
Whilst thou liest warm at home, secure and safe;
And craves no other tribute at thy hands
But love, fair looks, and true obedience—
Too little payment for so great a debt.
Such duty as the subject owes the prince,
Even such a woman oweth to her husband;
And when she is froward, peevish, sullen, sour,
And not obedient to his honest will,
What is she but a foul contending rebel
And graceless traitor to her loving lord?
I am ashamed that women are so simple
To offer war where they should kneel for peace,
Or seek for rule, supremacy, and sway,
Whey they are bound to serve, love, and obey.
Why are our bodies soft, and weak, and smooth,
Unapt to toil and trouble in the world,
But that our soft conditions and our hearts
Should well agree with our external parts?
Come, come, you froward and unable worms!
My mind hath been as big as one of yours,
My heart as great, my reason haply more,
To bandy word for word and frown for frown;
But now I see our lances are but straws,
Our strength as weak, our weakness past compare,
That seeming to be most which we indeed least are.
Then vail your stomachs, for it is no boot,

And place your hands below your husband's foot,
In token of which duty, if he please,
My hand is ready, may it do him ease. (V.ii.140–83)

Katherina's commentary on idealized femininity outstrips any expectations
Petruchio could have devised for her; she does not only what he says but
reaches beyond what he says, thus demonstrating the failures inherent in the
prescriptive system of identity. As Juliet Dusinberre acknowledges, Katherina's final "speech steals the show. Beneath an ostensible message of humility,
it generates the suppressed exhilaration of its stage power."[90] By accepting the
model of femininity foisted on her, Katherina gains autonomy. And, by
speaking the category of feminine virtue that masculine discourse would
define, she steps outside the boundaries of subjectivity imagined by
Petruchio. He cannot help but be pleased, because she makes literal his desire
for absolute feminine submission. But, by performing her subjection in such
independent terms, she exposes the illusory nature of the power he would
wield over her.

Despite the fact that Petruchio directs Katherina to school the other
women, her speech of wifely submission achieves a startling degree of independence. To be sure, Petruchio seeks to co-opt her strength for his own
benefit. But, because Katherina takes up a stance of radical obedience, he is
unable to direct her virtue to reinforce his own authority. This does not mean
Katherina is unchanged at the end of Shakespeare's play. She is neither shrew,
nor virtue—in a most unsettling fashion, she enacts both identities at once.
Her agency is evident, yet because it passes as passivity, it becomes intelligible
as virtue. Katherina's excellence, moreover, clearly derives from her body, for
it is her willingness to prostrate herself as she delivers prescriptions about
wifely subservience that proves her radical obedience.[91] Though it is a role
she did not fashion, Katherina *inhabits* virtue in a transformative fashion. In
keeping with Aristotelian ethics, she bodies forth the specifics of virtue in a
way that makes this ethical identity her own. In this moment she achieves
material virtue, an ethical stature that, as I have endeavored to demonstrate
across this study, resists oppression by withstanding and thereby overcoming
its imposition.

Given the power and pathos her performance requires, it is little wonder
that her final speech produces anxiety. Bernard Shaw acknowledges the dis-
comfort Katherina causes when he describes the final scene as embarrassing
and "altogether disgusting to modern sensibility."[92] Shaw's unease, however,

contradicts his sense that the shrew-taming plot gives "an honest and masterly picture of a real man, whose like we have all met."[93] Although Shaw is sympathetic to Katherina, his desire to apologize to the woman with whom he views Katherina's speech is yet another attempt to feel for the woman and hence to direct her agency through his own. Perhaps it is unsporting to isolate Shaw's comments, since there is a long critical and theatrical tradition that attempts to see behind the mask of Katherina's obedience.[94] Revisionist interpretations, though they recognize Katherina's plight, replay the same drama of dominance that Petruchio seeks to stage in Shakespeare's play.[95] When we insist that Katherina winks, or that she remains her old self, we attempt to see through the fictions of identity, and to direct Katherina's agency through a reality constructed for and imposed upon her.[96] Masculine authority might remain intact, but feminine passivity is surely an act. Yet, as Katherina's speech demonstrates, the poles of such a dichotomy do not split that neatly. Real or ruse, that is the frightening question; and Katherina's bearing suggests that the active/passive binary meant to authorize Petruchio's household dominance is really just a ruse.

If we read Katherina's final performance of abjection as a response to Petruchio's agency, then we miss the productive power that she wields through her performance of passivity. Katherina's repeated association with the category of shrew, read alongside the widow's and Bianca's protests against the masculine discourse defining them, demonstrates that male control depends on sustaining the myth of female insubordination. Exposing the implications of female subservience, on the other hand, reveals currents of feminine agency that cannot be contained by masculine discourse, desire, or representation. As Suzanne M. Tartamella so pithily puts it, "Petruchio has indeed *created* a submissive wife whom he cannot *contain* in that role."[97] Like the early modern Griseldas whose displays of patience outstrip oppression, Katherina is at her most subversive when she offers to place her hand under Petruchio's foot. These radical gestures of submission, I maintain, make visible the regimes of power that mark gender difference in patriarchal marriage.[98] When Katherina offers this extreme display, she exemplifies what Jacques Rancière calls "work[ing] the intervals" which, in Bonnie Honig's characterization, "neither conforms to the expected form nor simply violates it."[99]

When she steps into the role of submission, Katherina evades the categories—virtue or shrew—that her performative passivity instates. Petruchio can no longer manage Katherina, because by inhabiting the model

of virtue, she occupies the place of creator which Petruchio covets. Katherina
focuses attention on male domination, but, in so doing, she places herself
outside its domain. In Amy L. Smith's astute reading, "It is precisely *because*
Kate performs subjection that subjection is opened to critique in the play."[100]
Katherina undermines the male discourse that regulates women by identifying with it unreservedly; by taking on the ideology of femininity that
Petruchio promotes, she takes from Petruchio the feminine submission he
purports to desire. Katherina's performance limits Petruchio's response to
sanction: "Why, there's a wench! Come on, and kiss me, Kate" (V.ii.184).
Petruchio's attempt to redirect her agency, rather than asserting his dominance, admits that Katherina's performance of passivity does not need masculine intervention for its execution. Katherina's submission, which must be at
once sincere and artificial, is thus the most destabilizing aspect of the play.
Lucentio's bewilderment at Katherina's transformation—"'Tis a wonder, by
your leave, she will be tamed so" (V.ii.193)—bolsters the suspicion that
Petruchio's power is illusory. Katherina's speech exposes the agency involved
in passivity, and by reifying the masculine rhetoric that seeks to inscribe her,
she blurs the division of power designed to render women's virtue a masculine production in premodern England.

Reforming Virtue in Fletcher's *Woman's Prize, or the Tamer Tam'd*

Re-Turning Shrews

Taking Katherina's submission seriously vitiates the notion that women's
ethical action must be subject to masculine regulation. Instead of putting
Petruchio back together again, her final speech fragments his control. Besides
providing a powerful critique of masculine authority, Katherina's closing
monologue lays the groundwork for a material virtue that women can fully
embody and inhabit. When Katherina kneels and speaks, she bodies forth a
power that cannot be redirected to shore up masculine dominance. The spectacle of her submission is too extreme to legitimate Petruchio's authority.
That said, she is not allowed to enact this virtue until her last speech in the
play. We might see flashes of her strength throughout Shakespeare's drama,
and we might appreciate the ways her aggressive submission muddles the
virtue/shrew binary that justifies male control over women's identities.[101]
Shakespeare's *Shrew* reveals the rotten gender foundations of early modern

domestic ideology. But it is only with John Fletcher's play, *The Woman's Prize, or the Tamer Tam'd*, that Katherina's model of material virtue is afforded the power to make a positive difference in the premodern household.

Fletcher's play issues a strong answer to Shakespeare's folio-*Shrew*, though it does so, notably, without calling anyone a "shrew." The play's language is laced with terms of domestic revolt; there is talk of carting, cuffing, and cucking, the women are referred to as rebels, and Maria is accused of running a college for young scolds.[102] In the play's atmosphere of gendered insurrection, the absence of "shrew" as an organizing term is dramatically conspicuous. By eliminating what was part of an organizing dichotomy of feminine identity, Fletcher develops a model of material virtue that counters masculine tyranny. Material virtue is realized through the female body, but the excellence Maria enacts also reforms Petruchio, and challenges men's dominance. Throughout *The Woman's Prize*, the type of temperament Petruchio manifests, especially when exemplified by a ruler, points to the sovereign counterpart of the recalcitrant shrew in early modern discourse: the figure of the reckless tyrant.[103] In her analysis of Renaissance writings, Rebecca W. Bushnell invokes the figure of the shrew to explain representations of the tyrant: "With the exception of fearlessness, this description [of the shrew] corresponds to the typical portrait of the tyrant, who is a monster and a shifter of shapes, and who rules without rule, law, trust, or reason."[104] Fletcher utilizes the close connection between shrews and tyrants to critique Petruchio's marital authority.

As *The Woman's Prize* demonstrates, Petruchio's so-called patriarchalism involves irregular antics that render him a tyrant.[105] If Petruchio performs the role of shrew, which, in Shakespeare's play was part of his taming, "He kills her in her own humor" (*Shrew*, IV.i.168), he still acts the part of the tyrant, since dissembling was one mark of tyranny, theatricality another.[106] Yet, in recasting Petruchio as a tyrant, Fletcher creates a new model of embodied virtue, one with the power to reform both marital partners. By vesting Maria with the rational control required to bring order to the domestic body, *The Woman's Prize* affirms that the material virtue frequently associated with women also offers a more habitable model of excellence for men. Petruchio is saved when he is allowed to jettison the cultural expectation that mandated men's household governance. He concedes domestic control, yet he gains a substantial benefit when he becomes his wife's partner instead of her governor. Similarly, Maria's virtue is ultimately predicated on the ability to yield, not dominate. She decides upon deference not out of coercion, but from a position of reasoned responsiveness. In Fletcher's household drama, neither partner is forced to capitulate to the other. Rather, as *The Woman's Prize* affirms, when partners submit to one another, their virtues become shared, connective, and mutually enriching.

Rational Virtue

Although Maria rebels against her new husband, she is no shrew. Indeed, she manifests none of the violent, wasteful, or unproductive tendencies that Natasha Korda and Frances E. Dolan identify as features of shrews in early modern domestic literatures.[107] Notably, Maria uses rational control as a defense against her partner's excesses. Since Petruchio has surrendered the substance of himself to angry shows, Maria aims to recover him through a contrasting rebellion of contained withdrawal. With her declaration, "There's a fellow / Must yet . . . / Be made a man, for yet he is a monster" (I.ii.101–3), she insists that Petruchio has lost the constancy that would authorize his mastery.[108] By telling Livia, "Here must his head be," Maria affirms her ability to assume the position of reasonable governance that Petruchio has abandoned to reckless gestures of absolute domination (I.ii.104). To legitimate her tactics, Maria draws a strong contrast between her methods and those of her predecessor, suggesting that Katherina "was a foole, / And took a scurvy course" (I.ii.141–42). Maria's difference from Katherina, she insists, arises from her decision to assume domestic power in a manner that departs from the irrational unruliness traditionally associated with shrews.

As she makes clear, Maria's defiance does not derive from passionate imbalance, but instead arises from a calculated plan to preserve her identity within marriage. While marriage discourses circulate ideas of "commixtion" in their attempts to promote a companionate union, often enough these images of intermingling effectively dissolve feminine identity by fully incorporating a wife's position into her husband's.[109] As the classic example of the *femme covert* illustrates, women are covered over and potentially blotted out through their marital arrangements.[110] With this in mind, the suggestion that Petruchio will "bury" Maria means that her virtue will be covered over, blotted out by the prescriptive ethical authority Petruchio assumes. Maria's attempt to retain her own powers of discretion, rationality, and discernment, however, asserts the centrality of "fellowship" to marriage (I.ii.141). Affirming her personal dignity, Maria makes marriage into a bond that necessarily recognizes the power of both partners. As she explains,

> By the faith I have
> In mine own noble will, that childish woman
> That lives a prisoner to her husband's pleasure
> Has lost her making, and becomes a beast
> Created for his use, not fellowship. (I.ii.137–41)

To achieve this vision of conjugal parity, Maria rebalances marriage's power differential by valorizing women's embodied rationality.

Focused as it is on the female body as a locus of male profit and pleasure, Maria's taming scheme uncovers masculine authority's dependence upon women's domestic powers.[111] Her virtue arises explicitly from the sexual and procreative capacities of female materiality. Using curbing tactics that arise from the maternal, Maria laces her language of reform with a birthing vocabulary: "Nor never with thy secret hand make briefe / A mothers labour to me . . . Though it would pull another joincure from him, / And make him every day another man . . . till I have my will, / May I be barren of delights" (I.ii.111–12, 118–19, 120–21). Even as she explains her intention to withhold sex from Petruchio, Maria embraces the dignified power that sometimes accrues to maternity, validating a mother's ability to form her children, both physically and socially.[112] Yet the nightmarish potential of mothering also galvanizes Maria's rhetoric, for she clearly intends to infantilize Petruchio in order to unsettle his patriarchal presumption (I.ii.171–74). As she makes clear, until Petruchio becomes "easy as a child, / And tame as feare!" (I.ii.115–16), Maria will play the part of what Janet Adelman famously called the "suffocating mother."[113] In a departure from the tradition associating such maternal images with unchecked corruption, Maria's intention to rebirth her husband is a return to rational rule, a corrective force that will invest both partners with the moderate governance of self-control.[114]

Maria illustrates the virtues of (self-)rule through her measured program of marital reform. Notwithstanding the raucous band of alewives who rally in defense of Maria's cause, her claim for autonomy is moderate, both in logic and in affect. By withdrawing herself from the scene of sexual consummation that would visibly affirm Petruchio's ascendancy, Maria calls upon Petruchio to comport himself in a fashion that respects her agency. When

Petruchio insists that Maria owes him obedience because she is a wife, she claims their marital obligations should be mutual:

> I owe no more
> Then you owe back again. (I.iii.198–99)

Moreover, in asserting the "nobility" of woman's nature, Maria resists the corrupting admixture that marriage imposes upon wives:

> We are gold,
> In our own natures pure; but when we suffer
> The husband's stamp upon us, then alloys,
> And base ones, of you men are mingled with us,
> And make us blush like copper. (I.iii.243–47)

As Biancha later affirms, a community outside of the domain of "base men" protects women against what marital writers characterize as the degrading "conjunction" of marriage (II.i.39).[115]

Maria does not seek to escape the marital bonds she shares with Petruchio. Rather, by reforming Petruchio, she attempts to make marriage something other than bondage for both. As Petruchio's anger attests, he is equally in thrall to the expectations of hierarchical marriage. According with the image of the tyrant, who was a slave to the passions in ancient and early modern renderings, "Petruchio *Furius*" is defined by rage.[116] His reputation as a wife-breaker, both Maria and Petruchio affirm, requires him to assert dominance over his new wife. From the outset, Maria's explanation of her rebellion is responsive to Petruchio's successful career as tamer:

> You have been famous for a woman-tamer,
> And bear the feared-name of a brave wife-breaker:
> A woman now shall take those honours off, and tame you.
> (I.iii.266–69)

Similarly, Petruchio's reaction to Maria's insubordination is colored by his marital history. Because he is a notorious domestic autocrat, making peace with Maria would subject him to ridicule, or so Petruchio surmises. Petruchio is indignant that he would be challenged in such a fashion, for having tamed his former wife, who was "a fury to this Filly" (II.v.12), he believes he should be immune to wifely rebellion. Although the coercive taming involved in Petruchio's former marriage is meant to secure his power—investing him with a mythic cruelty that promotes wifely obedience—his excessive reputation provides the impetus for Maria's challenge. To prevent Petruchio from assuming the powers of domestic tyrant, Maria rebels against her husband's authority. Nevertheless, Maria's dramatic uprising promises to be short-lived. With startling economy, the feminine insurrection so unforgettable in this play comes to an end by the close of the second act.[117]

Active Obedience

Moving away from its celebration of female confederacy, *The Woman's Prize* shifts focus to concentrate on the reformation of masculine power. From the outset, Maria's plan moderates Petruchio's temper. Moved to calm by Sophocles's advice, Petruchio agrees to Maria's terms of peace, including money, liberty, and company. Yet, when Petruchio relents, so does Maria. Against the advice of her commanders, the city- and the country-wife, Maria accepts Petruchio's promise to fulfill her demands without further pledge. It is possible that Petruchio realizes that "nothing but repentance, and undoing / Can win her love" (II.v.147–48), and accepts Maria's conditions as a capitulation to marital concord. But Sophocles's subsequent assurance casts masculine submission as a strategic ploy that will allow Petruchio to gain the upper hand after the hierarchical imposition of marriage:

> When ye are once a-bed, all these conditions
> Lie under your own seale. (II.v.148–49)

Maria's decision to come down from her barricaded position, "Enough. I yield" (II.v.159), promises to reinstitute gender hierarchy after its temporary suspension. Yet this familiar comic structure, used with such comprehensive success elsewhere in Shakespeare, is radically reworked in Fletcher's handling.

For the remainder of *The Woman's Prize*, Maria wages a more comprehensive rebellion, the reformative aim of which is more than superficial display. Indeed, Maria's scheme affirms that virtue is more than a prescribed cover that is imposed from sources outside the subject. Accordingly, her sustained campaign of ethical renovation really gets underway only after the alewives are dispersed. The public visibility of staged rule, which Maria initially challenges with her orchestrated insurrection, is completely undermined by her domestic resistance. As Petruchio reports, Maria makes a distinction between outer and inner forms of domination and submission to challenge Petruchio's power. He might force her to submit her body to him, but she will not surrender her will to his.[118] In fact, Maria's inner resistance will be redoubled against Petruchio's physical coercion:

> She swore my force might weary her, but win her
> I never could, nor should, till she consented;
> And I might take her body prisoner,
> But for her mind or appetite—(III.iii.12–15)

As is the case for those who resist the coercive control of tyrants, Maria's autonomy is at stake in her negotiations.[119] Although other characters in Fletcher's oeuvre depose tyrants, Maria does not pit her will against her oppressor's desire in a permanent conflict of immutable resistance.[120] Instead, in a particularly subversive maneuver, considering the play's Jacobean milieu, Maria practices *active* obedience to reform a domestic tyrant.[121]

Indeed, Maria defends her character against the corruptions of an imbalanced marriage by recovering her husband from tyrannical distemper. In Geffrey Whitney's *A Choice of Emblemes* (1586), which recalls the story of "the tyraunt vile Mezentivs," who would kill his victims by binding "the quicke, and dead, togeather sure," mismatched marriage is characterized as a cruel union in which the decay of the one partner will grotesquely corrupt the other (see fig. 11).[122] Although early modern marriage literature suggests that this kind of contamination is only a danger to men, Maria's reaction to Petruchio's "illness" indicates the reverse. Outdone with his wife's refusals, Petruchio gives himself over to fury, as Maria explains, "My husband has it now, and raves extremely!" (III.v.28). Instead of attempting to recover him, Maria strips the house of all its goods, locking Petruchio away to prevent his infection from spreading. By suggesting the contagion of his condition, "No man that has been neere him come near me" (III.v.21), Maria protects herself from the dis-ease that taints her husband's temper.

This scene is fascinating for the ways in which it connects the maladies of tyrannical marriage with representations of contagious disease in early modern Europe. In a striking correspondence, Desiderius Erasmus's colloquy on mismatched marriage, "A Marriage in Name Only, or, The Unequal Match" (1529), also recalls the punishment of Mezentius for this deleterious

To Aphilus.

THE tyraunt vile MEZENTIVS, put in vre,
Amongſt the plagues, wherewith hee murthered men:
To binde the quicke, and dead, togeather ſure,
And then, to throwe them both into a denne.
 Whereas the quicke, ſhould ſtill the dead imbrace,
 Vntill with pine, hee turn'd into that caſe.

Thoſe wedding webbes, which ſome doe weaue with ruthe,
As when the one, with ſtraunge diſeaſe doth pine:
Or when as age, bee coupled vnto youthe,
And thoſe that hate, inforced are to ioyne,
 This repreſentes: and doth thoſe parentes ſhowe,
 Are tyrauntes meere, who ioyne their children ſoe.

Yet manie are, who not the cauſe regarde,
The birthe, the yeares, nor vertues of the minde:
For goulde is firſt, with greedie men prefer'de,
And loue is laſte, and likinge ſet behinde:
 But parentes harde, that matches make for goodes:
 Can not be free, from guilte of childrens bloodes.

  Quàm malè inæquales veniunt ad aratra iuuenci,
  Tam premitur magno coniuge nupta minor.

     N 2.   *Frontis*

Virg. 8. Æneid.
Mortua quinetiã iun-
gebat corpora viuis,
Componens manibúsque
manus atque oribus ora.

Ouid. Epiſt. 9.

FIGURE 11. Geffrey Whitney, *A Choice of Emblemes*, 1586, Mezentius the Tyrant,
"the mismatched marriage." Rare Books, 79714, The Huntington Library,
San Marino, California.

conjugal formation.[123] Yet the ill-matched coupling in this narrative is literally caused by disease, for the groom's dissolute habits have infected him with a fever that undoubtedly looks like syphilis. In lamenting the bride's misfortune, however, Erasmus's interlocutors recast Maria's reaction to Petruchio's illness in terms that affirm the devoted affection she proclaims: "In Italy, buildings are locked up at the first sign of pestilence; those who attend the sufferers are quarantined. Some call this inhumanity, though actually it is the highest humanity, for because of this precaution the plague is checked with few fatalities. How great the humanity of protecting the lives of so many thousands. . . . Yet how much less is the peril from plague than from this pox!"[124] Maria's treatment might be viewed as a further sign of her rebellion, except for the fact that *The Woman's Prize* treats masculine anger like any other disease born of intemperance. Although Petruchio declares his sanity with a curse upon his "damned wife Maria," the doctor verifies her household diagnosis: "[Petruchio] shews a general inflammation, / Which is the symptome of a pestilent feaver" (III.v.54 and 60–61).[125] Praying that "patience be his Angel" (III.v.37), Maria abandons her husband to his ill humor.

After this incident, Petruchio feels notoriously abused by his wife, but he cannot find an excuse to punish her because her behavior defies discrete classifications of wifely misconduct:

> Were she a whore directly, or a scold,
> An unthrift, or a woman made to hate me,
> I had my wish and knew which way to rein her. (IV.i.14–16)

His confusion is only compounded when, after he breaks free from his confinement, Maria pretends that it was Petruchio who forbade her to see him while he was sick (IV.ii.27–28). Since Juan Luis Vives uses the story of a wife who nursed her husband through a series of maladies (including the contagious pox) to exemplify wifely obedience, Maria's simulation of concern aligns her with this prescriptive strain of wifely virtue.[126] Through the contrast between her actions and avowals, then, Maria satisfies contradictory renderings of wifely devotion. But when she claims that it was Petruchio, who, in his delusion, would have sent away "all the household stuff, had I not crost it" (IV.i.60), Maria invents Petruchio's domestic power in order to suggest its folly.[127] Enacting the role of wife that Petruchio would have her play, Maria locates her agency as a product of her husband's (in)discretion.

Through her nonsensical redistribution, Maria simulates Petruchio's ideal of wedlock, as even he concedes:

> Though I doe know this falser then the devil,
> I cannot choose but love it. (IV.i.43–44)

Unmaking "The Shrew"

This exchange offers just one example of what we might call the comprehensive "unmaking" of Shakespeare's *Taming of the Shrew* in Fletcher's drama. In *The Woman's Prize*, Maria's refashioning of the household echoes Katherina's outfitting scene (WP, III.iii; *Shrew*, IV.iii), just as her later sexual forwardness recalls Petruchio's demand that Katherina kiss in the street (WP, IV.v; *Shrew*, V.ii.130–38). By undoing the control that Petruchio formerly secured through displays of dominance, Maria finally moves Petruchio to abandon the public authority his position as husband would impose. With wearied resignation, Petruchio finally relinquishes the cultural fantasy of masculine authority he sought to achieve through two marriages. His defeat ushers in a victory, however, for it is only after he disavows the tyrannical power of marital sovereignty that he achieves accord with Maria. In a dizzying reversal, immediately after Petruchio severs all ties to his wife, Maria proclaims her absolute marital devotion. Responding to Petruchio's complaint, Maria simply, if surprisingly, declares,

> Now I love ye,
> And now I see ye are a man, I'll talk to ye—,
> And I forgive your bitterness. (IV.iv.130–32)

Echoing Lucentio's surprise at Katherina's apparent transformation in Shakespeare's *Taming of the Shrew*, Maria eloquently affirms Petruchio's miraculous alteration:

> Methinks you look a new man to me now,
> A man of excellence, and now I see
> Some great design set in ye. (IV.iv.139–41)

Though it certainly turns Petruchio from his coercive taming, his dogged defeat recalls Katherina's harried suspicion after her isolation in Petruchio's house. Over and over again, Maria justifies her methods "under name of perfect love" (*Shrew*, IV.iii.12). Nevertheless, with her capital pronouncement upon Petruchio's departure, "I do commit your reformation. / And so I leave you to your *stilo novo*" (WP, IV.iv.227–28), Maria sounds as imperious as the tyrannical sovereign whom she has deposed. Petruchio is dispatched at the end of this scene, unsure whether to stay or go at his wife's command. The close of this exchange markedly reverses Petruchio's vaunting dismissal of women's shrewish power in Shakespeare's play:

> Have I not heard the sea, puffed up with winds,
> Rage like an angry boar chafèd with sweat? (*Shrew*, I.ii.200–201)

Here, Petruchio resigns himself to the sea, claiming that any perils it might offer are slight compared to those domestic storms he has weathered:

> Then, women, if there be a storm at sea
> Worse than your tongues can make, and waves more broken
> Than your dissembling faiths are, let me feel
> Nothing but tempests, till they crack my keel! (WP, IV.iv.233–36)

Although Maria is no brawling shrew, her domestic disobedience completely unmans Petruchio.

It is therefore no great surprise when, in the final act of Fletcher's play, Petruchio's men declare "His wife, his devil / . . . [has] killed him, killed him" (V.ii.46–48). The men in the play condemn Maria in an attempt to reinstate traditional gender hierarchy. When her father brings her to contemplate Petruchio's body, it is designed to shame her into submission. His accusation is direct and unwavering:

> There he that was Petruchio, too good for ye.
> Your stubborn and unworthy way has killed him. (V.iv.4–5)

As she gazes on the body of her deceased husband, the men search her emotions to see if she has "some good nature yet left in her" (V.iv.16). Yet Maria's performance of mourning once again defies public expectations for feminine behavior, once again because she embraces the conflicting prescriptions that define wifehood. Maria's sadness is not prompted by regret; she does not mourn the loss of Petruchio as he was. Indeed, she mourns Petruchio for the loss he was, for the complete waste of manhood that was Petruchio:

> To think what this man was, to think how simple,
> How far below a man, how far from reason,
> From common understanding, and all gentry. (V.iv.23–25)

Even here, she remains a wife who seeks her husband's betterment, for as she explains, her grief derives completely from Petruchio's loss, not her own.

Although Maria is not devoid of emotions, her feelings are fully governed in this scene. Moreover, as she explains her grief, it is also clear that the measure she exhibits is fully characterized as a product of her husband's (mis) rule. By situating her power in relation to her husband, finally, Maria avoids the charges of tyranny that her ascension to domestic governance might provoke. Maria attributes her power to Petruchio, elevating him to a position of household divine, as some marriage manuals recommended. Using the biblical analogy that related the husband's power over the wife to Christ's sovereignty over the church, the 1608 treatise entitled *Counsel to the husband: To the wife instruction,* claims that a husband is "King, Priest, and Prophet in his house."[128] When Petruchio arises—presumably from shock at his wife's measured lament—it is a comic resurrection that restores his domestic governance. Maria's regulated rule reforms house and state, even if Maria reverts to her submissive position in the marital hierarchy: "I have tamed ye, / And now am vowed your servant" (V.iv.45–6).

Homely Virtues

By limiting her own power, Maria avoids the charge against women's domestic tyranny, which *Counsel to the husband* likens to an inverted crucifixion: "The vvife in usurping authoritie crucifieth her husband, as it is said of S. Peter, vvith his heeles upvvard."[129] Maria maintains self-control throughout Fletcher's play, making manifest the rational power of women's autonomy, even in surrender. By reforming a domestic tyrant, Maria keeps herself from becoming one. Maria does more than justify women's governance in exceptional circumstances. Instead, she shows the value of material virtue for women and men. As Maria enacts it, rational rule entails temperance, responsiveness, and measure. It involves yielding, not dominating. It does not turn on the regulation of others. While this form of virtue accesses circuits of desire and emotion that derive from the body, the rational measure that forwards these powers develops a richer form of selfhood. Akin to Aristotelian virtue ethics, which recommends the mean between extremes as the basis for embodied action, this model of excellence relies on a synthesis of mind and body. It is not exclusively masculine. Rather, the material virtue Maria enacts is an ethical subjectivity that frees women as well as men from the pressures of hierarchical marriage.

This model of embodied action was largely unrecognized, but not completely unknown. Domestic manuals, particularly those that depend on women to manage the practical details of the household, recognize women's synthetic ability as part of a comprehensive moral program. Gervase Markham's *English housevvife* (1631) promises to describe "the inward and outward vertues which ought to be in a compleate woman."[130] Besides the "inward vertues of her minde," or a religious devotion that makes her an "incitement and spurre vnto all her family to pursue the same steppes," the treatise outlines the housewife's nuanced mastery of physical properties: "To begin then with one of the most principal vertues which doth belong to our English Houswife; you shall vnderstand, that sith the preseruation and care of the family touching their health and soundnesse of body, consisteth most in the diligence: it is meet that she haue a physicall kind of knowledge, how to administer many wholesome receits or medicines for the good of their healths, as well to preuent the first occasion of sicknesse, as to take away the effects and euill of the same when it hath made seasure on the body."[131] Other guides, such as John Partridge's *Treasurie of commodius Conceits* (1573), describes the housewife's knowledge of the "vertues" of a number of healing concoctions. He claims his book "doth instruct and teach all maner of persones & De|grees to know perfectly, the maner to make diuers & sundrie sortes of fine Conceits aswell of meates, as of Co~serues & Marmalades, as al|so, of sweete and pleasant Waters, of wonderfull Odours, Operation and Vertues."[132] Richard Surflet's translated *Countrey farme* (1616) calls such "vertues," "the natural remedies which shee shall acquaint her selfe withal for the succor of her folke in their sicknesses."[133] Household literatures require a wife to attend to the virtues of a dizzying array of diverse bodies, which means, as Surflet's treatise explains, "I Doe not find the state or place of a Huswife or Dairie-woman to be of lesse care and diligence than the office of her Husband."[134]

In her indispensable analysis, Wendy Wall observes that household guides frequently distinguish housewifery as a distinct province of women's work. Yet, as she further remarks, when writers of such manuals are "compelled to explain the simultaneous importance *and* inferiority of housewifery, they fall back on the default existence of 'mean' knowledges that the husband can't allow himself to know."[135] As she points out, William Perkins claims he, "ought not in modestie to challenge the priuiledge of prescri|bing and aduertising his wife in al mat|ters domesticall, but in some to leaue her, to her owne will and iudgement."[136] Furthermore, Dod and Cleaver admit there are some areas "in which the hus|band giueth ouer his right vnto his wife . . . to see to those things that belong vnto the kitchin, and to huswiferie, and to their houshold stuffe."[137] Though these guides clearly aim to classify domestic labor as beneath that of the husband, in the evidence Wall amasses, women's work offers an alternative ethical life based on the sustenance of proximate bodies. We might say that confining these powers to the interior, private life of the early modern household privileges the virtues ascribed to men, those public, outward duties of "the perfect Husbandman," whom Markham characterizes as "the Father and Master of the Family . . . whose office and imployments are euer for the most part abrod, or remoued from the house, as in the field or yarde."[138] But as comedies such as Fletcher's affirm, we do so only if we believe that ethical fitness is based on public exercises of individual agency.

To be sure, the fantasy of a publicly empowered (masculine) subjectivity is one domestic literatures promote, though they simultaneously acknowledge the crucial importance of women to the premodern household. Prescriptive guides are keen to insist, as William Whately writes, that a woman with a foolish husband "must needs either rebell against him, or contemne him, or both"[139] Again, however, Fletcher's play shows the folly in Petruchio's fantasy of enclosure: Maria's rebellion demonstrates the porous boundaries of the early modern household. Furthermore, as her taming program confirms, there is no way (or reason) to confine women's virtues within safe household space. The domestic, as the very existence of household manuals affirms, is a vital part of public life in this period. More importantly, Petruchio's renovation critiques the association of empowered masculinity with public governance for its ethical impoverishment. Maria offers him a richer existence, one in which spouses foster each other's excellences through their interconnection. While her refusal to concede absolute authority to Petruchio might seem radical, then, Maria's behavior is actually more in line with domestic literatures, which promoted mutuality as the ultimate goal of marriage. In taking the marital handbooks at their word, Maria shows a kinship with Katherina, who overthrows Petruchio's domestic tyranny by doing "*what is allowed*, that is, what the existing order explicitly allows, although it prohibits it at the level of implicit unwritten prohibitions."[140] Fletcher's play goes further than Shakespeare's, but only because *The Woman's Prize* embraces the more comprehensive ethical reformation that Maria's material virtue makes available.

The virtues that Maria and Katherina embody are homely. This means Katherina and Maria are like Griselda to the extent that they materialize an excellence that is neither glamorous, heroic, nor dominant. Material virtue, we might say, comprises a cultural underbelly of ethics—a way of understanding the ethical power of bodies that are usually understood as passive, disposable, and socially unimportant. Griselda's ability to evince strength in the face of oppression is frequently discounted because her virtue does not fulfill the expectation that ethical fitness be expressed through gestures of public autonomy, resistance, or sovereignty.[141] Hers is an unappealing form of virtue because it reinforces the dominant social order of patriarchal marriage. This is despite the fact that Griselda stories critique masculine power and reveal feminine strength. Like Shakespeare's Katherina, premodern Griseldas survived a masculinist ideology over which women wielded very little control. Maria might be said to depart from Griselda's model, except for her creative rebellion also operates within the boundaries of the premodern household. Acknowledging such limitations does not mean that these female characters are disappointing, or that these stories are complicit with the sexist ideology that oppressed women in premodern England; rather, Griselda stories, like late shrew plays, open up new ways to acknowledge the ethical action of the dispossessed. As I shall suggest in this book's conclusion, paying more attention to the embodied excellence of culturally disposable characters gives us a new way of thinking about what subjectivity became, and what it might yet become, through an ethical consideration of our material bonds with others.

Legends of Good Women

As a defense of women, essentialism destroys itself.
—Sheila Delany, *The Naked Text*

This book ends where it might have begun, with a consideration of Chaucer's *Legend of Good Women*. In his final dream vision, Chaucer grapples with problems common to writers featured in this study: in order to write within the limited discursive space allowed by an empowered masculinity, he represents good women according to traditional criteria for feminine virtue—principally fidelity, suffering, and self-sacrifice. Satisfying absolutist masculinity entails writing about femininity in only one way, even if female exemplars evince material virtues that supersede the prescriptive qualities assigned to them. Feminist critics have rightly identified the problematic gender politics of *The Seintes Legende of Cupide*; yet I suggest that the problem they identify has more far-reaching consequences for reappraising human subjectivity as it took shape over the period studied in this book.[1] More than a political difference, there is an ethical problem that produces the gender asymmetry of Chaucer's *Legend*. It is not just gender trouble, in other words, but virtue trouble that undermines Chaucer's attempt to enshrine women "trewe of love" (G.193).[2]

The stylistic repetition involved in Chaucer's gathering of female worthies is notable.[3] Over and over again, Chaucer trims feminine virtue to fit a model that gratifies totalized masculine authority.[4] This is despite the fact that these women show strength, compassion, fidelity, and bravery, among other laudable qualities. This is also despite the fact that this series features a string of faithless men, whose duplicity, exploitation, and violence are subject to critique. The narrator condemns heroes such as Jason, "Thow sly devourere and confusioun / Of gentil wemen, tendre creatures" (F.1369–70), but the masculinity the poem elaborates remains unfettered and empowered. In the same vein, the narrator praises heroines such as Hypermnestra, "Pyëtous, sad, wis, and trewe as stel, / As to these wemen it acordeth wel" (F.2582–83), yet the femininity the poem praises remains confined and dispossessed. Given this disparity, *The Legend of Good Women* raises the important question: Why do material virtues fail to invest good women with cultural power, especially when men's predatory abuses of their cultural privilege are simultaneously laid bare?[5] Chaucer confronts this question by connecting gender inequity to ethical disparity, by thinking about the difference poetry might make (or fail to make) to the ways that women's virtues become culturally legible. What we see with the *Prologue*'s portrait of a tyrannous king, then, is Chaucer coming to terms with the role of masculine dominance in the culture of books in which he works.[6]

The God of Love is all about books. In both forms of the *Prologue* Chaucer's trespass involves books: in the F-version Cupid observes, "And of Creseyde thou hast seyd as the lyste, / That maketh men to wommen lasse triste" (F.332–33), and in the G-version he asks, "Hast thow nat mad in Englysh ek the bok / How that Crisseyde Troylus forsok, / In shewynge how that wemen han don mis?" (G.264–66). In the latter, moreover, the God of Love frames Chaucer's failing in relation to an expansive narrative tradition:

> Yis, God wot, sixty bokes olde and newe
> Hast thow thyself, alle ful of storyes grete,
> That bothe Romayns and ek Grekes trete
> Of sundry wemen, which lyf that they ladde,
> And evere an hundred goode ageyn oon badde. (G.273–77)

If Cupid's vision of good women is limited, then so too are the stories that precede Chaucer's collection.[7] Chaucer's run-in with the God of Love establishes the masculine valence of traditional virtue. Like Christine de Pizan, sitting in her study pondering the antifeminist tradition, Chaucer's catalog affirms that writing about women's virtue has always been a male-dominated enterprise.[8]

Yet, by representing Chaucer's own precarity under the God of Love's gaze—"For sternely on me he gan byholde" (F.239)—*The Legend of Good*

Women challenges the artistic tradition that makes women's ethical action a support for men's cultural authority. It does so by demonstrating the need for material virtue as a countertradition of ethics that can be inhabited by the dispossessed—canonically women, but just as often men. Chaucer puts himself in the place of a vulnerable woman under a domineering masculine gaze as a way to acknowledge the restricted cultural frame within which the goodness of his abandoned heroines might be perceived.[9] Chaucer is vulnerable to a powerful male, whose excesses must be reined in by feminine intercession:

> I preye to God that evere falle she fayre,
> For ne hadde confort been of hire presence,
> I hadde be ded, withouten any defence,
> For dred of Loves words and his chere. (G.180–83)

In no small irony, Chaucer challenges the legacy of women's virtue as it is circulated in old books, but he is saved by a heroine who hails directly from this tradition. It is only because Alceste pleads for the poet, in other words, that Chaucer is allowed to answer the charges leveled against him.

Historicist analysis by Paul Strohm shows that Chaucer's emphasis on feminine intercession is not far off the cultural mark, since Queen Anne made several powerful intercessory pleas, and since she prostrated herself in a carefully scripted tableau of reconciliation between Richard and the City of London.[10] What Chaucer discloses with this interweaving is how stories of feminine virtue influenced women's potential for ethical action in late medieval culture.[11] Alceste puts herself between Cupid and Chaucer: she diverts the angry god's gaze, but her "feminine eloquence," to use David Wallace's formulation, also reframes the course of action the king might properly take.[12] The grounds of her instruction are ethical, but the authority she wields is based on her embodied history of suffering and sacrifice. As she explains, refusing leniency amounts to absolutist oppression, aligning the God of Love with the "tyraunts of Lumbardye" (G.354).[13] Cupid reveres her advice, as he instructs Chaucer's narrator to do, because "She that for hire husbonde ches to dye" (G.501). She has hazarded her body, sacrificing herself in the ultimate gesture of love. Her virtue, then, is staked on the substance of her body, even if she becomes the decorated icon of a masculinist tradition of women's goodness. Her willingness to die in her husband's place, though it relies on her embodied excellence, reinforces masculine authority. The power she accrues through submission substantiates a potent masculinist fantasy. Women's softness, according to Isidore of Seville's *Etymologiae*, is meant to moderate masculine *virtus*, as Richard Maidstone's late fourteenth-century repetition of this formula of gender division makes clear:

> Flectere regales poterit regina rigores,
> Mitis ut in gentem rex velit esse suam.
> Mollit amore virum mulier:
> Deus huic dedit illam;
> Tendat ad hoc vester, o pia dulcis amor.

> (Let the queen soften royal severity that the king may be forbearing
> to his people. A woman mellows a man with love: for this God gave
> her; for this, O blessed woman, may your sweet love aspire.)[14]

The virtues of femininity—those that accrue to the suffering female body—are imagined as a complement to those of hardheaded, and sometimes hardhearted, masculinity.

Alceste would appear to be the perfect complement, the feminine "help-meet" who moderates masculine harshness.[15] Yet, as Strohm persuasively argues, Alceste is also a good counselor whose opinion matters.[16] We should not be so quick, then, to dismiss what she sees as a valuable literary tradition. As Catherine Sanok convincingly demonstrates, Chaucer's *Legend* not only acknowledges a female audience for the poem, but credits its female readers, those "twenty thousand moo" (F.559) who are featured alongside Alceste, with powerful influence over the poem's meaning.[17] While some critics have blamed Cupid for imposing the *Legend*'s narrow masculinist perspective, Alceste shares his purview. The God of Love effectively transfers jurisdiction to "The grete goodnesse of the queene Alceste" (G.499), who may, as Cupid declares, "doth with hym what yow leste" (G.439). Accordingly, Alceste enjoins Chaucer to write "a glorious legende / Of goode wymmen, maydenes and wyves, / That weren trewe in lovyng al hire lyves" (F.483–85). Her participation recognizes women's investments in prescriptive ideals of feminine virtue, but it also affirms the reliance of this tradition on women's active endorsement. It further shows, more importantly, the ways in which an established tradition can be repurposed.[18] If Chaucer writes *The Legend of Good Women* for Queen Anne, as the F-Prologue seems to indicate when it suggests, "And whan this book ys maad, yive it the quene, / On my byhalf, at Eltham or at Sheene" (F.496–97), he also writes for an audience of elite women who could, Nicola F. McDonald argues, intervene in the prescriptive tradition of women's virtue.[19] To acknowledge that women's material virtue can be truncated or diminished by poetic formulation is also to recognize that women's embodied excellence can be reanimated or substantiated by reading practices.[20] Women who promote stories of good women, like Alceste, can reinvigorate even the most abstract, unenlivened narratives to make a case for women's material virtues.

When Shakespeare's Katherina voices prescriptions from marital handbooks, she does not simply reinforce masculine power. Rather, as the conversions that follow Chaucer's Custance affirm, women's ethical action takes strange, even uncanny forms. Women's ethical action remains unpredictable even when it follows script: with Spenser's thread of the two Florimells, a woman is imagined as an abstraction, but her embodied virtue remakes her beloved in a material transformation that is enriching for both partners. Similarly, Fletcher's Maria reforms Petruchio's masculine tyranny in a play that challenges the ethical worth of traditional virtue. If Dekker, Chettle, and Haughton's Grissel uncases masculine tyranny in premodern marriage, Phillip's Grissil shows that withstanding oppression is its own form of virtue. This is the most central idea of this book: as writers including Lydgate, Henryson, and Bokenham affirm, an embodied ability to withstand chaos, violence, and oppression is a world-(re)making excellence that affords equal benefits to women and men. Such a recognition, however, does not endorse political quietism. The writers studied across this book are interested in formulating material virtues that emerge from cultural vulnerability, even dispossession, yet there is no suggestion that the social conditions that produce these excellences should remain intact. In other words, these writers advocate change, even as they grapple with a tradition that has ensconced a model of virtue based on domination, governance, and (self-)regulation. Lodge is pointed in suggesting that women need intelligence and autonomy, while Fletcher demonstrates the virtues associated with yielding (not wielding) agency enrich men.

Women endowed with material virtues open a different vista on the ethical lives we share with others. They show that moral good does not simply amount to cultural power. Through their complex enactments, moreover, it becomes clear that men are diminished by traditional *virtus*, too. Even elite men, such as Troilus, suffer for their attempts to define their identities in relation to those feminized others they seek to control. And, while early modern light versifiers work to obscure masculine misery through a punitive program of poetic censure, Criseyde's ruined legacy far more poignantly indicts the forces of war that destroy both lovers. Chaucer might represent himself under the gaze of an imperious male ruler in his *Legend of Good Women*, yet, as all but a very few men would understand, that position is not exclusively feminized in premodern England. As Sheila Delany puts it, "The moral life may well be gender-blind, but social life is not."[21] Chaucer, like so many "new men" of his era, works within the domain of a powerful king.[22] Fifteenth-century writers, including Lydgate, Bokenham, Capgrave, and Henryson, lived in an arguably more tumultuous political environment.[23] And, though writers from the second half of the sixteenth century wrote under a powerful queen, their vulnerability was no less pronounced under the supposedly benevolent watch of Elizabeth I.[24] Stuart absolutism, finally, did nothing to alleviate the need to satisfy a powerful sovereign.[25] Thus, while the particulars of poetic production were obviously different in Chaucer's day, speaking from a precarious position is an experience that nearly all the writers featured in this book share with each other, and with their dispossessed female characters.[26] As Stephen Orgel reminds us, "this is a world in which masculinity is always in question."[27]

Chaucer's cycle of abandoned women provides insight into that historical experience. While critics have attended to the excisions and redactions of the *Legends*, the self-censorship that has been associated with negotiating the dangers of Ricardian court life has also been attributed to Chaucer's dissatisfaction with patronage writing more generally.[28] Because a powerful queen gives him a commission, in other words, he finds the task aesthetically restrictive. Chaucer's boredom with writing about good women, so the longstanding critical fiction goes, prompted him to abandon his gathering of betrayed heroines.[29] This explanation fails on aesthetic grounds: as R. W. Frank Jr. has shown, Chaucer dedicated impressive care to this collection of female worthies.[30] But it also does not match what we know about Chaucer's work habits. Like other writers, Chaucer needed the support of powerful patrons, and if his earlier *Book of the Duchess* is any indication, he was willing to gratify elites through his poetic productions.[31] The boredom explanation is also patently sexist: because Chaucer was commanded to write about good *women*—and by a powerful woman, no less—he must have found the task belittling.[32] Chaucer might be galled by the God of Love's directive, "Let be the chaf, and writ wel of the corn. / Why noldest thow han writen of Alceste, / And laten Criseide ben aslepe and reste?" (G.529–31), but as he

shows across the specific *Legends*, he is a good enough poet to adapt prescribed formulations to innovative reimaginings. Helen Phillips points out
that Chaucer "present[s] passion itself as an experience which can have, in
certain noble personalities, moral qualities."[33] By investing his heroines with
bodily resources of excellence—endurance, fidelity, and pity, for example—
Chaucer imagines the ways that vulnerability might recalibrate what qualifies
as a virtuous response to unjust treatment.[34]

    The Legend of Lucrece challenges the idea that rape is a political weapon,
or that rape is somehow generative for and even foundational to great Western cultures.[35] Unlike other versions of the story, Chaucer uncovers the social
utility of women's violation in patriarchal culture.[36] Chaucer initially distances his rendering from this story's traditional function as a Republican
fable, in which the "kynges / Of Rome"—the Tarquini—are overthrown for
their tyranny. Instead, the narrator claims, "But for that cause tell I nat this
storye, / But for to preyse and drawe to memorye / The verray wif, the
verray trewe Lucresse" (F.1684–86). To celebrate Lucrece's "wifhod and hire
stedefastness" (F.1687), however, is to recount a masculine contest that establishes the worth of husbands based on the quality of their wives. Of course,
this logic subtends numerous narratives—including Shakespeare's *Taming of
the Shrew*—but *The Legend of Lucrece* lays bare its ethical vacuity. Tarquin's
irrational desire reflects the masculinist indulgence of the homosocial contest
that introduces him to Lucrece. Chaucer captures the power asymmetry
involved in this encounter with a more general acknowledgment, "Wel wot
men that a woman hath no myght" (F.1801). Accordingly, Lucrece's plea for
grace is met with an even greater threat,

> And thus thow shalt be ded and also lese
> Thy name, for thow shalt non other chese. (F.1810–11)

In Chaucer's handling, women's consent, as well as their physical vulnerability, is mooted by the predatory abuses of dominant masculinity.

    To be sure, Chaucer's tale makes Lucrece's suicide a benefit to her
husband:

> She sayde that, for hir gylt ne for hir blame,
> Hir husbonde shulde nat have the foule name. (F.1844–45)

Likewise, his version endorses a preoccupation with feminine modesty drawn
directly from prescriptive discourse:

And as she fel adoun, she kaste hir lok,
And of hir clothes yet she hede tok.
For in hir fallynge yet she had a care,
Lest that hir fet or suche thing lay bare;
So wel she loved clennesse and eke trouthe. (F.1856–60)

And finally, Brutus converts the Roman populace's sympathy into political resistance against tyrannical rule:

And Brutus by hir chaste blood hath swore
That Tarquyn shulde ybanysshed be therefore
. . . .
Ne never was ther kyng in Rome toun
Syn thilke day. (F.1862–63, 1869–70)

Her story functions as a support for various masculine concerns. Nevertheless, Lucrece's material virtue also critiques the ethical system that establishes masculine dominance: the rape that prompts her self-destruction is explicitly linked to Tarquin's presumption of cultural privilege.[37] In describing him as "a wolf that fynt a lomb alone" (F.1798), Chaucer confronts the violence entailed by a *virtus* based on the exercise of agency over subordinates. Lucrece's care for her own name, which provoked dismissive disdain from Augustine, despite the *Legend*'s insistence that "The grete Austyn hath gret compassioun" (F.1690), achieves a dignity that equally extends to her body.[38] Her performance of modesty, more than rote adherence to an externally imposed code of conduct, affirms Lucrece's active investment in her own excellence.[39]

To view this story as silly, or to regard heroines such as Cleopatra or Thisbe as beset by "sheer stupidity and blindness," in Elaine Tuttle Hansen's words, is to express a wish that the virtue of these women could be accommodated by the tradition of *virtus* that defines heroism according to exercises of individual agency and personal control.[40] Hansen is correct to observe the critical treatment of classical heroes in Chaucer's *Legend*, but her indictment of "the pervasive and sometimes comic passivity, irrationality, and stupidity of the composite good woman depicted in the Legends[, which] tempts the reader to agree with the critic who thinks that these ladies only get what they ask for," is sustainable if we believe that only one model of virtue is conceivable, so that women's equality results from their inclusion within an ethical and social system that has traditionally depended upon their exploitation and degradation for its very ability to function.[41] Chaucer shows the impossibility, as well as the undesirability, of this egalitarian fantasy. In Nancy Bradley Warren's phrase, "[the legends] call into question not only official masculinist history but also masculine political dominance."[42] Chaucer is not interested in valorizing a classical model of virtue, but shows, rather, that this traditional model of ethics produces bad men, who in turn organize social structures in ways that are harmful to nearly everyone. In their dynasty-making sojourns, heroes including Jason, Theseus, and Demophon reveal that men's world-making power is staked on exploiting the bodies, brains, and virtues of those (women) who are more vulnerable than they are.

As Jill Mann argues, Chaucer's *Legend* answers the misogynist tradition by emphasizing the importance of women's "pite."[43] Mann breaks new ground with her contention that Chaucer is interested in rethinking the ethical foundations of the human. And, as Sarah McNamer has also shown, pity is a power that had particular feminine resonance in the Middle Ages.[44] So Mann is correct, and she makes an invaluable contribution to our understanding of the poem when she argues that Chaucer makes a quality traditionally associated with women foundational to a new ethical ideal.[45] Yet, in a deep irony given this book's feminist debts and aims, I suggest that Mann's treatment is too narrow because it focuses on gender. Chaucer does not just respond to misogyny in an effort to gain women greater recognition as ethical subjects; instead, he challenges the ethical organization of his culture, placing women at the center of human experience in an effort to rethink the ethical criteria for being human. By so doing, he suggests that women and men should be governed by a morality that includes pity for others. That women already evince this characteristic provides incontrovertible evidence that something is amiss in the value structure that awards men—especially predatory men—cultural dominance in premodern England.

The Legend of Good Women redresses Chaucer's *Troilus and Criseyde*, then, not by repudiating the latter's antifeminism, but by showing that Criseyde's betrayal is entailed by an ethics that makes women exchangeable even while those same women are enjoined to be true to the very men who have traded them in service to a cultural ideal of masculine dominance. If we wonder what would have happened if Criseyde had not been "slydinge of corage" (*T&C*, V.825), Chaucer's cycle of female worthies shows how faithful women fare within a heroic tradition. Women's dispossession within a world governed by heroic virtue ethics is even more pronounced considering the *Legend*'s notable gaps: Chaucer left out all instances of violent revenge in recounting these women's narratives. This is not, as some would have it, because he sought to make his women less able, less complex, or less venerable.[46] Instead, the virtues of Dido, Hypermnestra, or Ariadne—their courage, their long-suffering, their fidelity, and their pity—critique any notion that ethical life should be ordered so that men gain power at the expense of dispensable others. While some scholars believe Chaucer's narrator seems too unimpressed with the complaints of Medea or Dido to recount their words, his deferrals are just as much a refusal to use women's suffering as a titillating affirmation of masculine (poetic) power.[47] By suspending feminine complaint, "But who wol al this letter have in mynde, / Rede Ovyde, and in hym he shal it fynde" (F.1366–67), Chaucer departs from the tradition that makes women's pain a site of poetic production.[48] A different catalog of excellences, including endurance, pity, and compassion, is foregrounded. Because these heroines' virtues are as manifest as the abuses committed against them, Chaucer's narrator allows the excellences of his legendary women to speak for themselves.

By contrast, he is quite voluble about masculine trespass. Given the *Legend*'s direct censure of elite men, it is hard to compass the claim, made most directly by Carolyn Dinshaw, that Chaucer's narrator is allied with the God of Love.[49] Yet, her overarching proposition, "You can't found a tradition on the constraining of the feminine, Chaucer suggests here, because it will eventually silence men, too," remains not just right, but crucial for understanding the *Legend*.[50] But again, I suggest that Chaucer challenges the ethical conditions that underlie conventional gender hierarchy by critiquing the predations incumbent to empowered masculinity.[51] The God of Love is a prime target in this critique. Though Cupid may praise women, the heroes featured in these stories are part of the God of Love's retinue. These are men Chaucer's narrator condemns as "traytour[s]," who are "fals," and who practice "tirannye" (F.1328, 1169, 1883). They number among the foundational heroes of Western culture, moreover, whose privilege relies, the *Legends* reveal, on the mistreatment of women. In suggesting their ethical bankruptcy, Chaucer draws a moral distinction between those elite men who exploit others and the host of humanity who must attempt to remain true notwithstanding the chaos, violence, and degradation that follow from the acts of the privileged and powerful. Less commanding men, such as the narrator, are included in Chaucer's company of the vulnerable.

Through the formal restriction of *The Legend of Good Women*, Chaucer shows how little room there is to acknowledge an ethics founded on a common finitude, not the empowered individual. Phyllis exercises great courage when "She was hire owene deth ryght with a corde" (F.2485), and Cleopatra claims moving dignity when she declares, "And thilke covenant whil me lasteth breth / I wol fulfille" (F.693–94). V. A. Kolve rightly recognizes that "Chaucer's image of Cleopatra's death is heroic rather than didactic."[52] That such powers cannot be recognized as heroic only registers the limited ethical field that Chaucer's poem critiques. An important reason to end this book with a consideration of Chaucer's *Legend*, then, is because it lays bare the logic of gender that traditional virtue ethics supports: men are predatory, but they suffer no consequences for their exploitation of the vulnerable; women are virtuous, but they gain no social power from their embodied excellence. Alceste is rewarded for her virtue, "Hire grete bounte doubleth hire renoun" (G.510), but it is Cupid, whom Chaucer describes as "the myghty god of Love" (G.142), whose reign Chaucer's narrator must respect. Nevertheless, if Chaucer is different from other writers considered in this study, it is in his persistent insistence that poetry can transform the ethical foundations of human life. Though he is certainly not naïve about the vicissitudes of late Ricardian culture, his work suggests that poetry remakes the structures it critiques. Alceste's fidelity and pity—alongside her bravery and humility—provide a capacious ideal of material virtue that transforms the social disparities the poem records.

Later writers, I want to suggest in closing, are less optimistic about the possibility of wholesale ethical reformation, mainly because the social conditions that ensconce masculine authority continue unchanged. Shakespeare might share Chaucer's conviction that traditional virtue ethics impoverishes human moral experience—as I believe his *Troilus and Cressida* suggests—but he is less sanguine about the possibility of installing vulnerability as the ethical foundation of shared community. Just look at Ophelia. There is every good reason to see her material virtue—which entails protest, dignity, and forbearance—as a model of ethics with the power to resist violence, instability, and exploitation. Yet, as I argued in the introduction, the reparative power of her moral critique gains no social traction. Instead, Shakespeare's play features a competitive cycle of masculine vengeance—Hamlet vs. Claudius—which produces a cascade of destructive violence.

Shakespeare knew there might be a better way forward, and he is capable of imagining an alternative ethics that is *not* based on individual consciousness, but his work suggests that this countertradition of ethics will remain suppressed given contemporary political structures of personal power.

Just look at Polonius. His murder, as I noted in the introduction, begins the devastation of Shakespeare's play, and, as a consequence, it makes Ophelia's material virtue legible. Here, I return to Shakespeare's depiction of the old counselor's disposability because it provides an important contact with Chaucer's vulnerable narrator in his *Legend of Good Women*. Chaucer's narrator serves a volatile sovereign, in the same way, we might say, that Polonius advises an impetuous prince. Ophelia's father is in an even more precarious position, however, because Polonius also seeks to satisfy his sinister king, the murderous Claudius, who demands information about his dangerous nephew's state of mind. Rather obviously, Polonius is caught between dueling male elites. What Shakespeare shows us about how powerful men regard those who support their masculine privilege, however, provides an important final commentary on the need for material virtue as an alternative practice of ethics. Rather than presenting Polonius as a victim—as someone whose murder should be accounted for—*Hamlet* makes his death seem warranted, even justified. It does so by refusing to afford him respect or reverence. Because the play's protagonist disregards Polonius, the play treats his demise as unworthy of notice.

In other words, Polonius's death is a direct result of Hamlet's disrespect. To say that the old man is tedious is to offer an understated characterization of the young prince's attitude toward the senior courtier:

> This counsellor
> Is now most still, most secret, and most grave,
> Who was in life a foolish prating knave.—(*Hamlet*, III.iv.187–89)

Over the years, much ink has been spilled about Polonius's role: his proverbs echo teachings of the ancient rhetorician Isocrates, but scholars remain divided over whether these are just a tired recirculation of worn adages that every schoolboy might have known, or an upright deployment of respectable wisdom that a prudent father and counselor might have endorsed.[53] There is evidence that Polonius's counsel is still valued, since his instruction is frequently cited out of context:

> to thine own self be true,
> And it must follow, as the night the day
> Thou canst not then be false to any man. (*Hamlet*, I.iii.78–80)

It is only when this guidance is attached to Polonius that its wisdom becomes suspect. Because the Danish prince sees his wisdom as empty, Polonius ends up a discarded fool.

Polonius's foolishness is sinister because it supposedly excuses his murder. Icily if wittily, Saul Bellow remarks on the old man's demise: "One of the nice things about *Hamlet* is that Polonius gets stabbed."[54] Unlike the women included in Chaucer's *Legend*, Polonius is not a victim since his death does not even warrant recognition. His killing passes without notice because the play's focus—which has rightly attracted critical attention—is on the development of an individuated form of subjectivity, what Katharine Eisaman Maus investigates as "an unexpressed interior and a theatricalized exterior."[55] This subjectivity is ethically impoverished, as Polonius's murder affirms. Though *Hamlet* articulates a model of human consciousness that remains culturally empowered, even today, its emergence is predicated on a model of virtue that cheapens the lives of the less privileged.[56] This is an acute irony given that Hamlet's subjectivity is indebted, Tanya Pollard convincingly argues, to "a tradition of emotionally affecting tragedy that was female-centered, rooted in lament, and culminating in triumphant action."[57]

As Pollard details, female protagonists from Greek tragedy—in particular the grieving Hecuba—convert spectacles of vulnerability into performances of power.[58] Hamlet's engagement with the bereaved Trojan queen—"What's Hecuba to him, or he to Hecuba, / That he should weep for her?" (*Hamlet*, II.ii.536–37)—marks a transformation of tragedy, one that renders women's suffering a spectacle that enables masculine power. Watching a woman grieve, as Pollard observes, provides Hamlet with an impassioned model that ultimately forwards his revenge. He does not assume the same frenzied, affective distress as Hecuba, whom the player describes as a sight who fires the passions of her audiences:

> But who, O who had seen the mobbled queen,—
> . . . .
> Run barefoot up and down, threat'ning the flames
> With bisson rheum; a clout upon that head
> Where late the diadem stood, and for a robe,

About her lank and all o'erteemèd loins,
A blanket, in th'alarm of fear caught up—
Who this had seen, with tongue in venom steeped,
'Gainst Fortune's state would treason have pronounced.
But if the gods themselves did see her then,

. . . .

The instant burst of clamour that she made—
Unless things mortal move them not at all—?
Would have made milch the burning eyes of heaven,
And passion in the gods. (*Hamlet*, II.ii.483, 485–92, 495–98)

As Pollard explains, Hamlet occupies a reflective, metatheatrical position, which allows him to take up the role of revenger traditionally played by classical Greek women, but which does not require him to lose his sense of self-control as a component of the violence he enacts. Hamlet does not run mad, even if he is finally destroyed by his pursuit of revenge. With this role, Pollard concludes, "Shakespeare constructs Hamlet's distinctive innovation to the genre—a new focus on audiences' relationship with the moving spectacles they watch, at a moment when theaters were rapidly rising in prominence."[59]

This shift is not just due to the theater's rise, but also marks the demise of material virtue, an embodied mode of excellence usually, though not exclusively, enacted by women. The role of avenging woman is eclipsed, taken up by men who use female suffering to enable individualist (self-)governance. If Shakespeare's *Hamlet* marks the culmination of this transference, Chaucer looks forward to its arrival. In *Troilus and Criseyde* Chaucer endows his hero with a voice of complaint that most closely approximates female suffering. His final apotheosis, however, offers Troilus a distanced vantage point from which to reflect upon the worldly instability that led to his destruction. Chaucer's *Legend of Good Women*, by contrast, asks, what happens if virtue is recognized only in those with cultural power? His heroines bear up against oppression; they uncover the circuits of bodily desire, affect, and emotion that predicate effective action against tyrannical cultural powers. Yet women such as Philomela and Medea, unlike their classical namesakes, are afforded no powers of vengeance in Chaucer's collection. They suffer and they die, consolidating masculine control of the unruly, seductive feminine, in Dinshaw's argument.[60]

By suggesting that the narrator might be in the same position as his vulnerable heroines, I propose that Chaucer rejects a model of virtue that ensconces elite individualist power. His heroines do not take up traditional modes of violence, nor do they participate in classical cycles of retribution. Philomela and Procne, "In armes everych of hem other taketh" (F.2381), comfort one another rather than meting out vengeance against Tereus. The narrator emphasizes Philomela's innocence, "For this is al and som: thus was she served, / That nevere harm agilte ne deserved / Unto this crewel man, that she of wiste" (F.2384–86). Similarly, Medea's story ends with a lament wherein she questions her prior judgments:

> Whi lykede me thy yelwe her to se
> More than the boundes of myn honeste?
> Why lykede me thy youthe and thy fayrnesse,
> And of thy tonge, the infynyt graciousnesse? (F.1672–75)

Medea's self-awareness does not lead to a frenzy of violence, but, rather, substantiates the tale's denunciation of Jason's faithless exploitation. When she wishes him dead, "O, haddest thow in thy conquest ded ybe, / Ful mikel untrouthe hadde ther deyd with the!" (F.1676–77), Medea preserves her dignity in the face of Jason's mistreatment. And, while these women show the potential of material virtue—a model of ethics that connects bodies in nourishing alliance—their stories uncase the masculinist model of power that destroys such reparative "vertues."

All told, then, the *Legend* simultaneously critiques and gratifies elite masculine power: Chaucer's narrator serves the God of Love, while his standardized stories of good women uncover the ethical emptiness of a *virtus* that rewards the powerful at the expense of the vulnerable. If suicide is a good woman's only recourse, this is because, as *The Legend of Thisbe* reveals, there are no other cultural means of redress open to virtuous women. Most women cannot rely on the pity of the gods, who stellify Ariadne to save her from Theseus's abandonment:

> The goddess han hire holpen for pite,
> And in the signe of Taurus men may se. (F.2222–23)

The denunciation of Theseus in *The Legend of Ariadne* shows that pity is in short supply in the world of men. Indeed, like the later writers Lydgate and

Henryson, Chaucer evinces a canny awareness that ethical norms usually follow social power. As is clear from *The Legend of Cleopatra* and *The Legend of Thisbe*, good men also kill themselves, because, as Anthony and Pyramus demonstrate, forces of oppression frequently overwhelm vulnerable men, too. With Alceste Chaucer imagines another ethics, one that includes pity and compassion. It is predicated on yielding to others, yet it also elevates her stature. Due to her association with the daisy, "And she that is of alle floures flour / Fulfilled of al vertu and honour" (F.53–54), Alceste is meant to offer a perfect synthesis between material and immaterial excellences: "For also manye vertues hadde she / As Smal flourys in hyre coroun be" (G.516–17).

In Cupid's account, the material virtue Alceste realizes should be able to assimilate good women into the heroic tradition. Yet, as the *Legends* indicate, material virtue cannot be treated as an additive element, or a feminine complement, to a classical model of *virtus*. Neither are these women virile: they do not take on masculine characteristics when they demonstrate their constancy, pity, or strength. Rather, these women expose the fiction of the virile woman as a masculinist fantasy.[61] This problem is one that Chaucer has addressed before: his *Troilus and Criseyde* endeavors to invest Criseyde with a material virtue that credits her personal struggle against the social circumstances that beset her. Because the qualities that make her worthy—including pliancy, beauty, and pity—also make her exchangeable (and thereby disposable) within a masculinist society, the poem exposes a rift between heroic and material modes of virtue. Criseyde's vulnerability in heroic culture is something men exploit rather than protect. This signal incompatibility between material and heroic models of virtue occupies poets across this book: Lydgate's gatherings of virtuous women are meant to offer a protection against the kinds of instability that heroic culture visits upon good women; Bokenham similarly suggests the importance of networks of virtue as a way of nourishing those alternative forms of excellence that women enact in late medieval culture. Material virtues are not essentially feminine, however; Shakespeare and Fletcher insist, on the contrary, that men are also enriched when they yield rather than wield governance. In Spenser's *Faerie Queene*, likewise, Marinell flourishes when he hears Florimell's complaint and grants her his love.

This book is about women's ethical action, in particular, though, because women most often embody material virtues in premodern England. As I have argued, an ethics based on embodied vulnerability rather than cultural empowerment has more in common with women's social experience. This association need not be essential, since the writers featured herein were interested in rethinking the foundations of ethical life that supported certain social formations. This is attributable to the political upheaval that was a historical constant across this period. It is also due to a greater theological interest in human dependency during this era. My concern has been in thinking about the parallel between a confining ethics and a restrictive aesthetics in writers from Chaucer to Shakespeare. Chaucer avows his allegiance to his literary predecessors, "But wherefore that I spak, to yeve credence / To bokes olde and don hem reverence" (G.97–98), but in *The Legend of Good Women*, as elsewhere, he chafes against a confining aesthetic that reduces women's ethical action to prescriptive behavioral norms that reinforce masculine power. He is not alone. Poets including Capgrave and Henryson resist the belittling reinstatement of masculine power that gentleman poets take up in sixteenth-century Cressid poetry. Recirculations of Cressid by Gasgoigne, Turberville, and Whetstone, among others, confirm poetry's power to diminish women's virtues. Even so, Lodge's *A Margarite of America* warns against the dangers of making women into lifeless props in a saga of masculine achievement. As early modern Grissil narratives demonstrate, finally, the same story can enliven or deaden women's animate excellences.

The project I have considered here, which is the poetic invention of a counter-ethics that challenges classical *virtus*, is not just about adding women to or incorporating women within a heroic tradition. Shakespeare is not simply calling greater attention to Hecuba's centrality in the genre of tragedy. Rather, from Chaucer to Shakespeare, women's participation in ethical life remakes heroism itself.[62] To be sure, this participation is limited in the representations of female characters this book analyzes. Other stories, namely those by women, might show other ways through which an embodied model of virtue gains substance across this period. Margery Kempe's itinerant piety (fifteenth century), punctuated by wailing and characterized by humiliation, reveals the vulnerability that continually (1613) besets women's enactments of alternative virtues. In *The Tragedy of Mariam*, moreover, Elizabeth Cary links women's silence and excellence in a relationship that shows their constant endangerment. Yet this book pursues men's representations of material virtues, mainly because the feminism that emerges from rethinking women's ethical action is not deliberate—it does not derive from any attempt to call attention to women's vulnerability within patriarchal structures. Instead, when men write female characters, new forms of heroism emerge from the challenges these female characters face. That most men share something with these female characters—namely, their precarity—should prompt us to rethink what counts as virtue, and how ethical action transpires.

I propose that rethinking virtue according to representations of women's ethical action institutes a reparative ethics. Custance does not pursue vengeance or practice violence; instead, as Katherina's closing speech affirms, women have the capacity to remake the social norms that confine them by exposing their ethical vacuity. This is not, as one strain of contemporary self-help would have it, a suggestion that women's submission will reform men or improve marriage. Laura Doyle's (in)famous *Surrendered Wife* series, which includes book, sequel, website, and coaching service, treats men as individualist agents and women as complementary helpmeets.[63] By contrast, rethinking virtue from the standpoint of women's cultural vulnerability repudiates the dominant/submissive gender contract. The texts included here, I would like to insist in closing, are part of a much broader rethinking of ethical action. Other texts not treated in this study validate and expand material virtue's transformative potential—for women as well as men. For instance, Hermione in *The Winter's Tale* (1610–11) shows the uncanny, troubling, and reformative power of women's material virtue. This is not, I should add, because Hermione becomes an object: certain strains of posthumanist thought urge us to rethink our ethical classifications of agency in bodies once thought to be lacking such powers.[64] Hermione's ethical influence, unlike such posthumanist leveling, arises because her objectification makes masculine tyranny visible; this critique, in turn, gives her humanity a renewed, reparative power. The human is not discarded; rather, it is reframed. Throughout the play, Hermione remains virtuous; it is the rethinking of human good that her displacement uncovers, which the play ultimately restores through her reanimation.

Despite its promise, the story of material virtue is not a triumphalist narrative. Ophelia's destruction, like Cressida's degradation, marks the loss of an alternative model of "vertue," one with the power to repair the destruction wrought by ceaseless masculine competition. This model of material virtue is suppressed, ultimately, in favor of an individual subjectivity with the power to contemplate human fragility. Hamlet's meditations on Yorick's skull, for instance, arguably include a rational awareness of embodiment's pull on the ethical connections we make with others. Nevertheless, despite his acknowledgment of a common mortality, "Alexander died, / Alexander was buried, Alexander returneth into dust" (*Hamlet*, V.i.192–93), Hamlet still gets caught up in a cycle of vengeance that leads to total devastation. When Fortinbras remarks with bewildered shock, "This quarry cries on havoc. O proud death, / What feast is toward in thine eternal cell / That thou so many princes at a shot / So bloodily has struck!" (*Hamlet*, V.ii.308–11), Shakespeare's play affirms the failure of an ethical model that improves the traditional masculine concept of *virtus* by incorporating an awareness of mortality within its rational reflections.

Several of the writers included in this book are deeply invested in philosophical responses to vulnerability: Spenser's *Faerie Queene* is famously inflected by Aristotelianism *and* Platonism—not to mention Lucretian materialism.[65] Neostoicism is a useful resource for Chaucer and for Lydgate.[66] I have only nodded to the influence of voluntarism, Boethius, Luther, and other Reformation theologians.[67] Augustine comes up only in passing.[68] That is because this is not a book about philosophy's or theology's influence on literature. Nor is it a book that argues certain poets *are* philosophers or theologians.[69] When Chaucer's *Legend* invokes Aristotle's principle of the mean to describe virtue, "for vertu is the mene, / As Etik seith" (F.165–66), the poet does not bind himself to a moral calculus whereby different characters are judged as moderate, extreme, deficient, or what have you.[70] Rather, this book argues that poets including Chaucer construct an alternative foundation for ethics based on vulnerability. This occurs largely for formal reasons: as different poets represent characters whose actions reflect upon an ideal of human goodness, a reparative ethics based on embodied vulnerability emerges. Indeed, a different ethical world appears when the fact of our common finitude grounds our understanding of the human and its excellences. We can no longer act as if the discrete (masculine) subject who exercises rational governance is the ideal of and model for the human. Shifting the grounds of the human upends gender difference, and suggests that we need new modes of social organization. Through their female characters, poets from Chaucer to Shakespeare imagine new modes of ethical action based on intimacy and protection, not domination and governance. In arguing for "the matter of virtue," then, this book suggests that imagining women's ethical excellences as embodied, living, and connective remains a world-remaking project.

NOTES

INTRODUCTION

1. As I shall explain, this date range runs from the approximate date of Chaucer's birth to the print appearance of Shakespeare's First-Folio.

2. Shakespeare, *Hamlet, Norton Shakespeare*, 1683–1784. All further citations, noted parenthetically, are from this edition.

3. Aristotle, *Physics*, VII.iii (247a).

4. Foot, *Natural Goodness*, 51, recognizes that virtue requires us to consider "what kind of a living thing a human being is." Also see Annas, "Virtue Ethics," and Hursthouse, *On Virtue Ethics*, 192–239.

5. *MED*, s.v. "vertu(e)."

6. Hawes, *Pastime of Pleasure*, chap. xxv, chap. xxvi, chap. xxviii.

7. *Oxford English Dictionary*, s.v. "virtue," 5, 8 (a–d).

8. Cohen, "An Abecedarium for the Elements," 294.

9. *English Medieval Lapidaries*, ed. Evans and Serjeantson, 64.

10. Carruthers, "Sociable Text of the 'Troilus Frontispiece,'" 429. Carruthers makes no distinction between *virtus*, which she uses here, and its Middle English formulations.

11. Carruthers, "Virtue, Intention and the Mind's Eye," 86–87.

12. *Dives and Pauper*, 1.145.

13. For an important "capabilities approach," see Nussbaum, *Frontiers of Justice*; also see MacIntyre, *Dependent Rational Animals*.

14. Trevisa, *On the Properties of Things*, 102 a/b. *MED*, 6c.(b). [Add. MS. 27944].

15. Holthausen, "Rezepte, Segen u. Zauber-sprüche aus zwei Stockh. Hss." 75–88.

16. *admirable vertue, property and operation of the quintessence of rosemary flowers*, n.p.

17. *boke of the propreties of herbes called an herball*.

18. [*Pathway to Health*], *A right profitable booke for all diseases*, t.p.

19. *hospitall for the diseased*, t.p.

20. *Prepositas*, A1ʳ.

21. Chaucer, *Canterbury Tales, Riverside Chaucer*, 3–328. All further citations, noted parenthetically by fragment and line numbers, are from this edition.

22. Augustine, *Confessions* [*Confessiones*], Bk. III, chap. 2 (38).

23. Ibid.

24. Ibid., Bk. I, chap. 13 (13).

25. MacIntyre, *After Virtue*, 122–28, 182.

26. MacIntyre, *Whose Justice? Which Rationality?* 104.

27. Salkever, *Finding the Mean*, 165–204, provides an invaluable account of "gendered virtue" in ancient thought.

28. Ibid., 174.

29. Most virtue ethicists treat the exclusion of women, slaves, and children from the conditions of virtue as a historical inconvenience of Aristotle's cultural context, even though they also fully grant that virtues arise as an active product of deliberate education (and so presumably would still be available only to those fostered under the conditions that nourish the virtues). Besides those sources cited on the exclusions of heroic culture, above, see Annas, *Intelligent Virtue*, 8–10, for a discussion of virtue's active cultivation, and 52–54, on the importance of education and its cultural context. Hursthouse, 221–22, acknowledges the ways in which feminism has prompted us to recognize that "it is not in our nature or essence that female human beings are bound to do whatever they have, so far, done" (221).

30. Isidore, *Etymologies*, IX.v.6 (206).

31. Cadden, *Meanings of Sex Difference*, 169–88.

32. Guido Delle Colonne, *Historia Destructionis Troiae*, 14; qtd. in Blamires, *Woman Defamed*, 48.

33. Herdt, *Putting On Virtue*, 2.

34. See MacIntyre, *After Virtue*, 165–80. Also see Porter, "Virtue Ethics."

35. Here and elsewhere, I use the DRV translation.

36. Aquinas, *Treatise on the Virtues* [*Summa Theologiae*, qq. 49–67], 57 [q. LVI, art. 1].

37. Ibid., 144–45 [q. LXV, art. 3].

38. B. Newman, *God and the Goddesses*, 34–50, 78–81, 160–67.

39. Raskolnikov, *Body Against Soul*, 1–9, 22–26, surveys treatments of grammatical gender in medieval allegory and modern theory.

40. Wentzel, introduction, 7.

41. Ibid., 8.

42. Bloomfield, "Allegories of the Virtues and Vices," 494–96; Bloomfield, Guyot, Howard, and Kabealo, eds., *Incipits of Latin Works*; Newhauser, *Treatise*; Newhauser and Bejczy, eds., *Supplement to Morton W Bloomfield*.

43. Newhauser, *Treatise*, 58. For a discussion of Peraldus and his influence, see 127–30, 142–44.

44. *Summa Virtutum de remediis anime*, l.2.

45. E. A. Jones, "Literature of Religious Instruction," 406–22.

46. MacIntyre, *After Virtue*, 1–88; Herdt, 174–218; Frede, "Historic Decline of Virtue Ethics," 124–48.

47. Herdt, 173–96, 306–21; Russell, "Hume's Anatomy of Virtue," 92–123.

48. Frede, 133–40; Schneewind, "Misfortunes of Virtue," 42–63.

49. Schneewind.

50. Breen, *Imagining an English Reading Public*, 16–42. Works that consider the theological controversies surrounding virtue's performance include Aers, *Salvation and Sin*, 25–54; McGrath, *Intellectual Origins*, 67–117; MacIntyre, *After Virtue*, 165–80; and Kent, *Virtues of the Will*, 94–149.

51. Book II.1, 70–73.

52. For a compact survey, see Kent, "Virtue Theory," 493–505.

53. On dissimulation, see Benner, *Machiavelli's Ethics*, 63–97; and on the "impressiveness" of virtue, see Mansfield, *Machiavelli's Virtue*, 16–19, 25–27. Skinner, *Foundations of Modern Political Thought*, 1:118–38, focuses on Machiavelli's *virtù* as an ability to perform greatness.

54. Herdt, 173–96; Morrison, *Mimetic Tradition of Reform*, 230–35; McGrath, *Luther's Theology of the Cross*, 84; Ozment, *Age of Reform*, 292, 296–302.

55. McGrath, *Luther's Theology of the Cross*, 65–66, 77–78, 87–91, 119–28; also see Oberman, *Harvest of Medieval Theology*.

56. Breen, *Imagining an English Reading Public*, 45–48.

57. Ibid., 47. This point is from Aquinas, but other writers made the same moral distinction.

58. Herdt, 101–27.

59. Elliott, *Proving Woman*, studies Continental writers, while the following discuss this tradition in England: Bartlett, *Male Authors, Female Readers*; E. Robertson, *Early English Devotional Prose*; and Riddy, "'Women Talking about the Things of God,'" 104–27.

60. Surveys of medieval and early modern sources include Ashley and Clark, eds., *Medieval Conduct*; Nicholls, *Matter of Courtesy*; Staley, *Languages of Power*, 265–338; and Bryson *From Courtesy to Civility*. Studies of medieval and early modern conduct books for women include Ashley, "Medieval Courtesy Literature"; Bornstein, *Mirrors of Courtesy*; Collette, "Chaucer and the French Tradition Revisited"; Greco and Rose, "Maid to Order," 1–43; Hull, *Chaste, Silent and Obedient*; Kelso, *Doctrine for the Lady of the Renaissance*; K. Newman, *Fashioning Femininity*; and Riddy, "Mother Knows Best."

61. Goffman, *Presentation of Self*; see also Sponsler, *Drama and Resistance*, 50–74.

62. Caxton, *Book of the Knight*, 3.

63. Ibid., 145.

64. Christine de Pizan, *Here begynneth the boke of the cyte of ladyes*, bk. 3, chap. 3, R6^r, R5^r, and R4^v.

65. Vives, *Instruction*, I. x. L3^v.

66. Castiglione, *Courtyer*, bk. 3, 2F2^r.

67. Boccaccio, *Famous Women [De claris mulieribus]*, 3.

68. Castiglione, *Courtyer*, bk. 3, 2F2^v.

69. Stubbes, *Anatomie of abuses*, L8^v.

70. Ibid., E2^r.

71. Moriarty, *Disguised Vices*, 3.

72. *N-Town Passion Play I*, 111–16.

73. Skinner, "Thomas Hobbes," 1–61.

74. Plummer, "Logomachy of the N-Town Passion Play I," 318.

75. Qtd. in Owst, *Literature and the Pulpit*, 96.

76. *N-Town Passion Play I*, 101–2.

77. Pocock, *Machiavellian Moment*; Skinner, *Machiavelli*, 38–53.

78. Rich, *My Ladies Looking Glasse*, q2.

79. Breton, *Will of Wit*, A4^v.

80. Breton, *Soules Immortall Crowne*, A4^r, B3^v.

81. Averell, *dyall for dainty darlings*, E2^v.

82. Stubbes, *Christal Glas for christian women*, A2^v.

83. Salter, *Mirrhor of modestie*, A6^v.

84. Ibid., D7^r.

85. Vives, bk. 2, chap. 3, a4^v–b1^r.

86. Breen, *Imagining an English Reading Public*, 3, addresses the losses in translation of *hexis* as *habitus*.

87. Maus, *Inwardness and Theater*, 1–33.

88. Schwarz, *What You Will*, 4.

89. Katzenellenbogen, *Allegories of the Virtues and Vices*, plate 41. See Hamburger and Suckale, "Between This World and the Next"; and B. Newman, *God and the Goddesses*, 160–65, for analysis and variations on this motif.

90. Schwarz, *What You Will*, 1.

91. Glenn Burger, "Conduct Becoming," 123. Also see his *Conduct Becoming*, which argues that women's performative reading allowed them to take on moral improvement as more than a series of rote exercises imposed by men.

92. Aers, "Langland on the Church," 59–81.

93. Hildegard of Bingen, *Ordo Virtutum*, lines 7–8.

94. Newhauser, *Treatise*, 160–61.

95. Gray, "London, British Library, Additional MS 37049."

96. Hall, *Two guides to a good life*, B4^r. Hall claims virtue is ordered by reason, but he also claims it is a natural vestment of human perfection.

97. Langland, *Vision of Piers Plowman*, B XIX.355.

98. Tuve, *Allegorical Imagery*, 116.

99. Hanape, *ensamples of vertue and vice*.

100. Larke, *booke of wysdome*, Bi^r.

101. Mâle, *Religious Art in France*, 285–300, traces a new iconography of the virtues beginning ca. 1470. The artists of Rouen, he notes, begin to depict the virtues with different material possessions.

102. Becon, *gouernaunce of vertue*, Fii^v.

103. *Book of Vices and Virtues*, 92–96.

104. The former is the title to Part III of Whetstone's *rocke of regard*; R. Robinson, *vineyarde of vertue*.

105. Ritchey, *Holy Matter*, details the gendered significance of many texts that sought to make virtue more material for audiences. As she notes, the organic imagery in both the *Speculum Virginum* and Hildegard's *Ordo Virtutum* was designed to show women audiences how a life of enclosed virginity would foster embodied virtues.

106. *Mary Magdalene, from the Digby MS* 1079–85.

107. Cadden, 26.

108. Aristotle, *Generation of Animals*, I.XIX (727b), I.XX (729a).

109. As Butler remarks in her still-provocative *Bodies That Matter*: "[Reason] . . . requires that women and slaves, children and animals be the body, perform the bodily functions, that it will not perform" (49).

110. *Book to a Mother*, 175 (line 12).

111. Aquinas, *Summa Theologiae*, Art. 10, xxxiv, 149.

112. Bynum, *Christian Materiality*, 52, 213.

113. J. A. Phillips, *commemoration of the life and death*, A2^v.

114. See Bynum, *Jesus as Mother*; and Astell, *Song of Songs*. Walter Hilton's *Scale of Perfection* (late 1380s) is addressed to a female spiritual learner, but by Book 2, he uses that address to reach a wider audience of women and men.

115. Dronke, introduction to *Ordo Virtutum*," 147.

116. Prudentius, *Psychomachia*, 274–342. See Newhauser, *Treatise*, 161–63, for a discussion of this motif's persistence.

117. Cooper, "Gender and Personification," 34.

118. Ibid., 39.

119. Gibson, *Woman's Worth*, A2^r, A4^r.

120. *honour of vertue*, A2ʳ, B1ʳ.

121. Dekker, "Pleasant Comedie of Old Fortunatus."

122. Blake, "Allegorical Causation," 349.

123. Tilney, *Flower of friendshippe*, E5ʳ.

124. Rose, *Gender and Heroism*.

125. For groundbreaking investigations of Christ's representation in the cycle drama, see Beckwith, *Christ's Body*; and Fitzgerald, *Drama of Masculinity*, 145–64.

126. Sanchez, *Erotic Subjects*; Kuzner, *Open Subjects*; Campana, *Pain of Reformation*.

127. Fradenburg, *Sacrifice Your Love*, 2–4, makes an important, unacknowledged connection between virtue and sacrifice in traditional accounts. The material virtue I trace, because it is based on the body's substance and proximity, is not sacrificial, or determined by the pleasures of suffering.

128. M. Miller, *Philosophical Chaucer*, 4–12.

129. Lupton, *Thinking with Shakespeare*, 10.

130. J. Bennett, *Vibrant Matter*, 2.

131. J. Bennett, *Enchantment of Modern Life*, 14.

132. Lamb, *Popular Culture of Shakespeare, Spenser, and Jonson*, xvii.

133. Bialo, "Popular Performance," 295.

134. See Butler, *Precarious Life*, 128–51; and Butler, *Frames of War*, 1–32.

135. Honig, *Antigone Interrupted*, 17–18, 25–27.

136. Ibid., 30–31.

137. P. A. Brown, *Better a Shrew Than a Sheep*.

138. Alaimo and Hekman, "Introduction: Emerging Models of Materiality in Feminist Theory," 7.

139. *admirable vertue, property and operation of the quintessence of rosemary flowers* n.p.

140. Gerard, *herball*, 2.1257.

141. Ibid.

142. Ibid.

143. Laroche, "Ophelia's Plants."

144. Gerard, 2.850.

145. This iteration pays homage to Butler, *Bodies That Matter*, who rightly notes "that to invoke matter is to invoke a sedimented history of sexual hierarchy and sexual erasures," but it does not treat matter strictly as "a *sign* which in its redoublings and contradictions enacts an inchoate drama of sexual difference" (49).

146. Hanning, *Individual in the Twelfth-Century Romance*; Morris, *Discovery of the Individual*; Haidu, *Subject Medieval/Modern*. Aers, "Whisper in the Ear," 177–202, has cautioned early modernists not to overlook medieval instances of subjectivity, but, as I have argued recently in "The Premodern as Problem," the "we were there first" contention does not do service to medieval authors (139).

147. Medwall, *Nature*, 125–30.

148. Chaucer, *Troilus and Criseyde*, *Riverside Chaucer*, 471–585. All further citations, noted parenthetically by book and line numbers, are taken from this edition.

CHAPTER I

1. Chaucer, *Troilus and Criseyde*, *Riverside Chaucer*, 471–585. All further citations, noted parenthetically by book and line numbers, are taken from this edition.

2. See Hansen, *Chaucer and the Fictions of Gender*, 155–86, for a feminist reading of Chaucer's debts to Boccaccio.

3. Pearsall, *John Lydgate*; Lerer, *Chaucer and His Readers*; C. D. Benson, "Critic and Poet."

4. My argument is influenced by Lawton, "Dullness and the Fifteenth Century," who attributes once-maligned aspects of Lydgate's verse to deliberate literary strategies.

5. I would not go as far as N. Watson, "Outdoing Chaucer," but I would say that Lydgate challenges Chaucerian idealism.

6. See C. D. Benson, *History of Troy*; and Simpson, "Other Book of Troy," for studies of Guido's history and its influence. Renoir, *Poetry of John Lydgate*, 76–94, connects Lydgate's expressed views on women to his different audiences; Edwards, "Lydgate's Attitudes to Women," 436–37, grants that Lydgate's antifeminism might be connected to place and occasion, but objects to the neat categories (clerical, courtly, and humanist) that Renoir posits. Shutters, "Truth, Translation," tracks differences between Lydgate's various women in the *Troy Book*.

7. Lydgate, *Troy Book*. All further citations, noted parenthetically by book and line numbers, are taken from this edition.

8. Pearsall, "Lydgate as Innovator," emphasizes Lydgate's medievalism.

9. See Trigg, *Congenial Souls*, 93–99, for an analysis of Lydgate's fantasy of Chaucerian community. Meyer-Lee, *Poets and Power*, traces Lydgate's investment in Chaucer pursuant to his "laureate" ambitions.

10. MacIntyre, *After Virtue*, 23–35, suggests that "A moral philosophy . . . characteristically presupposes a sociology" (23). For the philosophical controversies involved in the moral reorganization of the medieval self, see Aers, *Salvation and Sin*; Courtenay, *Capacity and Volition*; Herdt, *Putting on Virtue*; Oberman, *Harvest of Medieval Theology*; Oberman, *Forerunners of the Reformation*; McGrath, *Intellectual Origins*, 67–117; and Kent, *Virtues of the Will*, 204–52.

11. Taylor's emphasis on inwardness in his seminal study *Sources of the Self* is at stake in Criseyde's representation. Although Chaucer might attempt to align Criseyde with a modern subjectivity as Taylor articulates it, "whereby we place 'within' the subject what was previously seen as existing, as it were, between knower/agent and world" (188), war's chaos circumvents this moral potential. In this, I suggest, Criseyde is explicitly not representative of late medieval ethical trends; instead, she represents the material inequities of social morality, to the extent that differences in political status, specifically gender, might prevent some members of society from assuming the same ethical prerogatives as culturally privileged elites.

12. In this project I follow Somerset, " 'Hard is with seyntis for to make affray,' " who calls for a "cross-comparison" of Lydgate's religious and secular writings (258). In my methods, I am influenced by Sanok, *Her Life Historical*, who claims "not only that ethics are historically specific, but also that they are inextricable from other categories of social practice and identity" (9).

13. As Colletti, "*Paupertas est donum Dei*," argues: "[Fifteenth-century] authors sought to model [religious figures] in accordance with the values and aspirations of their well-to-do patrons even as they engaged social, religious, and political issues that were relevant both to communities of lay readers and to the fortunes of church and nation" (343).

14. Winstead, *Virgin Martyrs*; K. J. Lewis, "Model Girls?"

15. By arguing that Osbern Bokenham's *Legendys of hooly wummen* was responsive to Chaucer's *Legend of Good Women*, Delany, *Impolitic Bodies*, obliquely acknowledges the broader

consolidation of secular and religious discourses of famous women in fifteenth-century England that I seek to acknowledge through Criseyde's excluded history.

16. Winstead, *Virgin Martyrs*, 113.

17. Sanok, *Her Life Historical*, 9.

18. Caxton, *Book of the Knight*, 44–45.

19. *Le Ménagier de Paris*, 69.

20. Lawton, 779–82; Patterson, "Making Identities." Strohm, "Hoccleve, Lydgate," 654–56, notes that Lydgate's pacifism often sits uneasily with his Lancastrian sympathies. Straker, "Rivalry and Reciprocity" and "Propaganda," is most direct in arguing that Lydgate critiqued Lancastrian policies, particularly (as I shall discuss later) those invested in marital alliance.

21. Baswell and Beekman Taylor, "*Faire Queene Eleyne.*"

22. Boccaccio, *Famous Women*, 150–51 [Ipsa autem quam diu post hec vixerit, aut quid egerit, seu quo sub celo mortua sit, nusquam legisse recordor].

23. Christine de Pizan, *Boke of the cyte of ladyes*, bk. 2, chap. 61, Dv^r.

24. Caxton, *Book of the Knight*, 164, 165.

25. Ibid., 163.

26. Ibid., 164.

27. Ibid., 167.

28. Simpson, *Reform and Cultural Revolution*, 121, 127.

29. In her discussion of classical catalogs of famous women, Glenda McLeod establishes the *Heroides* as one of several antique texts that formalize a "divorce between women and the active life" (*Virtue and Venom*, 28).

30. Simpson, *Reform and Cultural Revolution*, 131.

31. McLeod, 15, discusses the elevation of public duty over private in the Roman return to classical Greek heroes.

32. Aers, "Criseyde," remains one of the boldest acknowledgments of Chaucer's lack of ethical idealism regarding his heroine's social status.

33. Steinberg, "'We do usen here no wommen for to selle,'" 268.

34. Jacobs, "Mate or Mother," 59–73.

35. *Woman Defamed*, 135–44.

36. Rosenfeld, "Doubled Joys," 39–59, studies the moral complexity of the poem in relation to scholastic theories of pleasure; McAlpine, "Criseyde's Prudence," 119–224, offers a revisionist reading of Criseyde's practical wisdom.

37. Mitchell, *Ethics and Eventfulness*, 39–41, focuses on Criseyde's moral agency in a world of temporal change.

38. Collette, "Criseyde's Honor," 55.

39. *MED*, s.v. "vertu," 8(a.; V. Allen, "Mineral Virtue," 123. Akbari, "Death as Metamorphosis," connects such articulations of natural virtue to the ethical potential of the body.

40. *MED*, s.v. "vertu," 11(a. Caxton's preface to his translation of the *Book of the Knight of the Tower* makes this sense tautologically clear: "All vertuouse doctryne & techynge had & lerned of suche as haue endeuoured them to leue for a remembraunce after theyr deth to vs / by whiche we ben enfourmed in scyence / wysedom and understandyng of knowleche / hou we ought to rewle our self in this present lyf haue cavsed us to know many good reules / & vertuous maners to be gouerned by" (3).

41. Archibald, "Declarations of 'Entente'"; Campbell, "Figuring Criseyde's 'Entente.'"

42. Caxton, *Book of the Knight*, 163.

43. Christine de Pizan, *Medieval Woman's Mirror of Honor*, is especially pointed: "For God's sake, remember who you are! Consider your high position. Do not consent for the sake of any foolish pleasure to forget your soul and your honor. Do not put trust in vain fancies, as many young women do, allowing themselves to believe that there is no harm in loving with a tender passion provided that it is not accompanied by any sinful act" (141).

44. Scholars have long debated Criseyde's consent: if Criseyde has the power to consent, her autonomy also makes her culpable for betrayal. See E. Robertson, "Public Bodies and Psychic Domains," for an important articulation. See Cartlidge, "Criseyde's Absent Friends," McTaggart, "Shamed Guiltless," and Boboc, "Criseyde's Descriptions," for considerations of the ethical bind Criseyde faces.

45. See Dinshaw, *Chaucer's Sexual Poetics*, 57–61, for an important reading, and G. Rubin, "Traffic in Women," for its theoretical basis.

46. Strohm, *Politique*, 87–132.

47. For a sense of Lydgate's relations to his social milieu, see Strohm, *England's Empty Throne*, and Nolan, *John Lydgate*.

48. See Nolan, *John Lydgate*, 131–54; see also C. D. Benson, "Civic Lydgate," and Sponsler, "Lydgate and London's Public Culture," for discussions of the scope of Lydgate's civic interludes.

49. Tuve, *Allegorical Imagery*, 57–88; Katzenellenbogen, *Allegories of the Virtues and Vices*. The two most important sources for this tradition were Cicero, *De Inventione*, Bk. II, 53–55, 326–33, and Macrobius, *Commentary on the Dream of Scipio*, Bk. I, chap. 8 (Macrobius, vol. II, ed. J. Willis, 36–39).

50. See Scanlon, *Narrative*, 98–105, for analysis of the Fürstenspiegel tradition; see H. A. Kelly, *Chaucerian Tragedy*, and D. Wallace, *Chaucerian Polity*, for analysis of Boccaccio's *De Casibus Illustrium Virorum*.

51. Kantorowitz, *King's Two Bodies*, 468–83; Barron, *Medieval Guildhall of London*, 27, plates 9a, 9b, 10.

52. Watts, *Henry VI and the Politics of Kingship*, 23–26, 58–59, demonstrates a pronounced connection between the cardinal virtues and late medieval kingship.

53. Straker, "Rivalry and Reciprocity," argues that Lydgate granted only tacit approval to the marriage between Henry V and Katherine of Valois; Mitchell, "Queen Katherine," suggests that Katherine's contested remarriage is the topical subtext for Lydgate's puzzling allegory.

54. "That Now is Hay," Lydgate, *Minor Poems*, Part II, line 111.

55. Nolan, " 'Now Wo, Now Gladnesse,' " 532; Simpson, *Reform and Cultural Revolution*, 69–128.

56. Here, I follow Sidhu, "Henpecked Husbands," who urges scholars to consider gender in conjunction with other forms of politics evident in Lydgate's poetry. In an inversion of Nolan, "Lydgate's Worst Poem," and Andrea Denny-Brown, "Lydgate's Golden Cows," both of whom laudably expand their critical focus of several Lydgate poems beyond their traditional focus on women and household structures of labor, I consider the ways that femininity, in its symbolic and social deployments, might contribute to more traditional forms of politics, i.e., those that concern men and their makings of the world.

57. "That Now is Hay," Lydgate, *Minor Poems*, Part II, line 94.

58. Ibid., lines 49–56.

59. Meyer-Lee, "Emergence of the Literary," argues for Mary's "incarnational" powers, as well as her mediating pity and infused, divinely illumined virtues, in ways that are instructive for my broader thinking about Lydgate's representation of feminized excellence (329–31).

60. Lydgate, *Mumming at Eltham, Mummings and Entertainments*, lines 50–63.

61. Mitchell, "Queen Katherine," 56–58. For this general trend, see K. M. Phillips, "Maidenhood"; and M. Rubin, *Mother of God*, 285–331.

62. Mitchell, "Queen Katherine," 58.

63. Lydgate, "Floure of Courtesy," *Minor Poems*, Part II, lines 190–96.

64. Lydgate, "A Ballade, of Her that Hath all Virtues," *Minor Poems*, Part II, lines 8–13.

65. Lydgate, "A Ballade on an Ale-Seller," *Minor Poems*, Part II, lines 36–38.

66. Lydgate, "Horns Away," *Minor Poems*, Part II, line 25.

67. See Mitchell, "Queen Katherine."

68. Lydgate, "That Now is Hay," *Minor Poems*, Part II, line 50.

69. Lydgate, *Troy Book*, section heading, III.4641–42.

70. Blamires, *Chaucer, Ethics, and Gender*, 130–40, distinguishes between masculine largesse and feminine liberality.

71. Lydgate, *Amor vincit omnia, Minor Poems*, Part II, lines 17–22.

72. Ibid., line 20.

73. See *Riverside Chaucer*, 657, for this poem, as well as a discussion of its relation to the Chaucer canon.

74. Ibid., 17, 19.

75. Latin Vulgate, 1 Cor. 13:13: "nunc autem manet fides spes caritas tria haec maior autem his est caritas."

76. For examples, see Lydgate, *Minor Poems*, Part I, nos. 1, 2, 4, 6, 7, 21, 31, 34, 35, 37, 43, 45, 48, and 49.

77. Lydgate, "Ballad at the Reverence of Our Lady," *Minor Poems*, Part I, lines 16–18.

78. Lydgate, "The Fyftene Ioyes," *Minor Poems*, Part I, line 1; "*Gaude Virgo Mater Christi*," *Minor Poems*, Part I, line 43.

79. Ashley, "Medieval Courtesy Literature."

80. Caxton, *Book of the Knight*, 147.

81. Christine de Pizan, *Boke of the cyte of ladyes*, bk. 3, chap. 1, Riiii^v.

82. Ibid.

83. Shutters, "Truth, Translation," 87.

84. Indeed, as a direct inversion of Agamben's *homo sacer*, Polyxena can be sacrificed but not killed: to the extent that her life is not grievable (and Hecuba's madness, which lands her on an island and ultimately prompts the Greeks to stone her to death, is not grieving), Polyxena's existence never counts as a livable life, as Butler has theorized it. Agamben defines the *homo sacer* as the sacred man "who *may be killed* and yet *not sacrificed*" (*Homo Sacer*, 8; italics in the original); Butler, *Precarious Life* and *Frames of War*, defines the threshold of a "liveable life" as its "grievability."

85. Fradenburg, *Sacrifice Your Love*.

86. Lydgate, "Gloucester's Approaching Marriage," *Minor Poems*, Part II; Straker, "Propaganda, Intentionality."

87. Straker, Propaganda, Intentionality, 107–17.

88. Lydgate, "Gloucester's Approaching Marriage," *Minor Poems*, Part II, lines 71–75, 78.

89. Straker, "Propaganda, Intentionality," 113.

90. Lydgate, "Valentine to her that Excelleth All," *Minor Poems*, Part I, lines 50–56.

91. Lydgate, *"Life of Our Lady,"* I.302–8.

92. Critics including Strohm, Patterson, Lawton, and Straker have complicated and challenged the older view, propounded most influentially by Pearsall, that Lydgate was a propagandist for the Lancastrian regime.

93. Lawton; C. D. Benson "Civic Lydgate"; Sponsler, "Lydgate and London's Public Culture."

94. See Scarry, *Body in Pain*, 129–33. To destroy the social goods that virtuous women exemplify parallels what Scarry characterizes in a different context as a culture's ability to make its own meaning, to devise its own values, ideals, and ethics.

95. This idea is a truism of Chaucer criticism, but Scanlon, "Lydgate's Poetics," esp. 89, prompted me to rethink its relation to Lydgate.

CHAPTER 2

1. Lydgate, "That Now is Hay Some-Tyme Was Grase," *Minor Poems*, Part II.

2. Although this poem is not attributed to Chaucer in manuscript, scholars have generally accepted its authentic status as part of Chaucer's canon. See *Riverside Chaucer*'s explanatory notes, 1089–90.

3. Skelton uses Cressid to compliment his patron's beauty in "To my lady Elisabeth Howarde," a prefatory address to his *Garlande or Chaplet of Laurell* (1523), *Poetical Works of John Skelton*, 396–97 (lines 871–72). In 1507, however, in his *Philip Sparrow*, *Works*, 1:84, 85 (lines 695, 710–12), Skelton condemns Cressid: "For she dyd but fayne . . . She was moch to blame; / Disparaged is her fame, / And blemysshed is her name." Though Cressid might express a positive comparison, it was not straightforward even in the early sixteenth century.

4. Thynne, *Workes of Geffray Chaucer*. See Henryson, *Robert Henryson*, 3–13, and Sheridan, "Early Prints," 23–27, for a discussion of Henryson's anglicization and inclusion in this edition.

5. Mieszcowski, "Reputation of Criseyde," 135, argues that Henryson's portrayal is consistent with a longer tradition of negative typecasting. Also see Mapstone, "Origins of Criseyde," 131–47.

6. Thynne, Oqiiiʳ.

7. For example, see *A poore knight his pallace of private pleasures*. In this dream allegory, Cressid is a leper, but the poem also praises Chaucer as "The cheefest of all Englishmen" (Ciiiᵛ).

8. For examples, see Stearns, "Henryson and Chaucer"; Spearing, *Medieval to Renaissance*; and Strohm, "Fourteenth- and Fifteenth-Century Writers as Readers."

9. C. D. Benson, "Critic and Poet"; Watson, "Outdoing Chaucer."

10. Rollins argues that sixteenth-century poets misunderstood Henryson's sympathy for Cresseid. While I also believe that Henryson's poem is different from later versified accounts, my argument does not surmise or depend on authorial attitudes.

11. Much of the Elizabethan poetry I will treat is classed among what C. S. Lewis, *English Literature*, 222–317, calls "drab age verse," including Turberville, Howell, Whetstone, and Gascoigne, along with the English print miscellanies. Whetstone contributed to these collections, and the writers Turberville, Howell, and Gascoigne collected their own poetry in a fashion that is similar to that of the miscellanies. Besides these formal overlaps, my discussion also includes poems taken directly from the miscellanies. See Pomeroy, *Elizabethan Miscellanies*, for a discussion of the didactic and amusement value of different collections. Taken together, I consider these poems—written for preferment or entertainment—as popular or light prescriptive verse.

12. While much of the light verse I read takes up this sardonic tone, broadside ballads, which I touch on only briefly, are uniformly cutting in their assessment of Cressid. For the relation between broadside ballads and the print miscellanies, see Pomeroy, 8–12, 16, 26–27.

Also see Nebeker, "Broadside Ballads." Popular poetic forms were deeply invested in parodic mockery, as M. Jones demonstrates in his essay, " 'Such pretty things.' " Also see Sullivan and Woodbridge, "Popular Culture in Print."

13. Henryson, *Testament of Cresseid, Poems of Robert Henryson*, ed. Kindrick. All other citations, noted parenthetically, are taken from this edition. Henryson's poem was printed with *Troilus and Criseyde* beginning with Thynne's edition (1532).

14. Shakespeare, *Troilus and Cressida*, ed. Bevington. All further citations, noted parenthetically, are taken from this edition.

15. See Jacquart and Thomasset, *Sexuality and Medicine*, 77–94, and Brody, *Disease of the Soul*, for discussions of the medical and literary traditions. For discussions of Henryson's treatment, see Stearns, "Robert Henryson and the Leper Cresseid"; and Parr, "Cresseid's Leprosy Again." Hanna, "Cresseid's Dream," argues for cosmology's diminished importance since this episode is actually a dream. Kruger, *Dreaming*, 136–37, describes this type of dream as an "action dream," in which a deity acts upon a mortal. See H. A. Kelly, *Chaucerian Tragedy*, 235, for a discussion of this type of dream in relation to Henryson's poem. For discussions of humoral theory and medieval cosmology, see Thorndike, *History of Magic*; and Curry, *Chaucer and the Mediaeval Sciences*. B. Newman helpfully presents this information as it relates to medieval theories of gender in her invaluable book, *Sister of Wisdom*.

16. The "redemptive" position is prevalent. For examples, see Rollins, "Troilus-Cressida Story," 383–429; Fox, *Testament of Cresseid*; Mieszcowski, 71–153; Patterson, "Christian and Pagan"; Craun, "Blaspheming Her 'Awin God' "; and Aronstein, "Cresseid Reading Cresseid."

17. Riddy, " 'Abject Odious,' " offers a compelling argument that Troilus's heroism is predicated on Cresseid's suffering. Edmondson's insightful reading of Henryson's negation of *Troilus and Criseyde*, "Henryson's Doubt," informs my thinking about *why* Henryson might have subjected Cresseid to inhuman punishment.

18. The classic articulation of this position is by Tillyard, "Henryson: *The Testament of Cresseid*."

19. Patterson, 705.

20. Fox, 42–43.

21. Fumo, "Books of the Duchess," argues that the downfall of Eleanor Cobham increasingly made the complaint a vehicle for thinking about feminine suffering in terms that move beyond the traditional Chaucerian (or Ovidian) models.

22. Edmondson's analysis, "Henryson's Doubt," 176, is indebted to Margherita, "Criseyde's Remains," and Strohm, *England's Empty Throne*, 101–27. Connecting Cresseid to Lacan's *Ethics*, as Edmondson does, shows the consequences of her status as a leper in terms that are both symbolic and tangible.

23. Pearsall, " 'Quha wait,' " 177.

24. A failed encounter between once-lovers here denotes what Jacques Rancière calls a "distribution of the sensible," since the basic conditions of visuality are dispensed in radically unequal, explicitly gendered measures. See *Politics of Aesthetics*, 12–13.

25. Riddy, 281.

26. The extensive astrological lore Henryson employs is explained in Grant, *Planets, Stars, and Orbs*, and Duhem, *Medieval Cosmology*. See Mann, "Planetary Gods," for Henryson's usage. Fumo, 465, argues that astrological knowledge was coming under scrutiny in the fifteenth century, and suggests Henryson's awareness of its misuse in his *Fox and the Wolf*. It could be said, actually, that the entirety of the *Testament* shows the cultural shackles provided

by astrology, particularly as a tool for asserting women's wantonness. Notwithstanding potential skepticism, it was still the case that astrology was part of accepted scientific knowledge in
Henryson's day.

27. Matter, "Passions and Ecstasies," 25, includes a helpful diagram of the elements,
dispositions, and directions in humoral theory.

28. For a discussion of the importance of place in medieval cosmology, see selections in
Duhem, 137–91. Also see Lilley's fascinating study, *City and Cosmos* (131–57), which examines
the relationship between medieval cosmology, morality, and urban planning—including leper
laws.

29. See Douglas, *Purity and Danger*, 44, for a discussion of "matter out of place," and its
function as cultural "dirt." Douglas also talks about uncleanness in relation to contagion in
ways that relate to Cresseid's constructed sexual impurity.

30. Lacan, *Four Fundamental Concepts*, 95: "if what Petit-Jean said to me, namely, that
the can did not see me, had any meaning, it was because in a sense, it was looking at me, all
the same."

31. Lacan, *Ethics of Psychoanalysis*, 55.

32. Kent, "Virtue Theory."

33. Butler, *Frames of War*, 62.

34. Boffey, "Lydgate, Henryson, and the Literary Testament," details the legal precision
of Cresseid's testament, while Mathews, "Land, Lepers, and the Law," demonstrates its lack of
legal standing.

35. Cressid is occasionally invoked as a model mistress by frustrated suitors, but these
writers also suggest that her sexual availability is a given: in *Tottel's Miscellany* (1557), *Richard
Tottel's "Songes and Sonettes,"* #206 (lines 71–72), notably, the speaker urges his beloved, "To
graunt me grace and so to do, / As Creside then did Troylus to." Elderton's ballad, "The panges
of Loue and louers fittes" (1559), refers to Cressid's pity. And Fullwood's speaker muses, *Enime
of Idlenesse* (1568), not without irony, "Therfore graunt grace, as Cressida, / did vnto Troylus
true" (138).

36. Proctor, *Gorgious gallery*, Eii^v.

37. Proctor, Ci^v.

38. Gascoigne, "Dan Bartholomewes Dolorous discourses," 109 (line 110), and "The
Reporter's Conclusion," 126 (line 52); both in Gascoigne, *Complete Works*, vol. 1.

39. Turberville, *Epitaphes*, 139^r.

40. Rollins, 410. He also notes Helen's negative appraisals in such collections, but since
her story is also contained in defenses of women, it would seem that her divided history remains
consistent.

41. Gybson, *Very proper dittie.*

42. Proctor, Gii^r.

43. Turberville, *Epitaphes*, 61^v.

44. Proctor, Ci^v.

45. Proctor, Eiii^v.

46. Edwards, *Paradise of daintie devises*, L4^v.

47. Howell, *Newe sonets*, 6 (emphasis mine).

48. Ibid., 6.

49. Howell, *His devises*, Biiii^v.

50. Turberville, *Tragicall tales*, 182^v.

51. C. Robinson, *Handefull of pleasant delites*, B8^v.

52. J. G. Harris, *Sick Economies*, 83–107.

53. Brody, 175–77.

54. J. G. Harris, 2.

55. *OED*, s.v. "moralize." The term doesn't become a verb until the fifteenth and six-teenth centuries.

56. *Poore knight*, F^r.

57. Proctor, "Lover in the prayse of his beloved," Fiv^v.

58. Gascoigne, "This question being propounded," *Complete Works*, 1:89 (lines 13–14).

59. Gascoigne, "Dan Bartholomew his first Triumphe," *Complete Works*, 1:101–2 (lines 29–30, 32, 35–37).

60. Dorrell, *Willobie his Auisa*, 65^r.

61. Proctor, "Lover forsaken," *Gorgious gallery*, C^r.

62. See Jehan le Fèvre, *The Lamentations of Matheolus*, in *Woman Defamed, Woman Defended*, 177–97, for an example.

63. Ibid.

64. Turberville, *Epitaphes*, 49^v.

65. In many early modern poems, Troilus is true to the point of naiveté.

66. Proctor, "Lover forsaken," C^v.

67. George Whetstone, *Rocke of regard*.

68. Ibid., t.p.

69. Ibid., "Epistle," ¶i^v.

70. Ibid., "R.C. in praise of Whetstons and his Rocke of Regard," ¶ii^v.

71. Ibid., "Argument, for Cressids complaint," 17.

72. Ibid.

73. Ibid., 18.

74. Ibid.

75. Ibid.

76. Ibid.

77. Ibid., 19.

78. Shakespeare, *Taming of the Shrew, Complete Works*, ed. Bevington, IV.i.84. All further citations, noted parenthetically, are taken from this edition.

79. Whetstone, 19.

80. Kent, *Virtues of the Will*; Ozment, *Age of Reform*, 292, 296–302.

81. Zeeman, *'Piers Plowman'*; Freinkel, *Reading Shakespeare's Will*; Schwarz, *What You Will*.

82. Schwarz, *What You Will*, 32–37.

83. Gowing, *Common Bodies*, 82–110.

84. Whetstone, 20, 21.

85. Ibid., 21.

86. Ibid.

87. Ibid.

88. Ibid., 22.

89. Gascoigne, "The Shield of Love," *Complete Works, Hearbes*, 1:340 (lines 13–16).

90. Turberville, "Lover finding his Love," *Epitaphes*, 91^r.

91. R. Johnson, "Phillidaes kind replye," *Crowne garland of goulden roses*, Evii^v.

92. Dorrell, 59^r.

93. R. Greene, *Euphues, Complete Works*, 6:166.

94. Elyot, *Of the Knowledge*, 52. After telling Caninius of Zenobia's martial virtues, Candidus explains, "I have boden her to supper, it wyll not nowe be longe or she come hyther. And whan ye doo here her, I dare well saye, ye wyll be chaunged frome your opinion, and confesse, that in womenne is both courage, constance, and reason."

95. Charnes, *Notorious Identity*, 72. James, *Shakespeare's Troy*, 95, observes, "Cressida does not shoulder full responsibility for the play's failures of value, and we are denied an edifying moral."

96. James, 88.

97. Charnes, *Notorious Identity*, 72.

98. S. M. Harris, "Feminism and Shakespeare's Cressida: 'If I be false . . .'" provides a thorough if shocking catalog of assessments of Cressida-as-whore from the 1940s to the 1980s. Also see Adelman, "'This is and is not Cressid'"; and G. Greene, "Shakespeare's Cressida," for responses.

99. G. Greene, "Language and Value." Altman, "Practice of Shakespeare's Text," sees Cressida as a symbol of the play's failed values.

100. It should be noted that almost all manuals for young women present women's isolation as a defensive posture. See Caxton, *Book of the Knight*, 167, for a representative admonition.

101. Hodgdon, "He Do Cressida," 284.

102. Sanchez, *Erotic Subjects*, 88.

103. Gil, *Before Intimacy*, 78–81, rightly notes the heroes' weariness with homosocial traffic in women, though I believe he is wrong to conclude that the asocial affair between Troilus and Criseyde exceeds this system. Engle, *Shakespearean Pragmatism*, 147–63, and Grady, *Shakespeare's Universal World*, 58–94, read the play's negation of grand categories of meaning, such as love and war.

104. Tiffany, "Not Saying No," offers a powerful and provocative argument that Cressida should be held accountable for her moral choices, since "a female character can be false without being wanton" (44). She fails to acknowledge that the men in Shakespeare's play foreclose this disjunction, however.

105. R. Greene, *Mamillia*, 2.

106. "My luve was fals and full of flattry" (ca. 1568), *Five Hundred Years of Chaucer Criticism*, vol. 3, IV, 37.

107. Feylde, *Contrauersye bytwene a louer and a Jaye*.

108. In the late sixteenth- or early seventeenth-century poem, Fowler, "Laste Epistle of Creseyd to Troylus," *Poems of Robert Henryson*, appendix, 283–300, which survives in the Hawthornden MSS in the National Library of Scotland, and is associated with the court of James VI of Scotland, James I of England, and is sometimes attributed to William Fowler, Secretary to Queen Anne, Cressid gives Troilus permission to write her epitaph:

And on my tombe some epitaphe
Engrave as lykes the beste.
So fayre the well: this lipers knight
Can showe of me the rest. (lines 305–9)

CHAPTER 3

1. Yunck, "Religious Elements," 257.

2. David, "Man of Law vs. Chaucer," 222.

3. Clasby, "Chaucer's Constance," 223: "Her virtue is human virtue, and her suffering is human suffering. The point at issue in the tale is precisely the meaning of her suffering as it reflects on her virtue and on the justice of God."

4. Raybin, "Custance and History," 70.

5. Delany, "Womanliness in *The Man of Law's Tale*," 63.

6. For a discussion of "actants" see Latour, *Reassembling the Social*, 154–55. My understanding of distributed agency, and of actants being collective and individual at alternating points, is influenced by Latour. My thinking about networks as open systems, as opposed to closed grids, is influenced by Latour, but also Connolly, *World of Becoming*, 17–42, and Massumi, *Parables for the Virtual*, 71–82.

7. Mann, *Geoffrey Chaucer*, 131.

8. *Book of Vices and Virtues*, 168.

9. Winstead, *Virgin Martyrs*, 6–7, 40–56; B. Newman, *From Virile Woman to Woman-Christ*, 77–107; Wogan-Browne, "Saints' Lives and the Female Reader"; Millett, "Audience of the Saints' Lives."

10. Aristotle, *Nicomachean Ethics*, VI.13, par. 3 (pp. 370–71). As Irwin explains in his notes to Book VI, chap. 13 (par. 6), "Though Aristotle rejects the Socratic belief in the unity and identity of all the virtues, he thinks (a) each virtue is inseparable from prudence (1107a1, 1138b18–34, 1178a16–19), and since (b) prudence is inseparable from all the virtues, it follows that (c) each virtue is inseparable from all the other virtues" (255).

11. Aquinas, *Treatise on the Virtues*, 140.

12. *Jacob's Well*, 3.

13. *John Myrc's Instructions for Parish Priests*, 48–51. Tuve's *Allegorical Imagery* emphasizes the importance of the remedial virtues as dynamic sources of strength. See my introduction for a discussion of the virtues' materiality.

14. *Lay Folks' Catechism*, 78.

15. See the influential article by Wogan-Browne, "Virgin's Tale"; also see Jenkins, "Reading Women Reading," who acknowledges the differences between secular women's everyday lives and the virgin martyrs' legends they read as part of a program of spiritual devotion.

16. See essays included in Salih, ed., *Companion to Middle English Hagiography*, as well as those in Bernau, Salih, and Evans, eds., *Medieval Virginities*; also see Wogan-Browne, *Saints' Lives and Women's Literary Culture*; Mills, *Suspended Animation*; Bernau, *Virgins*; Salih, *Versions of Virginity*; and Camp, *Anglo-Saxon Saints' Lives as History*; K. C. Kelly, *Performing Virginity and Testing*, and McInerney, *Eloquent Virgins*, for treatments of the power of virgins (including female saints) to solidify notions of community, region, and nation.

17. K. J. Lewis, "Model Girls?"; Winstead, *Virgin Martyrs*, 98–99, 116–46; Sanok, *Her Life Historical*, 6–23.

18. Paull, "Influence of the Saint's Legend Genre," 185.

19. For visual representations, see Duffy, *Stripping of the Altars*, plates 59, 60, 68. For analysis of textual changes, see Winstead, *Virgin Martyrs*; K. J. Lewis, "Model Girls?"; and Sanok, *Her Life Historical*. Also see Jenkins, "Lay-Devotion and Women Readers."

20. Winstead, *Virgin Martyrs*, 113.

21. K. J. Lewis, "Model Girls?," 25–46.

22. Block, "Originality, Controlling Purpose, and Craftmanship," Paull, "Influence of the Saint's Legend Genre," and Clogan, "Narrative Style," trace the influence of hagiography, but these articles generally treat the genre as abstract and ahistorical.

23. K. Davis, "Time Behind the Veil," 115. See also Kisor, "Moments of Silence," who links the Emperor's dispensation of Custance in marriage to the incest excised from the tale, since both acts feature "a father asserting control over his daughter's body" (142).

24. See Dawson, "Custance in Context," who analyzes Custance's speeches for their ability to move audiences despite their submissive rhetoric.

25. NLS Adv MS 19.2.1, f.17vb (lines 119–22).

26. Ibid., f.18vb (lines 206, 214–15).

27. For helpful discussions of the figurative and material power of relics, see Chaganti, *Medieval Poetics of the Reliquary*; and Bynum, *Christian Materiality*, 131–39.

28. Larsen, "Who is the Master of This Narrative?," 94–104.

29. NLS Adv MS 19.2.1, f.16vb (line 31).

30. *South English Legendary*, 316 (lines 22–23).

31. Ibid., 323 (lines 232–34).

32. Capgrave, *Life of St. Katherine*, I.801–6.

33. Ibid., I.36–49.

34. Ibid., I.302–5.

35. Ibid., I.327–28.

36. Caxton, *Book of the Knight*, 121.

37. Capgrave, I.271–73.

38. Bokenham, *Legendys of hooly wummen*, 2413–14.

39. Ibid., 2423–28, 2435–36.

40. Ibid., 673–76.

41. A. Allen, *Politics of Our Selves*, 47. Jürgen Habermas's account of autonomy, Allen further explains, should be "understood as the capacity for rational accountability or critical reflexivity with respect to existing norms, beliefs, practices, institutions" (98).

42. Capgrave, II.1407.

43. There were over forty-eight manuscripts and two printed copies of the *Legend of St. Katherine* in medieval England. For surveys, see D'Evelyn and Foster, "Saints' Legends," 410–39, 553–65; Pickering, "Saints' Lives," 249–70; for more detailed discussion, see K. J. Lewis, *Cult of St. Katherine of Alexandria*, 14–25, 73–77.

44. Capgrave, I.190–91.

45. Bokenham, *Legendys of hooly wummen*, 2115–22.

46. Wogan-Browne, *Saints' Lives and Women's Literary Culture*, 57–90.

47. Capgrave, IV.1327.

48. See Barlow, "Thrifty Tale," who argues, "the tale repeatedly equates or conflates spiritual and political authority and systems of value" (404–5).

49. Cooper, *English Romance in Time*, chap. 3.

50. Though I claim that imperialism exposes the Emperor's militarist patriarchal aggression, critics have admirably demonstrated the tale's investment in England's national identity as it relates to issues of sovereignty, conquest, and empire. See Heng, *Empire of Magic*, 178–237; Nakley, "Sovereignty Matters"; Schibanoff, "Worlds Apart"; and K. Davis, "Time Behind the Veil," esp. 113–17.

51. See Dinshaw, *Chaucer's Sexual Poetics*, 88–112; and Wetherbee, "Constance and the World," 76. Both show how the Man of Law's immoderate rhetoric sustains a suffocating, incestuous relation between teller and tale. Schlauch, *Chaucer's Constance*, details the narrative's emergence from two incest plots; see also Black, *Medieval Narratives of Accused Queens*, who also studies the visual and literary trajectories of this story. Archibald, "Flight from Incest,"

argues that incest was a well-known element of this story, the absence of which would have been conspicuous; Elizabeth Scala, "Canacee and the Chaucer Canon," views incest as an origin that emerges from its disavowal in *The Man of Law*'s introduction.

52. NLS Adv MS 19.2.1, f.10vb (lines 685–93).

53. See Nelson, "Premodern Media and Networks of Transmission," who persuasively argues that *The Man of Law's Tale* "thematizes mobility" by situating "human agency . . . within a network of . . . mediating forces" (212).

54. Kolve, *Chaucer and the Imagery of Narrative*, influentially observes, "what comes immediately to mind when one thinks of the tale . . . [is] the image of a woman in a rudderless boat, afloat on the sea" (302). Kolve's chapter, 297–358, remains an impressive and enduring reading of this image in medieval art and literature.

55. For a comprehensive treatment, see Jansen, *Making of the Magdalen*.

56. Lavezzo, "Beyond Rome," provides a brilliant discussion of the Man of Law's nationalist exceptionalism in the tale.

57. Bale, "'A maner Latyn corrupt,'" suggests that the tale "collapse[s] distinctions between the personal, national, and religious," which results in "a vagrant cosmopolitanism, of shared traditions and Mediterranean miscegenation" (63; 62).

58. Dinshaw, "Pale Faces," 28, describes Custance as "utterly passive," and "unacquainted with the language," after "her husband and all [his] court [are] slaughtered."

59. E. Robertson, "'Elvyssh' Power of Constance," 164.

60. Nelson, 221.

61. Morgan, "Chaucer's Man of Law," 29.

62. See Jenkins, "Reading Women"; Wogan-Browne, "Saints' Lives and the Female Reader"; Meale, "'. . . alle the bokes that I haue of latyn, englisch, and frensch'"; Riddy, "'Women Talking About the Things of God'"; and Krug, *Reading Families*.

63. Besides sources listed above, see Edwards, "Transmission and Audience"; Driver, "Nuns as Patrons, Artists, Readers"; and essays collected in the invaluable volume, McCash, ed., *Cultural Patronage of Medieval Women*.

64. Delany, *Impolitic Bodies*, 15–22, 127–84.

65. Sanok, *Her Life Historical*, 50–82.

66. Ibid., 58.

67. Duffy, "Holy Maydens, Holy Wyfes," 189. Also see Waters, "Power and Authority," who suggests that there were "attempts to contain the potential energies of saintly authority—by promoting saintly admiration instead of imitation, or by diverting audiences' attention to the saint's self-control rather than his or her earthly disruptiveness" (82).

68. Heffernan, *Sacred Biography*, 7, observes that saints were viewed as interconnected on account of their collective share in Christ's life. Lifshitz, "Beyond Positivism and Genre," emphasizes the particularity of these networks of sanctity.

69. Lydgate, *Legend of Seynt Margarete*, *Minor Poems*, Part I, 192.

70. Meale, "'. . . alle the bokes that I haue of latyn, englisch, and frensch,'" 128–58; Riddy, "'Women Talking About the Things of God,'" 104–27; Krug, 153–206. Jacqueline Jenkins is also completing a study of women readers and vernacular book production in the late Middle Ages.

71. Kempe, *Book of Margery Kempe*, 215, lines 12–17.

72. Caxton, 147.

73. James and Tristram, "Wall Paintings in Eton College Chapel"; Martindale, "Wall-Paintings in the Chapel of Eton College." Also see Borenius and Tristram, *English Medieval Painting*, 44–49.

74. Black, 109–37.

75. All figures are kindly reproduced by Historic England Archive, part of the Historic Buildings and Monuments Commission for England.

76. James and Tristram, 41.

77. Delany, *Impolitic Bodies*, 127–84; Sanok, *Her Life Historical*, 50–82; Hilles, "Gender and Politics."

78. See Lyte, *History of Eton College*, 1–98, for an account of the intrigues that surrounded Henry VI's establishment of Eton. Though there were earlier threats to Eton, during the 1480s all reigning monarchs secured the college. The political struggles between Lancastrian and Yorkist forces, which often involved connections to powerful women (e.g., Elizabeth Woodville and Margaret Beaufort), were not as peaceful.

79. Goldstein, "Future Perfect," 89. Also see Zeeman, *'Piers Plowman,'* who traces the ways in which human agency was mitigated even as spiritual experience was imagined as increasingly internalized and personalized.

80. Goldstein, 101–4.

81. See Mann, *Geoffrey Chaucer*, 138, 139, who argues that this power derives from pity, which "is the pressure brought to bear by the sufferer on the beholder . . . pity cancels power, uniting beholder with sufferer."

82. Robertson connects Custance's power to reformist movements in late fourteenth-century Christianity, especially Lollardy.

83. Heng, 205.

84. [Voragine], *Legenda aurea sanctorum*, CCxvij.

85. Bokenham, 5766–72.

86. Cross, "Weakness and Grace," 449.

87. Augustine, *City of God* [*De civitate Dei*], XIX, 14, 873; *Confessions* [*Confessiones*], VIII; Cross, 441–43; McGrath, *Iustitia Dei*, 24–31; Herdt, *Putting on Virtue*, 66–71.

88. Rolle, *Psalter*, 16.1.

89. Duns Scotus and William of Ockham went further than other thinkers by claiming that God could save anyone he pleases, even if any such person had no habit of charity. See Cross, 452.

90. Aquinas, *Summa contra Gentiles*, III, 149.1. Also see Cross, 452; and Ozment, *Age of Reform*, 31–33. McGrath, *Iustitia Dei*, 81–82, relates Aquinas's maturing views on grace to his views of justification.

91. The literature on this topic is vast. For the basics, see Pink, *Free Will*; "Medieval Theories of Free Will," *Internet Encyclopedia of Philosophy*, http://www.iep.utm.edu/freewi-m/; and "Foreknowledge and Free Will," *Stanford Encyclopedia of Philosophy (SEP)*, http://plato.stanford.edu/entries/free-will-foreknowledge/.

92. Pecock, *Reule of crysten religioun*, 7.

93. Regan influentially delineates this distinction in *The Case for Animal Rights*:

> Moral agents are individuals who have a variety of sophisticated abilities, including in particular the ability to bring impartial moral principles to bear on the determination of what, all considered, morally ought to be done and, having made this determination, to freely choose or fail to choose to act as morality, as they conceive it, requires. Because moral agents have these abilities, it is fair to hold them morally accountable for what they do, assuming that the circumstances of their acting as they do in a particular case do not dictate otherwise. . . . In contrast to

moral agents, *moral patients* lack the prerequisites that would enable them to control their own behavior in ways that would make them morally accountable for what they do. A moral patient lacks the ability to formulate, let alone bring to bear, moral principles in deliberating about which one among a number of possible acts it would be right or proper to perform. Moral patients, in a word, cannot do what is right nor can they do what is wrong. (151–52)

94. Bentham, *Introduction to the Principles of Morals and Legislation*, chap. XVII, note (p. 311).

95. Nussbaum, *Frontiers of Justice*.

96. MacIntyre, *Dependent Rational Animals*.

97. Marenbon, "When Was Medieval Philosophy?" 2.

98. Ibid.

99. Wolfe, *What Is Posthumanism?* 77. See 49–98 for intellectual context.

100. Porter, "Virtue Ethics," 78.

101. [Voragine], *Legenda aurea sanctorum*, CCxviij.

102. See Kisor, who reads Custance's speech and silence as tactical resistance against paternal tyranny.

103. See McGrath, *Iustitia Dei*, 87–91; Kent, "Rethinking Moral Dispositions"; and Ozment, *Age of Reform*, 35–44, 55–62.

104. Custance's ultimate reunion with the Emperor is an instance of what I have described as "performative passivity," wherein a woman enacts submission. Crocker, "Performative Passivity."

105. Gravdal, *Ravishing Maidens*, suggests a parallel between hagiography and pornography, since both emphasize the prurient display of female flesh. Salih, *Versions of Virginity*, 80–86, contests this view. Mills, "'Whatever you do is a delight to me!,'" points out that male martyrs are subject to the same treatment, and reads the erotics of the genre as less one-sided in its power dynamics. Burrus, *Sex Lives of Saints*, argues that extreme physical punishment transforms into erotic power in early examples of the genre.

106. As Goldstein explains, in *De gratia et libero arbitrio* (426 CE), Augustine addresses his claim that the will must depend on grace to a small monastic community, but he nevertheless suggests that his argument "applies to those seculars who, not given the more perfect gift of continence, choose to marry and observe marital chastity by avoiding prohibited sexual practices" (95–96). This group was bigger, but was by no means socially dominant.

107. See Hudson, *Premature Reformation*, 314–15, who points out that Wyclif believed the true church was comprised of a small group that consisted of those predestined for salvation.

108. Riddy, "Middle English Romance," identifies a new emphasis on the dynastic family as a locus of heroic achievement in late Middle English romance. Winstead, "Saints, Wives, and Other 'Hooly Thynges.'" I follow Winstead in focusing on the social reintegration this tale requires, but, in distinction to her position, I suggest that the patriarchal family is transformed over the course of this narrative.

109. Sheingorn, "Appropriating the Holy Kinship," traces an important shift in the family as represented by the Holy Kinship in medieval art. As she observes, matrilineal networks tracing Mary's rich family connections to other women (and the extensive biography created for Saint Anne) gave way to new motifs that recuperated Joseph's status as patriarch: "But the meaning of the Holy Kinship underwent a virtual reversal as kinship patterns and religious structures changed, until eventually it championed fatherhood and the isolation of women in

nuclear families" (194). Robertson, "'Elvyssh' Power of Constance," 168–73, traces Custance's affinities with Lollard ideas about women's ability to effect spiritual change through her unmediated ability to convert others to a pacifist, apostolic Christianity. Custance's remarriage at the end of the tale complicates these parallels, however. As McSheffrey details, *Gender and Heresy*, 81–107, women in Lollard families were visibly subject to their husbands' authority. Custance's public affirmation of deference to Alla, then, is in keeping with Lollard ideas about family structure.

110. McGrath, *Iustitia Dei*, 65–66, 77–78, 87–91, 119–28; also see Oberman, *Harvest of Medieval Theology.*

111. Nicholls, *Matter of Courtesy*, 8–9.

112. Caxton, *Book of the Knight*, 3 (lines 19, 10–11).

113. "Why I Can't Be a Nun," 80, 84–87.

CHAPTER 4

1. Salter, *Mirrhor of Modestie*, Dvii^v.

2. Clark, "Margarite of America," 405. Clark does not provide a source for this characterization, which she claims is not her own.

3. Lodge, *"A Margarite of America 1596,"* 186. All further citations, noted parenthetically, are taken from this edition.

4. See Dees, "Spenser's Anti-Neoplatonism," who argues that Spenser develops "an ethic of love grounded in a simultaneous giving and receiving" (276). More recently, D. Miller, "Chastity of Allegory," calls attention to Spenser's awareness of the delicate gender politics of his ethical project: "For a male poet to speak about any woman's sexual interiority is potentially invasive, coercive, or presumptuous, and therefore demands exquisite tact" (4).

5. Campana, *Pain of Reformation*, 24.

6. Quilligan, *Milton's Spenser*, 38–41, 181, points out that Spenser opens the poem's fashioning project to women with this phrase. In doing so, though, she argues that Spenser specifies the difference between masculine and feminine ethical action—"virtuous and gentle discipline." As she suggests, *virtus* is differentiated from a more "gentle" form of action, but unlike Quilligan, I do not see the function of this alternative mode of ethics as purely a support for masculine achievement. Thanks to David Lee Miller for reminding me of this insight.

7. Campana, 74–104.

8. See Gregerson, *Reformation of the Subject*, 44, who remarks that, in donning the armor of the Saxon warrior Angela, Britomart "has revived the lineage of female warriors in order to defend the prerogatives of patriarchy." Also see Anderson, "Britomart's Armor."

9. This chapter will survey this critical tradition. Here, I mention two articles central to my thinking about Platonism's relation to the Florimells thread: Borris, "Platonism and Spenser's Poetic"; and P. Cheney, "'And Doubted Her to Deeme an Earthly Wight.'"

10. Pollack, "Lodge's *A Margarite of America*"; Falke, "'Marguerite' and the 'Margarita.'" For Elizabeth I's connection to the "cult of the virgin," formed mainly in the later years of her reign, see Hackett, *Virgin Mother, Maiden Queen.*

11. Linton, *Romance of the New World*, 39–61; Roberts, "Lodge's *A Margarite of America*."

12. In their introduction to *A Margarite of America*, 11–70, Beecher and Janzen argue that Lodge's romance is merely brought back from America. On account of place names, and the proximity of Cusco and Musco, they are unconvinced that Cusco refers to the Incan kingdom,

and therefore reject the idea that Lodge critiques New World exploration through his romance. It remains clear, however, that Lodge sets up a contrast of values, new and old, that might be figured by a colonialist allegory.

13. Vives, *Instruction*, I.xvi.Riv^r.

14. Vives, I.xv.Nii^r.

15. Bruto, *Necessarie, Fit, and Conuienient Education*, Fvi^{r-v}.

16. Salter, Avii^r.

17. Stallybrass, "Patriarchal Territories," 133.

18. Lodge was a member of Thomas Cavendish's doomed second voyage to South America (1591–92). In his dedicatory epistle, "To the Gentlemen Readers," he claims, "it was my chance in the librarie of the Jesuits in Sanctum to find this historie in the Spanish tong, which as I read delighted me and delighting me, wonne me, and in winning me, made me write it. The place where I began my worke, was a ship" (42).

19. Here, we see the negative consequences of turning the physical body into a province of external regulation. See Elias, *Civilizing Process*.

20. Ralegh, *Discouerie*, 96.

21. Fenton, *Forme of Christian Pollicie*, 287.

22. Mulcaster, *Positions*, 176.

23. Classic articulations of this position include Montrose, "Elizabethan Subject"; Helgerson, *Self-Crowned Laureates*, 55–100; and Jones and Stallybrass, "Politics of Astrophil and Stella."

24. Montrose, "Spenser and the Elizabethan Political Imaginary," 934. For Montrose, Spenser's poetry, like that of other Elizabethan courtiers, records "the discourse of a vigilant masculine virtue that is under pressure from the omnipresent threat of effeminization" on account of a powerful female sovereign (932).

25. Qtd. in Kelso, 280. D'Aubigné, "Mes filles touchant les femmes doctes de nostre siecle," 446–47: "C'est qu'elle respondit en un jour à huiet Ambassadeurs aux langues qui leur estoyent les plus propres; mais le plus louable de cette ame benitte de Dieu e esté la prattique de sa theorie, ayant si bien employé les Ethiques & Politiques, qu'elle a tenu la nef de son royaume en calme quarante ans en une mer fort troublee & en un siecle tempestueux."

26. Spenser, *The Faerie Queene*, ed. Hamilton, 737. All citations, noted parenthetically by book, canto, stanza, and line number, are taken from this edition.

27. S. Miller, " 'Mirrours More Then One,' " shows that Spenser's poem provided women with an increased measure of literary autonomy. Eggert, *Showing Like a Queen*, 22–50, offers an important argument that establishes the reign of Elizabeth I as a positive poetic resource for Spenser. In a witty and learned argument, Wilson-Okamura, "Belphoebe and Gloriana," 67, uses the Letter to Ralegh's distinction, "between royal queen and virtuous lady . . . the well-known image of the king's two bodies" to clarify the boundaries of Spenser's critique in *The Faerie Queene*. As Wilson-Okamura argues, "when Spenser criticizes Elizabeth, it is the woman that he reprimands, not Her Highness; Elizabeth T., not Elizabeth R. . . . Gloriana is the queen, and Belphoebe is the lady."

28. See the classic analysis of Elizabethan pageantry, including its relation to Spenser's poetic perspective: Strong, *Cult of Elizabeth*, 43, 68–69.

29. Anderson, " 'In liuing colours and right hew,' " demonstrates the limitations of Spenser's female sovereign; also see Berry, *Of Chastity and Power*, 153–65, for a discussion of Spenser's critical attitude toward his queen. Wilson-Okamura, "Spenser and the Two Queens," reminds us that by the time Spenser's *Faerie Queene* was published, the queen's virginity was itself a

moot cultural point. Here, I suggest that her impossible idealization creates the possibility of material virtue in *other women*.

30. Schwarz, *Tough Love*, 138–74.

31. See Augustine, *City of God*, Book I, 10:18 (p. 22).

32. Rich, *Excellency of good women*, 21 (Dii^r).

33. Tuke, *Discourse against painting and tincturing of women*, 16.

34. Ibid., 57.

35. Buoni, *Problemes of beauty*, 7, claims that "Beauty is a certaine diuine splendour . . . and that doth most participate of the diuine Nature." But Romei, *Courtiers academie*, "Of Beautie," 27, makes the strongest statement: "There can not bee good in the vniversall world, without proportion . . . and as good can not without proportion procure desire; so can not beautie without proportion cause loue: In that loue is not generate in the louer, but by symetrie, which the thing beloued hath with the louer." Gellar, "Venus and the Three Graces."

36. Kelso, *Doctrine*, 198.

37. Averell, *Dyall*, Fi^v.

38. Bentley, *Monument of matrones*, 307.

39. *Here foloweth a lytell treatyse of the beaute of women*, n.p.

40. Vives, I.xi.Mii^r.

41. C. Smith, "Ethical Allegory," begins the critical trend of seeing the two Florimells in terms of beauty's doubleness (true and false). See also Norhnberg, *Analogy of "The Faerie Queene,"* 461–70, 573–92.

42. Evans, *Spenser's Anatomy of Heroism*, 166–76; Sims, "Cosmological Structure"; Bahr, "Misery of Florimell."

43. Roche, *Kindly Flame*, 150–94.

44. Hamilton, *Structure of Allegory*, 78.

45. Quilligan, 186–88, argues that the poem's direct address to women means that Britomart cannot sympathize with Florimell's predicament.

46. Borris, 235.

47. Ibid., 230–32.

48. See Kaske, "Hallmarks of Platonism," 31–32, who discusses the concomitance of beauty and goodness in Platonist thought and Spenser's poetry.

49. Murdoch, *Sovereignty of Good*, 84.

50. Scarry, *On Beauty*, 12–18.

51. Berry, 9–38, gives an invaluable account of this tradition as it culminates in Renaissance Neoplatonism.

52. Greenblatt, *Shakespeare's Freedom*, 19–48.

53. Castiglione, *Courtyer*, Bbii^v.

54. Ibid., Et.iiii^r.

55. Tilney, *Briefe and Pleasant Discourse*, Eiv^v.

56. Ficino, qtd. in Rees, "Ficinian Ideas," 87.

57. See Rees, 73–134, who surveys Spenser's debts to Ficino, and provides evidence that Spenser takes up some of the most common tenets of Ficinian Platonism.

58. Cavanaugh, *Wanton Eyes and Chaste Desires*, 26.

59. Castiglione, Ii.i^v.

60. Buncombe, "Faire Florimell as Faire Game."

61. Silberman, *Transforming Desire*, 29.

62. Vives, I.xii.Nii^r-^v.

63. Hamilton, "Our New Poet," 114.

64. D. L. Miller, in his commentary on this passage for the *Oxford Spenser* (forthcoming), notes that the witch is afraid of Florimell (not vice versa). Indeed, as he points out, the witch is astonished by Florimell's supernatural beauty, wondering "what devill" appears when she is struck by her dazzling appearance. Florimell, by contrast, is composed, and answers the witch with a prepossession that suggests "her control over the encounter with the witch." My thanks to Miller for sharing an advance copy of the commentary on this passage.

65. Nussbaum, *Fragility of Goodness*, 419.

66. P. Cheney, "'And Doubted Her to Deeme an Earthly Wight,'" 332–33. As Borris points out, "despite beauty's visionary, divinely authorized force in Spenser's view, it only has a soft power, as it were, vulnerable to abuses, misrepresentations, and misapprehensions" (232).

67. P. Cheney, 324–25, claims that Florimell's experience with masculine aggression makes her afraid of her own desire. I see no evidence of her fear of desire per se; instead, she flees from the destructive masculine fantasies Cheney so precisely catalogs.

68. Christian, "'Waves of Weary Wretchedness,'" argues that Florimell's trials represent the traditional spiritual trials, of the world, the flesh, and the devil. I find this argument unconvincing for its refusal to recognize Florimell's resilience, even if Christian is right to notice the episode's ultimate emphasis on divine providence.

69. Nussbaum, *Fragility of Goodness*, 420.

70. Ibid.

71. Evans, 170, points out that many of the materials the witch uses to construct False Florimell were commonly used by women for cosmetic purposes during Spenser's era.

72. P. Cheney, "'And Doubted Her to Deeme an Earthly Wight,'" 325, 329–30.

73. Romei, 9, 27.

74. Buoni, 22.

75. Tate, "Haunted by Beautified Beauty," 197–98.

76. Goldberg, *Endlesse Work*, 129, argues that the cestus is like a chain that binds together the organizing elements of heroic culture.

77. Yearling, "Florimell's Girdle," insightfully returns to this issue, which is frequently ignored by critics. Gough's dismissal, Yearling notes, is characteristic: "How [False Florimell] is able to wear [the girdle] now is not explained, but such inconsistencies are frequent in the *Faerie Queene*" (qtd. in Yearling, 138).

78. Yearling, esp. 139–40.

79. Oram, *Edmund Spenser*, 222.

80. Yearling, 140.

81. Berger, *Revisionary Play*, 21.

82. MacIntyre, *Dependent Rational Animals*; Foot, 27.

83. Annas, *Intelligent Virtue*, 14.

84. *Here foloweth*, n.p.

85. Bahr, 116–22.

86. Stubbes, *Anatomy of abuses*, Fvii^r.

87. Dees, 293, suggests that False Florimell extends and intensifies an ambivalence that has always been present with regard to true beauty.

88. Knapp, *Image Ethics*, 1–31, 67–98, tackles the challenges of vision's duality in early modern thought, and argues that Spenser devises an image ethics that calls upon the body's registers in a way that is similar to that of modern phenomenology.

89. *Here foloweth*, n.p.

90. Lacan, *Ethics of Psychoanalysis*, 149–50.

91. Žižek, *Metastases of Enjoyment*, 90. The best exploration of courtly love's relation to masochism in medieval literature is Cohen, "Masoch/Lancelotism."

92. Bruto suggests that it is imperative to train children in good manners, so that beloved daughters, "their mindes being pure and cleane, filled with bountie and diuine beautie, be not found spotted and soiled with great and eminent faults" (n.p.).

93. *Here foloweth*, n.p., describes beauty as an external condition, which requires bounty, humility, and simplicity so that its appearance will not be marred.

94. Buoni, 12.

95. Agrippa, *Treatise*, Bvi[v].

96. Gibson, *Woman's Worth*, 60[v].

97. Stump, "Slow Return to Eden," argues that Spenser uses the traditional distinction between nature and grace to endorse women's natural capacity to rule in furtherance of divine providence: "Spenser sees [women's subordination] being gradually relaxed as grace brings sanctification and renewal" (413).

98. Buoni, 29.

99. Goldberg, *Endlesse Worke*, suggests that virtue is always composite. Coles, "'Perfect Hole,'" 55–56, argues that Belphoebe, because she practices lone virginity rather than conjugal chastity, exemplifies dead virtue in Spenser's poem.

100. Celovsky, "Early Modern Masculinities," discusses Marinell's reformed masculinity, but she does not acknowledge Florimell's shaping role in his transformation.

101. Scarry, *On Beauty*, 48.

102. Bersani, "Is the Rectum a Grave?" Also see his "Sociality and Sexuality," which provides an explicitly Platonist account of "new relational modes."

103. Kuzner, *Open Subjects*, makes the convincing argument that Spenser utilizes vulnerability to establish and suspend personal boundaries at once. My thinking about how vulnerability might allow characters to undo one another, to be undone by one another, and to open themselves up to one another, all as a means of nourishing less discrete, more fulfilled subjectivities, is deeply indebted to his brilliant study, particularly chaps. 1–2.

104. Frantz, "Union."

105. Nancy, *Listening*, 40.

106. Murdoch, 85–86.

107. Ibid., 84.

108. Parker, *Inescapable Romance*, 92.

109. King, *Spenser's Poetry*; Mallette, *Spenser and the Discourses*; Weatherby, *Mirrors*; Hume, *Edmund Spenser*.

110. See Steinmetz, "Reformation and Grace."

111. A necessary caveat: Red Crosse Knight's encounter with Despair in Book I offers the most vivid example in which Spenser seeks to illuminate the helplessness of his protagonist. See Moss, "Spenser's Despair and God's Grace," for a searching discussion of the proximity of despair and grace in a reformed theological framework. For discussions of Spenser's reliance on Nature and Grace as components of human virtue, see Woodhouse, "Nature and Grace"; and Hoopes, "'God Guide Thee, Guyon.'"

112. Wells, "Spenser's Christian Knight," makes a useful comparison between Erasmus's *Enchiridion Militis Christiani* and Spenser's apparent conception of human agency as a complement to divine grace. Schiavone, "Spenser's Augustine," proves that Spenser had access to Erasmus's edition of Augustine, the organization of which might have prompted Spenser to

combine alternating images of spiritual agency and dependency in Book I. Prescott, "Complicating the Allegory," provides an invaluable survey of arguments concerning Spenser's religious
outlook to observe "Spenser's own slipperiness" on religious issues including grace and free
will.

113. Wind, *Pagan Mysteries*, chaps. 2–3, provides a detailed discussion of the Neoplatonic
tradition that associates the three Graces with Venus.

114. Danner, "Courteous Virtù in Book 6 of the *Faerie Queene*," surveys connections
between Spenser and Machiavelli to develop a striking division in Spenser's virtue ethics: "The
late episodes of the Dance of the Graces and Calidore's muzzling of the Blatant Beast typify
the book's contrast between symbolic visions of courtesy and the largely violent practice of
courteous heroes" (2).

115. K. Williams, "Courtesy and Pastoral," and *Spenser's 'Faerie Queene,'* 212–18; Gellar,
"Acidalian Vision." Other critics, particularly D. Cheney, *Spenser's Image of Nature*, 190, and
Hough, *Preface to 'The Faerie Queene,'* 210, are more cautious about equating the three
Graces—or the fourth Grace in Calidore's vision—to particular forms of Christian grace.

116. Gellar, "Acidalian Vision," 268.

117. Ibid., 269n1.

118. Rees, 92–93, 96.

119. P. Benson, "Florimell at Sea," rightly sees Florimell's wandering, especially her extension of the "rudderless boat" motif taken up in Chaucer's tale of Custance and elsewhere, as
the operation of divine grace in *The Faerie Queene*. My reading resists Benson's displacement
of human agency, however, since I find evidence that Florimell achieves a virtue that is based
on her own mental perseverance and physical endurance.

120. D. L. Miller, "Chastity of Allegory," 15.

121. D. D. Wallace, *Puritans and Predestination*; also see Collinson, *Religion of Protestants*.

122. See D. D. Wallace, *Puritans and Predestination*, viii–ix, 42–55; also see Kevan, *Grace
of Law*.

123. Castiglione, Ggiiiᵛ.

CHAPTER 5

1. As Jardine, *Still Harping*, 103, and Wayne, "Refashioning the Shrew," acknowledge,
"shrew" was not gendered feminine before the early modern period. I trace this history in my
essay, "Engendering Shrews."

2. Chaucer, *Canterbury Tales*, *Riverside Chaucer*. All further citations, noted parenthetically by fragment and line number, are taken from this edition.

3. See Jardine, 182–93, who claims of Griselda, "'Virtue' here is silent enduring of whatever patriarchal fortune brings" (182). Though she recognizes the importance of Griselda as a
model for women's excellence, she uses her as a negative figure throughout her argument.

4. In a characteristic "us vs. them" "modernity vs. premodernity" move, Keyishian,
"Griselda on the Elizabethan Stage," 259, juxtaposes the known popularity of this story with
moderns' presumed objections. In the opposition he builds, "the Griselda story is a piece of
sentimentalism at best, an affront to human dignity with pathological implications at worst"
(261).

5. See Belsey, *Subject of Tragedy*, 166, who claims the story, "can have appealed only,
one would suppose, to the most vehemently misogynistic audience." Elsewhere, however, she

recognizes that the story "leaves the audience to confront the problem of the moral duty to submit to an immoral power, and to ponder the question whether there is any proper limit to the silent endurance of patriarchal tyranny" (171). McLuskie, *Dekker and Heywood*, 104, calls Griselda a "puppet," though elsewhere she also recognizes Griselda's integrity.

6. C. C. Brown, "Katherina of *The Taming of the Shrew*."

7. Here, I follow Sedgewick's logic of the beside, *Touching Feeling*, 8.

8. P. A. Brown, *Better a Shrew*, 178–204, sees these identities as juxtaposed, though she does make a larger argument for the cultural validation of shrewishness in wives: "Proverbs about the profitability of shrews (and by implication the undesirability of Griseldas) issue regularly from male mouths in household manuals" (206).

9. Dekker, Chettle, and Haughton, *Pleasant Comodie of Patient Grissil*, ed. Fredson Bowers. All further citations, noted parenthetically, are taken from this edition.

10. All quotations, hereafter noted parenthetically, are from Phillip, *Play of Patient Grissell*.

11. Comensoli, "Refashioning," 200.

12. *Patient Grisel* [chapbook], ed. Wheatley, 13.

13. D. Wallace, *Chaucerian Polity*, 261–98, provides an invaluable analysis of this story's commentary on tyranny as it relates to the humanist tradition.

14. Deloney, "Patient Grissel," n.p., http://ebba.english.ucsb.edu/ballad/33585/ transcription.

15. Ibid.

16. Ibid.

17. Ibid.

18. Bliss, "Renaissance Griselda." I am deeply indebted to Bliss's article, which offers the most comprehensive analysis of all the texts under consideration here. See 304–15 for her analysis of Phillip.

19. Ibid., 313.

20. Jewel, *Second Tome of Homilies, Homily of the State of Matrimony*, 482, suggests that wives should "perfourme subiection" in order to promote harmony with their husbands.

21. Taylor, qtd. in Comensoli, 204.

22. McLuskie, *Dekker and Heywood*, 104.

23. Comensoli, 202, 203n18.

24. Dod and Cleaver, *Godly forme*, A6ʳ.

25. T. Smith, *De republica anglorum*, 13, claimed that, "in the house and familie is . . . one of the best kindes of a common wealth." See Stone, *Family, Sex, and Marriage in England*, 109–46, for a discussion of the "positive reinforcement of the despotic authority of husband and father—that is to say, of patriarchy" that accompanied the shift to a nuclear family structure in the sixteenth and seventeenth centuries (109).

26. Whately, *Care Cloth*, qtd. in Orlin, *Private Matters*, 31.

27. Gouge, *Of Domesticall Duties*, 353.

28. Orlin, 97. She persuasively argues, 85–136, that drama of the late 1590s problematized patriarchalism.

29. See Ozment, *When Fathers Ruled*, 50–72, 144–76, Schücking, *Puritan Family*, and Haller and Haller, "Puritan Art of Love," for discussions of men's familial responsibilities.

30. P. A. Brown, *Better a Shrew*, 192.

31. Dunworth, "'Bosom Burnt Up with Desires,'" 338–39, argues that the mother role is split to allow Grissell to remain placid while her children are taken from her.

32. Levin, *Multiple Plot*, 50, complains that the storial threads work at "cross-purposes."

33. This pressure, I would suggest, accounts for the preponderance of men's wagering about women—and the deleterious consequences of such wagering—in early modern English literatures. *The Rape of Lucrece* provides a classical model, which Robert Greene takes up in his *Penelope's Web* (1587), 5:137–234; Penelope's third tale tells the story of three princes whose inheritance depends on the obedience of their wives. In Shakespeare's *Taming of the Shrew* and Fletcher's *Woman's Prize*, the wagers are meant to affirm masculine control, but, and especially in Fletcher, they simply uncover men's desire to be seen in positions of power over women. Schroeder, "A New Analogue," suggests that the wager scene in *A Shrew* might have been drawn from the "Queen Vastis" episode included in Caxton's translation of *Le Livre du chevalier de la Tour Landry*: after the queen refuses to appear three times after her husband, the king, summons her, he imprisons her with very little food and water for a year.

34. Hoy, *Introductions, Notes, and Commentaries*, 1:140. Hoy goes on to observe that the play suggests rational motives for irrational behavior (142).

35. Wheatley, 18.

36. Belsey, 167.

37. Rutter, "Patient Grissil," argues that the character of Laureo figures the role of the poet-satirist.

38. Jones and Stallybrass, *Renaissance Clothing*, chap. 9.

39. McLuskie, *Renaissance Dramatists*, 140.

40. Wheatley, 30.

41. Dunworth, 344.

42. Pechter, "Patient Grissil and the Trials of Marriage," 92.

43. Comensoli, 206, argues that Gwalter's "coercive behavior generally stemmed from outmoded social values."

44. Belsey, 168.

45. Wheatley, 36–37.

46. D. M. Greene, "Welsh Characters in *Patient Grissil*," argues that Dekker did not write these scenes based on their (phonetically spelled) accuracy, and suggests that Haughton might have written them instead (though any definitive assignment must remain speculative due to the paucity of the Haughton canon that survives).

47. Champion, "Shakespeare and Dekker," 53, observes that the humor of the Welsh scenes "[is] carefully placed to temper our attitude toward the more serious relationship between Gwalter and Grissil."

48. Ovid, *Metamorphoses*, III.339–401.

49. Pechter, 95, remarks: "In giving him satisfaction, she withholds it by pointing precisely to the hidden area of an interior self he can never be sure he has found." While I am not arguing for a depth-model of subjectivity, it is true that her self-articulating submission gives and denies Gwalter satisfaction.

50. Deloney, "Patient Grissel."

51. Dunworth, 335.

52. Reference appears in John Bale's *Scriptorum illustrium maioris Brytanniae* (1557–59). See Hoy, 1:131–32, for a discussion.

53. Forrest, *History of Grisild the Second*.

54. Ibid., 130.

55. Potter, "Tales of Patient Griselda and Henry VIII," qtd. on 13.

56. Ibid., 17–25.

57. Ibid., 24.

58. Wright, "Political Reflection," links the play to Elizabeth's lack of an heir.

59. Champion, 54, suggests that these two plays mirror one another, but sees Shakespeare as entirely comic, and Dekker, Chettle, and Haughton as entirely earnest. Also, P. A. Brown, *Better a Shrew*, 213, calls *Taming of the Shrew* a "Griseldine parable."

60. Shakespeare, *Taming of the Shrew, Complete Works*, ed. Bevington. All further citations, noted parenthetically, are taken from this edition.

61. For a discussion of Petruchio's union of "symbolic" and "economic" capital, in the terms identified by Pierre Bourdieu, see Korda, "Household Kates."

62. See Hull, *Chaste, Silent, and Obdient*, 31–70, and Hull, *Women According to Men*, 31–51, for a survey of prescriptive literature for early modern women.

63. Marcus, *Unediting the Renaissance*, 108.

64. Important treatments include, Amussen, "'Being Stirred to Much Unquietness'"; and Underdown, "Taming of the Scold."

65. Boose, "Scolding Brides and Bridling Scolds."

66. Detmer, "Civilizing Subordination." See *Mery Jest*; and *Tom Tiler*. In both texts, husbands use methods of taming supposedly appropriate for animals to train their unruly wives. For a discussion of such methods, see Hartwig, "Horses and Women."

67. See the *MED*, s.v. "shreue," 1(a)–(c): The entries continuously associate bodily malfeasance and disorder with shrewishness.

68. Feinstein, "Shrews and Sheep," acknowledges that men were more frequently called "shrew" in the Middle Ages.

69. Hile, "Disability and the Characterization of Katherine," provocatively suggests that Katherine's limp, almost universally taken to be a figurative disfigurement, might be connected to her shrewishness.

70. Sirluck, "Patriarchy, Pedagogy, and the Divided Self," 420.

71. A. L. Smith, "Performing Marriage," treats this optimistic sort of performativity, and the possibilities for gender fluidity it creates within the play.

72. Bean claims that the play is a game, one that revises the farcical fabliau elements of earlier shrew-taming stories with a "humanizing" program of matrimonial reform in his essay, "Comic Structure." Katherina is released from "the fabliau stereotype of the shrew turned household drudge" (66), but her transformation destabilizes the masculine control that Petruchio seeks.

73. Baumlin, "Petruchio the Sophist," takes an optimistic view of Petruchio's rhetorical agility, arguing that he gives Katherina a new, more free identity through his language creation.

74. Fenton, *Forme of Christian Pollicie*, 270.

75. In this, Petruchio follows prescriptive form, viz., Fenton claims that it is more honorable for a man to correct his wife without violence: "Tobie and Job endured with pacience the reproches of their wyues, without beatinge them, but with gentle declaration they corrected them, and had them afterwardes very obedient" (269).

76. See Rebhorn, "Petruchio's 'Rope Tricks.'" My reading of Petruchio's desire is greatly indebted to Rebhorn's analysis. Richard Rainolde, *Foundacion of Rhetoric*, claims that a rhetorician's purpose is "to drawe un|to theim the hartes of a multitude" (A1ᵛ).

77. Kahn, *Man's Estate*, 117.

78. Chamberlain, "Domestic Economies," argues that Petruchio needs to tame Katherina publicly to prove that he has control over his household, which would in turn allow him to establish his economic credit.

79. Shea and Yachnin, "Well-Hung Shrew," 109.

80. Topsell, *Historie of foure-footed beastes*, t.p., 536.

81. Tilney, *Flower of Friendship*, 112.

82. This is in keeping with early modern household ideology, since Dod and Cleaver assert the preeminence of the husband's perspective: "For as men should obey the laws of their ci|ties, so women the manners of their husbands. . . . For an honest Ma|tron hath no neede of any greater staffe, but of one word, or one sowre countenance" (95).

83. Garner, "Taming of the Shrew: Inside or Outside the Joke?" suggests the play's values are outmoded, and that its humor is directed against women in a way which no longer sits with modern sensibilities. P. A. Brown, " 'Fie,' " also suggests the play is directed against women, but she argues that the play would have been equally problematic to its early modern female audiences.

84. Laurie E. Maguire, " 'Household Kates,' " makes the interesting point "that the name Kate assumes an almost generic quality and becomes a synecdoche for 'woman' " (130).

85. In a reading that acknowledges the bodily circuits of connection which theater relies upon, Nunn, "Playing with Appetite," argues that the play's denial of food to Katherina might have stirred a (hungry) theater audience's empathy for Katherina.

86. Vives, *Instruction*, II.iv. X3ᵛ.

87. Fineman, "Turn of the Shrew," 139.

88. A. L. Smith, "Performing Marriage," 308.

89. Dolan, *Dangerous Familiars*; K. Newman, *Fashioning Femininity*, 33–50.

90. Dusinberre, "*Taming of the Shrew*: Women, Acting, Power," 80.

91. Zajko, "Petruchio is 'Kated,' " remarks that the "questions [the play] raises about dominance and submission are uncomfortable for those who like to believe that love resides in mutuality and not in coercion" (33).

92. Shaw, *Shaw on Shakespeare*, 188.

93. Ibid.

94. As Ranald, "Performance of Feminism," affirms, the embarrassment that Shaw identifies has "not evaporated" (325).

95. Heilman, "Taming the Untamed," identifies what he calls a "revisionist" impulse in critical interpretations of *The Taming of the Shrew*: these interpretations explain Katherina's behavior as a product of male aggression and work to celebrate the strength of character that makes her undesirable in Padua. Stephen Bretzius, *Shakespeare in Theory*, 51–62, also provides a helpful overview of different theoretical approaches to the play.

96. Mary Pickford winks at the audience when she delivers Katherina's final speech. *The Taming of the Shrew*, dir. Sam Taylor (United Artists, 1929). See Freeman, "Mary Pickford as Shakespearean Shrew," for a discussion of how this film sought to subvert gender roles (early modern and early twentieth century). Novy, *Love's Argument*, sees Katherina's delivery as part of a game that she and Petruchio play with one another. Burns, "Ending of the Shrew," 89, views the final speech as a practice in irony; though she is correct, I think, when she observes "the speech continuously displays strength and animation," Katherina is not enacting her opposite just for a humorous show.

97. Tartamella, "Reinventing the Poet and Dark Lady," 471.

98. Boose traces a historical parallel with the marriage ceremony, which required brides to prostrate themselves before grooms. As she notes, however, this practice was no longer current; at best it shows Petruchio's throwback attitude toward absolutist masculine authority.

99. Qtd. in Honig, "Antigone's Two Laws," 22.

100. A. L. Smith, "Performing Marriage," 307 (emphasis in original).

101. Barkan, *Gods Made Flesh*, 281, and Bate, *Shakespeare and Ovid*, 123–24, both see Katherina's transformation as part of a larger process of subjectivity formation. Bate, however, articulates the dangers that Katherina faces in his Ovidian articulation: "As the only release for Daphne was to become a tree, is not the only release for Kate to become a branch of Petruchio, bent to his will?" (120–21).

102. P. A. Brown, *Better a Shrew*, 141, points out that the language of John Fletcher's play is more violent than its Shakespearean predecessor(s).

103. Bushnell, 1–75.

104. Bushnell, 66.

105. In *Patriarchalism in Political Thought*, 37–53, Schochet discusses the persistence of and challenges to patriarchalism as a justification for men's domestic dominance. Orlin, *Private Matters*, 85–130, and Ezell, *Patriarch's Wife*, 48–61, discuss the problematic totality of patriarchalism for early modern women. Wendy Wall's *Staging Domesticity*, suspends patriarchalism in order to attend to the power housework afforded lesser family members, such as women and servants (7–9).

106. Bushnell, 56–63. See also Armstrong, "Elizabethan Conception of the Tyrant"; and Armstrong, "Influence of Seneca and Machiavelli." Armstrong explains hereditary succession's influence upon notions of tyranny during this period. If a ruler ascended to the throne by right of succession, then the monarch was no tyrant. This figure of the rightful ruler was contrasted with the reckless tyrant, who nevertheless accumulated a "fatal grandeur" through the extremity of his character ("Elizabethan Conception," 20).

107. Korda, *Shakespeare's Domestic Economies*, 35, 53; Dolan, *Marriage and Violence*, 100.

108. Fletcher, *Tamer Tamed*, ed. Daileader and Taylor. All further citations, noted parenthetically, are taken from this edition.

109. Primaudaye, *French Academie*, 460. Later, Primaudaye tells the story of Seneca's wife Paulina, who was so wedded to the idea of commixture in marriage that, after Seneca was killed by the opening of his veins in the bath, "did the like to her selfe in the same bath, mingling togither their blood for a greater vnion and coronation of their long and perfect loue" (491). See Dolan, *Marriage and Violence*, 26–66, for a discussion of the "one flesh" theory of marriage.

110. See Dolan, "Battered Women," for the political valence of woman's domestic insurgency as it relates to the *femme covert* status.

111. Korda, *Shakespeare's Domestic Economies*, 42–51, notes the subversive potential of women's household responsibilities. Wall offers a comprehensive look at women's "estranged" relations to domesticity: experts in household management, women were also expected to submit themselves to husbands' domestic governance (2, 18–53).

112. See Ste. B., *Counsel to the husband*, which suggests that the wife is the husband's "Lieutenant" in child rearing (49). Dod and Cleaver acknowledge mothers' formative influence: "for euen as a child cockered and made a wanton by the mother, will be more vntractable, when the father will seeke to bend him to good: so on the other side, a child wisely trained vp by the mother in the yong yeares, will be the easilier brought to goodnesse by the fathers godly care" (60).

113. See Adelman, *Suffocating Mothers*, 11–34.

114. Maria's politicized maternity points squarely to the challenge that female sovereignty posed to political theology, particularly the theory of "the King's Two Bodies." See Kantorowicz, *King's Two Bodies*, 3–60, for the sacral aspects of this theory. By comparing the sovereign to Christ, this theory leaves little room for the reproductive powers of the maternal. See Axton,

Queen's Two Bodies, 11–25, on the complications female sovereignty (particularly Elizabeth I's marriage and succession) held for this tradition.

115. Ste. B. uses the term "coniunction" to characterize happy and unhappy marital unions (2–5).

116. In *Of the Knowledge which Maketh a Wise Man*, Thomas Elyot suggests that the rule of the passions degenerates into beastly tyranny: "but after if it happen that the appetites and desy|res of the body so moch do increase, that they haue the hole possession of the body / and that the affections of the soule, that is to saye / vertues be suppressed or putte to silence / than the lyfe becommeth beastely" (24 [64]).

117. See Daileader, *Eroticism on the Renaissance Stage*, 53–65, for an insightful reading of this episode's significance. I would only emphasize that the control over space that marks Maria's personal autonomy in Daileader's reading is prominent throughout Fletcher's play.

118. Moretti, *Signs Taken for Wonders*, 47, sees the opposition between king and tyrant as a contest between reason and will.

119. See Shannon, *Sovereign Amity*, 54–89, for a discussion of resistance to marital tyranny in Elizabeth Cary's *Tragedy of Mariam*. For a treatment of the subversive power of the women's revolt, see M. E. Smith, "John Fletcher's Response to the Gender Debate."

120. Turner, "Responses to Tyranny," traces this motif across Fletcher's career, although it does not explicitly consider *The Woman's Prize*.

121. See Goldberg, *James I and the Politics of Literature*, 15–54, 85–112, for an analysis of the king's demand for passive obedience, which he implemented using a complex familial rhetoric.

122. Whitney, *Choice of Emblemes and Other Devises*, 99.

123. Erasmus, "Marriage in Name Only," 401–12, 405.

124. Erasmus, 410–11.

125. Wall, 161–88, notes the power that women's medicinal responsibilities entailed; members of the household, including husbands, would be subjected to a housewife's medical care. Here, we see Maria's diagnostic power confirmed.

126. Vives, *Instruction*, II.iii. This discussion is intricately bound up with Vives's meditations on other husbandly infirmities that follow in his treatise, including ill temper and dissolute habits.

127. See Korda, *Shakespeare's Domestic Economies*, 15–51, and Wall, 18–52, for analyses of injunctions for wives to keep the goods of the household; Panek, *Widows and Suitors*, 13–39, notes that widows were desirable because they already knew how to keep a household.

128. Ste. B., 2–5, 64.

129. Ibid., 71, marginal gloss.

130. Markham, *English housevvife*, t.p.

131. Ibid., 2, 4–5.

132. Partridge, *Treasurie of commodious conceits*, A.iii^v.

133. Surflet, *Maison rustique*, 39.

134. Ibid., 38.

135. Wall, 32.

136. Perkins, *Christian Oeconomie*, 126.

137. Dod and Cleaver, L6^v–L7^r.

138. Markham, *English housevvife*, 1.

139. Whately, *bride bush*, 153.

140. Žižek, *Fragile Absolute*, 147.

141. P. A. Brown, " 'Fie,' " argues that Griselda would have been alienating to early modern women as well. Many arguments that invoke Griselda as a figure for feminine passivity do so by way of Caryl Churchill's *Top Girls* (1982), which presents Griselda as patriarchal history's doormat.

CONCLUSION

1. Key treatments include Delany, *Naked Text*; Dinshaw, *Chaucer's Sexual Poetics*, 65–87; Hansen, "Irony and the Antifeminist Narrator," 11–31; Mann, *Geoffrey Chaucer*, 26–38; Martin, *Chaucer's Women*, 196–210. Recently, the special issue of the *Chaucer Review* 52, no.1 (2017), ed. McCormick, Schwebel, and Shutters, has returned critical attention to *The Legend of Good Women*. While this book was drafted before this issue appeared, I have sought to acknowledge the brilliant interventions of this collection and its contributors.

2. Chaucer, *The Legend of Good Women, The Riverside Chaucer*, 587–630. All further citations, noted parenthetically by version and line number, are taken from this edition.

3. Sanok, "Reading Hagiographically," convincingly associates the abbreviation and thematic continuity of individual *Legends* with the genre of hagiography. Also see Minnis, *Oxford Guides to Chaucer*, 312–22.

4. As Shutters, "Griselda's Pagan Virtue," observes, "pagan women are often the best sorts of wives precisely because they are pagans and therefore freer to devote themselves fully to their husbands than were their Christian counterparts" (66).

5. Shutters, "Thought and Feel," and Dumitrescu, "Beautiful Suffering," suggest that this poem is part of a tradition that idealizes the suffering of women. I depart from these readings because I see the narrator as vulnerable in the same fashion as the heroines featured in Chaucer's collection.

6. Simpson, "Ethics and Interpretation," argues that Cupid is a tyrannical reader and ruler in *The Legend of Good Women*. Later, in *Reform and Cultural Revolution*, Simpson claims that the poem "describe[s] tyranny in terms of a willful appropriation of discursive power" (171).

7. Kiser, *Telling Classical Tales*, gives an extensive account of these sources; McLeod, *Virtue and Venom*, studies the *Legend*'s indebtedness to a tradition of "famous women." Percival, *Chaucer's Legendary Good Women*, situates the poem as part of a cultural game/debate about the "matter of women." Getty, " 'Other smale ymaad before,' " argues that the poem is about the problems of writing from historical sources.

8. Laird, "Good Women and *Bonnes Dames*," Meale, "Legends of Good Women," and Delany, *Naked Text*, 94–100, all agree that Christine's project is less masculinist than Chaucer's. Martin argues that Chaucer calls attention to the fact that "the accounts of women are mediated to us through a tradition which is mainly masculine" (210).

9. As Ganim, "Chaucerian Ritual," remarks, "the poet [is] in the position of the good women themselves, bereft of any choice but one so severely limited as to verge on self-destruction" (81).

10. Strohm, *Hochon's Arrow*, 105–11. Percival argues that "the *Legend of Good Women* is cheerfully biased in favour of the poet's own gender" (15). The doubleness Percival finds in the poem—idealized defense and ironic skepticism—"colludes with the expectations of a preponderantly male audience" (15).

11. Accordingly, for Collette, "Chaucer's Poetics and Purposes," Chaucer's story moves away from female exemplarity to social good.

12. D. Wallace, *Chaucerian Polity*, 338, 349–56, 365–78. He argues that Anne of Bohemia is a powerful "historical surrogate" (376) for imagining Alceste.

13. D. Wallace, 367–68, connects this attribution to Richard's proposed marriage to Caterina Visconti (whose father was Bernabò Visconti). See Percival, 113–29, for a discussion of Chaucer's representation of the God of Love as a tyrant in the context of late medieval political and moral theory, especially as that was applied to Richard II's reign. See Simpson, *Reform*, 171–72, for a brief discussion of the poem's resonance with charges of tyranny brought against Richard II, along with Hanrahan, "Seduction and Betrayal," for a longer discussion. Also see H. Phillips, "Register, Politics."

14. Isidore, *Etymologies*, XI, ii.18 (p. 242): "But the word woman (*mulier*) comes from softness (*mollities*), as if *mollier* (cf. *mollior*, "softer"), after a letter has been cut and a letter changed, is now called *mulier*. Maidstone, "Concordia facta inter regem Riccardum II et civitatem Londonie," 190, lines 229–332.

15. See Bloch, *Medieval Misogyny*, 65–92, for a discussion of women's representation in oppositional terms, as either man's complement or his opponent.

16. Strohm, *Hochon's Arrow*, 111–19.

17. Sanok, "Reading Hagiographically," 326–33. Boffey, " 'Twenty thousand more,' " suggests that the poem might have influenced a "nine worthies" tradition in the following centuries.

18. See Glenn Burger, " 'Pite renneth soone in gentil herte,' " whose concept of performative reading in the *Legend* is especially instructive.

19. McDonald, "Chaucer's *Legend of Good Women*"; her more recent essay, "Games Medieval Women Play," connects the elite female audiences of the poem to a series of ludic games included in several manuscripts. Coleman, "Flower, the Leaf, and Philippa of Lancaster," connects John of Gaunt's eldest legitimate daughter to the poetic circulation of the "flower and the leaf" that informs the *Legend*. Taken together, this research suggests the powerful, playful influence of elite women on the generation and reception of Chaucer's poem.

20. Sanok, "Reading Hagiographically," 330–33, 352–54, emphasizes the poem's acknowledgment of the agency of women readers. McCormick, "Remembering the Game," argues that readers are forced into assuming a "pro-active stance" in the poem.

21. Delany, *Naked Text*, 158.

22. See Strohm, "Chaucer's Audience," Brewer, "Class Distinction in Chaucer," and Howard, "Chaucer the Man," for a discussion of Chaucer's upward mobility and its influence on his writing. Middleton, "Chaucer's 'New Men,' " famously argues that Chaucer dramatizes this social position as a literary outlook espoused by several of his pilgrims in *The Canterbury Tales*.

23. See Strohm, *Politique*; Nolan, *John Lydgate*; Delany, *Impolitic Bodies*; and Winstead, *John Capgrave's Fifteenth Century*.

24. Montrose, *Subject of Elizabeth*; Helgerson, *Forms of Nationhood*. Simpson, "Sacrifice of Lady Rochford," compares Parker's translation to Chaucer's *Legend* in a way that makes manifest the dangers of working under a powerful sovereign (in Parker's case, Henry VIII).

25. Goldberg, *James I and the Politics of Literature*.

26. See Warren, "Chivalric Men and Good(?) Women," and Cook, "Author, Text, and Paratext," for helpful analyses of the *Legend*'s status, circulation, and intersection with early modern gender politics.

27. Orgel, *Impersonations*, 153.

28. Fyler, *Chaucer and Ovid*, claims that the *Legend* is "a wonderfully comic exercise in censorship" (99). See Minnis, 379–81, for a discussion of the excisions.

29. Fradenburg, "Beauty and Boredom," offers an invaluable analysis of the connection between desire, sacrifice, and repetition as foundational to the poem's appeal.

30. Frank, *Chaucer and "The Legend of Good Women,"* 189–210.

31. Carlson, *Chaucer's Jobs*; also see Strohm, *Chaucer's Tale*, for Chaucer's relationships with the powerful in late medieval England.

32. As Sanderlin, "Chaucer's 'Legend of Dido,'" points out, Chaucer presented his Dido in the same way in his *House of Fame* as he does in the *Legend*, "so he did not need to be ordered by Alceste, or Anne, to write from a feminist point of view" (332).

33. H. Phillips, "Morality in the Canterbury Tales," 167.

34. Nowlin, "*Legend of Good Women* and the Affect of Invention," argues that the poem represents invention as an affective force, one that is linked in his analysis to the heroines' intensities of feeling.

35. Unlike Ovid's *Metamorphoses*, the complaints of abandoned women featured in Chaucer's sources, principally the *Heroides*, at least recognize another perspective on the sexual predations of powerful men. As Desmond, "*Translatio* of Memory and Desire," suggests, Chaucer's poem "records Chaucer's recognition of the *auctoritas* of the *Heroides*" (186). Hagedorn, *Abandoned Women*, 21–46, provides a helpful survey of medieval receptions of the *Heroides*.

36. See Saunders, *Rape and Ravishment*, 265–74; and Galloway, "Chaucer's *Legend of Lucrece*."

37. See Schwebel, "Livy and Augustine," which shows how Chaucer rejects earlier renderings of Lucrece.

38. Augustine, *City of God*, 1.18–19, claims that Lucrece committed a crime with her self-slaughter (and speculates that she might have done so because she felt guilt—guilt induced by pleasure at her own sexual violation). See Delany, *Naked Text*, 203–6, who gives the full passage from Augustine, and discusses its problematic implications in the context of Chaucer's poem.

39. Annas, *Intelligent Virtue*, insists that Aristotelian virtue ethics is not about the rote repetition of externally imposed moral norms. McCormick, 128–29, argues that the uncertainty of the poem, and *The Legend of Lucrece*, in particular, asks readers to decide upon the grounds of the ethical itself. My thinking about the entanglement of ethical and erotic normativity is indebted to M. Miller, *Philosophical Chaucer*.

40. Hansen, "Irony and the Antifeminist Narrator," 24.

41. Ibid., 25. Hansen, "Feminization of Men," takes up the poem's critical treatment of men.

42. Warren, "'Olde Stories' and Amazons," 86.

43. Mann, *Geoffrey Chaucer*, 32–38.

44. McNamer, *Affective Meditation*, 1–10, 208–12.

45. As Meecham-Jones argues, Chaucer "questions whether the heroism of Chaucer's 'seintes' lies in the active commission of acts, or wehther it can be seen also in the patient (albeit involuntary) bearing of suffering." Meecham-Jones, "Intention, Integrity, and 'Renoun,'" 144.

46. See Hansen, "Irony and the Antifeminist Narrator," Martin, *Chaucer's Women*, and Dinshaw, *Chaucer's Sexual Poetics*, for this charge.

47. See Desmond, 182–84, 205–7, who discusses how Chaucer enlists readers in the circulation of desire by directing readers to the original letters.

48. Simpson, *Reform*, argues "that elegy produces the Renaissance" (127), but he does not credit women's centrality to this tradition, even when he describes *The Legend of Good Women*

as a poem with "an elegiac and Ovidian sympathy with the demands of the grieving and/or loving self, provisionally set above the relentless demands of 'history' " (161).

49. Dinshaw, *Chaucer's Sexual Poetics*, 66, 68, 72, and 86, repeatedly speaks of the narrator's "control of the feminine," a position of privilege the God of Love also assumes for himself.

50. Ibid., 87.

51. After reflecting on her earlier, still groundbreaking, reading of the *Legend*, "Afterword: Re-reading, or, When You Were Mine," Dinshaw has more recently claimed, "my own binary gender analysis . . . does not account for the breadth and complexity of human experience" (164). My claim is that a focus on the ethics rather than gender shows the problematic ideal of the human (and its virtues) that would enforce a binary gender structure.

52. Kolve, "From Cleopatra to Alceste," 151.

53. A debate over Polonius's stature broke out in the 1950s. J. W. Bennett started the debate, "Characterization in Polonius' Advice to Laertes." Responses included O. B. Davis, "Note on the Function of Polonius' Advice"; Hunter, "Isocrates' Precepts and Polonius' Character"; and Wilson, "Polonius in the Round."

54. Qtd. in Stimpson, "Polonius, Our Pundit," 99.

55. Maus, *Inwardness and Theater*, 2.

56. Charnes, *Hamlet's Heirs*.

57. Pollard, "What's Hecuba to Shakespeare?," 1077.

58. Ibid., 1063–74.

59. Ibid., 1088.

60. Dinshaw, *Chaucer's Sexual Poetics*, 85–86.

61. See Minnis, 424–25, for a discussion of the virile woman in Chaucer's *Legend*. B. Newman, *From Virile Woman to Woman-Christ*, discusses this association as it pertains to medieval religious women. See Isidore, XI, ii.22 (p. 242), who separates the kind of feminine virtue I have been discussing in this book from "virile," or "manly" behavior: "A 'heroic maiden' (*virago*) is so called because she 'acts like a man' (*vir* + *agere*), that is, she engages in the activities of men and is full of male vigor. The ancients would call strong women by that name. However, a virgin cannot be correctly called a heroic maiden unless she performs a man's task. But if a woman performs manly deeds, then she is correctly called a heroic maiden, like an Amazon."

62. As Green, "Chaucer's Victimized Women," argues, Chaucer shows how women are excluded from the chivalric cultures of "trouthe" in the *Legend*.

63. Doyle, *Surrendered Wife*. For the website and affiliated services, see http://www.sur renderedwife.com (last accessed May 23, 2018).

64. For examples, see Cohen, *Stone*; Wolfe, *Animal Rites*; and Morton, *Humankind*. Alaimo, *Bodily Natures* and *Exposed*, is most attuned to the intersection of gender and posthumanism.

65. For the latter, see Ramachandran, "Edmund Spenser, Lucretian Neoplatonist"; Goldberg, *Seeds of Things*, 31–62; and Lezra and Blake, eds., *Lucretius and Modernity*. Ramachandran is particularly helpful with this approach to Spenser's materialism, since she treats topics relevant to my argument, but which I do not address: Spenser's *Hymn of Beautie*, and the Temple of Venus and the Gardens of Adonis episodes in *The Faerie Queene*.

66. See Blamires, *Chaucer, Ethics, and Gender*; and Strohm, *Politique*.

67. See E. Johnson, *Practicing Literary Theory*; Freinkel, *Reading Shakespeare's Will*; and Shuger, *Renaissance Bible*.

68. Robertson, *Preface to Chaucer*, remains the most important statement of "exegetical" criticism inflected by Augustine, but work important to this study, namely *The Naked Text* and *Impolitic Bodies*, both by Sheila Delany, is heavily Augustinian.

69. Lynch, *Chaucer's Philosophical Visions*; Beauregard, *Virtue's Own Feature*; Rhodes, *Poetry Does Theology*.

70. Tupper, "Chaucer and the Seven Deadly Sins," tied Chaucer's *Canterbury Tales* to the virtues and vices tradition. Lowes, "Chaucer and the Seven Deadly Sins," argued against the shortcomings of a totalizing moral schema. Tupper defended his approach in "Chaucer's Sinners and Sins." Justice, "Who Stole Robertson?," reviews the problems with and strengths of exegetical criticism as it was practiced by D. W. Robertson Jr., and his followers. At its worst, this school of criticism evaluated whether certain characters were in a state of *caritas*, and whether they were therefore good or bad, sinful or justified. Moral criticism, medievalist or early modernist, has gotten a bad rap as a result of its propensity to judge characters, works, or authors according to externally generated ideals.

BIBLIOGRAPHY

PRIMARY TEXTS

Manuscripts

Baltimore, Walters Art Museum, MS W.72
Edinburgh, National Library of Scotland, Adv. MS 19.2.1
London, British Library, MS Additional 37049

Early Imprints (EEBO)

The admirable virtue, property and operation of the quintessence of rosemary flowers. 1615. STC
    2nd ed. 24844.7.
Agrippa, Henricus Cornelius. *A treatise of the nobilitie and excellencye of vvoman kynde.* Trans.
    Dauid Clapam. 1542. STC 2nd ed. 203.
Averell, William. *A dyall for dainty darlings, rockt in the cradle of securitie: A glasse for all disobedi-
    ent sonnes to looke in; A myrrour for vertuous maydes.* 1584. STC 2nd ed. 978.
Becon, Thomas. *The gouernaunce of vertue teaching all faythful christia[n]s, how they oughte daily
    to leade their lyfe, & fruitfully to spend their time vnto the glorye of God & the health of their
    owne soules.* 1566. STC 2nd ed. 1727.
Bentley, Thomas. *The monument of matrones.* 1582. STC 2nd ed. 1892.
*A boke of the propreties of herbes called an herball wherunto is added the time [the] herbes, floures
    and sedes shold be gathered to be kept the whole yere, wyth the vertue of [the] herbes when
    they are stilled.* 1552. STC 2nd ed. 13175.15.
Breton, Nicholas. *The Soules Immortall Crowne.* 1605. STC 2nd ed. 3701.
———. *The Will of Wit.* 1597. STC 2nd ed. 3705.
Bruto, Giovanni Michele. *The Necessarie, Fit, and Conuienient Education of a Yong Gentle-
    woman.* 1598. STC 3947.
Buoni, Tommaso. *Problemes of beauty, loue, and all humane affections.* Trans. Samson Lennard.
    1618. STC 2nd ed. 4103.5.
Castiglione, Baldassare. *The courtyer of Count Baldessar Castilio diuided into foure books.* Trans.
    Thomas Hoby. 1561. STC 2nd ed. 4778.
Christine de Pizan. *Here begynneth the boke of the cyte of ladyes.* London, 1521. STC 2nd ed.
    7271.

Deloney, Thomas. "Patient Grissel: An Excellent Ballad." *The Garland of Good Will*. 1593, 1631. n.p. http://ebba.english.ucsb.edu/ballad/33585/transcription.

Dod, John, and Robert Cleaver. *A godly forme of houshold government*. 1598, 1621. STC 2nd ed. 5387.5.

Dorrell, Hadrian. *Willobie his Auisa: Or the true picture of a modest maid, and of a chast and constant wife*. 1594. STC 2nd ed. 25755.

Edwards, Richard. *The paradise of daintie devises containyng sundrie pithie preceptes, learned counsails and excellent inventions*. 1585. STC 2nd ed. 7520.

Elderton, William. "The panges of Love and louers fittes." 1559. STC 2nd ed. 7561.

Fenton, Geoffrey. *A Forme of Christian Pollicie*. 1574. STC 10793a.

Feylde, Thomas. *A contrauersye bytwene a louer and a Jaye*. Ca. 1508. STC 10839.

Fulwood, William. *The Enime of Idlenesse*. 1568. STC 2nd ed. 11476.

Gerard, John. *The herball or Generall historie of plantes*. 1597, 1633. STC 2nd ed. 11751.

Gibson, Anthony. *A Woman's Worth, defended against all the men in the world Proouing them to be more perfect, excellent, and absolute in all vertuous actions, then any man of what qualitie soeuer*. 1599. STC 2nd ed. 11831.

Gouge, William. *Of Domesticall Duties*. 1622. STC 2nd ed. 12119.

Greene, Robert. *Mamillia: A Mirrour or looking-glasse for the Ladies of Englande*. 1583. STC 12269.

Gybson, Leonarde. *A very proper dittie: To the tune of lightie loue*. 1571. STC 2nd ed. 11836.

Hall, Joseph. *Two guides to a good life: The genealogy of vertue and the nathomy of sinne*. 1604. STC 2nd ed. 12466.

Hanape, Nicholas. *The ensamples of vertue and vice, gathered oute of holye scripture. By Nicolas Hanape patriarch of Ierusalem. Very necessarye for all christen men and women to loke vpon. And Englyshed by Thomas Paynell*. 1561. STC 2nd ed. 12742.

Hawes, Stephen. *The historie of graunde Amoure and la bell Pucel, called the Pastime of pleasure*. 1554. STC 2nd ed. 12950.

Here foloweth a lytell treatyse of the beaute of women. 1525. STC 1696.

The honour of vertue: Or the monument erected by the sorowfull husband, and the epitaphes annexed by learned and worthy men, to the immortall memory of that worthy gentle-woman Mrs Elizabeth Crashawe. 1620. STC 2nd ed. 6030.

An hospitall for the diseased VVherein are to be found most excellent approoued medicines, as well emplaisters of speciall vertue, as also notable potions or drinkes, and other comfortable receipts, for the restitution and preseruation of bodily health. 1610. STC 2nd ed. 4307.5.

Howell, Thomas. *His devises, for his owne exercise, and his friends pleasure*. 1581. STC 2nd ed. 13875.

———. *Newe sonets, and pretie pamphlets*. 1570. STC 2nd ed. 13876.

Jewel, John. *A Homily of the State of Matrimony. The Second Tome of Homilies*. 1563, 1582. STC 2nd ed. 13669.

Johnson, Richard. *A crowne garland of goulden roses Gathered out of Englands royall garden*. 1612. STC 2nd ed. 14672.

Larke, John. *The boke of wisdome otherwise called the flower of vertue*. 1565. STC 2nd ed. 3358.

Markham, Gervase. *The English housevvife: Containing the inward and outward vertues which ought to be in a compleate woman*. 1631. STC 2nd ed. 17353.

Mulcaster, Richard. *Positions*. 1581. STC 2nd ed. 18253.

Partridge, John. *The treasurie of commodious conceits, & hidden secrets and may be called, the huswiues closet, of healthfull prouision*. 1572. STC 2nd ed. 19425.5.

[*The Pathway to Health*]. *A right profitable booke for all diseases: Called The path-way to health Wherein are to be found most excellent and approoued medicines, of great vertue.* 1587. STC 2nd ed. 15533.

Perkins, William. *Christian oeconomie.* 1609. STC 2nd ed. 19677.

Phillips, John. *A commemoration of the life and death of the right worshipfull and vertuous ladie: Dame Helen Branch.* 1594. STC 2nd ed. 19863.7.

A poore knight his pallace of private pleasures. 1579. STC 2nd ed., 4283.

Prepositas his practise a vvorke very necessary to be vsed for the better preseruation of the health of man. 1588. STC 2nd ed. 20180.7.

Primaudaye, Pierre [recorded as Peter] de La. *The French Academie.* 1589. STC 2nd ed. 15234.

Proctor, Thomas. *A gorgious gallery, of gallant inuentions.* 1578. STC 2nd ed. 20402.

Ralegh, Sir Walter. *The discouerie of the large, rich, and bevvtiful empire of Guiana.* 1596. STC 2nd ed. 20634.

Rich, Barnabe. *The excellency of good women.* 1613. STC 2nd ed. 20982.

———. *My Ladies Looking Glasse.* London, 1616. STC 2nd ed. 20991.7.

Robinson, Clement. *A handefull of pleasant delites containing sundrie new sonets and delectable histories, in divers kindes of meeter.* 1584. STC 2nd ed. 21105.

Robinson, Richard. *The vineyarde of vertue collected, composed, and digested into a tripartite order, conteining XXXII. most excellent plants of fruitful vertue.* 1579. STC 2nd ed. 21121.

Romei, Annibale. "Of Beauty." *The courtiers academie comprehending seuen seuerall dayes discourses: Wherein be discussed, seuen noble and important arguments, worthy by all gentlemen to be perused.* 1598. STC 2nd ed. 21311.

Salter, Thomas. *A Mirrhor mete for all mothers, matrones, and maidens, intituled the Mirrhor of Modestie no lesse profitable and pleasant, then necessarie to bee read and practiced.* 1579. STC 2nd ed. 21634.

Smith, Thomas. *De republica anglorum.* 1583. STC 2nd ed. 22857.

Ste. B. *Counsel to the husband: To the wife instruction.* 1608. STC 2nd ed. 1069.

Stubbes, Philip. *The anatomie of abuses.* 1583. STC 2nd ed. 23376.

———. *A Christal Glas for christian women.* London, 1592. STC 2nd ed. 23382.

Surflet, Richard. *Maison rustique, or The countrey farme: Compyled in the French tongue by Charles Steuens, and Iohn Liebault, Doctors of Physicke. And translated into English by Richard Surflet, practitioner in physicke.* 1616. STC 2nd ed. 10549.

Thynne, William. *The workes of Geffray Chaucer.* 1532. STC 2nd ed. 5068.

Tilney, Edmund. *A briefe and pleasant discourse of duties in mariage, called the flower of friendshippe.* 1571. STC 2nd ed. 24077.

Topsell, Edward. *The historie of foure-footed beastes.* 1607. STC 2nd ed. 24123.

Tuke, Thomas. *A discourse against painting and tincturing of women.* 1616. STC 2nd ed. 24316a.

Turberville, George. *Epitaphes, epigrams, songs and sonets.* 1567. STC 2nd ed. 24326.

———. *Tragicall tales translated by Turberuile in time of his troubles out of sundrie Italians.* 1587. STC 2nd ed. 24330.

Vives, Juan Luis. *A very frutefull and pleasant boke called the Instructio[n] of a Christen woma[n].* Trans. Richard Hyrd. 1529. STC 2nd ed. 24856.5.

[Voragine, Jacobus]. *Legenda aurea sanctorum, sive, Lombardica historia.* Trans. Wyllyam Caxton. 1483. STC 2nd ed. 24873.

Whately, William. *A bride-bush: or, A direction for married persons.* 1619. STC 2nd ed. 25297.

Whetstone, George. *The rocke of regard.* 1576. STC 2nd ed. 25348.

Whitney, Geffrey. *A choice of emblemes, and other deuises, for the moste parte gathered out of sundrie writers, Englished and moralized.* 1586. STC 2nd ed. 25438.

Modern Editions

Aquinas, Thomas. *Summa contra Gentiles. Opera Omnia.* Editio Leonina manualis. Vol. 11. Rome, 1878.
———. *Summa Theologiae.* Vol. 34. Trans. R. J. Batten. London: Blackfriars, 1975.
———. *Treatise on the Virtues.* Trans. John A. Oesterle. South Bend, IN: Notre Dame University Press, 1984.
Aristotle. *The Generation of Animals.* Trans. A. L. Peck. Loeb Classical Library, 366. Cambridge, MA: Harvard University Press, 1943.
———. *Nicomachean Ethics.* Intr. and trans. Terrence Irwin. Indianapolis, IN: Hackett, 1999.
———. *Nicomachean Ethics.* Trans. H. Rackham. Loeb Classical Library, 1. Cambridge, MA: Harvard University Press, 1926.
———. *Physics, Books 5–8.* Trans. P. H. Wicksteed and F. M. Cornford. Loeb Classical Library, 255. Cambridge, MA: Harvard University Press, 1934.
d'Aubigné, Théodore Agrippa. "A mes filles touchant les femmes doctes de nostre siècle." *Oeuvres complètes de Théodore Agrippa d'Aubigné.* Ed. Françoise de Caussade, Eugène Réaume, and A. Legouëz. Vol. 1. Paris: A. Lemerre, 1873–92.
Augustine. *The City of God [De civitate Dei].* Trans. Henry Bettenson. 1972. Reprint, London: Penguin, 1984.
———. *Confessions [Confessiones].* Trans. F. J. Sheed. Indianapolis, IN: Hackett, 1942.
Boccaccio, Giovanni. *Famous Women [De claris mulieribus].* Ed. and trans. Virginia Brown. Cambridge, MA: Harvard University Press, 2001.
Bokenham, Osbern. *Legendys of hooly wummen, ed. from ms. Arundel 327.* Ed. Mary S. Serjeantson. EETS, 206. London: H. Milford for Oxford University Press, 1938.
Book to a Mother: An Edition with Commentary. Ed. Adrian James McCarthy. Salzburg: Institut für Anglistik und Amerikanistik, Universität Salzburg, 1981.
The Book of Vices and Virtues. Ed. W. Nelson Francis. EETS, o.s., 217. London: Humphrey Milford, Oxford University Press for the EETS, 1942.
Capgrave, John. *The Life of St. Katherine.* Ed. Karen A. Winstead. Kalamazoo, MI: Medieval Institute Publications, 1999.
Caxton, William, trans. *The Book of the Knight of the Tower.* Ed. M. Y. Offord. EETS, s.s., 2. London: Oxford University Press, 1971.
Chaucer, Geoffrey. *The Canterbury Tales. The Riverside Chaucer.* Ed. Larry Benson. Boston: Houghton-Mifflin, 1987.
———. *The Legend of Good Women. The Riverside Chaucer.*
———. *Troilus and Criseyde. The Riverside Chaucer.*
Christine de Pizan. *The Book of the City of Ladies.* Ed. and trans. Rosalind Brown-Grant. London: Penguin, 1999.
———. *A Medieval Woman's Mirror of Honor: The Treasury of the City of Ladies.* Trans. Charity Cannon Willard. Ed. Madeleine Pelner Cosman. New York: Persea, 1989.
Cicero. *De Inventione.* Trans. H. M. Hubbell. Loeb Classical Library, 386. Cambridge, MA: Harvard University Press, 1949.

Dekker, Thomas. *The Pleasant Comedie of Old Fortunatus. Thomas Dekker.* Ed. Ernest Rhys. London: T. Fisher Unwin, n.d. [ca. 1900]. 288–384.

Dekker, Thomas, Henry Chettle, and William Haughton. *The Pleasant Comodie of Patient Grissil. The Dramatic Works of Thomas Dekker.* Ed. Fredson Bowers. Vol. 1. Cambridge: Cambridge University Press, 1953. 208–98.

Dives and Pauper. Ed. P. H. Barnum. EETS, 275, 280. 1976. Reprint, Oxford: Oxford University Press for EETS, 1980.

Elyot, Thomas. *Of the Knowledge which Maketh a Wise Man.* London, 1533. Ed. Edwin Johnston Howard. Facsimile ed. Oxford, OH: Anchor Press, 1946.

English Medieval Lapidaries. Ed. J. Evans and M. Serjeantson. EETS, o.s., 190. London: Oxford University Press for EETS, 1933.

Erasmus, Desiderius. "A Marriage in Name Only, *or,* The Unequal Match." *The Colloquies of Erasmus.* Trans. Craig R. Thompson. Chicago: University of Chicago Press, 1965.

Five Hundred Years of Chaucer Criticism. Ed. Caroline F. E. Spurgeon. Vol. 3. Cambridge: Cambridge University Press, 1925.

Fletcher, John. *The Tamer Tamed: or, The Woman's Prize.* Ed. Celia R. Daileader and Gary Taylor. Revels Student Editions. Manchester: Manchester University Press, 2006.

Forrest, William. *The History of Grisild the Second: A Narrative, in Verse, of the Divorce of Queen Katharine of Arragon.* Ed W. D. Macray. London, Chiswick Press, 1875.

Fowler, William. "The Laste Epistle of Creseyd to Troylus." *The Poems of Robert Henryson.* Ed. Robert L. Kindrick. Kalamazoo, MI: TEAMS Middle English Series, 1997. Appendix, 283–300.

Gascoigne, George. *The Complete Works.* Ed. John W. Cunliffe. Vol. 1. Cambridge: Cambridge University Press, 1907.

Greene, Robert. *Euphues: The Life and Complete Works in Prose and Verse of Robert Greene.* Vol. 6, *1881–1886.* Ed. Alexander B. Grosart. New York: Russell & Russell, 1964.

———. *Penelope's Web: Life and Complete Works.* Vol. 5.

Guido delle Colonne. *Historia Destructionis Troiae.* Bloomington: Indiana University Press, 1974.

Henryson, Robert. *The Testament of Cresseid: The Poems of Robert Henryson.* Ed. Robert L. Kindrick. Kalamazoo, MI: TEAMS Middle English Texts Series, 1997.

Hildegard of Bingen. *Ordo Virtutum: Nine Medieval Latin Plays.* Ed. and trans. Peter Dronke. Cambridge: Cambridge University Press, 1995.

Hilton, Walter. *The Scale of Perfection.* Ed. Thomas H. Bestul. Kalamazoo, MI: TEAMS Middle English Series, 2000.

The History of Patient Grisel, 1619. [Chapbook.] Ed. Henry B. Wheatley. London: Printed for the Villon Society, 1885.

Isidore of Seville. *The Etymologies of Isidore of Seville.* Trans. and ed. Stephen A. Barney, W. J. Lewis, J. A. Beall, and Oliver Berghof. Cambridge: Cambridge University Press, 2006.

Jacob's Well: An English Treatise on the Cleansing of Man's Conscience. Part I. Ed. Arthur Brandeis. EETS, o.s., 115. London: Kegan Paul, Trench, Trübner for EETS, 1900.

John Myrc's Instructions for Parish Priests. Ed. Edward Peacock. EETS, o.s., 31. London: Kegan Paul, Trench & Trübner for EETS, 1868.

Kempe, Margery. *The Book of Margery Kempe.* Ed. Sanford Brown Meech and Hope Emily Allen. EETS, 212. London: Oxford University Press for EETS, 1940.

Langland, William. *The Vision of Piers Plowman.* Ed. A. V. C. Schmidt. London: Everyman, 1978.

The Lay Folks' Catechism. Ed. Thomas Frederick Simons and Henry Edward Nolloth. EETS, o.s., 118. London: Kegan Paul, Trench & Trübner for EETS, 1901.

Lodge, Thomas. *An Old-Spelling Critical Edition of Thomas Lodge's "A Margarite of America 1596."* Ed. James Clyde Addison Jr. Elizabethan Studies, 96. Salzburg: Institut für Anglistik und Amerikanistik, 1980.

Lydgate, John. *A Critical Edition of John Lydgate's "Life of Our Lady."* Ed. Joseph A. Lauritis, Ralph A. Klinefelter, and Vernon F. Gallagher. Pittsburgh, PA: Duquesne University Press, 1961.

———. *The Minor Poems of John Lydgate*. Part I. Ed. Henry Noble MacCracken. EETS, e.s., 107. London: Kegan Paul, Trench, Trübner & Co., 1911.

———. *The Minor Poems of John Lydgate*. Part II. Ed. Henry Noble MacCracken. EETS, e.s., 107. Oxford: Humphrey Milford, Oxford University Press, 1934.

———. *Mummings and Entertainments*. Ed. Claire Sponsler. Kalamazoo, MI: Medieval Institute Publications, 2010.

———. *The Troy Book: A.D. 1412–20*. Ed. Henry Bergen. 4 vols. in 3. 1906–35. Reprint, London: EETS, 1975.

Macrobius. [Commentary on the Dream of Scipio.] *Opera*. Vol. 2. Ed. James Willis. 1970. Reprint, K. G. Saur Verlag, 1998.

Mary Magdalene, from the Digby MS. Medieval Drama. Ed. David Bevington. Boston: Houghton Mifflin, 1975. 687–753.

Medwall, Henry. *Nature. The Plays of Henry Medwall*. Ed. Alan H. Nelson. Suffolk: D. S. Brewer, 1980.

Le Menagier de Paris. Ed. G. L. Greco and C. M. Rose. *The Good Wife's Guide (Le Menagier de Paris): A Medieval Household Book*. Ithaca, NY: Cornell University Press, 2009.

A Mery Jest of a Shrewd and Curst Wife Lapped in Morel's Skin, for Her Good Behavior. The Taming of the Shrew: Texts and Contexts. Ed. Frances E. Dolan. Boston: Bedford Books, 1996. 254–88.

N-Town Passion Play I. Medieval Drama. Ed. David Bevington. Boston: Houghton Mifflin, 1975. 477–535.

Ovid. *Metamorphoses*. Ed. G. P. Goold. Trans. Frank Justus Miller. Loeb Classical Library. Ovid, vol. 3. 3rd ed. Cambridge, MA: Harvard University Press, 1984.

Pecock, Reginald. *The reule of crysten religioun*. Ed. William Cabell Greet and H. Milford. 1927. Millwood, NY: Kraus Reprint, 1987.

Phillip, John. *The Play of Patient Grissell by John Phillip*. Ed. W. W. Greg and Ronald B. McKerrow. London: Malone Society Reprints, 1909.

Prudentius. *Psychomachia. Prudentius*, vol. 1. Trans. H. J. Thomson. Loeb Classical Library, 387. Cambridge, MA: Harvard University Press, 1949.

Rainolde, Richard. *The Foundacion of Rhetoric*. Ed. R. C. Alston. 1563. Reprint, Menston, UK: Scolar Press, 1972.

Richard Tottel's "Songes and Sonettes": The Elizabethan Version. Ed. Paul A. Marquis. Renaissance English Text Society, 7th ser., vol. 32. Tempe, AZ: ACMRS, 2007.

Rolle, Richard. *The Psalter, or Psalms of David and certain canticles / with a translation and exposition in English by Richard Rolle of Hampole*. Ed. H. R. Bramley. 1884. Reprint, Ann Arbor: University of Michigan Press, 2006.

Shakespeare, William. *Hamlet. The Norton Shakespeare*. Ed. Stephen Greenblatt, Walter Cohen, Jean E. Howard, and Katharine Eisaman Maus. 2nd ed. New York: W. W. Norton, 2015. 1683–1784.

————. *The Taming of the Shrew. The Complete Works of Shakespeare.* Ed. David Bevington. 4th ed. New York: Harper Collins, 1992.

————. *The Tempest.* Ed. Peter Hulme and William Sherman. Norton Critical Edition. New York: W. W. Norton, 2003.

————. *Troilus and Cressida.* The Arden Shakespeare. Ed. David Bevington. London: Methuen, 1982.

Skelton, John. *Garlande or Chaplet of Laurell. The Poetical Works of John Skelton.* Ed. Alexander Dyce. Vol. 2. 1855. Reprint, New York: AMS Press, 1965.

————. *Philip Sparrow, Poetical Works of John Skelton.* Vol. 1.

South English Legendary. Ed. Charlotte D'Evelyn and Anna J. Mill. Vol. 1. EETS, o.s., 235. London: Oxford University Press, 1956–59.

Spenser, Edmund. *The Faerie Queene.* Ed. A. C. Hamilton. 7th ed. London: Longman, 1980.

Summa Virtutum de remediis anime. Ed. Siegfried Wentzel. Athens: University of Georgia Press, 1984.

The Taming of the Shrew (film). Dir. Sam Taylor. United Artists, 1929. Starring Mary Pickford and Douglas Fairbanks.

Tilney, Edmund. *The Flower of Friendship: A Renaissance Dialogue Contesting Marriage.* Ed. Valerie Wayne. 1573. Reprint, Ithaca, NY: Cornell University Press, 1992.

Tom Tiler and His Wife in Two Tudor "Shrew" Plays. Ed. John S. Farmer. London: Early English Drama Society, 1908.

Whitney, Geffrey. *A Choice of Emblemes and Other Devises.* Leyden: imprinted in the House of Christopher Plantyn by Francis Raphelengius, 1586. The English Experience, Its Record in Early English Books Published in Facsimile 161. New York: De Capo Press, 1969.

"Why I Can't Be a Nun." *Six Ecclesiastical Satires.* Ed. James Dean. Kalamazoo, MI: Medieval Institute Publications, 1991.

Woman Defamed, and Woman Defended: An Anthology of Medieval Texts. Ed. Alcuin Blamires. Oxford: Oxford University Press, 1992.

SECONDARY SOURCES

Adelman, Janet. *Suffocating Mothers: Fantasies of Maternal Origin in Shakespeare's Plays, "Hamlet" to "The Tempest."* New York: Routledge, 1992.

————. "'This is and is not Cressid': The Characterization of Cressida." *The (M)other Tongue: Essays in Feminist Psychoanalytic Interpretation.* Ed. Shirley Nelson-Garner, Claire Kahane, and Madelon Sprengnether. Ithaca, NY: Cornell University Press, 1985. 119–41.

Aers, David. "Criseyde: Woman in Medieval Society." *Chaucer Review* 13 (1978–79): 177–200.

————. "Langland on the Church and the End of the Cardinal Virtues." *Journal of Medieval and Early Modern Studies* 42 (2012): 59–81.

————. *Salvation and Sin: Augustine, Langland, and Fourteenth-Century Theology.* South Bend, IN: University of Notre Dame Press, 2009.

————. "A Whisper in the Ear of Early Modernists; or, Reflections on Literary Critics Writing the 'History of the Subject.'" *Culture and History, 1350–1600: Essays on English Communities, Identities and Writing.* Ed. David Aers. Detroit, MI: Wayne State University Press, 1992. 177–202.

Agamben, Giorgio. *Homo Sacer: Sovereign Power and Bare Life.* Trans. Daniel Heller-Roazen. Stanford, CA: Stanford University Press, 1998.

Akbari, Suzanne Conklin. "Death as Metamorphosis in the Devotional and Political Allegory of Christine de Pizan." *The Ends of the Body: Identity and Community in Medieval Culture.* Ed. Suzanne Conklin Akbari and Jill Ross. Toronto: University of Toronto Press, 2013. 283–318.

Alaimo, Stacy. *Bodily Natures: Science, Environment, and the Material Self.* Bloomington: Indiana University Press, 2010.

———. *Exposed: Environmental Politics and Pleasures in Posthuman Times.* Minneapolis: University of Minnesota Press, 2016.

Alaimo, Stacy, and Susan Hekman. "Introduction: Emerging Models of Materiality in Feminist Theory." *Material Feminisms.* Ed. Stacy Alaimo and Susan Hekman. Bloomington: Indiana University Press, 2008. 1–19.

Allen, Amy. *The Politics of Our Selves: Power, Autonomy, and Gender in Contemporary Critical Theory.* New York: Columbia University Press, 2008.

Allen, Valerie. "Mineral Virtue." *Animal, Vegetable, Mineral: Ethics and Objects.* Ed. Jeffrey Jerome Cohen. Washington, DC: Oliphant Books, 2012. 123–52.

Altman, Joel. "The Practice of Shakespeare's Text." *Style* 23 (1989): 466–500.

Amussen, Susan Dwyer. " 'Being Stirred to Much Unquietness': Violence and Domestic Violence in Early Modern England." *Journal of Women's Studies* 6 (1994): 70–89.

Anderson, Judith H. "Britomart's Armor in Spenser's *Faerie Queene*: Reopening Cultural Matters of Gender and Figuration." *English Literary Renaissance* 39 (2009): 74–96.

———. " 'In liuing colours and right hew': The Queen of Spenser's Central Books." *Poetic Traditions of the English Renaissance.* Ed. Maynard Mack and George de Forest Lord. New Haven, CT: Yale University Press, 1982. 47–66.

Annas, Julia. *Intelligent Virtue.* Oxford: Oxford University Press, 2011.

———. "Virtue Ethics: What Kind of Naturalism?" *Virtue Ethics Old and New.* Ed. Stephen M. Gardiner. Ithaca, NY: Cornell University Press, 2005. 11–29.

Archibald, Elizabeth. "Declarations of 'Entente' in *Troilus and Criseyde*." *Chaucer Review* 25 (1991): 190–213.

———. "The Flight from Incest: Two Late Classical Precursors of the Constance Theme." *Chaucer Review* 20 (1986): 259–72.

Armstrong, W. A. "The Elizabethan Conception of the Tyrant." *Review of English Studies* 22 (1946): 161–81.

———. "The Influence of Seneca and Machiavelli on the Elizabethan Tyrant." *Review of English Studies* 24 (1948): 19–35.

Aronstein, Susan. "Cresseid Reading Cresseid: Redemption and Translation in Henryson's *Testament*." *Scottish Literary Journal* 21 (1994): 5–22.

Ashley, Kathleen. "Medieval Courtesy Literature and Dramatic Mirrors of Female Conduct." *The Ideology of Conduct.* Ed. Nancy Armstrong and Leonard Tennenhouse. New York: Routledge, 1987. 25–38.

Ashley, Kathleen, and Robert Clark, eds. *Medieval Conduct.* Minneapolis: University of Minnesota Press, 2001.

Astell, Anne. *The Song of Songs in the Middle Ages.* Ithaca, NY: Cornell University Press, 1995.

Axton, Marie. *The Queen's Two Bodies: Drama and the Elizabethan Succession.* London: Royal Historical Society, 1977.

Bahr, Howard W. "The Misery of Florimell: The Ladder of Temptation." *Southern Quarterly* 4 (1965): 116–22.

Bale, Anthony. "'A maner Latyn corrupt': Chaucer and the Absent Religions." *Chaucer and Religion*. Ed. Helen Phillips. Cambridge: D. S. Brewer, 2010. 52–64.

Barkan, Leonard. *The Gods Made Flesh: Metamorphosis and the Pursuit of Paganism.* New Haven, CT: Yale University Press, 1986.

Barlow, Gania. "A Thrifty Tale: Narrative Authority and the Competing Values of the *Man of Law's Tale*." *Chaucer Review* 44 (2010): 397–420.

Barron, Caroline M. *The Medieval Guildhall of London*. London: Corporation of London, 1974.

Bartlett, Anne Clark. *Male Authors, Female Readers: Representation and Subjectivity in Middle English Devotional Literature.* Ithaca, NY: Cornell University Press, 1995.

Baswell, Christopher C., and Paul Beekman Taylor. "The *Faire Queene Eleyne* in Chaucer's *Troilus*." *Speculum* (1988): 293–311.

Bate, Jonathan. *Shakespeare and Ovid*. Oxford: Clarendon Press, 1993.

Baumlin, Tita French. "Petruchio the Sophist and Language as Creation in *The Taming of the Shrew*." *Studies in English Literature, 1500–1900* 29 (1989): 237–57.

Bean, John C. "Comic Structure and the Humanizing of Kate in *The Taming of the Shrew*." *The Woman's Part: Feminist Criticism of Shakespeare*. Ed. Carolyn Ruth Swift Lenz, Gayle Greene, and Carol Thomas Neely. Urbana: University of Illinois Press, 1980. 65–78.

Beauregard, David N. *Virtue's Own Feature: Shakespeare and the Virtue Ethics Tradition.* Newark: University of Delaware Press, 1995.

Beckwith, Sarah. *Christ's Body: Identity, Culture, and Society in Late Medieval Writings.* London: Routledge, 1993.

Beecher, Donald, and Henry D. Janzen. Introduction. *A Margarite of America*, by Thomas Lodge. Ed. Donald Beecher and Henry D. Janzen. Publications of the Barnabe Riche Society, 17. 1596. Reprint, Toronto: Toronto Centre for Reformation and Renaissance Studies, 2005. 11–70.

Belsey, Catherine. *The Subject of Tragedy: Identity and Difference in Renaissance Drama.* London: Methuen, 1985.

Benner, Erica. *Machiavelli's Ethics*. Princeton, NJ: Princeton University Press, 2009.

Bennett, Jane. *The Enchantment of Modern Life: Attachments, Crossings, and Ethics.* Princeton, NJ: Princeton University Press, 2001.

———. *Vibrant Matter: A Political Ecology of Things.* Durham, NC: Duke University Press, 2010.

Bennett, Josephine Waters. "Characterization in Polonius' Advice to Laertes." *Shakespeare Quarterly* 4 (1953): 3–9.

Benson, C. David. "Civic Lydgate: The Poet and London." *John Lydgate: Poetry, Culture, and Lancastrian England*. Ed. Larry Scanlon and James Simpson. South Bend, IN: University of Notre Dame Press, 2006. 147–68.

———. "Critic and Poet: What Lydgate and Henryson Did to Chaucer's 'Troilus and Criseyde.'" *Modern Language Quarterly* 53 (1992): 23–40.

———. *The History of Troy in Middle English Literature: Guido delle Colonne's "Historia Destructionis Troiae" in Medieval England.* Totowa, NJ: Rowman & Littlefield, 1980.

Benson, Pamela. "Florimell at Sea." *Spenser Studies* 6 (1985): 83–92.

Bentham, Jeremy. *An Introduction to the Principles of Morals and Legislation.* Oxford: Clarendon Press, 1907.

Berger, Harry, Jr. *Revisionary Play: Studies in the Spenserian Dynamics.* Berkeley: University of California Press, 1988.

Bernau, Anke. *Virgins: A Cultural History.* London: Granta, 2007.

Bernau, Anke, Sarah Salih, and Ruth Evans, eds. *Medieval Virginities*. Toronto: University of Toronto Press, 2003.

Berry, Phillipa. *Of Chastity and Power: Elizabethan Literature and the Unmarried Queen*. New York: Routledge, 1994.

Bersani, Leo. "Is the Rectum a Grave?" *October* 43 (1987): 197–222.

———. "Sociality and Sexuality." *Critical Inquiry* 26 (2000): 641–56.

Bialo, Caralyn. "Popular Performance, the Broadside Ballad, and Ophelia's Madness." *Studies in English Literature, 1500–1900* 53 (2013): 293–309.

Black, Nancy B. *Medieval Narratives of Accused Queens*. Gainesville: University Press of Florida, 2003.

Blake, Liza. "Allegorical Causation and the Nature of Allegory in Henry Medwall's *Nature*." *Studies in English Literature, 1500–1900* 55 (2015): 341–63.

Blamires, Alcuin. *Chaucer, Ethics, and Gender*. Oxford: Clarendon Press, 2006.

Bliss, Lee. "The Renaissance Griselda: A Woman for All Seasons." *Viator: Medieval and Renaissance Studies* 23 (1992): 301–43.

Bloch, R. Howard. *Mediaeval Misogyny and the Invention of Western Romantic Love*. Chicago: University of Chicago Press, 1992.

Block, Edward A. "Originality, Controlling Purpose, and Craftmanship in Chaucer's *Man of Law's Tale*." *PMLA* 68 (1953): 572–616.

Bloomfield, Morton. "Allegories of the Virtues and Vices in Medieval Art from Christian Times to the Thirteenth Century." *Speculum* 16 (1941): 494–96.

Bloomfield, M. W., B.-G. Guvot, D. R. Howard, and T. B. Kabealo, eds. *Incipits of Latin Works on the Virtues and Vices, 1100–1500 A.D., Including a Section of Incipits of Works on the Pater Noster*. Cambridge, MA: Medieval Academy of America, 1979.

Boboc, Andreea. "Criseyde's Descriptions and the Ethics of Feminine Experience." *Chaucer Review* 47 (2012): 63–83.

Boffey, Julia. "Lydgate, Henryson, and the Literary Testament." *Modern Language Quarterly* 53 (1992): 41–56.

———. " 'Twenty thousand more': Some Fifteenth- and Sixteenth-Century Responses to *The Legend of Good Women*." *Middle English Poetry: Texts and Traditions; Essays in Honour of Derek Pearsall*. Ed. A. J. Minnis. Woodbridge: York Medieval Press, 2001. 279–97.

Boose, Lynda E. "Scolding Brides and Bridling Scolds: Taming the Woman's Unruly Member." *Shakespeare Quarterly* 42 (1991): 179–213.

Borenius, Tancred, and E. W. Tristram. *English Medieval Painting*. New York: Hacker Art Books, 1976.

Bornstein, Diane. *Mirrors of Courtesy*. Hamden, CT: Archon Books, 1975.

Borris, Kenneth. "Platonism and Spenser's Poetic: Idealized Imitation, Merlin's Mirror, and the Florimells." *Spenser Studies* 24 (2009): 209–68.

Breen, Katharine. "Discipline and Doctrine: Inculcating Moral Habits in *Le livre de éthiques d'Aristote*." *New Medieval Literatures* 12 (2010): 209–50.

———. *Imagining an English Reading Public, 1150–1400*. Cambridge: Cambridge University Press, 2010.

Bretzius, Stephen. *Shakespeare in Theory: The Postmodern Academy and the Early Modern Theatre*. Ann Arbor: University of Michigan Press, 1997.

Brewer, D. S. "Class Distinction in Chaucer." *Speculum* 43 (1968): 290–305.

Brody, Saul. *The Disease of the Soul: Leprosy in Medieval Literature*. Ithaca, NY: Cornell University Press, 1974.

Brown, Carolyn E. "Katherina of *The Taming of the Shrew*: 'A Second Grissel.'" *Texas Studies in Language and Literature* 37 (1995): 285–313.

Brown, Pamela Allen. *Better a Shrew Than a Sheep: Women, Drama, and the Culture of Jest in Early Modern England*. Ithaca, NY: Cornell University Press, 2003.

———. "'Fie, What a Foolish Duty Call You This?': *The Taming of the Shrew*, Women's Jest, and the Divided Audience." *A Companion to Shakespeare's Works*. Vol 3, *The Comedies*. Ed. Richard Dutton and Jean E. Howard. Malden, MA: Blackwell, 2006. 289–306.

Bryson, Anna. *From Courtesy to Civility: Changing Codes of Conduct in Early Modern England*. Oxford: Clarendon Press, 1998.

Buncombe, Marie. "Faire Florimell as Faire Game: The Virtuous, Unmarried Woman in *The Faerie Queene* and *The Courtier*." *College Language Association Journal* 28 (1984): 164–75.

Burger, Glenn. "Conduct Becoming: Gender and the Making of an Ethical Subject in *The Book of the Knight of the Tower*." *Medieval Literature: Criticism and Debates*. Ed. Holly A. Crocker and D. Vance Smith. London: Routledge, 2014. 117–25.

———. *Conduct Becoming: Good Wives and Husbands in the Later Middle Ages*. Philadelphia: University of Pennsylvania Press, 2018.

———. "'Pite renneth soone in gentil herte': Ugly Feelings and Gendered Conduct in Chaucer's *Legend of Good Women*." *Chaucer Review* 52 (2017): 66–84.

Burns, Margie. "The Ending of the Shrew." *The Taming of the Shrew: Critical Essays*. Ed. Dana E. Aspinall. London: Routledge, 2002. 84–105.

Burrus, Virginia. *The Sex Lives of Saints: An Erotics of Ancient Hagiography*. Philadelphia: University of Pennsylvania Press, 2007.

Bushnell, Rebecca W. *Tragedies of Tyrants: Political Thought and Theater in the English Renaissance*. Ithaca, NY: Cornell University Press, 1990.

Butler, Judith. *Bodies That Matter: On the Discursive Limits of 'Sex.'* New York: Routledge, 1993.

———. *Frames of War: When Is Life Grievable?* London: Verso, 2009.

———. *Precarious Life: The Powers of Mourning and Violence*. London: Verso, 2004.

Bynum, Carolyn Walker. *Christian Materiality: An Essay on Religion in Late Medieval Europe*. New York: Zone Books, 2011.

———. *Jesus as Mother: Studies in the Spirituality of the High Middle Ages*. Berkeley: University of California Press, 1984.

Cadden, Joan. *Meanings of Sex Difference in the Middle Ages: Medicine, Science, and Culture*. Cambridge: Cambridge University Press, 1993.

Camp, Cynthia Turner. *Anglo-Saxon Saints' Lives as History Writing in Late Medieval England*. Woodbridge: D. S. Brewer, 2015.

Campana, Joseph. *The Pain of Reformation: Spenser, Vulnerability, and the Ethics of Masculinity*. New York: Fordham University Press, 2012.

Campbell, Jennifer. "Figuring Criseyde's 'Entente': Authority, Narrative, and Chaucer's Use of History." *Chaucer Review* 27 (1993): 342–58.

Carlson, David R. *Chaucer's Jobs*. New York: Palgrave Macmillan, 2004.

Carruthers, Mary. "The Sociable Text of the 'Troilus Frontispiece': A Different Mode of Textuality." *ELH* 81 (2014): 423–41.

———. "Virtue, Intention and the Mind's Eye in Chaucer's *Troilus and Criseyde*." *Traditions and Innovations in the Study of Medieval English Literature: The Influence of Derek Brewer*. Ed. Charlotte Brewer and Barry Windeatt. Cambridge: D. S. Brewer, 2013. 73–87.

Cartlidge, Neil. "Criseyde's Absent Friends." *Chaucer Review* 44 (2010): 227–45.

Cavanaugh, Sheila. *Wanton Eyes and Chaste Desires: Female Sexuality in "The Faerie Queene."* Bloomington: Indiana University Press, 1994.

Celovsky, Lisa. "Early Modern Masculinities and the *Faerie Queene.*" *English Literary Renaissance* 35 (2005): 210–47.

Chaganti, Seeta. *The Medieval Poetics of the Reliquary: Enshrinement, Inscription, Performance.* New York: Palgrave Macmillan, 2008.

Chamberlain, Stephanie. "Domestic Economies in *The Taming of the Shrew*: Amassing Cultural Credit." *Upstart Crow* 28 (2009): 50–69.

Champion, Larry S. "Shakespeare and Dekker: Creative Interaction and the Form of Romantic Comedy." *Upstart Crow* 5 (1984): 50–63.

Charnes, Linda. *Hamlet's Heirs: Shakespeare and the Politics of a New Millennium.* New York: Routledge, 2006.

———. *Notorious Identity: Materializing the Subject in Shakespeare.* Cambridge, MA: Harvard University Press, 1993.

Cheney, Donald. *Spenser's Image of Nature: Wild Man and Shepherd in "The Faerie Queene."* New Haven, CT: Yale University Press, 1966.

Cheney, Patrick. " 'And Doubted Her to Deeme an Earthly Wight': Male Neoplatonic 'Magic' and the Problem of Female Identity in Spenser's Allegory of the Two Florimells." *Studies in Philology* 86 (1989): 310–40.

Christian, Margaret. " 'Waves of Weary Wretchedness': Florimell and the Sea." *Spenser Studies* 14 (2000): 133–61.

Clark, Sandra. "A Margarite of America." *University of Toronto Quarterly* 76 (2007): 405–7.

Clasby, Eugene. "Chaucer's Constance: Womanly Virtue and the Heroic Life." *Chaucer Review* 13 (1979): 221–33.

Clogan, Paul M. "Narrative Style of *The Man of Law's Tale.*" *Medievalia et Humanistica* 8 (1977): 217–33.

Cohen, Jeffrey Jerome. "An Abecedarium for the Elements." *postmedieval: a journal of medieval cultural studies* 2 (2011): 291–303.

———. "Masoch/Lancelotism." *Medieval Identity Machines.* Minneapolis: University of Minnesota Press, 2003. 78–115.

———. *Stone: An Ecology of the Inhuman.* Minneapolis: University of Minnesota Press, 2015.

Coleman, Joyce. "The Flower, the Leaf, and Philippa of Lancaster." Collette, ed., *Legend of Good Women.* 33–58.

Coles, Kimberly Anne. " 'Perfect Hole': Elizabeth I, Spenser, and Chaste Productions." *English Literary Renaissance* 32 (2002): 31–61.

Collette, Carolyn P. "Chaucer and the French Tradition Revisited: Philippe de Mézières and the Good Wife." *Medieval Women: Texts and Contexts in Late Medieval Britain; Essays for Felicity Riddy.* Ed. Jocelyn Wogan-Browne, Rosalynn Voaden, Arlyn Diamond, Ann Hutchison, Carol Meale, and Lesley Johnson. Turnhout: Brepols, 2000. 151–68.

———. "Chaucer's Poetics and Purposes in the *Legend of Good Women.*" *Chaucer Review* 52 (2017): 12–28.

———. "Criseyde's Honor: Interiority and Public Identity in Chaucer's Courtly Romance." *Literary Aspects of Courtly Culture.* Rochester, NY: Boydell & Brewer, 1994. 47–55.

———, ed. *The Legend of Good Women: Context and Reception.* Cambridge: D. S. Brewer, 2006.

Colletti, Theresa. "*Paupertas est donum Dei*: Hagiography, Lay Religion, and the Economics of Salvation in the *Digby Mary Magdalene.*" *Speculum* 76 (2001): 337–78.

Collinson, Patrick. *The Religion of Protestants: The Church in English Society, 1559–1625*. Oxford: Clarendon Press, 1983.

Comensoli, Viviana. "Refashioning the Marriage Code: The *Patient Grissil* of Dekker, Chettle and Haughton." *Renaissance and Reformation/Renaissance et Reforme* 13 (1989): 199–214.

Connolly, William. *A World of Becoming*. Durham, NC: Duke University Press, 2011.

Cook, Megan. "Author, Text, and Paratext in Early Modern Editions of the *Legend of Good Women*." *Chaucer Review* 52 (2017): 124–42.

Cooper, Helen. *The English Romance in Time: Transforming Motifs from Geoffrey of Monmouth to the Death of Shakespeare*. Oxford: Oxford University Press, 2004.

———. "Gender and Personification in *Piers Plowman*." *Yearbook of Langland Studies* 5 (1991): 31–48.

Courtenay, William J. *Capacity and Volition: A History of the Distinction of Absolute and Ordained Power*. Bergamo: Perluigi Lubrina, 1990.

Craun, Edwin D. "Blaspheming Her 'Awin God': Cresseid's Lamentation in Henryson's *Testament*." *Studies in Philology* 82 (1985): 24–41.

Crocker, Holly A. "Engendering Shrews, Medieval to Early Modern." *Gender and Power in Shrew-Taming Narratives, 1500–1700*. Ed. David Wootton and Graham Holderness. London: Palgrave Macmillan, 2010. 48–69.

———. "Performative Passivity and Fantasies of Masculinity in the *Merchant's Tale*." *Chaucer Review* 38, no. 2 (2003): 178–98.

———. "The Premodern as Problem." *Journal of Early Modern Cultural Studies* 16 (2016): 139–45.

Cross, Richard. "Weakness and Grace." *The Cambridge History of Medieval Philosophy*. Ed. Robert Pasnau. Vol. 1. Cambridge: Cambridge University Press, 2010. 441–53.

Curry, Walter Clyde. *Chaucer and the Mediaeval Sciences*. Oxford: Oxford University Press, 1926.

Daileader, Celia R. *Eroticism on the Renaissance Stage: Transcendence, Desire, and the Limits of the Visible*. Cambridge: Cambridge University Press, 1998.

Danner, Bruce. "Courteous Virtù in Book 6 of the *Faerie Queene*." *Studies in English Literature, 1500–1900* 38 (1998): 1–18.

David, Alfred. "The Man of Law vs. Chaucer: A Case in Poetics." *PMLA* 82 (1967): 217–25.

Davis, Kathleen. "Time Behind the Veil: The Media, the Middle Ages, and Orientalism Now." *The Postcolonial Middle Ages*. Ed. Jeffrey Jerome Cohen. New York: Palgrave Macmillan, 2000. 105–22.

Davis, O. B. "A Note on the Function of Polonius' Advice." *Shakespeare Quarterly* 7 (1956): 275–76.

Dawson, Robert B. "Custance in Context: Rethinking the Protagonist of the *Man of Law's Tale*." *Chaucer Review* 26 (1992): 293–308.

Dees, Jerome S. "Spenser's Anti-Neoplatonism: The Evidence of Florimell." *Spenser: Classical, Medieval, Renaissance, and Modern*. Ed. David A. Richardson. Cleveland, OH: Cleveland State University Press, 1977. 271–305.

Delany, Sheila. *Impolitic Bodies: Poetry, Saints, and Society in Fifteenth-Century England; The Work of Osbern Bokenham*. Oxford: Oxford University Press, 1997.

———. *The Naked Text: Chaucer's "Legend of Good Women."* Berkeley: University of California Press, 1994.

———. "Womanliness in *The Man of Law's Tale*." *Chaucer Review* 9 (1974): 63–71.

Denny-Brown, Andrea. "Lydgate's Golden Cows: Appetite and Avarice in *Bycorne and Chychev-ache*." *Lydgate Matters: Poetry and Material Culture in the Fifteenth Century*. Ed. Lisa H. Cooper and Andrea Denny-Brown. New York: Palgrave Macmillan, 2007. 35–56.

Desmond, Marilynn R. "The *Translatio* of Memory and Desire in *The Legend of Good Women*: Chaucer and the Vernacular *Heroides*." *Studies in the Age of Chaucer* 35 (2013): 179–207.

Detmer, Emily. "Civilizing Subordination: Domestic Violence and *The Taming of the Shrew*." *Shakespeare Quarterly* 48 (1997): 273–94.

D'Evelyn, Charlotte, and Frances A. Foster. "Saints' Legends." *A Manual of the Writings in Middle English, 1050–1500*. Vol. 2. Ed. J. Burke Severs. Hamden, CT: Archon Books, 1970. 410–39, 553–65.

Dinshaw, Carolyn. "Afterword: Re-Reading, or, When You Were Mine." *Chaucer Review* 52 (2017): 162–66.

———. *Chaucer's Sexual Poetics*. Madison: University of Wisconsin Press, 1989.

———. "Pale Faces: Race, Religion, and Affect in Chaucer's Texts and Their Readers." *Studies in the Age of Chaucer* 23 (2001): 19–41.

Dolan, Frances E. "Battered Women, Petty Traitors, and the Legacy of Coverture." *Feminist Studies* 29 (2003): 249–77.

———. *Dangerous Familiars: Representations of Domestic Crime in England, 1550–1700*. Ithaca, NY: Cornell University Press, 1994.

———. *Marriage and Violence: The Early Modern Legacy*. Philadelphia: University of Pennsylvania Press, 2008.

Douglas, Mary. *Purity and Danger: An Analysis of Concepts of Pollution and Taboo*. London: Routledge, 2002.

Doyle, Laura. *The Surrendered Wife: A Practical Guide to Finding Intimacy, Passion, and Peace*. New York: Touchstone, 2001.

Driver, Martha. "Nuns as Patrons, Artists, Readers: Brigettine Woodcuts in Printed Books Produced for the English Market." *Art into Life: Collected Papers from the Kresge Art Museum Medieval Symposia*. Ed. Carol Garrett Fisher and Kathleen L. Scott. East Lansing: Michigan State University Press, 1995. 237–67.

Dronke, Peter. Introduction to *Ordo Virtutum: Nine Medieval Latin Plays*, by Hildegard of Bingen. Ed. and trans. Peter Dronke. Cambridge: Cambridge University Press, 1995.

Duffy, Eamon. "Holy Maydens, Holy Wyfes: The Cult of Women Saints in Fifteenth- and Sixteenth-Century England." *Studies in Church History* 27 (1990): 175–96.

———. *The Stripping of the Altars: Traditional Religion in England, c. 1400–1580*. New Haven, CT: Yale University Press, 1992.

Duhem, Pierre. *Medieval Cosmology: Theories of Infinity, Place, Time, Void, and the Plurality of Worlds*. Ed. and trans. Roger Ariew. Chicago: University of Chicago Press, 1985.

Dumitrescu, Irina. "Beautiful Suffering and the Culpable Narrator in Chaucer's *Legend of Good Women*." *Chaucer Review* 52 (2017): 106–23.

Dunworth, Felicity. "A 'Bosom Burnt Up with Desires': The Trials of Patient Griselda on the Elizabethan Stage." *Paragraph* 21 (1998): 330–53.

Dusinberre, Juliet. "*The Taming of the Shrew*: Women, Acting, Power." *Studies in the Literary Imagination* 26 (1993): 67–84.

Edmondson, George. "Henryson's Doubt: Neighbors and Negation in *The Testament of Cresseid*." *Exemplaria* 20 (2008): 165–96.

Edwards, A. S. G. "Lydgate's Attitudes to Women." *English Studies* 51 (1970): 436–37.

———. "The Transmission and Audience of Osbern Bokenham's *Legendys of Hooly Wummen*." *Late-Medieval Religious Texts and Their Transmission: Essays in Honour of A. I. Doyle*. Ed. A. J. Minnis. Cambridge: D. S. Brewer, 1994. 157–67.

Eggert, Katherine. *Showing Like a Queen: Female Authority and Literary Experiment in Spenser, Shakespeare, and Milton*. Philadelphia: University of Pennsylvania Press, 2000.

Elias, N. *The Civilizing Process: Sociogenetic and Psychogenetic Investigations*. Cambridge, MA: Blackwell, 2000.

Elliott, Dyan. *Proving Woman: Female Spirituality and Inquisitional Culture in the Later Middle Ages*. Princeton, NJ: Princeton University Press, 2004.

Engle, Lars. *Shakespearean Pragmatism: Market of His Time*. Chicago: University of Chicago Press, 1993.

Evans, Maurice. *Spenser's Anatomy of Heroism*. Cambridge: Cambridge University Press, 1970.

Ezell, Margaret J. M. *The Patriarch's Wife: Literary Evidence and the History of the Family*. Chapel Hill: University of North Carolina Press, 1987.

Falke, Anne. "The 'Marguerite' and the 'Margarita' in Thomas Lodge's *A Margarite of America*." *Neophilogus* 70 (1986): 142–54.

Feinstein, Sandy. "Shrews and Sheep in 'The Second Shepherd's Play.' " *Pacific Coast Philology* 36 (2001): 64–80.

Fineman, Joel. "The Turn of the Shrew." *Shakespeare and the Question of Theory*. Ed. Patricia Parker and Geoffrey Hartman. New York: Methuen, 1985. 139–59.

Fitzgerald, Christina. *The Drama of Masculinity and Medieval English Culture*. New York: Palgrave Macmillan, 2007.

Foot, Phillipa. *Natural Goodness*. Oxford: Oxford University Press, 2003.

Fox, Denton, ed. *Testament of Cresseid*. London: Thomas Nelson, 1968.

Fradenburg, L. O. Aranye. "Beauty and Boredom in *The Legend of Good Women*." *Exemplaria* 22 (2010): 65–83.

———. *Sacrifice Your Love: Psychoanalysis, Historicism, Chaucer*. Minneapolis: University of Minnesota Press, 2002.

Frank, R. W., Jr., *Chaucer and "The Legend of Good Women*." Cambridge, MA: Harvard University Press, 1972.

Frantz, David. O. "The Union of Florimell and Marinell: The Triumph of Hearing." *Spenser Studies* 6 (1986): 115–27.

Frede, Dorothea. "The Historic Decline of Virtue Ethics." D. C. Russell, ed., *Cambridge Companion to Virtue Ethics*. 124–48.

Freeman, Sonia Loftis. "Mary Pickford as Shakespearean Shrew: Redefining the Image of America's Sweetheart." *Shakespeare Bulletin: A Journal of Performance Criticism and Scholarship* 28 (2010): 331–45.

Freinkel, Lisa. *Reading Shakespeare's Will: The Theology of Figure from Augustine to the Sonnets*. New York: Columbia University Press, 2002.

Fumo, Jamie. "Books of the Duchess: Eleanor Cobham, Henryson's Cresseid, and the Politics of Complaint." *Viator* 37 (2006): 447–77.

Fyler, John. *Chaucer and Ovid*. New Haven, CT: Yale University Press, 1979.

Galloway, Andrew. "Chaucer's *Legend of Lucrece* and the Critique of Ideology in Fourteenth-Century England." *ELH* 60 (1993): 813–32.

Ganim, John. "Chaucerian Ritual and Patriarchal Romance." *Chaucer Yearbook* 1 (1992): 65–86.

Garner, Shirley Nelson. "The Taming of the Shrew: Inside or Outside the Joke?" *"Bad" Shakespeare: Revaluations of the Shakespeare Canon*. Ed. Maurice Charney. Rutherford, NJ: Fairleigh Dickinson University Press, 1988. 105–19.

Gellar, Lila. "The Acidalian Vision: Spenser's Graces in Book VI of *The Faerie Queene*." *Review of English Studies*, n.s., 23 (1972): 267–77.

———. "Venus and the Three Graces: A Neoplatonic Paradigm for Book III of *The Faerie Queene*." *Journal of English and Germanic Philology* 75 (1976): 56–74.

Getty, Laura J. "'Other smale ymaad before': Chaucer as Historiographer in the *Legend of Good Women*." *Chaucer Review* 42 (2007): 48–75.

Gil, Daniel Juan. *Before Intimacy: Asocial Sexuality in Early Modern England*. Minneapolis: University of Minnesota Press, 2006.

Goffman, Erving. *The Presentation of Self in Everyday Life*. New York: Anchor, 1957.

Goldberg, Jonathan. *Endlesse Work: Spenser and the Structures of Discourse*. Baltimore: Johns Hopkins University Press, 1981.

———. *James I and the Politics of Literature: Jonson, Shakespeare, Donne, and Their Contemporaries*. Baltimore: Johns Hopkins University Press, 1983.

———. *The Seeds of Things*. New York: Fordham University Press, 2009.

Goldstein, James. "Future Perfect: The Augustinian Theology of Perfection and the *Canterbury Tales*." *Studies in the Age of Chaucer* 29 (2007): 87–140.

Gowing, Laura. *Common Bodies: Women, Touch, and Power in Seventeenth-Century England*. New Haven, CT: Yale University Press, 2003.

Grady, Hugh. *Shakespeare's Universal World: Studies in Early Modern Reification*. Oxford: Clarendon Press, 1996.

Grant, Edward. *Planets, Stars, and Orbs: The Medieval Cosmos, 1200–1687*. Cambridge: Cambridge University Press, 1994.

Gravdal, Kathryn. *Ravishing Maidens: Writing Rape in Medieval French Literature and Law*. Philadelphia: University of Pennsylvania Press, 1991.

Gray, Douglas. "London, British Library, Additional MS 37049—A Spiritual Encyclopedia." *Text and Controversy from Wyclif to Bale*. Ed. Helen Barr and Ann M. Hutchinson. Turnhout: Brepols, 2005. 99–116.

Greco, Gina L., and Christine M. Rose. "Maid to Order: The Good Wife of Paris." *The Good Wife's Guide: "Le Ménagier de Paris"; A Medieval Household Book*. Ed. and trans. Gina L. Greco and Christine M. Rose. Ithaca, NY: Cornell University Press, 2009. 1–43.

Green, Richard F. "Chaucer's Victimized Women." *Studies in the Age of Chaucer* 10 (1988): 3–21.

Greenblatt, Stephen. J. *Shakespeare's Freedom*. Chicago: University of Chicago Press, 2010.

Greene, David Mason. "The Welsh Characters in *Patient Grissil*." *Boston University Studies in English* 4 (1960): 171–80.

Greene, Gayle. "Language and Value in Shakespeare's Troilus and Cressida." *Studies in English Literature, 1500–1900* 21 (1981): 271–85.

———. "Shakespeare's Cressida: 'A kind of self.'" *The Woman's Part: Feminist Criticism of Shakespeare*. Ed. Carolyn Ruth Swift Lenz, Gayle Greene, and Carol Neely. Urbana: University of Illinois Press, 1980. 133–49.

Gregerson, Linda. *The Reformation of the Subject: Spenser, Milton, and the English Protestant Epic*. Cambridge: Cambridge University Press, 1995.

Hackett, Helen. *Virgin Mother, Maiden Queen: Elizabeth I and the Cult of the Virgin Mary*. London: Macmillan, 1995.

Hagedorn, Suzanne. *Abandoned Women: Rewriting the Classics in Dante, Boccaccio, and Chaucer*. Ann Arbor: University of Michigan Press, 2004.

Haidu, Peter. *The Subject Medieval/Modern: Text and Governance in the Middle Ages*. Stanford, CA: Stanford University Press, 2004.

Haller, Mandeville, and William Haller. "The Puritan Art of Love." *Huntington Library Quarterly* 5 (1942): 235–72.

Hamburger, Jeffrey F., and Robert Suckale, "Between This World and the Next: The Art of Religious Women in the Middle Ages." *Crown and Veil: Female Monasticism from the Fifth to the Fifteenth Centuries*. Ed. Jeffrey Hamburger and Susan Marti. New York: Columbia University Press, 2008. 76–106.

Hamilton, A. C. "Our New Poet: Spenser 'Well of English Undefyld.' " *A Theatre for Spenserians*. Ed. Judith M. Kennedy and James A. Reither. Toronto: University of Toronto Press, 1973. 101–23.

———. *The Structure of Allegory in "The Faerie Queene."* Oxford: Clarendon Press, 1971.

Hanna, Ralph. "Cresseid's Dream and Henryson's *Testament*." *Chaucer and Middle English Studies in Honour of Rossell Hope Robbins*. Ed. Beryl Rowland and Lloyd A. Duchemin. London: Allen & Unwin, 1974. 288–97.

Hanning, Robert W. *The Individual in the Twelfth-Century Romance*. New Haven, CT: Yale University Press, 1977.

Hanrahan, M. "Seduction and Betrayal: Treason in the Prologue to the *Legend of Good Women*." *Chaucer Review* 30 (1996): 229–40.

Hansen, Elaine Tuttle. *Chaucer and the Fictions of Gender*. Berkeley: University of California Press, 1992.

———. "The Feminization of Men in Chaucer's *Legend of Good Women*." *Seeking the Woman in Late Medieval and Renaissance Writings: Essays in Feminist Contextual Criticism*. Ed. Sheila Fisher and Janet E. Halley. Knoxville: University of Tennessee Press, 1989. 51–70.

———. "Irony and the Antifeminist Narrator in Chaucer's *Legend of Good Women*." *Journal of English and Germanic Philology* 82 (1983): 11–31.

Harris, Jonathan Gil. *Sick Economies: Drama, Mercantilism, and Disease in Shakespeare's England*. Philadelphia: University of Pennsylvania Press, 2004.

Harris, Sharon M. "Feminism and Shakespeare's Cressida: 'If I be false . . .' " *Women's Studies* 18 (1990): 65–82.

Hartwig, Joan. "Horses and Women in *The Taming of the Shrew*." *Huntington Library Quarterly* 45 (1982): 285–94.

Heffernan, Thomas J. *Sacred Biography: Saints and Their Biographers in the Middle Ages*. Oxford: Oxford University Press, 1998.

Heilman, Robert. "Taming the Untamed, or, The Return of the Shrew." *Modern Language Quarterly* 27 (1966): 14–61.

Helgerson, Richard. *Forms of Nationhood: The Elizabethan Writing of England*. Chicago: University of Chicago Press, 1992.

———. *Self-Crowned Laureates: Spenser, Jonson, Milton, and the Literary System*. Berkeley: University of California Press, 1983.

Heng, Geraldine. *Empire of Magic: Medieval Romance and the Politics of Cultural Fantasy*. New York: Columbia University Press, 2003.

Herdt, Jennifer A. *Putting on Virtue: The Legacy of the Splendid Vices*. Chicago: University of Chicago Press, 2008.

Hile, Rachel. "Disability and the Characterization of Katherine in *The Taming of the Shrew*." *Disability Studies Quarterly* 29 (2009): n.p.

Hilles, Carol. "Gender and Politics in Osbern Bokenham's *Legendary*." *New Medieval Literatures* 4 (2001): 189–212.

Hodgdon, Barbara. "He Do Cressida in Different Voices." *English Literary Renaissance* 20 (1990): 254–86.

Holthausen, F. "Rezepte, Segen u. Zauber-sprüche aus zwei Stockh. Hss." *Anglia* 19 (1897): 75–88.

Honig, Bonnie. *Antigone, Interrupted*. Cambridge: Cambridge University Press, 2013.

———. "Antigone's Two Laws: Greek Tragedy and the Politics of Humanism." *New Literary History* 41 (2010): 1–33.

Hoopes, Robert. " 'God Guide Thee, Guyon': Nature and Grace Reconciled in *The Faerie Queene*, Book II." *Review of English Studies*, n.s., 5 (1954): 14–24.

Hough, Graham. *A Preface to 'The Faerie Queene.'* New York: W. W. Norton, 1963.

Howard, Donald. "Chaucer the Man." *PMLA* 80 (1965): 337–43.

Hoy, Cyrus. *Introductions, Notes, and Commentaries to Texts in 'The Dramatic Works of Thomas Dekker.'* Ed. Fredson Bowers. Vol. 1. Cambridge: Cambridge University Press, 1980. 129–31.

Hudson, Anne. *The Premature Reformation: Wycliffite Texts and Lollard History*. Oxford: Clarendon Press, 1988.

Hull, Suzanne. *Chaste, Silent and Obedient: English Books for Women, 1475–1640*. San Marino, CA: Huntington Library, 1982.

———. *Women According to Men: The World of Tudor-Stuart Women*. New York: Altamira, 1996.

Hume, Anthea. *Edmund Spenser: Protestant Poet*. Cambridge: Cambridge University Press, 1984.

Hunter, G. K. "Isocrates' Precepts and Polonius' Character." *Shakespeare Quarterly* 8 (1957): 501–6.

Hursthouse, Rosalind. *On Virtue Ethics*. Oxford: Oxford University Press, 2001.

Jacobs, Kathryn. "Mate or Mother: Positioning Criseyde Among Chaucer's Widows." *New Perspectives on Criseyde*. Ed. Cindy L. Vitto and Marcia Smith Marzec. Asheville, NC: Pegasus Press, 2004. 59–73.

Jacquart, Danielle, and Claude Thomasset. *Sexuality and Medicine in the Middle Ages*. Trans. Matthew Adamson. Princeton, NJ: Princeton University Press, 1988. 177–94.

James, Heather. *Shakespeare's Troy: Drama, Politics, and the Translation of Empire*. Cambridge: Cambridge University Press, 1997.

James, M. R., and E. W. Tristram. "The Wall Paintings in Eton College Chapel and in the Lady Chapel of Winchester Cathedral." *Walpole Society* 17 (1928–29): 1–43.

Jansen, Katherine Ludwig. *The Making of the Magdalen: Preaching and Popular Devotion in the Later Middle Ages*. Princeton, NJ: Princeton University Press, 2000.

Jardine, Lisa. *Still Harping on Daughters: Women and Drama in the Age of Shakespeare*. Totowa, NJ: Barnes and Noble, 1983.

Jenkins, Jacqueline. "Lay-Devotion and Women Readers of the Middle English Prose Life of St. Katherine (MS. Harley 4012)." *Saint Katherine of Alexandria: Texts and Contexts in Western Medieval Europe*. Ed. Katherine J. Lewis and Jacqueline Jenkins. Turnhout: Brepols, 2003. 53–170.

———. "Reading Women Reading: Feminism, Culture, and Memory." *Maistresse of My Wit: Medieval Women, Modern Scholars*. Ed. Louse D'Arcens and Juanita Feros Ruys. Turnhout: Brepols, 2004. 317–34.

Johnson, Eleanor. *Practicing Literary Theory in the Middle Ages: Ethics and the Mixed Form in Chaucer, Gower, Usk, and Hoccleve*. Chicago: University of Chicago Press, 2013.

Jones, Ann Rosalind, and Peter Stallybrass. "The Politics of Astrophil and Stella." *Studies in English Literature, 1500–1900* 24 (1984): 53–68.

———. *Renaissance Clothing and the Materials of Memory*. Cambridge: Cambridge University Press, 2000.

Jones, E. A. "Literature of Religious Instruction." *A Companion to Medieval English Literature and Culture, c. 1350–c. 1500*. Ed. Peter Brown. London: Wiley-Blackwell, 2009. 406–22.

Jones, Malcolm. "'Such pretty things would soon be gone': The Neglected Genres of Popular Verse, 1480–1650." *A Companion to English Renaissance Literature and Culture*. Ed. Michael Hattaway. London: Blackwell, 2000. 442–63.

Justice, Steven. "Who Stole Robertson?" *PMLA* 124 (2009): 609–15.

Kahn, Coppèlia. *Man's Estate: Masculine Identity in Shakespeare*. Berkeley: University of California Press, 1981.

Kantorowitz, Ernst. *The King's Two Bodies: A Study in Medieval Political Theology*. Princeton, NJ: Princeton University Press, 1957.

Kaske, Carol. "Hallmarks of Platonism and the Sons of Agape (*Faerie Queene* IV, ii–iv)." *Spenser Studies* 24 (2009): 15–71.

Katzenellenbogen, Adolf. *Allegories of the Virtues and Vices in Mediaeval Art: From Early Christian Times to the Thirteenth Century*. London: Warburg Institute, 1939.

Kelly, Henry Ansgar. *Chaucerian Tragedy*. Cambridge: D. S. Brewer, 1997.

Kelly, Kathleen Coyne. *Performing Virginity and Testing Chastity in the Middle Ages*. London: Routledge, 2002.

Kelso, Ruth. *Doctrine for the Lady of the Renaissance*. 1956. Reprint, Urbana: University of Illinois Press, 1978.

Kent, Bonnie. "Rethinking Moral Dispositions: Scotus on the Virtues." *Cambridge Companion to Duns Scotus*. Ed. Thomas Williams. Cambridge: Cambridge University Press, 2003. 352–76.

———. "Virtue Theory." *The Cambridge History of Medieval Philosophy*. Vol. 1. Ed. Robert Pasnau. Cambridge: Cambridge University Press, 2010. 493–505.

———. *Virtues of the Will: The Transformation of Ethics in the Late Thirteenth Century*. Washington, DC: Catholic University of America Press, 1995.

Kevan, Ernest F. *The Grace of Law: A Study in Puritan Theology*. London: Carey Kingsgate Press, 1964.

Keyishian, Harry. "Griselda on the Elizabethan Stage: The *Patient Grissil* of Chettle, Dekker, and Haughton." *Studies in English Literature, 1500–1900* 16 (1976): 253–61.

King, John N. *Spenser's Poetry and the Reformation Tradition*. Princeton, NJ: Princeton University Press, 1990.

Kiser, Lisa J. *Telling Classical Tales: Chaucer's "Legend of Good Women."* Ithaca, NY: Cornell University Press, 1983.

Kisor, Yvette. "Moments of Silence, Acts of Speech: Uncovering the Incest Motif in the *Man of Law's Tale*." *Chaucer Review* 40 (2005): 141–62.

Knapp, James A. *Image Ethics in Shakespeare and Spenser*. New York: Palgrave Macmillan, 2011.

Kolve, V. A. *Chaucer and the Imagery of Narrative: The First Five Canterbury Tales*. Stanford, CA: Stanford University Press, 1984.

———. "From Cleopatra to Alceste: An Iconographic Study of the *Legend of Good Women*." *Signs and Symbols in Chaucer's Poetry*. Ed. J. P. Hermann and J. J. Burke. Tuscaloosa: University of Alabama Press, 1981. 130–78.

Korda, Natasha. "Household Kates: Domesticating Commodities in *The Taming of the Shrew.*" *Shakespeare Quarterly* 47 (1996): 109–31.

———. *Shakespeare's Domestic Economies: Gender and Property in Early Modern England.* Philadelphia: University of Pennsylvania Press, 2002.

Krug, Rebecca. *Reading Families: Women's Literate Practice in Late Medieval England.* Ithaca, NY: Cornell University Press, 2002.

Kruger, Steven F. *Dreaming in the Middle Ages.* Cambridge: Cambridge University Press, 1992.

Kuzner, James A. *Open Subjects: English Renaissance Republicans, Modern Selfhoods and the Virtue of Vulnerability.* Edinburgh Critical Studies in Renaissance Culture. Edinburgh: Edinburgh University Press, 2011.

Lacan, Jacques. *The Ethics of Psychoanalysis, 1959–60: The Seminar of Jacques Lacan, Book VII.* Ed. Jacques-Alain Miller. Trans. Dennis Porter. New York: W. W. Norton, 1997.

———. *The Four Fundamental Concepts of Psychoanalysis: The Seminar of Jacques Lacan, Book XI.* Ed. Jacques-Alain Miller. Trans. Alan Sheridan. New York: W. W. Norton, 1998.

Laird, Judith. "Good Women and *Bonnes Dames*: Virtuous Females in Chaucer and Christine de Pizan." *Chaucer Review* 30 (1995): 58–70.

Lamb, Mary Ellen. *The Popular Culture of Shakespeare, Spenser, and Jonson.* London: Routledge, 2006.

Laroche, Rebecca. "Ophelia's Plants and the Death of Violets." *Ecocritical Shakespeare.* Ed. Lynne Bruckner and Daniel Brayton. Burlington, VT: Ashgate, 2011. 211–22.

Larsen, Wendy S. "Who Is the Master of This Narrative?: Maternal Patronage of the Cult of St. Margaret." *Gendering the Master Narrative.* Ed. Mary C. Erler and Maryanne Kowaleski. Ithaca, NY: Cornell University Press, 2003. 94–104.

Latour, Bruno. *Reassembling the Social: An Introduction to Actor-Network-Theory.* Oxford: Oxford University Press, 2007.

Lavezzo, Kathy. "Beyond Rome: Mapping Gender and Justice in the *Man of Law's Tale.*" *Studies in the Age of Chaucer* 24 (2002): 149–80.

Lawton, David. "Dullness and the Fifteenth Century." *ELH* 54 (1987): 761–99.

Lerer, Seth. *Chaucer and His Readers: Imagining the Author in Late-Medieval England.* Princeton, NJ: Princeton University Press, 1993.

Levin, Richard. *The Multiple Plot in English Renaissance Drama.* Chicago: Chicago University Press, 1971.

Lewis, C. S. *English Literature in the Sixteenth Century, Excluding Drama.* Oxford: Clarendon Press, 1954.

Lewis, Katherine J. *The Cult of St. Katherine of Alexandria in Late Medieval England.* Woodbridge: Boydell & Brewer, 2000.

———. "Model Girls?: Virgin-Martyrs and the Training of Young Women in Late Medieval England." *Young Medieval Women.* Ed. Katherine J. Lewis, Noël James Menuge, and Kim M. Phillips. New York: St. Martin's Press, 1999. 25–46.

Lezra, Jacques, and Liza Blake, eds. *Lucretius and Modernity: Epicurean Encounters Across Time and Disciplines.* New York: Palgrave Macmillan, 2016.

Lifshitz, Felice. "Beyond Positivism and Genre: Hagiographical Texts as Historical Narrative." *Viator* 25 (1994): 95–113.

Lilley, Keith D. *City and Cosmos: The Medieval World in Urban Form.* London: Reaktion Books, 2009.

Linton, Joan Pong. *The Romance of the New World.* Cambridge: Cambridge University Press, 1998.

Lowes, John Livingston. "Chaucer and the Seven Deadly Sins." *PMLA* 30 (1915): 237–371.

Lupton, Julia Reinhardt. *Thinking with Shakespeare: Essays on Politics and Life.* Chicago: University of Chicago Press, 2011.

Lynch, Kathryn L. *Chaucer's Philosophical Visions.* Cambridge: D. S. Brewer, 2000.

Lyte, H. C. Maxwell. *A History of Eton College, 1440–1875.* London: Macmillan, 1877.

MacIntyre, Alasdair. *After Virtue: A Study in Moral Theory.* 2nd ed. South Bend, IN: University of Notre Dame Press, 1984.

———. *Dependent Rational Animals: Why Human Beings Need the Virtues.* The Paul Carus Lectures. Chicago: Open Court Press, 1999.

———. *Whose Justice? Which Rationality?* South Bend, IN: University of Notre Dame Press, 1989.

Maguire, Laurie E. "'Household Kates': Chez Petruchio, Percy and Plantagenet." *Gloriana's Face: Women, Public and Private, in the English Renaissance.* Ed. S. P. Cerasano and Marion Wynne-Davies. Detroit, MI: Wayne State University Press, 1992. 129–65.

Maidstone, Richard. "Concordia facta inter regem Riccardum II et civitatem Londonie Per Fratrum Riccardum Maydiston, Carmelitum, Sacre theologie Doctorem, Anno Domine 1393." Ed. and trans. Charles Roger Smith. PhD diss., Princeton University, 1972.

Mâle, Émile. *Religious Art in France: The Late Middle Ages; A Study of Medieval Iconography and Its Sources.* Ed. Harry Bober. Trans. Marthiel Mathews. Princeton, NJ: Princeton University Press, 1986.

Mallette, Richard. *Spenser and the Discourses of Reformation England.* Lincoln, NE: University of Nebraska Press, 1997.

Mann, Jill. *Geoffrey Chaucer.* Atlantic Highlands, NJ: Humanities Press, 1991.

———. "The Planetary Gods in Chaucer and Henryson." *Chaucer Traditions: Studies in Honor of Derek Brewer.* Ed. Ruth Morse and Barry Windeatt. Cambridge: Cambridge University Press, 1990. 91–106.

Mansfield, Harvey C. *Machiavelli's Virtue.* Chicago: University of Chicago Press, 1966.

Mapstone, Sally. "The Origins of Criseyde." *Medieval Women: Texts and Contexts in Late Medieval Britain; Essays for Felicity Riddy.* Ed. Jocelyn Wogan-Browne, Rosalynn Voaden, Arlyn Diamond, Ann Hutchison, Carol Meale, and Lesley Johnson. Turnhout: Brepols, 2000. 131–47.

Marcus, Leah S. *Unediting the Renaissance: Shakespeare, Marlowe, Milton.* New York: Routledge, 1996.

Marenbon, John. "When Was Medieval Philosophy?" Inaugural lecture, University of Cambridge, Faculty of Philosophy, November 30, 2011. 1–11. http://www.sms.cam.ac.uk/media/1191806.

Margherita, Gayle. "Criseyde's Remains: Romance and the Question of Justice." *Exemplaria* 12 (2000): 257–92.

Martin, Priscilla. *Chaucer's Women: Nuns, Wives, and Amazons.* London: Macmillan, 1990.

Martindale, Andrew. "The Wall-Paintings in the Chapel of Eton College." *England and the Low Countries in the Late Middle Ages.* Ed. Caroline Barron and Nigel Saul. New York: St. Martin's Press, 1995. 133–52.

Massumi, Brian. *Parables for the Virtual: Movement, Affect, Sensation.* Durham, NC: Duke University Press, 2002.

Mathews, Jana. "Land, Lepers, and the Law in *The Testament of Cresseid.*" *The Letter of the Law: Legal Practice and Literary Production in Medieval England.* Ed. Emily Steiner and Candace Barrington. Ithaca, NY: Cornell University Press, 2002. 40–66.

Matter, E. Ann. "Passions and Ecstasies of Late Medieval Religious Women." *The Representation of Women's Emotions in Medieval and Early Modern Culture.* Ed. Lisa Perfetti. Gainesville: University Press of Florida, 2005. 22–42.

Maus, Katharine Eisaman. *Inwardness and Theater in the English Renaissance.* Chicago: University of Chicago Press, 1995.

McAlpine, Monica. "Criseyde's Prudence." *Studies in the Age of Chaucer* 25 (2003): 119–224.

McCash, June Hall, ed. *The Cultural Patronage of Medieval Women.* Athens: University of Georgia Press, 1996.

McCormick, Betsy. "Remembering the Game: Debating the *Legend*'s Women." Collette, ed., *Legend of Good Women.* 105–31.

McCormick, Betsy, Leah Schwebel, and Lynn Shutters. "Introduction: Looking Forward, Looking Back on the *Legend of Good Women.*" *Chaucer Review* 52 (2017): 3–11.

McDonald, Nicola F. "Chaucer's *Legend of Good Women*, Ladies at Court, and the Female Reader." *Chaucer Review* 35 (2000): 22–42.

———. "Games Medieval Women Play." Collette, ed., *Legend of Good Women.* 176–97.

McGrath, Alister E. *The Intellectual Origins of the European Reformation.* 2nd ed. Oxford: Blackwell, 2004.

———. *Iustitia Dei: A History of the Christian Doctrine of Justification.* Vol. 1, *From the Beginnings to 1500.* Cambridge: Cambridge University Press, 1986.

———. *Luther's Theology of the Cross.* Oxford: Basil Blackwell, 1985.

McInerney, Maud. *Eloquent Virgins from Thecla to Joan of Arc.* New York: Palgrave Macmillan, 2003.

McLeod, Glenda. *Virtue and Venom: Catalogs of Women from Antiquity to the Renaissance.* Ann Arbor: University of Michigan Press, 1991.

McLuskie, Kathleen. *Dekker and Heywood: Professional Dramatists.* London: Palgrave MacMillan, 1994.

———. *Renaissance Dramatists: Feminist Readings.* London: Harvester Wheatsheaf, 1989.

McNamer, Sarah. *Affective Meditation and the Invention of Medieval Compassion.* Philadelphia: University of Pennsylvania Press, 2010.

McSheffrey, Shannon. *Gender and Heresy: Women and Men in Lollard Communities, 1420–1530.* Philadelphia: University of Pennsylvania Press, 1995.

McTaggart, Anne. "Shamed Guiltless: Criseyde, Dido, and Chaucerian Ethics." *Chaucer Review* 46 (2012): 371–402.

Meale, Carol M. "'. . . alle the bokes that I haue of latyn, englisch, and frensch': Laywomen and Their Books in Late Medieval England." *Women and Literature in Britain, 1150–1500.* Ed. Carol M. Meale. Cambridge: Cambridge University Press, 1993. 128–58.

———. "Legends of Good Women in the European Middle Ages." *Archiv für das Studium der neueren Sprachen und Literaturen* 229 (1992): 55–70.

Meecham-Jones, Simon. "Intention, Integrity, and 'Renoun': The Public Virtue of Chaucer's Good Women." Collette, ed., *Legend of Good Women.* 132–56.

Meyer-Lee, Robert. J. "The Emergence of the Literary in John Lydgate's *Life of Our Lady.*" *Journal of English and Germanic Philology* 109 (2010): 322–48.

———. *Poets and Power from Chaucer to Wyatt.* Cambridge: Cambridge University Press, 2007.

Middleton, Anne. "Chaucer's 'New Men' and the Good of Literature in the *Canterbury Tales.*" *Chaucer, Langland, and Fourteenth-Century Literary History.* Ed. Steven Justice. Variorum Collected Studies. Burlington, VT: Ashgate, 2013. 27–60.

Mieszcowski, Gretchen. "The Reputation of Criseyde, 1155–1500." *Transactions of the Connecticut Academy of the Arts and Sciences* 43 (1971): 71–153.

Miller, David Lee. "The Chastity of Allegory: The Kathleen Williams Lecture, 2014." *Spenser Studies: A Renaissance Poetry Annual* 39 (2014): 1–20.

Miller, Mark. *Philosophical Chaucer: Love, Sex, and Agency in the "Canterbury Tales."* Cambridge: Cambridge University Press, 2007.

Miller, Shannon. "'Mirrours More Then One': Edmund Spenser and Female Authority in the Seventeenth Century." *Worldmaking Spenser: Explorations in the Early Modern Age.* Ed. Patrick Cheney and Lauren Silberman. Lexington: University of Kentucky Press, 1999. 125–47.

Millett, Bella. "The Audience of the Saints' Lives of the Katherine Group." *Reading Medieval Studies* 16 (1990): 127–55.

Mills, Robert. *Suspended Animation: Pain, Pleasure and Punishment in Medieval Culture.* London: Reaktion, 2005.

———. "'Whatever you do is a delight to me!': Masculinity, Masochism, and Queer Play in Representations of Male Martyrdom." *Exemplaria* 13 (2001): 1–37.

Minnis, Alastair. *Oxford Guides to Chaucer: The Shorter Poems.* Oxford: Clarendon Press, 1995.

Mitchell, J. Allen. *Ethics and Eventfulness in Middle English Literature.* New York: Palgrave Macmillan, 2009.

Montrose, Louis. "Spenser and the Elizabethan Political Imaginary." *ELH* 69 (2002): 907–46.

Morgan, Gerald. "Chaucer's Man of Law and the Argument for Providence." *Review of English Studies* 61 (2010): 1–33.

Moriarty, Michael. *Disguised Vices: Theories of Virtue in Early Modern French Thought.* Oxford: Oxford University Press, 2011.

Morris, Colin. *The Discovery of the Individual, 1050–1200.* New York: Harper and Row, 1972.

Morrison, Karl. F. *The Mimetic Tradition of Reform in the West.* Princeton, NJ: Princeton University Press, 1982.

Morton, Timothy B. *Humankind: Solidarity with Nonhuman People.* London: Verso, 2017.

Moss, Daniel. "Spenser's Despair and God's Grace." *Spenser Studies* 23 (2008): 73–102.

Murdoch, Iris. *The Sovereignty of Good.* 1970. Reprint, London: Routledge, 1991.

Nakley, Susan. "Sovereignty Matters: Anachronism, Chaucer's Britain, and England's Future's Past." *Chaucer Review* 44 (2010): 368–96.

Nancy, Jean-Luc. *Listening.* Trans. Charlotte Mandell. New York: Fordham, 2007.

Nebeker, Eric. "Broadside Ballads, Miscellanies, and the Lyric in Print." *ELH* 76 (2009): 989–1013.

Nelson, Ingrid. "Premodern Media and Networks of Transmission in the *Man of Law's Tale*." *Exemplaria* 25 (2013): 211–30.

Newhauser, Richard. *The Treatise on Vices and Virtues in Latin and the Vernacular.* Turnhout: Brepols, 1993.

Newhauser, Richard, and I. P. Bejczy, eds. *A Supplement to Morton W. Bloomfield et al., 'Incipits of Latin Works on the Virtues and Vices, 1100–1500 A.D.'* Turnhout: Brepols, 2008.

Newman, Barbara. *From Virile Woman to Woman-Christ: Studies in Medieval Religion and Literature.* Philadelphia: University of Pennsylvania Press, 1995.

———. *God and the Goddesses: Vision, Poetry, and Belief in the Middle Ages.* Philadelphia: University of Pennsylvania Press, 2005.

———. *Sister of Wisdom: St. Hildegard's Theology of the Feminine.* Berkeley: University of California Press, 1987.

Newman, Karen. *Fashioning Femininity and English Renaissance Drama*. Chicago: University of Chicago Press, 1991.

Nicholls, Jonathan. *The Matter of Courtesy: Medieval Courtesy Books and the Gawain Poet*. London: D. S. Brewer, 1985.

Nolan, Maura B. *John Lydgate and the Making of Public Culture*. Cambridge: Cambridge University Press, 2005.

———. "Lydgate's Worst Poem." *Lydgate Matters: Poetry and Material Culture in the Fifteenth Century*. Ed. Lisa H. Cooper and Andrea Denny-Brown. New York: Palgrave Macmillan, 2007. 71–88.

———. " 'Now Wo, Now Gladnesse': Ovidianism in the *Fall of Princes*." *ELH* 71 (2004): 531–58.

Norhnberg, James. *The Analogy of 'The Faerie Queene.'* Princeton, NJ: Princeton University Press, 1976.

Novy, Mariane. *Love's Argument: Gender Relations in Shakespeare*. Chapel Hill: University of North Carolina Press, 1984.

Nowlin, Steele. "The *Legend of Good Women* and the Affect of Invention." *Exemplaria* 25 (2013): 16–35.

Nunn, Hillary M. "Playing with Appetite in Early Modern Comedy." *Shakespearean Sensations: Experiencing Literature in Early Modern England*. Ed. Katherina A. Kraik and Tanya Pollard. Cambridge: Cambridge University Press, 2013. 101–17.

Nussbaum, Martha. *The Fragility of Goodness: Luck and Ethics in Greek Tragedy and Philosophy*. Cambridge: Cambridge University Press, 1986.

———. *Frontiers of Justice: Disability, Nationality, Species Membership*. Cambridge, MA: Harvard University Press, 2007.

Oberman, Heiko. *Forerunners of the Reformation: The Shape of Late Medieval Thought*. London: Lutterworth Press, 1967.

———. *The Harvest of Medieval Theology*. Cambridge, MA: Harvard University Press, 1963.

Oram, William Allan. *Edmund Spenser*. New York: Twayne, 1997.

Orgel, Stephen. *Impersonations: The Performance of Gender in Shakespeare's England*. Cambridge: Cambridge University Press, 1996.

Orlin, Lena Cowen. *Private Matters and Public Culture in Post-Reformation England*. Ithaca, NY: Cornell University Press, 1994.

Owst, G. R. *Literature and the Pulpit in Medieval England*. 2nd ed. Oxford: Basil Blackwell, 1961.

Ozment, Steven E. *The Age of Reform (1250–1550): An Intellectual and Religious History of Late Medieval and Reformation Europe*. New Haven, CT: Yale University Press, 1980.

———. *When Fathers Ruled: Family Life in Reformation Europe*. 6th ed. Cambridge, MA: Harvard University Press, 1985.

Panek, Jennifer. *Widows and Suitors in Early Modern English Comedy*. Cambridge: Cambridge University Press, 2004.

Parker, Patricia. *Inescapable Romance: Studies in the Poetics of a Mode*. Princeton, NJ: Princeton University Press, 1979.

Parr, Johnstone. "Cresseid's Leprosy Again." *Modern Language Notes* 60 (1945): 487–91.

Patterson, Lee. "Christian and Pagan in *The Testament of Cresseid*." *Philological Quarterly* 52 (1973): 696–714.

———. "Making Identities in Fifteenth-Century England: Henry V and John Lydgate." *New Historicist Literary Study*. Ed. Jeffrey N. Cox and Larry J. Reynolds. Princeton, NJ: Princeton University Press, 1993. 69–107.

Paull, Michael R. "The Influence of the Saint's Legend Genre in the 'Man of Law's Tale.'" *Chaucer Review* 5 (1971): 179–94.

Pearsall, Derek. *John Lydgate*. London: Routledge and Kegan Paul, 1970.

———. "Lydgate as Innovator." *Modern Language Quarterly* 53 (1992): 5–22.

———. "'Quha wait gif all that Chaucer wrait was trew?': Henryson's *Testament of Cresseid*." *New Perspectives on Middle English Texts: A Festschrift for R. A. Waldron*. Ed. Susan Powell and Jeremy J. Smith. Cambridge: D. S. Brewer, 2000. 169–82.

Pechter, Edward. "*Patient Grissil* and the Trials of Marriage." *The Elizabethan Theatre*. Vol. 14. Ed. A. L. Magnusson and C. E. McGee. Toronto: Meany, 1996. 83–108.

Percival, Florence. *Chaucer's Legendary Good Women*. Cambridge: Cambridge University Press, 1998.

Phillips, Helen. "Morality in the 'Canterbury Tales,' Chaucer's Lyrics, and the *Legend of Good Women*." *Chaucer and Religion*. Ed. Helen Phillips. Cambridge: D. S. Brewer, 2010. 156–72.

———"Register, Politics, and the *Legend of Good Women*." *Chaucer Review* 37 (2002): 101–28.

Phillips, Kim M. "Maidenhood as the Perfect Age of Woman's Life." *Young Medieval Women*. Ed. Katherine J. Lewis, Noël James Menuge, and Kim M. Phillips. New York: St. Martin's Press, 1999. 1–24.

Pickering, Oliver. "Saints' Lives." *A Companion to Middle English Prose*. Ed. A. S. G. Edwards. Cambridge: D. S. Brewer, 2004. 249–70.

Pink, Thomas. *Free Will: A Very Short Introduction*. Oxford: Oxford University Press, 2004.

Plummer, John F. "The Logomachy of the N-Town Passion Play I." *Journal of English and Germanic Philology* 88 (1989): 311–31.

Pocock, J. G. A. *The Machiavellian Moment: Florentine Political Thought and the Atlantic Republican Tradition*. 1975. Reprint, Princeton, NJ: Princeton University Press, 2003.

Pollack, Claudette. "Lodge's *A Margarite of America*: A Renaissance Medley." *Renaissance and Reformation* 12 (1976): 1–11.

Pollard, Tanya. "What's Hecuba to Shakespeare?" *Renaissance Quarterly* 65 (2012): 1060–93.

Pomeroy, Elizabeth W. *The Elizabethan Miscellanies: Their Development and Conventions*. Berkeley: University of California Press, 1973.

Porter, Jean. "Virtue Ethics in the Medieval Period." D. C. Russell, ed., *Cambridge Companion to Virtue Ethics*. 70–91.

Potter, Ursula. "Tales of Patient Griselda and Henry VIII." *Early Theatre* 5 (2002): 11–28.

Prescott, Anne Lake. "Complicating the Allegory: Spenser and Religion in Recent Scholarship." *Renaissance and Reformation / Renaissance et Réforme* 25, no. 4 (2001): 9–23.

Quilligan, Maureen. *Milton's Spenser: The Politics of Reading*. Ithaca, NY: Cornell University Press, 1979.

Ramachandran, Ayesha. "Edmund Spenser, Lucretian Neoplatonist: Cosmology in the *Fowre Hymnes*." *Spenser Studies* 24 (2009): 373–411.

Ranald, Margaret Loftus. "The Performance of Feminism in *The Taming of the Shrew*." *The Taming of the Shrew: Critical Essays*. Ed. Dana E. Aspinall. London: Routledge, 2002. 318–30.

Rancière, Jacques. *The Politics of Aesthetics: The Distribution of the Sensible*. Trans. Gabriel Rockhill. London: Continuum, 2004.

Raskolnikov, Masha. *Body Against Soul: Gender and "Sowlehele" in Middle English Allegory*. Columbus: Ohio State University Press, 2009.

Raybin, David. "Custance and History: Woman as Outsider in Chaucer's 'Man of Law's Tale.'" *Studies in the Age of Chaucer* 12 (1990): 60–82.

Rebhorn, Wayne A. "Petruchio's 'Rope Tricks': *The Taming of the Shrew* and the Renaissance Discourse of Rhetoric." *Modern Philology* 92 (1995): 294–327.

Rees, Valery. "Ficinian Ideas in the Poetry of Edmund Spenser." *Spenser Studies* 24 (2009): 73–134.

Regan, Tom. *The Case for Animal Rights*. 1983. Reprint, Berkeley: University of California Press, 2004.

Renoir, Alain. *The Poetry of John Lydgate*. London: Routledge and K. Paul, 1967.

Rhodes, Jim. *Poetry Does Theology: Chaucer, Grosseteste, and the Pearl-Poet*. South Bend, IN: University of Notre Dame Press, 2001.

Riddy, Felicity. "'Abject Odious': Feminine and Masculine in Henryson's *Testament of Cresseid*." *Chaucer to Spenser: A Critical Reader*. Ed. Derek Pearsall. Oxford: Blackwell, 1999. 280–96.

———. "Middle English Romance: Family, Marriage, Intimacy." *The Cambridge Companion to Medieval Romance*. Ed. Roberta Krueger. Cambridge: Cambridge University Press, 2000. 235–52.

———. "Mother Knows Best: Reading Social Change in a Courtesy Text." *Speculum* 71 (1996): 66–86.

———. "'Women Talking About the Things of God': A Late Medieval Sub-Culture." *Women and Literature in Britain, 1150–1500*. Ed. Carole Meale. Cambridge: Cambridge University Press, 1993. 104–27.

Ritchey, Sara. *Holy Matter: Changing Perceptions of the Material World in Late Medieval Christianity*. Ithaca, NY: Cornell University Press, 2014.

Roberts, Josephine A. "Lodge's *A Margarite of America*: A Dystopian Vision of the New World." *Studies in Short Fiction* 17 (1980): 407–14.

Robertson, D. W., Jr. *A Preface to Chaucer: Studies in Medieval Perspectives*. Princeton, NJ: Princeton University Press, 1962.

Robertson, Elizabeth. *Early English Devotional Prose and the Female Audience*. Knoxville: University of Tennessee Press, 1990.

———. "The 'Elvyssh' Power of Constance: Christian Feminism in Geoffrey Chaucer's *The Man of Law's Tale*." *Studies in the Age of Chaucer* 23 (2001): 143–80.

———. "Public Bodies and Psychic Domains: Rape, Consent, and Female Subjectivity in Geoffrey Chaucer's *Troilus and Criseyde*." *Representing Rape in Medieval and Early Modern Literature*. Ed. E. Robertson and C. M. Rose. New York: Palgrave Macmillan, 2001. 281–310.

Roche, Thomas P., Jr. *The Kindly Flame: A Study of the Third and Fourth Books of Spenser's "Faerie Queene."* Princeton, NJ: Princeton University Press, 1964.

Rollins, Hyder. "The Troilus-Cressida Story from Chaucer to Shakespeare." *PMLA* 32 (1917): 383–429.

Rose, Mary Beth. *Gender and Heroism in Early Modern English Literature*. Chicago: University of Chicago Press, 2001.

Rosenfeld, Jessica. "The Doubled Joys of *Troilus and Criseyde*." *The Erotics of Consolation: Desire and Distance in the Middle Ages*. New York: Palgrave Macmillan, 2008. 39–59.

Rubin, Gayle. "The Traffic in Women: Notes on the 'Political Economy' of Sex." *Toward an Anthropology of Women*. Ed. Rayna Reiter. New York: Monthly Review Press, 1975. 157–210.

Rubin, Miri. *Mother of God: A History of the Virgin Mary*. New Haven, CT: Yale University Press, 2009.

Russell, Daniel C., ed. *The Cambridge Companion to Virtue Ethics*. Cambridge: Cambridge University Press, 2013.

Russell, Paul. "Hume's Anatomy of Virtue." D. C. Russell, ed., *Cambridge Companion to Virtue Ethics*. 92–123.

Rutter, Tom. "*Patient Grissil* and Jonsonian Satire." *Studies in English Literature, 1500–1900* 48 (2008): 283–303.

Salih, Sarah, ed. *A Companion to Middle English Hagiography*. Cambridge: Boydell & Brewer. 2010.

———. *Versions of Virginity in Late Medieval England*. Cambridge: Boydell & Brewer, 2001.

Salkever, Stephen G. *Finding the Mean: Theory and Practice in Aristotelian Political Philosophy*. Princeton, NJ: Princeton University Press, 1990.

Sanchez, Melissa. *Erotic Subjects: The Sexuality of Politics in Early Modern English Literature*. Oxford: Oxford University Press, 2011.

Sanderlin, George. "Chaucer's 'Legend of Dido': A Feminist Exemplum." *Chaucer Review* 20 (1986): 331–40.

Sanok, Catherine. *Her Life Historical: Exemplarity and Female Saints' Lives in Late Medieval England*. Philadelphia: University of Pennsylvania Press, 2007.

———. "Reading Hagiographically: The *Legend of Good Women* and Its Feminine Audience." *Exemplaria* 13 (2001): 323–54.

Saunders, Corinne. *Rape and Ravishment in the Literature of Medieval England*. Cambridge: D. S. Brewer, 2001.

Scala, Elizabeth. "Canacee and the Chaucer Canon: Incest and Other Unnarratables." *Chaucer Review* 30 (1995): 15–39.

Scanlon, Larry. "Lydgate's Poetics: Laureation and Domesticity in the *Temple of Glas*." *John Lydgate: Poetry, Culture, and Lancastrian England*. Ed. Larry Scanlon and James Simpson. South Bend, IN: University of Notre Dame Press, 2006. 61–97.

———. *Narrative, Authority and Power: The Medieval Exemplum and the Chaucerian Tradition*. Cambridge: Cambridge University Press, 1994.

Scarry, Elaine. *The Body in Pain: The Making and Unmaking of the World*. New York: Oxford University Press, 1987.

———. *On Beauty and Being Just*. Princeton, NJ: Princeton University Press, 1999.

Schiavone, James. "Spenser's Augustine." *Spenser Studies* 20 (2005): 277–89.

Schibanoff, Susan. "Worlds Apart: Orientalism, Antifeminism, and Heresy in Chaucer's *Man of Law's Tale*." *Exemplaria* 8 (1996): 59–96.

Schlauch, Margaret. *Chaucer's Constance and Accused Queens*. 1923. Reprint, New York: Gordian Press, 1969.

Schneewind, J. B. "The Misfortunes of Virtue." *Ethics* 101 (1990): 42–63.

Schochet, Gordon J. *Patriarchalism in Political Thought: The Authoritarian Family and Political Speculation and Attitudes Especially in Seventeenth-Century England*. Oxford: Basil Blackwell, 1975.

Schroeder, John W. "A New Analogue and Possible Source for *The Taming of a Shrew*." *Shakespeare Quarterly* 10 (1959): 251–55.

Schücking, Levin L. *The Puritan Family: A Social Study from Literary Sources*. Trans. Brian Battershaw. New York: Schocken Books, 1970.

Schwarz, Kathryn. *Tough Love: Amazon Encounters in the English Renaissance.* Durham, NC: Duke University Press, 2000.

———. *What You Will: Gender, Contract, and Shakespearean Social Space.* Philadelphia: University of Pennsylvania Press, 2011.

Schwebel, Leah. "Livy and Augustine as Negative Models in the *Legend of Good Women.*" *Chaucer Review* 52 (2017): 29–45.

Sedgwick, Eve. *Touching Feeling: Affect, Pedagogy, Performativity.* Durham, NC: Duke University Press, 2002.

Shannon, Laurie. *Sovereign Amity: Figures of Friendship in Shakespearean Contexts.* Chicago: University of Chicago Press, 2002.

Shaw, George Bernard. *Shaw on Shakespeare: An Anthology of Bernard Shaw's Writing on the Plays and Production of Shakespeare.* Ed. Edwin Wilson. New York: E. P. Dutton, 1961.

Shea, J. A., and Paul Yachnin. "The Well-Hung Shrew." *Ecocritical Shakespeare.* Ed. Lynne Bruckner and Dan Brayton. Surrey: Ashgate, 2011. 105–22.

Sheingorn, Pamela. "Appropriating the Holy Kinship: Gender and Family History." *Interpreting Cultural Symbols: Saint Anne in Late Medieval Society.* Ed. Kathleen Ashley and Pamela Sheingorn. Athens: University of Georgia Press, 1990. 169–98.

Sheridan, Christian. "The Early Prints of the *Testament of Cresseid* and the Presentation of Lines 577–91." *ANQ* 20 (2007): 23–27.

Shuger, Deborah. *The Renaissance Bible: Scholarship, Sacrifice, and Subjectivity.* Berkeley: University of California Press, 1994.

Shutters, Lynn. "Griselda's Pagan Virtue." *Chaucer Review* 44 (2009): 61–83.

———."The Thought and Feel of Virtuous Wifehood: Recovering Emotion in the *Legend of Good Women.*" *Chaucer Review* 52 (2017): 85–105.

———. "Truth, Translation, and the *Troy Book* Women." *Comitatus* 32 (2001): 69–98.

Sidhu, Nicole Nolan. "Henpecked Husbands, Unruly Wives, and Royal Authority in Lydgate's *Mumming at Hertford.*" *Chaucer Review* 42 (2008): 431–60.

Silberman, Lauren. *Transforming Desire: Erotic Knowledge in Books III and IV of "The Faerie Queene."* Berkeley: University of California Press, 1995.

Simpson, James W. "Ethics and Interpretation: Reading Wills in Chaucer's *Legend of Good Women.*" *Studies in the Age of Chaucer* 20 (1998): 73–100.

———. "The Other Book of Troy: Guido delle Colonne's *Historia destructionis Troiae* in Fourteenth- and Fifteenth-Century England." *Speculum* 73 (1998): 397–423.

———. *Reform and Cultural Revolution. The Oxford English Literary History.* Vol. 2, *1350–1547.* 2nd ed. Oxford: Oxford University Press, 2004.

———. "The Sacrifice of Lady Rochford: Henry Parker's Translation of *De claris mulieribus.*" *"Triumphs of English": Henry Parker, Lord Morley, Translator to the Tudor Court; New Essays in Interpretation.* Ed. Marie Axton and James P. Carley. London: British Library Publications, 2000. 153–69.

Sims, Dwight. "Cosmological Structure in *The Faerie Queene,* Book III." *Huntington Library Quarterly* 40 (1977): 99–117.

Sirluck, Katherine A. "Patriarchy, Pedagogy, and the Divided Self in *The Taming of the Shrew.*" *University of Toronto Quarterly* 60 (1991): 417–34.

Skinner, Quentin. *The Foundations of Modern Political Thought.* Vol. 1. Cambridge: Cambridge University Press, 1978.

———. *Machiavelli: A Very Short Introduction.* Oxford: Oxford University Press, 2000.

————. "Thomas Hobbes: Rhetoric and Construction of Morality." *Proceedings of the British Academy* 76 (1990): 1–61.

Smith, Amy L. "Performing Marriage with a Difference: Wooing, Wedding and Bedding in *The Taming of the Shrew*." *Comparative Drama* 36 (2002): 289–320.

Smith, Charles. "The Ethical Allegory of the Two Florimells." *Studies in Philology* 31 (1934): 140–51.

Smith, Molly Easo. "John Fletcher's Response to the Gender Debate: *The Woman's Prize* and *The Taming of the Shrew*." *Papers in Language and Literature* 31 (1995): 38–60.

Somerset, Fiona. " 'Hard is with seyntis for to make affray': Lydgate the 'Poet-Propagandist' as Hagiographer." *John Lydgate: Poetry, Culture, and Lancastrian England*. Ed. Larry Scanlon and James Simpson. South Bend, IN: University of Notre Dame Press, 2006. 258–78.

Spearing, A. C. *Medieval to Renaissance in English Poetry*. Cambridge: Cambridge University Press, 1985.

Sponsler, Claire. *Drama and Resistance: Bodies and Theatricality in Late Medieval England*. Minneapolis: University of Minnesota Press, 1997.

————. "Lydgate and London's Public Culture." *Lydgate Matters: Poetry and Material Culture in the Fifteenth Century*. Ed. Lisa H. Cooper and Andrea Denny-Brown. New York: Palgrave Macmillan, 2008. 13–34.

Staley, Lynn. *Languages of Power in the Age of Richard II*. University Park: Pennsylvania State University Press, 2005.

Stallybrass, Peter. "Patriarchal Territories: The Body Enclosed." *Rewriting the Renaissance: The Discourse of Sexual Difference in Early Modern Europe*. Ed. Margaret W. Ferguson. Chicago: University of Chicago Press, 1986. 123–42.

Stearns, Marshall W. "Henryson and Chaucer." *Modern Language Quarterly* 6 (1945): 271–84.

————. "Robert Henryson and the Leper Cresseid." *Modern Language Notes* 59 (1944): 265–69.

Steinberg, Dianne Vanner. " 'We do usen here no wommen for to selle': Embodiment of Social Practices in *Troilus and Criseyde*." *Chaucer Review* 29 (1995): 259–73.

Steinmetz, David. "Reformation and Grace." *Grace upon Grace: Essays in Honor of Thomas A. Langford*. Nashville, TN: Abingdon Press, 1999. 75–86.

Stimpson, Catharine R. "Polonius, Our Pundit." *American Scholar* 71 (2002): 97–108.

Stone, Lawrence. *The Family, Sex, and Marriage in England, 1500–1800*. Abridged ed. London: Penguin, 1979.

Straker, Scott-Morgan. "Propaganda, Intentionality, and the Lancastrian Lydgate." *John Lydgate: Poetry, Culture, and Lancastrian England*. Ed. Larry Scanlon and James Simpson. South Bend, IN: University of Notre Dame Press, 2006. 98–128.

————. "Rivalry and Reciprocity in Lydgate's *Troy Book*." *New Medieval Literatures* 3 (2002): 119–47.

Strohm, Paul. "Chaucer's Audience." *Literature and History* 5 (1977): 26–41.

————. *Chaucer's Tale: 1386 and the Road to Canterbury*. New York: Viking, 2014.

————. *England's Empty Throne: Usurpation and the Language of Legitimation, 1399–1422*. New Haven, CT: Yale University Press, 1998.

————. "Fourteenth- and Fifteenth-Century Writers as Readers of Chaucer." *Genres, Themes, and Images in English Literature from the Fourteenth to the Fifteenth Century*. Ed. Piero Boitani and Anna Torti. Tübingen: Gunter Narr, 1988. 90–104.

————. "Hoccleve, Lydgate, and the Lancastrian Court." *The Cambridge History of Medieval English Literature*. Ed. David Wallace. Cambridge: Cambridge University Press, 1999. 640–61.

———. *Hochon's Arrow: Social Imagination of Fourteenth-Century Texts.* Princeton, NJ: Princeton University Press, 1992.

———. *Politique: Languages of Statecraft Between Chaucer and Shakespeare.* South Bend, IN: University of Notre Dame Press, 2005.

Strong, Roy. *The Cult of Elizabeth: Elizabethan Portraiture and Pageantry.* London: Thames and Hudson, 1977.

Stump, Donald. "A Slow Return to Eden: Spenser on Women's Rule." *English Literary Renaissance* 29 (1999): 401–21.

Sullivan, Garrett, and Linda Woodbridge. "Popular Culture in Print." *The Cambridge Companion to English Literature, 1500–1600.* Ed. Arthur F. Kinney. Cambridge: Cambridge University Press, 2000. 265–86.

Tartamella, Suzanne M. "Reinventing the Poet and Dark Lady: Theatricality and Artistic Control in Shakespeare's *The Taming of the Shrew.*" *English Literary Renaissance* 43 (2013): 446–77.

Tate, Robert W. "Haunted by Beautified Beauty: Tracking the Images of Spensers Florimell(s)." *Spenser Studies: A Renaissance Poetry Annual* 39 (2014): 197–218.

Taylor, Charles. *Sources of the Self: The Making of the Modern Identity.* Cambridge, MA: Harvard University Press, 1992.

Thorndike, Lynn. *A History of Magic and Experimental Science.* New York: Macmillan, 1923.

Tiffany, Grace. "Not Saying No: Female Self-Erasure in *Troilus and Cressida.*" *Texas Studies in Literature and Language* 35 (1993): 44–56.

Tillyard, E. M. W. "Henryson: *The Testament of Cresseid.*" *Five Poems: 1470–1870; An Elementary Essay on the Background of English Literature.* London, 1848. 5–29.

Trigg, Stephanie. *Congenial Souls: Reading Chaucer from Medieval to Postmodern.* Minneapolis: University of Minnesota Press, 2002.

Tupper, Frederick. "Chaucer and the Seven Deadly Sins." *PMLA* 29 (1914): 93–128.

———. "Chaucer's Sinners and Sins." *Journal of English and Germanic Philology* 15 (1916): 56–106.

Turner, Robert Y. "Responses to Tyranny in John Fletcher's Plays." *MRDE* 4 (1989): 123–41.

Tuve, Rosamund. *Allegorical Imagery: Some Medieval Books and Their Posterity.* Princeton, NJ: Princeton University Press, 1966.

Underdown, D. E. "The Taming of the Scold: The Enforcement of Patriarchal Authority in Early Modern England." *Order and Disorder in Early Modern England.* Ed. Anthony Fletcher and John Stevenson. Cambridge: Cambridge University Press, 1985.

Utley, Francis Lee. *The Crooked Rib: An Analytical Index to the Argument About Women in English and Scots Literature to the End of the Year 1568.* 1944. Reprint, New York: Octagon, 1970.

Wall, Wendy. *Staging Domesticity: Household Work and English Identity in Early Modern Drama.* Cambridge: Cambridge University Press, 2002.

Wallace, David. *Chaucerian Polity: Absolutist Lineages and Associational Forms in England and Italy.* Stanford, CA: Stanford University Press, 1997.

Wallace, Dewey D., Jr., *Puritans and Predestination: Grace in English Protestant Theology, 1525–1695.* Chapel Hill: University of North Carolina Press, 1982.

Warren, Nancy Bradley. "Chivalric Men and Good(?) Women: Chaucer, Gender, and John Bossewell's *Workes of Armorie.*" *Chaucer Review* 52 (2017): 143–61.

———. "'Olde Stories' and Amazons: The *Legend of Good Women,* the 'Knight's Tale,' and Fourteenth-Century Political Culture." Collette, ed., *Legend of Good Women.* 83–104.

Waters, Claire M. "Power and Authority." *A Companion to Middle English Hagiography*. Ed. Sarah Salih. Cambridge: D. S. Brewer, 2006. 70–86.

Watson, Nicholas. "Outdoing Chaucer: Lydate's *Troy Book* and Henryson's *Testament of Cresseid* as Competitive Imitations of *Troilus and Criseyde*." *Shifts and Transpositions in Medieval Narrative: A Festschrift for Dr. Elspeth Kennedy*. Ed. Karen Pratt. Cambridge: Boydell & Brewer, 1994. 89–108.

Watts, John. *Henry VI and the Politics of Kingship*. Cambridge: Cambridge University Press, 1996.

Wayne, Valerie. "Refashioning the Shrew." *Shakespeare Studies* 17 (1985): 159–87.

Weatherby, Harold L. *Mirrors of Celestial Grace: Patristic Theology in Spenser's Allegory*. Toronto: University of Toronto Press, 1994.

Wells, Robin Headlam. "Spenser's Christian Knight: Erasmian Theology in *The Faerie Queene*, Book I." *Anglia* 97 (1979): 350–66.

Wentzel, Siegfried. Introduction. *Summa Virtutum de remediis anime*. Athens: University of Georgia Press, 1984. 1–45.

Wetherbee, Winthrop. "Constance and the World in Chaucer and Gower." *John Gower: Recent Readings*. Ed. R. F. Yeager. Kalamazoo: Western Michigan University, 1989. 65–93.

Williams, Kathleen. "Courtesy and Pastoral in 'The Faerie Queene,' Book VI." *Review of English Studies*, n.s., 13 (1962): 342–45.

———. *Spenser's 'Faerie Queene': The World of Glass*. London: Routledge and K. Paul, 1966.

Williams, Tara. *Inventing Womanhood: Gender and Language in Later Middle English Writing*. Columbus: Ohio State University Press, 2010.

Wilson, Elkin Calhoun. "Polonius in the Round." *Shakespeare Quarterly* 9 (1958): 83–85.

Wilson-Okamura, David Scott. "Belphoebe and Gloriana." *English Literary Renaissance* 39 (2009): 47–73.

———. "Spenser and the Two Queens." *English Literary Renaissance* 32 (2002): 62–84.

Wind, Edgar. *Pagan Mysteries of the Renaissance*. 2nd ed. rev. London: W. W. Norton, 1968.

Winstead, Karen A. *John Capgrave's Fifteenth Century*. Philadelphia: University of Pennsylvania Press, 2006.

———. "Saints, Wives, and Other 'Hooly Thynges': Pious Laywomen in Middle English Romance." *Chaucer Yearbook* 2 (1995): 137–54.

———. *Virgin Martyrs: Legends of Sainthood in Late Medieval England*. Ithaca, NY: Cornell University Press, 1997.

Wogan-Browne, Jocelyn. "Saints' Lives and the Female Reader." *Forum for Modern Language Studies* 27 (1991): 314–32.

———. *Saints' Lives and Women's Literary Culture, c. 1150–1300*. Oxford: Oxford University Press, 2001.

———. "The Virgin's Tale." *Feminist Readings in Middle English Literature: The Wife of Bath and All Her Sect*. Ed. Lesley Johnson. London: Routledge, 1994. 165–94.

Wolfe, Cary. *Animal Rites: American Culture, the Discourse of Species, and Posthumanist Theory*. Chicago: University of Chicago Press, 2003.

———. *What Is Posthumanism?* Minneapolis: University of Minnesota Press, 2010.

Woodhouse, A. S. P. "Nature and Grace in *The Faerie Queene*." *ELH* 16 (1949): 194–228.

Wright, Louis B. "A Political Reflection in Phillip's *Patient Grissell*." *Review of English Studies* 4 (1928): 424–28.

Yachnin, Paul. "'The Perfection of Ten': Populuxe Art and Artisanal Value in *Troilus and Cressida*." *Shakespeare Quarterly* 56 (2005): 306–27.

Yearling, Rebecca. "Florimell's Girdle: Reconfiguring Chastity in *The Faerie Queene.*" *Spenser Studies* 20 (2005): 137–44.

Yunck, John A. "Religious Elements in Chaucer's *Man of Law's Tale.*" *ELH* 27 (1960): 249–61.

Zajko, Vanda. "Petruchio is 'Kated': *The Taming of the Shrew* and Ovid." *Shakespeare and the Classics*. Ed. Charles Martindale and A. B. Taylor. Cambridge: Cambridge University Press, 2004. 33–48.

Zeeman, Nicolette. *'Piers Plowman' and the Medieval Discourse of Desire*. Cambridge: Cambridge University Press, 2006.

Žižek, Slavoj. *The Fragile Absolute, or Why Is the Christian Legacy Worth Fighting For?* London: Verso, 2000.

———. *The Metastases of Enjoyment: Six Essays on Women and Causality*. London: Verso, 1994.

ACKNOWLEDGMENTS

I have been writing this book for nearly my entire intellectual life, and I have had a lot of help as I formulated these arguments. Even after all these years, I would like to thank Leah Marcus, Lynn Enterline, Kathryn Schwarz, and John Plummer for giving me the guidance and confidence to develop a cross-period, feminist project. Tommy Crocker taught me about virtues, and Ambrose Crocker taught me why they matter.

Good friends and colleagues helped me every step of the way. Glenn Burger offered patience, support, and wisdom, and I couldn't be more grateful to have his friendship and collaboration. Beth Robertson gave me guidance, confidence, and insight, and I will always cherish her mentorship and affection.

Anke Bernau, Cary Howie, Wan-Chuan Kao, Will Robins, Steven Kruger, Noah Guynn, Patricia Ingham, Liz Scala, Cynthia Turner Camp, and Tara Williams invited me to workshop portions of these arguments at the Freie Universität Berlin, Cornell University, Washington and Lee University, the Canada Chaucer Seminar (University of Toronto), the Medieval Club (New York City), the Exemplaria Theory Symposium (University of Texas at Austin), the UGA Symposium on the Book (University of Georgia), and the Critical Questions Lecture (Oregon State University). Ruth Evans, Katherine Jager, Tison Pugh, Holly Pickett, Kellie Robertson, Christopher Michael Roman, Nicole Nolan Sidhu, and Fiona Somerset invited me to present developing arguments at a series of generative panels at Kalamazoo, Medieval Academy, NCS, and the MLA. Thanks, too, for helpful advice from Valerie Allen, Anthony Bale, Candace Barrington, Harry Berger Jr., Matthew Boyd-Goldie, Jennifer N. Brown, Seeta Chaganti, Jay Clayton, Anne Coldiron, Andrew Cole, Suzanne Conklin Akbari, Lisa H. Cooper, Isabel Davis, Carolyn Dinshaw, Bob Eagleston, Jennifer Garrison, Tom Goodman, Frank Grady, Roland Greene, Bruce Holsinger, Jim Knowles, Karma Lochrie,

Robyn Malo, David Mathews, Bobby Meyer-Lee, Bob Mills, Julie Orleman-
ski, Gail Paster, Kristen Poole, Myra Seaman, James Simpson, Vance Smith,
Sarah Stanbury, Karl Steel, Emily Steiner, Paul Strohm, Marion Turner, and
Lawrence Warner. My online writing group helped me stay on track at a
crucial time.

Grants and leave were also crucial for bringing this project to fruition.
Thanks to the Folger Shakespeare Library, the Forschungskolleg Humanwis-
senschaften, Johann Wolfgang Goethe Universität, Frankfurt am Main, the
Fulbright Commission, and the Institute for Advanced Studies in the
Humanities, Edinburgh University, for fellowship support. The Provost's
Office at the University of South Carolina awarded me three Humanities
Faculty Fellowships, and the English Department of the University of South
Carolina granted me the Morrison Fellowship, all of which allowed me time
to think, read, and write. I was also grateful to spend a year as a visiting
scholar at Vanderbilt University, where I was welcomed with intellectual gen-
erosity by friends old and new.

Thanks, also, to William Rivers, Mary Ann Fitzpatrick, Michael Amiri-
dis, and Nina Levine for administrative wizardry in support of my scholarly
endeavors. Finally, dear friends at the University of South Carolina saw me
through this project: thanks to Tony Jarrells, Gretchen Woertendyke, Debra
Rae Cohen, Bob Brinkmeyer, Elise Blackwell, David Bajo, Eli Jelly-Shapiro,
Zsofia Jilling, John Muckelbauer, David Shields, Anne Gulick, Catherine
Keyser, Brian Glavey, Sam Amadon, Liz Countryman, Jennifer Frey, and Ed
Gieskes. Scott Gwara has been an inimitable colleague and champion: he has
promoted my career in every way possible, and he has been a model of profes-
sional courtesy, collegiality, and generosity.

Portions of this project have appeared in earlier iterations: thanks to the
Journal of Medieval and Early Modern Studies, Shakespeare Quarterly, and
Studies in English Literature: 1500–1900, for permission to include ideas that
originally appeared in these journals. Jerry Singerman is an editor with many
virtues: he's kind, intelligent, engaged, and patient. Likewise, the readers for
the press gave involved, challenging, and invigorating feedback; I thank them
for helping me make this a better book. Finally, this book is written for
an audience of premodernist feminist scholars. It invites debate about what
feminism might become, and in so doing, it affirms that feminism is just
getting going as a critical practice that might help us see the premodern past
differently.